GENERATIVE
/ STUDIES
IN
ROMANCE
LANGUAGES

Edited by:

Jean Casagrande and Bohdan Saciuk
University of Florida

NEWBURY HOUSE PUBLISHERS, INC.

NEWBURY HOUSE PUBLISHERS, INC.

Language Science
Language Teaching
Language Learning

68 Middle Road, Rowley, Massachusetts 01969

Library of Congress Catalogue Card Number: 72-94394
ISBN: 912066-72-5

Cover design by Holly Nichols

Printed in the United States of America.   First printing: December, 1972

To Danylo, Marie and Paul

FOREWORD

This book represents, at least partially, the written record of a
conference held at the University of Florida, Gainesville, Florida,
February 17-20, 1971, under the name of Linguistic Symposium of Romance
Languages: Application of Generative Grammar to Their Description and
Teaching.

The aim of the Symposium was to bring forth novel contributions in
the description of Romance languages, to draw attention to phenomena
that might be of importance in the constant re-evaluation of our theoretical views, and to make available some insights into the nature of Romance
languages which might be useful in the teaching of those languages.

The central objective of both the Symposium and this volume is the
dissemination of knowledge. One goal of the conference was to provide
well-established scholars and younger researchers with a forum for the
exchange of ideas. Papers were invited, or selected on the basis of
submitted abstracts. The reading of papers, the subsequent discussions,
and especially the many opportunities all participants had to speak with
colleagues also well acquainted with generative theory and the Romance
Languages resulted in a most successful meeting.

The Symposium was composed of seven sessions. Three papers were read
at each session, followed by a single lengthy discussion period. The
discussions were recorded and have been transcribed but they do not appear
in this book. They were left out mainly because of their bulk and the ensuing cost of the volume. All papers read at the Symposium appear herein.
The present volume consists of three parts: 1. Syntax, 2. Phonology,
3. Applied, representing the organizational division of the Symposium.

The Linguistic Symposium on Romance Languages was sponsored jointly
by the Graduate School, the Department of Romance Languages and Literatures, and the Program in Linguistics at the University of Florida. We
are deeply indebted to Harold P. Hanson, then Dean of the Graduate School,
to J. Wayne Conner, Chairman of the Department of Romance Languages and
Literatures, and to John Algeo, then Chairman of the Program in Linguistics,
for their generous support and their encouragement. We wish for the

success of the Symposium and the anticipated success of this volume to reflect on these three men. We want to thank James W. Harris, Ronald W. Langacker, David M. Perlmutter and John F. Vigorita who were kind enough to join us on the Program Committee and Edward N. Burstynsky, R. Joe Campbell, Weber D. Donaldson, Ernest Haden and Robert L. Trammell who served as Session Chairmen at the Symposium. We are also endebted to the Division of Sponsored Research at the University of Florida which supported the typing of the manuscript in its final, camera-ready form; to our typist, Gaylia Boerner; to our proofreader, Juanita Casagrande; to Donald H. Albury and Shannon T. Anderson, our students, who recorded and transcribed the discussions, and to our colleagues in the Department of Romance Languages and Literatures and in the Program in Linguistics for their interest and encouragement. Our deep appreciation goes to the one hundred-odd participants in the Symposium and, in particular to our speakers, who, when all is said and done, are responsible for the high quality of the meeting and for the atmosphere of earnest cooperative effort which prevailed throughout the conference.

Gainesville, Florida   J.C.
September 1972   B.S.

CONTENTS

SYNTAX

PHONOLOGY

SYNTAX

JEAN CASAGRANDE
UNIVERSITY OF FLORIDA

SYNTACTIC STUDIES IN ROMANCE

0. INTRODUCTION

The purpose of this paper is to serve as introduction to the syntactic contributions in this volume by outlining the development of syntactic studies in the Romance languages within the theoretical framework of this anthology. This paper will consist of two parts. In the first part I will sketch the chronological development of generative grammar, distinguishing between three stages: transformational baroque, classical transformational grammar, and the neo-classical period. This first part will constitute the substantial and organizational portion of the paper. In the second part of the paper the situation in generative Romance syntax will be examined.

In a broad sense, linguistic investigations in Romance began with Varro[1] and have appeared in large numbers since. For our narrower purposes, to place the studies included here within the proper context, I will briefly allude to outstanding studies and scholars in Romance studies since the last century. Grammatical studies at the beginning of the nineteenth century are characterized by their bulk and their purpose: they are long-winded reference texts. The tone and outlook of these grammars are traditional. Based on a combination of parts of speech and sentence structure theories, these grammars are but the continuation of Greek, Latin, and medieval grammatical thought.[2] Friedrich Diez's *Grammatik des romanischen Sprachen* (1836-1843), now a classic, opened the way for an area of study known since as Romance linguistics. Emulating Diez, Wilhem Meyer-Lubke authored an identically titled multi-volume work (1890-1902). Their approach was the one prevalent at that time in Germany: the historical comparative method. The trend they set has continued to this day thanks to important contributions by outstanding scholars like Bourciez, Iordan, Rohlfs, von Wartburg, and Malkiel, to name a few. De Saussure contributed to linguistics the distinction between diachronic and synchronic studies, giving rise to a split now several decades old.[3] On the synchronic side Sechehaye, Brunot, and Bally are the champions of the psychological approach while Tesnière, de Boer, and Martinet are the standard bearers

of the functional method.[4] By and large, the differences between their
views are minimal, deriving more from a different outlook rather than
depending on conflicting theories (Cf. Ruwet 1967:66 et passim).
    American structuralism failed to yield any novel work in syntax. This
failure results from the very nature of its theories and the interest of
the structuralists in phonology, the latter being dependent on the former.
Even tagmemics, the most syntactically developed structural system, remains
uninspiring   (Cf. Postal 1964, Roulet 1969, Lamérand, 1970). Only the work
of Zellig Harris   (Harris 1970), addressed itself to syntax in a novel
way. So, more than a hundred years after Diez's pioneering work Romance
syntax had not found a better theoretic vehicle on which it could make
headway.

1. GENERATIVE GRAMMAR

1.1. THE BAROQUE PERIOD

    The concept of transformation as a rule of language first appeared in
the work of Zellig Harris, who viewed this operation as a link relating
bi-directionally two observable strings of elements in a language: this
was transformational grammar in its embryonic form.   Noam Chomsky, then
Harris' student,   investigated and slightly modified this concept by
introducing the notion of unidirectional derivation which he integrated
with a generative device. *Syntactic Structures* (Chomsky, 1957), a summary
of Chomsky's dissertaion, is the central event in a period of investigation
which will be referred to as transformational baroque. Like much of structuralism, this period is characterized by emphasis on formalism both in
a deep and superficial sense. Formalism in the deep sense is illustrated
in Chomsky (1957, 1964) and Postal (1964) where the generative model is
compared to other formal models. Illustrations of formalism in its
superficial manifestation can be found in countless generalized transformations, page-long derivations, and rules involving as many as a dozen indices.
Transformational baroque is also characterized by an enthusiasm akin to that
of a recent convert: in most writings one finds controversy and preaching.
Substantially, everything remains to be done. The theory needs to be expanded and tested but few seem to concern themselves with this expansion
and testing. On the other hand, criticism abounds; some of it is valid--
especially from those who decry the lack of interest in semantics and the
disregard of stylistics--and some of it is pointless. But neither is
heeded. In short, transformational baroque is a period of investigatory
heroism, a period that saw ill-equipped linguists bravely and squarely
attack the giant of language, an adversary which turned out less like
Goliath and more like Hydra.[5]

1.2. CLASSICAL TRANSFORMATIONAL GRAMMAR

    Baroque was followed by a period marked by the uncontested rule of the
Massachusetts Institute of Technology, a rule which fostered order, harmony,

universality, and fecundity. There was order and harmony because the vast
majority of linguists agreed with the sweeping reforms that a handful of
MIT'ers brought to the theory. There was universality not only in grammatical claims but also in attempts at showing that generative transformational grammar has roots in the universalist tradition, and fecundity because
during the classical period a great deal of work was done on syntax, mostly
English syntax.

Among major improvements over the theory of *Syntactic Structures* are
the introduction of such concepts as competence and performance, which at
least afforded us with a less arbitrary means of discrimination of data
than otherwise, and the organization of grammar into three discrete components; a central syntactic component, and two interpretive ones, one phonological and one semantic (Cf. Chomsky 1964). Other improvements include the pioneering work of Katz and Postal on the integration of semantics to grammar, resulting in the principle of immutability of meaning in
a derivation (Katz and Postal 1964). The height of classicism was reached
in 1965 with the publication of Chomsky's *Aspects of the Theory of Syntax*.
This most influential book summarizes the principles of the classical
period, principles with which linguists throughout the world went about classifying languages. The bulk of the work, however, was on English syntax.
So secure and established was classical transformational grammar that it
began to solidify its position, not just within the expected arguments of
adequacy but in a search for ideological ancestors. *Cartesian Linguistics*
(1966') the result of this search by Chomsky, was critized from various
quarters for being a biaised account (Cf. Percival 1968) and for not looking
enough back in history (R. Lakoff 1969). Its great contribution lies in
that it has raised enough questions and problems to suggest to the linguistic community the cyclic nature of advances in the history of its thought
and scholarship (Salus 1969, 1971). Issued from *Aspects,* of which it was
a theoretical revision, Fillmore's theory of deep case relation (Fillmore
1966 a and b, 1968a, 1971a) has known great success. Dissertations and
monographs applying Fillmore's case theory to the description of a variety
of languages have swollen the already large output of the classical era.

Classical transformational grammar is the fruit of over a decade of
serious thought about the generative model of language. Many of the principles on which it rests are recurrent in the baroque and neoclassical
periods; some of them can be traced back to modistic grammar and even to
the Alexandrians. A cornerstone of classical generative transformational
grammar is regularity. Many of the issues of the present period depend
to a great degree on varying views of what constitutes regularity.

1.3. NEOCLASSICISM

The work which is at the roots of a number of controversies in neoclassical generative theory started out as an attempt to systematize irregularities. "It was begun as a minor revision and extension of the conception
of grammar presented in Noam Chomsky's *Aspects of the Theory of Syntax*.
Before the work was completed it had become apparent that the revision
was anything but minor." (Lakoff 1970b ix).

In his effort to characterize irregularities in terms of regular processes of language, George Lakoff

..."noticed along the way that the proposed exception mechanism, which this work attempts to motivate on independent grounds, would (1) allow certain sentences to be derived from underlying structures that more closely reflected their semantic representation; (2) permit one to reformulate transformational rules by removing idiosyncratic restrictions, thus permitting transformations in one language to resemble more closely transformations in other languages; and (3) permit the base rules to be simplified, seemingly in the direction of providing universal base rules." (Lakoff 1970b, ix)

I suggested above that the arguments on both sides of the great controversy[6] of neoclassicism in transformational grammar have to do with regularity. I am using regularity in a broad sense, including relatedness, universality and similarity. Generative semantics claims that some processes of language are similar, others related, yet others universal, while interpretive semantics views the same processes as different, unrelated, and language specific, respectively.[7] G. Lakoff and Ross (1968) argued that syntactic rules and semantic rules are similar, but the interpretivists have maintained the componential distinction outlined in Chomsky (1965) where syntax is a central generative component and semantics is interpretive (Jackendoff 1968, 1970). McCawley (1968b) has argued that selectional restrictions are semantic and not syntactic. He has also argued (McCawley 1971, and McCawley, in press) hand in hand with Quang Phuc Dong (1971) that syntactic rules must precede lexical insertion. The interpretivists retain the lexicon as an input to their deep structure (Chomsky 1970b, 1971, Jackendoff 1968). Furthermore generative semantics assumes lexical decomposition (McCawley 1968a, 1971, Fillmore 1971b, Postal 1971b), whereas interpretive semantics does not.
In short, syntactic and semantic processes are the same for the generativists but different for the interpretivists; underlying representation is semantic and likely to be more universal for the generativists but it is syntactic and likely to be more language specific for the interpretivists; deep structure is not a necessary level of linguistic description for the generativists but it remains the base of the interpretivist's grammar.
As all the above are empirical claims, truth *should* come to light through empirical examination. Yet neither the analogists not the anomalists of neoclassical generative grammar have succeeded in convincing the linguistic world of the appropriateness of their claims. A reason for this failure may be found in Postal's introduction to *Cross-Over Phenomena* (Postal 1971a).

"My position is that serious grammatical investigation at the moment is rather like traveling in quicksand. There are no firm supports. Every step is uncertain. Every move is questionable. There are no well worked, out unshakeable analyses of particular

portions of individual languages from which general principles of
grammar can be inferred. ... We are in short really almost at the
beginning of the study of the incredibly complex and still largely
unknown domain of natural language grammar."

Adding to this frustrating state of affairs, Peters and Ritchie (forthcoming a and b) point out inadequancies in the universal base hypothesis,
a point against the theory of generative semantics. Wall (1971) recommends
constraining generative theory as did Ross (1967b) rather than allowing it
to be less restricted.[8] So on the one hand mathematical linguistics tells
us to constrain our theory while on the other we find cases requiring reference to non-adjacent points in a derivation or to another derivation
altogether.
Neoclassicism is reminiscent of the baroque period in that it is marked
by controversy. But this controversy, it should be noted, has been an
internal one. The interpretivists, for example, have maintained that generative semantics is but a notational variant of the "standard theory." As
things stand, considering the efforts of generativists to search beyond
the classical scope of linguistic investigation it appears that the awaited
revolutionary change may come from the side of generative semantics.
Perhaps it has already come and we have not had sufficient historical perspective to recognize it.

2. ROMANCE GENERATIVE STUDIES

In the second part of this introduction we will concern ourselves with
work on the syntax of Romance languages as they apply and test the various
theories of generative transformational grammar. The three stages of transformational grammar in Romance studies are not bound in time by the same
dates as they are in the development of the theory.[9] Unlike English, which
often is both the linguistic vehicle of the exposition of the theory and
the illustrative language, the Romance languages often suffer from a lag.
It will not be surprising then to find recently published work categorized
in the baroque period.

2.1. BAROQUE STUDIES IN ROMANCE SYNTAX.

For nearly a decade after the publication of *Syntactic Structures* little
attention was paid to Chomsky's theory from within the ranks of grammarians
and linguists interested in the Romance languages. The scholars who eval-
uated Chomsky's principles demanded a degree of sophistication not yet
attained (Belasco 1961, Dubois 1969b). Baroque studies in Romance syntax
have recent publication dates. Ruwet (1967), Nivette (1970), Roulet (1969)
and Lamérand (1970) represent efforts by European linguists to acquaint
their colleagues with generative transformational theory.[10] Despite their
dates of publication and the inclusion in some cases of an outline of classical theory, they remain characteristic of the baroque period. All are
echos of Chomsky (1957) and Postal (1964).

Ruwet (1967), a revised "thèse de doctorat," is a lengthy introduction
to generative theory from 1955 to 1964 as it applies to syntax. This book,
intended for European linguists, "retrace, en quelque sorte le chemin que
j'ai suivi pour me familiariser avec une théorie nouvelle et difficile"
(Ruwet 1967:9). As pointed out by Langacker, Ruwet sticks "closely to
the content and approach of the standard published sources on generative
grammar" (Langacker 1969d:104). In so doing "Ruwet succeeds in evoking
the same attitude to linguistic description that sometimes predominates
in these sources...that linguistic theory and description are relatively
short-term engineering tasks, that linguistic problems can be solved by
tinkering with extant formalism and by hammering out more and more ...
rules" (Langacker 1969d:104). This book characterizes one attitude of the
baroque period. Its chapter on the goals of linguistics is the most successful. Because of its nature it has been spared the assaults of more recent
work in syntax and semantics. In spite of its shortcomings, *Introduction
à la grammaire générative* is a valuable and almost unique text. "To my
knowledge, it is the only work in any language which summarizes so thoroughly
the major works on generative grammar." (Asselin 1970). After serving
as an introductory text to generations of French linguists it will take an
important place as a chapter in the development of generative theory.

Nivette (1970) is also an introduction to the theory of transformational
grammar. This short book covers approximately the same time-span as Ruwet's.
Unlike Ruwet's book, *Principes de grammaire générative* aims to be an introduction to all three components of Chomsky's classical grammar. Like Ruwet,
Nivette chose to remain close to his sources, especially in their chronology.
There results a superficial and very brief survey[11] of generative grammar
which the reader will experience as a trip at high speeds through a laby-
rinth of Markov mazes, mathematical formulae, several theoretical blind
alleys, all in the half-light of superficial explanations. In short,
Nivette attempted to do too much in too few pages. This is unfortunate
because much of the book shows clarity and method (Cf. Casagrande, forthcoming
b). Nivette could have written, in about the same space, a clear introduction to transformational syntax directed to the lay reader. Such a book
would not have duplicated the work of Ruwet, a work of much grander proportions, and would have served the apparently intended purpose of *Principes
de grammaire générative*.

In many ways, Roulet's (Roulet 1969) and Lamérand's (Lamérand 1970)
books go hand in hand. In their substance, they are both founded on the
odd belief that tagmemics and generative grammar can be coupled and achieve
a happy marriage. To this aim, both books have, as point of departure,
a finite corpus which their taxonomic descriptions are intended to "handle"
and their transformational grammars to generate. Both contrast the applications of the two theories and draw heavily from generative grammar,
applying it (badly) rather than testing it. Faithful to chronology, Roulet
presents in separate sections the first (baroque) and the second (classical)
version of generative grammar, making sure *not* to spare his reader the
painful acquisition of such concepts as kernels and transforms, generalized
transformations, and transformation markers though they will be subsequently

discarded with the triumphal arrival of *la nouvelle théorie* (Roulet 1969: 117): classical transformational grammar.

Whereas the introduction to generative theory is confusing because of its slavish faithfulness to chronology, the original part on French syntax is often just wrong (Cf. Casagrande 1971, Langacker 1971). Transformations proposed are generally superficial, the kind one might have a computer apply to extract the correct surface output regardless of any grammar-internal justifications and independently of the intuition of the speaker of French. There is a rule that adds *ci* and *là* to voi in order to form *voici* and *voilà*, a rule that sticks in a morpheme ESK (est-ce que) to form some questions, a rule that deletes *pas* in negative sentences to avoid **il n'a pas rien vu,* a rule that deletes *subject* NP's because many French passives are agentless. All these rules are neither motivated directly nor independently. They are ad hoc means of producing superficial strings of French.

Lamérand's treatment of *if clauses* in French (Lamérand 1970) represents a further step backwards into baroque (Cf. Donaldson 1971, Casagrande 1971). This book, an extension of Roulet's, abounds with excessive formalism. In the first part, which treats the problem from the tagmemic point of view, the reader will find formulas like [KHS122:N], G123CTM that represents sentences like:

Si on l'avait laissé faire, il nous lisait tout Diderot dans la soirée.

Formulae instead of representative sentences are referred to and compared throughout the book.[12]

The part on generative grammar is an amalgam of formulae like the above with complex constituent structure rules and hopeless transformations. One such rule (Lamérand 1970:91) contains no less than fourteen indices in the structural description and three (3) possible output readings involving disjunctive sets linearly arranged with the conventional (baroque) square brackets. In all, excluding abbreviations, there are no less than 74 symbols crowded in that rule. Lamérand's P-markers are no clearer. On page 69 one can find an upside down[13] P-marker with the following as terminal string:

#INT ESK S SNOM TM mode indic tm pres AUX V_4DET NC # K_4 INT nom#
K_0 INT D S SNOM TM mode indic pres V_1 SA PR DET NC # # # K INT D TM
u s snom 3 3.

The P-marker in question is not a deep structure because *non* (as shown in the P-marker) is the result of morphophonemic rules; it cannot be a derived P-marker at the surface level because no lexical items are given and the double crosses are not erased; finally some lines overlap. A far clearer representation would have been a P-marker which abbreviates the irrelevant portions of the structure under consideration and allows the reader to rapidly locate and evaluate the illustrated bit of structure. But, as we know, the frame of mind of transformational baroque requires detailed illustrations of the whole.

As for his analysis of *if-clauses*, it is clear that Lamérand bogged down, not because of the complexity of the phenomenon[14], but rather because of the inconsistency and the complexity of principles he decided to burden himself with: the impossible reconciliation of theories[15] that differ on a multitude of fundamental points (Cf. Postal 1964) and the bulky baroque paraphernalia.

And so it is with baroque studies in Romance syntax. In contrast with a great deal of work and effort little resulted by way of clearer understanding of language. The baroque is clearly a period of transition, one which set higher standards than did previous theories but which was hindered by too bulky a vehicle and failed to reach the desired goals. As all transition periods it has proven to be a necessary and worthwhile evolutionary step.

2.2. CLASSICAL TRANSFORMATIONAL GRAMMAR IN ROMANCE

When generative Romance syntax first appeared the classical period was only blossoming, but the two studies which marked this beginning, Schane (1964) and Langacker (1965), were themselves both formally and doctrinally within the classical period.

Although it was written in 1964, Schane's article has a degree of theoretical sophistication which surpasses many subsequent works in transformational Romance. Schane's purpose was to show that historical change 'can be described by means of grammatical transformations.' He examines three stages of the Ce ETRE noun/pronoun construction. His data, taken from Lucien Foulet's "Comment on est passé de Ce suis je à C'est moi ," (Foulet, 1921) consisted of (I)

(1) *Declarative* *Interrogative*   *Negative*   *Interro-negative*
    ce es tu   es tu ce   ce ne es tu pas   ne es tu pas ce
    ce es Jean   est ce Jean   ce ne est pas Jean ne est pas ce Jean

for the first stage, of (II)

(II) *Declarative* *Interrogative*   *Negative*   *Interro-negative*
    ce est tu   est ce tu   ce ne est tu pas   ne est ce tu pas
    ce est Jean est ce Jean   ce ne est pas Jean ne est ce pas Jean

for the second stage, and (III)

(III) *Declarative* *Interrogative* *Negative*   *Interro-negative*
    c'est toi   est-ce toi   ce n'est pas toi   n'est-ce pas toi
    c'est Jean est-ce Jean ce n'est pas Jean n'est-ce pas Jean

for the third stage of the construction. He points out that for stage I the verb inflection is determined by the following subject while the verb inflection in stages II and III is determined by the preceding subject, that *ce* is inverted in questions for all stages, that for stages

I and II the pronoun subject precedes *pas* and/or *ce* in negation and/or interrogation, but not in stage III, and that noun subject follows the other elements in negation and/or interrogation. Consequently he proposes a set of rules which will generate the form in the first stage, and shows how the four transformations needed can be reordered, and some of them deleted to account for stages II and III.

Schane's purpose in this paper was not to describe a chunk of French but rather to illustrate some principles of the generative approach to historical linguistics as they were being investigated at the time at M.I.T. The rules which he used have since been improved upon but the argument is of interest.

In his 1965 article entitled "French Interrogatives: a transformational description," Langacker argues that a formalized account of the traditional descriptions of yes/no questions in French is inappropriate because it fails to unify the interrogative process. More precisely, a rule that permutes a subject with verb or auxiliary (relating the following a and b sentences)

(a) Tu es fou.
(b) Es-tu fou?

(a) Il pleut.
(b) Pleut-il?

(a) Elle est arrivée.
(b) Est-elle arrivée?

and a rule that reduplicates an NP and pronominalizes it, (relating the a and c sentences below)

(a) Le medecin va venir.
(b) *Va venir le medecin?
(c) Le medecin va-t-il venir?

(a) Cette femme est folle.
(b) *Est cette femme folle?
(c) Cette femme est-elle folle?

fail to characterize interrogation in a unique way because they apply to different strings. The former applies to pronouns and the latter to nouns in interrogation, appending a nominal element after V.

To remedy this shortcoming Langacker proposed a three step analysis: Reduplication, Pronominalization, and Elipsis. Reduplication, which applies only in interrogative structures copies a subject NP and attaches it as a sister node of V. Pronominalization changes the N of the newly created NP node into a pronoun, deleting the rest of that NP structure. Elipsis deletes the original subject NP. The three step analysis is designed so as to operate on all interrogative structures (excluding, of course, the intonation conditioned questions). He then considers WH/d syntactic forms in light of both the two-rule and the three-rule analyses. He shows how a minor change of content in the first of the three step system can account for sentences like

> Quel tableau préfère Henri?
> Quel tableau Henri préfère-t-il?
> A quelle heure arrivera le courrier?
> A quelle heure le courrier arrivera-t-il?

Both rules of the integrated analysis require major revision to account for the same facts. He grants that the two alternatives are of equal complexity (by symbol counts) but notes that the revised rules of the non-integrated analysis are even more redundant than before the revision. So he states his preference for the three step analysis. Although the evidence is scanty, substantial critical evaluation[16] of this article had to wait until Hirschbühler (1970). Further study (Kayne, in this volume) shows that the redundant analysis is preferable.

Year 1966 saw the completion at the University of Illinois of two dissertations in Romance syntax: one on the relative clauses of Mexican Spanish (Cressey 1966) and the other on several related aspects of French Syntax (Langacker 1966a). Part of Cressey's thesis, in an extended form, was published in *Language* (Cressey 1968). There, Cressey argues that traditional grammar analyses which distinguish between sentences like a and b

(a) Salió del lugar donde estaba
(b) Salió de donde estaba

fail to capture an important generalization, namely that they are related in underlying structure. He suggests a derivation for these and a deletion rule to relate them. A bonus of this analysis is that it also allows another rule to be motivated, namely that concerned with the use of the subjunctive in sentences of type a and b.

(c) Yo ire donde usted va.
(d) Yo ire donde usted vaya.
(e) Estoy buscando un libro que tiene un forro rojo.
(f) Estoy buscando un libro que tenga un forro rojo.

He proposes a feature [±specific] to distinguish the two types of antecedents and further suggests that according to 'this view no symbol ADV would, be introduced by the phrase structure rules' (Cressey 1968. 499). His last suggestion is a move towards the eventual simplification of the base and a semantically more appropriate account of adverbials (George Lakoff 1970b 1967, Robin Lakoff 1968, Casagrande 1968, 1969, Rivero 1970b).

Langacker's dissertation (Langacker 1966a) is divided into three main parts. In part one he considers the complement system of French. This part is an evaluation of the universality of Rosenbaum's analysis of predicate complements in English (Rosenbaum 1967). The second part deals with the determiner system of French where he argues the pros and cons of two plausible alternatives. The third part has to do with pronominal expressions. He considers interrogation and negation as they pertain to the sentence (yes/no questions and sentential negation), to the determiner system and to the pronominal system. Also considered are relativization, infinitive clauses, reflexives, pronominalization, pro-forms, clitic placement, agreement, imperative, and a number of language specific rules.

This work became quickly outdated, through the author's own subsequent work and through other people's too. Evidently a few inadequacies have caused him to refrain from publishing the work as is. Fortunately, however, scholars have had access to this clearly written and broadly based dissertation in xerographic form. In that form it has served many a student of language interested in a broad classical analysis of French syntax. Another of Langacker's contributions to the field of Romance syntax is an article entitled 'Observations on French Possessives' (Langacker 1968). To derive a - j,

(a) ma maison
(b) cette maison est la mienne
(c) la mienne
(d) ma maison à moi
(e) un ami à moi
(f) Elle a levé la main.
(g) Je lui ai cassé le bras
(h) la maison de Pierre
(i) Elle a les yeux bleus
(j) la femme aux yeux bleus

he proposes and discusses a dozen explicitly stated rules. The theoretic framework of this article is essentially the same as that of his dissertation. In the last part of his article Langacker makes use of Fillmore's case theory to solve a problem involving the *avoir/être* dichotomy and the prepositions *à* and *de*. This last part, in Langacker's own admission, is 'highly tentative.'

Maurice Gross's *Grammaire transformationnelle du français: le verbe* (1968) is difficult book to place within any of the three periods referred to here. These periods are distinguished on the basis of the formalism used and on the relative emphasis on regularity. Gross chooses to avoid using the formalism characteristic of any of the three periods, probably a plus in the evaluation of his book, and he limits his investigation to a classification of many surface phenomena. The end result is a book vaguely based on principles of transformational grammar which limits itself to an inventory of complementation as it manifests itself in surface structure. However, because his inventory is thorough and detailed Gross succeeds in bringing out a wealth of facts about verbs that has provided a basis for

other important investigations, notably Perlmutter's work on surface
structure constraints (Perlmutter 1969, 1970, 1971).

Jean Dubois and Françoise Dubois Charlier's *Eléments de linguistique
française: syntaxe* (1970) contrasts strikingly with Gross's book. The
latter is nearly all free of transformational formalism while the former
is written precisely for the purpose of giving a detailed account of the
formalism of classical transformational grammar. Excluding a few points
which the Dubois adapted from *Syntactic Structures*, *Eléments de linguistique
française: syntaxe* owes its theoretical basis to Chomsky (1965). This
book constitutes an excellent introduction to the mechanics of classical
transformational grammar. It is lacking, however, in argumentation for
or against the analyses adopted in the book. A number of the rules proposed, it should be said in all fairness, are of the language specific,
shallow structure type, the kind which it is most difficult to find
arguments to support. The emphasis on formalism takes away from space
which two grammarians as talented as the Dubois could have used, as they
do a few places in the book, to impart particularly interesting information
about French. *Eléments* is not a book which tells its readers about French
syntax, as Gross (1968) does, instead it tells about the formalism of
classical transformational syntax and how some portions of French syntax
can be made to fit within the classical model. Hopefully, a subsequent
book will take up a number of syntactic and semantic facts not described
or explained by the classical theory.

Works on Romance have, like those on other languages, been influenced
by the theoretic currents of the discipline. Fillmore's theory of deep
case relations (Fillmore 1966a,b, 1968a), a revision of the standard
classical theory (Chomsky 1965), has influenced Mark Goldin's *Spanish
Case and Function* (Goldin 1968), Donald Dugas (Dugas 1969), Ana McCoy
(McCoy 1970) and Web Donaldson (Donaldson 1970b). This last dissertation
is a particularly clear and informative study. Donaldson argues that
essentially and accidentally reflexive verbs are in fact manifestations
of quite regular processes of abstract syntax. Their surface irregularity
is simply due to a lexical constraint. As for so-called 'pronominal
passives,'

La porte s'est ouverte brusquement.
Ses ouvrages se vendent uniquement en librairie.

Donaldson shows them to be neither reflexive nor passive. Instead, he
proposes that they are intransitive verbs and that the reflexive particle
se is introduced late, by rule.

Other thinkers have influenced Romance syntactic studies. Katz's notion
of semantic interpretation (Katz and Postal 1964, Katz 1966, 1967) is used
extensively in Ursula Stephany's *Adjektivische Attributkonstruktionen des
Französischen* (Stephany 1970). Klima's syntactic approach to negation
(Klima 1964') and a number of McCawley's notational improvements to
classical theory show up in Claire Asselin's dissertation on negation in
French (Asselin 1968).

Two dissertations on Italian syntax were written at Cornell. They are Maria Swenson's 'The Nominal Phrase in Italian: a transformational approach' (Swenson 1969), and Annarita Puglielli's (Puglielli 1968) which has appeared in print in Italian: *Strutture sintatiche del predicato in italiano* (Puglielli 1970).[17]

Also to be placed in the classical period in spite of its recent publication date is a book put together by a team of dynamic linguists in Montreal. *Description syntaxique élémentaire du français* (A. Dugas et al., 1969) is a set of team produced contributions, the main one being a syntax of French. The other contributions in Dugas et al. (1969) appear in the form of articles.

The grammar which constitutes the substantial part of the book combines baroque and classical traits. Next to syntactic and semantic features, it makes use of generalized, double-based transformations. A good part of the volume, in fact, is aimed at defending the generalized transformation. One of the appended contributions argues against recursion in the base. Another places referential indices on determiners in an attempt to control the scope of reference so as to distinguish between complex sentences whose relative clauses are embedded in different order. One of the appended contributions is particularly interesting. It treats the relationship of the determiner of an antecedent with the type of relative clause that can occur with it. The grammar proper is not very informative and at times it is misleading: not informative in that rules are given with no arguments as to why they exist and often with no illustration, misleading because some rules are simply wrong.[18]

Of the several theses and dissertations published by the Studies in Linguistics and Language Learning at the University of Washington, four deal with Spanish syntax. Claire Steven's dissertation, 'A Characterization of Spanish Nouns and Adjectives' (Stevens 1966), constitutes a hesitant step out of the baroque. The major improvement over baroque transformational grammar seems to be the use of syntactic features. Why nouns and adjectives (rather than verbs and adverbs or pronouns and conjunctions) are treated together remains unclear. A more felicitous choice would have been adjectives and verbs or prepositional phrases and adverbials; but Stevens did not have access to Lakoff's dissertation (1970b/65). Her work was particularly useful, however, in that it proposed a large amount of transformational rules on which subsequent studies were able to build.

The third volume of the University of Washington Studies series is John Lackstrom's thesis (1967). It is concerned with pro-forms in Spanish noun-phrases. This is another detailed study of an aspect of Spanish. Following the classical view of pronouns, Lackstrom distinguishes between pronouns which are formed transformationally by PRONOMINALIZATION from *pro-nouns* which 'are introduced into the grammar at the deepest level, the base component' (Lackstrom 1967.115), and shows the abstract structure of these forms. He concludes with interesting generalizations about pro-nouns and takes issue with Postal (Postal 1966) as to the derivation of pro-nouns.

Falk (1968), another volume in the same series, deals with nominalizations Falk discusses fact, manner, abstract and non-abstract nominalizations[19] as illustrated respectively by a-d.

(a) el construir el hombre la casa . . .
(b) el construir del hombre . . .
(c) la construction del la casa por el hombre . . .
(d) *la construction del hombre* es alta

Testing the theory of transformational grammar available to her as she
attempted to formulate the principles responsible for generating the
above nominalizations she discovered that nominalization in Spanish and in
English constitute counterexamples to the theory of classical transformational
grammar. The points she raises and others are still debated however, as
nominalization continues to be a burning issue in modern grammatical studies.
(Chomsky 1970b, Fraser 1970, G. Lakoff 1969, 1970b, R. Lakoff 1968, Menzel
1969, Newmeyer 1970, 1971, Albury, in progress).
   Philip Klein's thesis (Klein 1968) is a particularly lucid piece of
work. He starts out by giving accounts of traditional analyses of modal
auxiliaries as an independent class. Then he points to an argument (a
morphological argument) by Stockwell, Bowen and Martin (1965) that unlike
English, Spanish modals behave like main verbs. Klein himself gives clear
syntactic arguments to show that within the so-called class of modal
auxiliaries the modals do not behave alike, thus creating either (1) subclasses of modals or (2) doubts about the existence of a modal class.
He points to a suggestion by Bolinger in his review of Stockwell, Bowen
and Martin (1965) (Bolinger 1967) to the effect that a syntactic feature
[+M] could distinguish between *poder* and *deber* on the one hand, from
querer on the other. The former would carry [+M] while the latter would
not. Klein proceeds to show that the feature solution is inadequate and,
lo and behold, he opts for a solution calling for modals as main verbs.
This is particularly interesting since there is no evidence in the body
of the work or in the bibliography that Klein ever set eyes on John Ross's
'Auxiliaries as Main Verbs' (Ross 1967a). The rest of this M.A. thesis is
devoted to syntactic arguments in favor of the 'verb phrase complementation' solution. Klein's last consideration has to do with the possible
extension of that solution to other auxiliaries. He concludes that such
an extension is not possible because the complement S of a copula cannot
be negated while the complement S of a modal may.

 (a) puedo no cantar
*(b) he no ido
*(c) esta no aqui

There is little doubt in my mind that Klein has since changed his mind
about these last two points.
   The passage from the classical era to the contemporary period took
place over several years with no clear break, all the more reason to label
the contemporary period neo-classicism. In Romance studies the passage
from one period to the other is also very gradual. Throughout the
classical period there were efforts to alter the theory. Phillip Klein's
fascinating thesis is an example of efforts to go beyond the model of

language proposed in Chomsky (1965). His claim that auxiliaries are main verbs is an important move in the direction of a more regular, and more universal grammar. In the attempt to simplify the base and to better integrate syntactic processes, Casagrande (1968) proposed that negation is a verb. A similar claim was arrived at by G. Lakoff (1966). Neither of these two (slightly different) proposals can remain in their original form but they represented a step in the direction of regularity and generalization. Casagrande (1969) is an attempt along the lines of performatives. It argues for a derivation of *est-ce que* not discussed elsewhere, and relates imperatives, questions, negation, and emphasis. Along similar lines, Mercedes Roldan's '*Ser* and *Estar* in a new light' (Roldan, 1970) leads her reader through the dense forest of the two so-called copulas of Spanish. In this amply illustrated article she concludes that *ser* only is a copula, while *estar* is really a stative verb.

St. Clair (1971) shows that DISLOCATION in Rumanian is a copying rule and not a chopping rule. He gives evidence from Rumanian for generalizing Ross's (1967b) copying rule. Unlike Ross's copying rule which simultaneously Chomsky-adjoins a copy of an NP and pronominalizes the unmoved NP, St. Clair's version does only the former of the two. St. Clair claims that PRONOMINALIZATION does not take place at that point but later in derivation. Hence, in St. Clair's view, his own version of DISLOCATION is more general than Ross's because it does not entail a simultaneous pronominalization. The argument would be more convincing if DISLOCATION was shown to precede PRONOMINALIZATION on independent grounds.

Reviewing the accomplishments of the classical period in Romance syntax, we see that a number of perceptive studies have contributed to a better understanding of language. By demonstrating that a particular process is present in a variety of superficially different sentences, by pointing to similarities between apparently different constructions, by showing that apparently idiosyncratic constructions are manifestations of deep regularity, researchers of the classical era in Romance have suceeded in tearing down the barriers of superficial analysis. The ways in which these accomplishments parallels those of students of other languages, notably English, are more numerous than might appear at first. This similarity of direction should not surprise the observer. It proceeds from the yet greater regularity of language, which is coming to light after years of concerted effort in attempting to find the principles which underly language as it manisfests itself around us.

NEO-CLASSICISM

I will not enumerate the many excellent books and articles which fall under the category of neo-classicism. Articles on Romance syntax have appeared at a fast rate and cover too wide a range of topics to be discussed individually. For a listing of contributions in the last four or five years the bibliography at the end of this volume will suffice. Instead, this part will outline a few of the areas of contemporary research which are of interest to the world of linguistics and to Romance syntax in particular. These will be clitics and surface structure constraints, abstract syntax and global constraints.

From the earliest efforts in explaining languages transformationally it has been obvious to researchers that constraints needed to be placed on rule application, on derivation, on the form of structures, on the vocabulary of the metatheory, etc. Among the constraints that have been shown to be needed in grammar are surface structure constraints (Perlmutter, 1969, 1970, 1971). Surface structure constraints can be found operating in many different languages, governing the behavior of a variety of items. Arguments for the existence of surface constraints, however, were first given on evidence principally from Spanish and French clitics. Perlmutter argued that there is no way of constraining the order of clitics in Spanish and French other than setting up as output conditions on syntax filtering constraints whose purpose is to allow through the proper sequence and to block from further derivation any sequence which does not match the order of elements prescribed in the constraint. Perlmutter distinguished between what he called global and non-global surface structure constraints. Global constraints are not restricted with regard to a contextual occurrence of any sort: they apply in all cases. Non-global constraints are restricted in that they are context sensitive: for clitic pronouns in Spanish and French, their context is defined in terms of the verbs under which they cliticize. Some verbs do not allow certain clitic co-occurrences. In a paper in this volume Dinnsen denies the necessity of any distinction between global and non-global surface structure constraints for Spanish. He claims that it is possible to formulate constraints that characterize Perlmutter's set of Spanish data and he further argues that Perlmutter's distinction between global and non-global surface structure constraints is impossible to integrate in a theory allowing surface structure constraints.

Another work on clitics which leads to Perlmutter's pioneering work on output constraints is Roldan's 'Double object constructions in Spanish' (Roldan, 1971). Roldan investigates several logically possible derivations for the subject+verb+direct-object+indirect object construction and its various topicalized and cliticized equivalents. She discards each alternative on grammar internal grounds and concludes that the surface structure constraints solution is the only one that meets descriptive adequacy.

Other works on clitics, although not involving surface structure constraints, have left a mark in neo-classical studies in Romance syntax. Kayne's dissertation, to appear in a revised form (Kayne, forthcoming d), argues for the cyclic application of transformations on the basis of the distribution of the clitic pronouns of French as they appear in the *fair/laisser* +INFINITIVE construction. Among the topics discussed are the behavior of the quantifiers *tous/tout* , clitic placement, the construction mentioned above, along with a wealth of related facts such as a syntactic-deletion rule which must disregard case distinction but take phonological identity into account, the A over A principle as applied to prepositional phrases, apparent similarities in different dative constructions, and the idiosyncratic behavior of the clitic 'se', to mention a few. Ruwet (1970) also makes use of clitics (as well as some quantifiers) to argue convincingly for the existence of *Subject Raising*. This most clever syntactic argument derives from the fact that the whole subject NP or only the head noun can be raised. In the latter case, a cliticized pronoun or a quantifier remains in the S from which the head noun is raised, leaving a shadow, as it were, in the lower S.

One of the characteristics of the neo-classical period in contemporary syntactic studies is the emphasis placed by a number of scholars on abstract explanation of superficially idiosyncratic facts. This trend in abstractness has been inherent in transformational grammar since 1957 but only relatively recently has it become an issue (Chomsky, 1970b). The trend towards radically more abstract explanation started with the work of George and Robin Lakoff. The latter's dissertation, published by MIT Press (R. Lakoff, 1968), is concerned precisely with abstract explanation. Lakoff's book is of greatest importance to those interested in Romance syntax. Concentrating her study on complementation and related matters, she points to the many affinities shared by Latin and the Romance languages, and shows that the syntax of Latin and that of English are also very similar, thus demonstrating that the more abstract the description the more likely it is to be near-universal. Lakoff's book is also important for other reasons, her theory of syntactic change, in particular. For a good evaluation of Lakoff's book see Green (1970).

Abstract syntax is, of course, a broad term and can therefore cover a number of different though parallel directions. One example of abstract description is McCawley's claim about the deep order of constituents in English (McCawley, 1970'). A similar claim is made by Meyer (this volume) regarding Spanish. She reaches her conclusion on the basis of different arguments than did McCawley. Yet another example of abstract underlying structures is (Gulstad, this volume) where a number of deep relations are explicitly represented. All these efforts converge in an attempt to find greater regularity in language.

Among Romance syntacticians Maria-Luisa Rivero has been most active in the area of abstract syntax. In 'La concepción de los modos en la grammatica de Andrés Bello y los verbos abstractos en la grammatica generativa', Maria-Luisa Rivero (1970a) draws a parallel between the insightful work of Andrés Bello regarding the subjunctive and that of the generativists in general and of the Lakoffs in particular. In the thorough treatment that we have come to expect from her, Rivero illustrates the above mentioned parallel in the use of independent subjunctives, of the optative subjunctive, of the subjunctive in subordinate classes. She goes on to show that the syntactic structures discussed in connection with the subjunctive and the abstract verb that governs it are also paralleled by similar structures involving the indicative, namely the performative structures first discovered by Ross (1970). She concludes that mood is not 'una categoría sintáctico-semántica con significado propio sino que el modo es un cambio morfológico que experimenta un verbo de manera automática en función de su posición subordinada.'

Continuing her work on abstract syntax and in particular on the differences between the indicative and the subjunctive, Rivero (1971) gives evidence that the presuppositional nature of a complement affects its

syntactic behavior. Her arguments are based on NEG-TRANSPORTATION,
EQUI-NP DELETION, NEG-INCORPORATION, SUBJECT RAISING, and tense restrictions.
She shows that complements which involve a positive presupposition with
respect to their truth value and are in the indicative mood are not subject
to tense restrictions. These complements also behave differently from
complements involving no positive presuppostion about the truth value of
their contents in that the former block the above mentioned rules, while
the latter undergo those rules.
   She further argues that the prepositional nature of the complement
cannot be attributed to the matrix verb and discards the possibility of
surface structure interpretation rules because the nature of the presupposition must be known at the time of application of the rules mentioned
above. She painstakingly reviews means of saving this interpretive
solution and concludes that the presuppositions she is discussing are
unlikely to be accounted for by late interpretive rules. She then takes
up the problem of the form in which presuppositions are to be incorporated
in a generative grammer and argues for the presuppostion as a conjunct, as
suggested by Morgan (Morgan, 1969).
   One issue in Romance syntax which separates the abstractist from the
lexicalist is the nature of French interrogation, particularly of the
est-ce que construction. Back in the classical days Langacker (1965)
proposed a transformational solution for the derivation of *est-ce que*,
qu'est-ce, etc   (See also Langacker's article in this volume where he
attempts to defend his position). A number of arguments have been put forth
arguing against the transformational solution in favor of one that would
simply insert these forms as syntactic markers (Roulet, 1969, Hirschbühler,
1970, Huddleston and Uren, 1969). Casagrande (forthcoming a) shows that
fossilization may well constitute the common ground on which both views can
be reconciled.
   One of the least popular proposals of the generative semantics approach
has been that of global rules. First proposed by G. Lakoff (1970a) and
also argued for by Lakoff and Perlmutter (MS), Casagrande (1970), Andrews
(1971), and Postal (1972), these rules apply to non-adjacent trees in a
derivation; global rules differ from classical transformations which are
restricted to apply to adjacent trees in a derivation. The main criticism
of global rules (Brame & Baker, 1972) has been that global rules are not
sufficiently constrained. Instead of attempting to constrain these rules,
however, critics have tried to use some coding device in an attempt to
by-pass this new theoretical device. This reaction to global rules, it
has been pointed out by Lakoff (1972), is reminiscent of that of the
structuralists against Chomsky's transformation. In his brilliant dissertation, however, Fauconnier (1971a) found that there are pronominalization
and agreement phenomena in French which neither global rules nor interpretive
rules can account for while his unexpanded NP solution does account for
those phenomena. In effect what Fauconnier's solution claims is that
some coreferential phenomena are really a complex of two processes: one
which establishes relations between certain nodes but does nothing else,
and later another which effects the proper feature copying. Fauconnier's

solution resembles that of Brame & Baker and was arrived at independently. Fauconnier also distinguishes between two types of global constraints: (1) those that are language specific and describe only the data they were formulated to describe;and (2) those which are more general (not language or phenomena specific) and which predict the behavior of a greater range of phenomena than those they were intended to explain. In his estimation the first type does not require global apparatus while the latter is justified. It seems, however, that the argument against global constraints would be stronger if it were possible to show that no global constraints of any sort are necessary nor sufficient. To do otherwise is to claim that there are universal (or metatheoretical) processes which cannot have language specific equivalents. If global constraints of a universal nature are to be incorporated in the theory of language, it only seems natural to have global constraints of a language specific nature as well. Similarly, it would seem odd to deny transformational status to a language specific rule on the grounds that it predicts no more than what it is intended to describe.

From all that precedes, one thing is certain. Syntax has been experiencing a degree of excitement which characterizes scientific revolutions and a good deal of this excitement comes from work in Romance languages. As we look back and study the exciting controversies which raged at various times in the history of language study, we need not feel that 'those were the days.' Excitement is with us here and now. *Carpe diem!*

NOTES

1. There is little doubt that the study of Latin can shed light on the nature of the Romance languages. A variety of phenomena are shared by Latin and its descendants (Robin Lakoff 1968). That the Romance languages, and in fact all languages, share many of their features is a belief common among transformationalists. We know also that this same belief was held before, during the Middle Ages, for example. However, investigating the works of Peter of Seville, Albert the Great, Sanctius and Arnauld for the purpose of illustrating the similarity of their studies to ours is a task of proportions too grand to be even outlined here.

2. For an example of these grammars see Girault Duvivier's *Grammaire des Grammaires*, probably the epitome of these works. It is a compilation of the salient points of several other traditional grammars of French.

3. It is encouraging to see in contemporary work a rejuvenated interest in the study of diachronic phenomena. This should not, however, be interpreted as a return to old beliefs and methods (King 1969, Kiparsky 1968b, Robin Lakoff 1968).

4. For a detailed study of the developments of Romance syntax in the nineteenth and twentieth century ending before the generative-transformational period see Patiño (1965) of which some of the above comments were paraphrases.

5. Typical of baroque descriptions are Lees's *Grammar of English Nominalization* (Lees 1960) and Klima's "Negation in English" (Klima 1964). Both squarely tackled problems of English grammar which are still to be solved.

6. Actually there are more than two sides to this controversy. Theories about the interrelation of meaning and syntax are likely to be as numerous as there are people seriously asking themselves questions about that relationship. By and large, however, there are two tendencies with Chomsky, Dougherty, and Jackendoff defending the lexicalist interpretive position and Ross, the Lakoffs, McCawley, and Postal the generative one. The term 'interpretivist' refers to a linguist who contends that meaning is assigned in an interpretive semantic component. Interpretivists also believe that words are basic entities in language; consequently they place the lexicon in the base of their transformational grammar. For this reason they are called lexicalists. The term generative semantics has to do with the contention that syntactic and semantic processes are alike, and that they should be characterized in the same way; consequently the base is a set of semantic structures represented in the form of tree diagrams—the same diagrams as used to represent syntactic structure.

Among thinkers who have expressed themselves on the question of the relation of syntax and semantics, Katz (Fodor and Katz 1963, Katz and Postal 1964, Katz 1966, 1967, 1972) holds to interpretive rules which apply in deep structure. With componentiality and interpretiveness on the one hand and deep meaning on the other Katz seems to be straddling the fence.

7.   These arguments over the nature of language structure are reminiscent of those of the Analogists and Anomalists of Alexandria and Pergamon. The difference between the ancient controversy and that of contemporary thought is that the former argued over morphology while the latter argue over the nature and scope of rules of language as they affect syntax and meaning.

8.   In various lectures on generative semantics George Lakoff has pointed out that global and transderivational constraints are not do-anything devices (Cf. also Postal, 1972). But even properly constrained, such rules do increase the generative capacity of grammars: a dilema.

9.   Rather than following in strict chronological order the appearance of works in Romance syntax, I have placed them into one of the three categories outlined in the first part of the paper. Also, I will not follow chronology too closely within each of the three parts in order to keep together works which share direction or inspiration. Consequently the reader may experience a feeling of regression at times but I think that this order will prove less uncomfortable than a chronological harum-scarum, a meanwhile-back-at-the-ranch approach.

10.   Not discussed here is the last volume of J. Dubois' *Grammaire structural du français* in which the author injects his personal type of transformationalism. For an evaluation of Dubois's structural trilogy see Micheline Sainte-Marie's brilliant review (1971).

11.   In seven chapters crammed into a mere 120 pages, Nivette reviews the principles of the structural method and illustrates the various difinitions of the term grammar in 7 pages, expedites the *Syntactic Structures* in 9 pages, and discards phonology and semantics in 7 and 3 pages respectively.

12.   Actually, Lamérand is not solely accountable for this cryptic manner of refering to construction-types. This extensive use of formalism is a remnant of structural influence. Tagmemic analysis and Gross's *Grammaire transformationnelle du français* (1968), both sources in Lamérand's book, identify constructions precisely in that way.

13.   There is no truth to the belief that Lamérand attempted to sneak in levity in his book by arranging it so that an uprooted and a down rooted tree are pictured on page 69.

14.   Maria-Luisa Rivero, in this volume, shows that clear and methodical arguments can shed light on the same topic.

15.   I do not mean here to imply that integration of theories is not a desirable goal. In fact such conciliatory efforts are laudable, but they are not exempt from critical evaluation. As new theoretical proposals they are subject to empirical and logical scrutiny.

16.   A number of useful remarks were made to Langacker about this article on interrogatives (1965). They are mentioned in his dissertation (1966. 74, fn. 18).

17.   For a review of Puglielli (1970), see Wanner (1971).

18.   To place all agreement rules pre-cyclically, for example, is wrong because gender and number agreement in French is a global rule (Casagrande, 1970). For yet another argument against pre-cyclic agreement one might simply refer to subject raising and passive. Subject raising and passive are cyclic rules and must apply before agreement.

Les manifestants sembl*aient* encore plus acharnés.
Il sembl*ait* que les manifestants étaient encore plus acharnés.
La porte *fut* ouverte par les manifestants.
Les manifestants ouvrir*ent* la porte.

So agreement is not pre-cyclic.
19. Cf. Lees (1960)

GEORGE W. PATTERSON
UNIVERSITY OF ALBERTA

FRENCH INTERROGATIVES: A DIACHRONIC PROBLEM

1. INTRODUCTION

The traditional concept of analogy has been replaced by simplification or lexical restructuring in generative grammars. This paper will examine this replacement in respect to diachronic data from French.[1] The central character of French interrogatives since at least the twelfth century has been an inversion transformation. Many minor changes have occurred in the specific formulation of inversion and in an accompanying deletion transformation. A single recent modification challenges the generative interpretation of analogy.[2]

2. ANALOGY AND SIMPLIFICATION

Analogy has played an important role in traditional linguistic literature.[3] Most treatments have viewed analogy as a proportional relation of the type:

(1) $a:a' = b:x$

Where x is the analogically modified or created item. The change manifested in x is such that x is made to bear the same relationship to b as a' holds to a. Typical examples are (2) and (3).

(2)   sing:sang = bring:x
            brought = x > brang

(3)   dog:dogs = cow:x
            kine = x > cows

The problems with this conception have been: (1) determining the conditions under which analogy applies; (2) the provision of appropriate partners for the two sides of the proportion; and, (3) an explanation of the division between occasional and sporadic application to suitable items and instances where all appropriate items are affected.[4] These problems have remained unanswered in spite of various attempts at delineating the conditions under which analogy operates and the direction analogical changes take.[5]

In generative transformational theory it has been contended that analogical changes can be described as simplification within grammars.[6] Halle (1962:344-5) suggested that the sources of changes are minor additions to the grammars of adults. Adults are presumed to be incapable of constructing an optimum grammar or of restructuring an already existing grammar. Children, learning from adults or other persons with nonoptimal grammars, construct the simplest grammar consistent with the data to which they are exposed. The basic process of change is simplification. Special instances of simplification may be any of the following: rule reordering, rule loss, rule addition or lexical restructuring.[7] Simplification includes levelling, or loss of an alternation, which is represented either as as rule loss or as loss of special markers--as in (3)--and extension of alternations to new instances--as in (2)--which is represented as generalization of rules. Generalization can take the form of changes in the structural descriptions of transformations.

Complication is the introduction of new structural conditions. These new conditions might be features which are entirely new to the language. They are probably more often features which occur elsewhere in the language and are added to the environment of a rule so that the rule applies to fewer items. This is a reduction in the scope of the rule. It is not a difference in the lexical redundancies or other features of the items previously affected by the rule. In Old French, a sentence or clause initial adverb or object pronoun usually entailed an inversion of the subject and verb:[8]

(4) a. Là est-il.
     b. Il est là.
         He is (over) there.

(5) a. Dont *dist li dus* au chevalier....
     b. Alors le duc dit au chevalier....
         Then the Duke said to the knight....

Two transformations were involved in the derivation of these sentences. The following evidence indicates that it was a two step process. The first step was left movement of the appropriate constituent from the verb phrase. The second was inversion. Sentence (6) contains a relative clause. Left movement has applied but inversion has not. The inversion transformation did not apply to relative clauses.

(6) a. ...se tres douce amie qu'il tant amoit. (Aucassin)
     b. ...sa chère amie qu'il aimait tellement.
         ...his dearest lover who(m) he loved so much.

Later,[9] inversion became optional in the environment of adverbs.
This change is neither simplification, nor complication--there is no
increase or loss of generality. It was only a modification from
obligatory to optional status of the inversion rule in the environment
of initial adverbs.

Modern French has introduced considerable complication. Only a
few sentence initial adverbs are accompanied by inversion:[10]

(7)   A peine l'*avait-il* quittée qu'elle....
        He had hardly left her when she....

(8)   Peut-être *était-elle* une des ces....
        Maybe she was one of those....

(9)   Ils étaient grands, aussi *trouvais-je*....
        They were big so I thought....

The portion of the inversion rule which is sensitive to inital adverbs
contains some very detailed information--probably the specific lexical
items. This portion of the grammar has therefore been complicated.

  Complication does not include a change such as

(10) ME *werede* > *wore,*

which merely depicts a change in the category of the verb so that different
rules apply to it. The rules which apply were already in the grammar.
The change in (10) does not appear in the simplification-complication
dichotomy.[11]

  The third general category of change is rule loss and rule addition.
An example of rule loss has occurred in non-literary Modern French.
There are no inverted subjects and verbs following sentence initial
adverbs in declarative sentences. The inversion rule, as it applied in
this environment, has been lost.

  An example of rule addition is the vocalization of pre-consonantal *l*
to *u* (Pope 1966:154-5) in Old French.

  Beyond the outline presented by Halle (see above), no attention has
been directed to the structural conditions under which rule additions
are made. Labov (1963) and Weinreich, *et al.* (1968) have pointed out
the necessity for determining the structural conditions in which changes
occur.[12] Labov presents what he calls the "transition problem" (1963:261)
as a fundamental problem for diachronic studies. This problem requires
that the steps involved in the progression from one diachronic state to
another be explicitly understood and formulated.

  This requirement looms as especially important when considering rule
additions. Rule additions are fundamentally different from simplifications
and other changes. It is not at all clear what type of information must
appear in the data to which a child is exposed in order for him to con-

struct a rule which has no analog in the grammar of his parents.[13]
Simplifications and other internal modifications operate within the
systematic relationships specified in parental grammars--and which are
manifested in their output data. Although it may well be impossible to
determine the factors inducing the change, for example, of a given rule
from obligatory to optional status, the information appropriate to the
change is present in the data to which children learning the language
are exposed: the data show obligatory (or uniform) relationships and
children change this feature. Similarly, rule loss can occur without
obvious motivation--cf. the loss of the adverbial environment of inversion
in popular Modern French.

The remainder of this paper outlines an instance of rule addition for
which the structural context is clear, but for which it is impossible
to provide a generative account.

3. FRENCH INTERROGATIVES

In twelfth century French, yes/no questions were formed by a process
of inversion: the subject and the verb (or auxiliary) were inverted.[14]

(11) a. Sire cumpainz, *faites* le *vus* de gret?
                  (Roland)
      b. Mon compagnon, le faites-vous exprès?
          Comrade, are you doing it on purpose?

(12) a. *A* chi *este Morgue li fée?*
                (Le Jeu de la Feuillée)
      b. Morgue le fée a-t-elle été ici?
          Has Morgue the fairy been here?

(13) a. i) Mes qui *est cil* que vos haez?
                (Renart)
        ii) Mais qui est-ce que c'est que vous haissez?
            But *who* is it that you hate?
      b. i) Qui *est ce,* diex, qui m'aparole.[15]
                (Renart)
        ii) Qui est celui, dieux, qui me parle?
            Who, gods, is speaking to me?

The examples (11-13) show that there were no restrictions on the type
of subject that was inverted. In (11), the second person pronoun *vus*
is in inverted position--the intervening object *le* is not relevant here.
In (12), the subject is the phrase *Morgue li fee,* which follows the verb
a estè. The sentences in (13) have inverted demonstrative pronouns as
subjects. They also show that inversion occurs in *WH* questions.

This situation is approximated in the transformation in (14).[16]

(14) S.D. X Q Y NP VP Z
            1 2 3 4 5 6 ==>

      S.C. 1 2 3 ∅ 5+4 6

By the sixteenth century a change had taken place: only pronoun
subjects could appear in inverted position and sentences like (15) (from
the fifteenth century) with the reduplicated inverted pronoun were
obligatory.

(15) a. *Ces harnois* cy sont *ilz* pourrys?
          Ces salades nous sieent *ilz* mal.
                    (Greban, *La Passion*)
      b   Cet équipement est-ce qui'il est usé?
          Ces casques, est-ce qu'ils nous vont mal?
          Are these outfits worn out?
          Do these helmets not fit us?

The sixteenth century, then, required a transformation like (16).

(16) S.D. X Q Y NP VP Z
            1 2 3 4 5 6 ==>

      S.C. 1 2 3 4 5 + $\begin{vmatrix} 4 \\ +PRO \end{vmatrix}$ 6

This change is a complication because it requires either the introduction of a NP deletion rule, or a restriction of the environment of
a previous NP deletion rule (see footnote 16). In either case the NP
deletion applies only to pre-verbal NP nodes containing the feature [+PRO].
     The situation established by (16) in the sixteenth century has been
maintained essentially intact into Modern Standard French. During
the seventeenth century, however, the alternate, though closely related,
est-ce que construction became prominent. *Est-ce que* contains an inverted
verb and demonstrative subject. It had its origins in sentences like
(13). Since its appearance before any sentence made the sentence an
interrogative, it is assumed for the purposes of this paper that all
sentences contained the declarative equivalent, *c'est que,* in underlying
structure.
     There was a *c'est que* deletion transformation which applied in appro-
priate conditions.[17] When *c'est que* was not deleted, the inversion transformation applied to it and *est-ce que* resulted. Apart form the altered
sense of *ce,* the situation is approximated in Modern French. Given (17a)
as an approximate underlying structure, (17c) would result if *c'est que*
deletion applied.

(17) a. Q C'est que Jean part.
              C'est que deletion ==>

b.   Jean part.
           Inversion ==>
c.   Jean part-il?

If, on the other hand, *C'est que* deletion does not occur, then a derivation like (18) results.

(18) a. Q C'est que je chante.
           Inversion ==>
     b. Est-ce que je chante?

In pre-sixteenth century French *C'est que* appeared in surface structure only as an explanatory or focusing device. The role of the demonstrative as an emphatic in (13) has been lost. In accordance with the
reduced function of *ce*, inverted *est-ce que* lost its rhetorical force
and gradually became an interrogative marker through the following stages.

During the seventeenth century *c'est que* deletion was forbidden when
the following subject NP was first person singular with most verbs. This
change was a clear complication since it added features to the grammar:
c'est que deletion was no longer dependent solely on previous conditions
but on the person of the subject NP and the verb. This change prevented
the inversion of the first person singular pronoun *je*. Shortly after
the inception of these conditions on *c'est que* deletion, inverted *est-ce
que* could optionally occur as a first person plural interrogative marker.

This second change is presumably an analogical extension. It is a
case of simplification since it marks the change from specification (19)
to specification (20) as part of the environment for *c'est que* retention.

(19) $\begin{bmatrix} + \text{ First person} \\ - \text{ Plural} \end{bmatrix}$

(20) ____ $\begin{bmatrix} + \text{ First person} \end{bmatrix}$

Subsequent simplifications removed even the person features from the
environment and *est-ce que* optionally appeared in front of all sentences
as an interrogative marker. This general situation still prevails in
Modern Standard French. Sentences (21) - (23) are examples.

(21) Est-ce que je chante bien?
     *Chante-je bien?
     Do I sing well?

(22) Chantons-nous bien?
     Est-ce que nous chantons bien?
     Do we sing well?

(23) Ta mère viendra-t-elle?
      *Viendra ta mère?
      Will your mother come?

4. THE DIACHRONIC PROBLEM

In some dialects[18] of French, however, there has evolved an entirely novel means of forming interrogatives. Examples from a Canadian dialect are:[19]

(24) Les filles *sont ti* en train de dîner?
      Are the girls eating?

(25) a. T'*as ti* un char?
          Do you have a car?
      b. Vous *avez ti* un char?
          Do you (formal) have a car?

(26) Je *sais ti* ton nom?
      Do I know your name?

(27) Ta soeur *est ti* marié?
      Is your sister married?

(28) Les gars *seront ti* rentrés?
      Will the boys be back?

(29) *Ou c'est ti* que tu vas?
      Where are you going?

(30) *Qui c'est ti* qui est là?
      Who is that over there?

(31) *Pourquoi c'est ti* que les cochons courent?
      Why are the pigs running?

(32) *Quand c'est ti* que tu nourris tes bêtes?
      When do you feed the stock?

(33) a. *Quel* jour *c'est ti*??
      b. *Quel* jour que *c'est ti* aujourd'hui?
          What day is it today?

(34) *Quel* char tu *vas ti* acheter?
      Which car are you going to buy?

(35) Ta fille, *quel* age *a ti*?
      How old is your daughter?

(36) *Que c'est ti* que tu leurs a donné?
      What did you give them?

Examples (24) - (28) are yes/no questions. The particle *ti* has replaced
the inversion found in Standard French dialects. This *ti* is simply placed
after the verb (24) - (26) or after the auxiliary (27, 28).
   Examples (29) - (36) are *WH* questions. In these examples the *WH* word
is front shifted as in Standard French but inversion is replaced by post-
verbal *ti*.
   For the purposes of this paper it is assumed that the dialects with the
ti particle have a common historical basis with standard dialects.[20] The generally accepted explanation of the origin of *ti* was first proposed by Paris
(1877). Regular third person masculine inversions yield $t + i$ sequences.

(37) a. Vient-il?
          Is he coming?
      b. Parlait-il?
          Was he talking?
      c. Sont-ils?
          Are they?
      d. Arrivent-ils?
          Do they arrive?

In many dialects of French the l of il is not pronounced. In these dialects
all the examples in (37) end with the sequence [ti] or [t`i] or [tsi].
This post verbal *ti* sequence, occurring exclusively in interrogatives, was
interpreted as an interrogative marker and was analogically extended to
all interrogatives.[21] The proportional model would depict the change as
in (38).

(38) [ləg'ar p'ar] : [ləg'ar part'i] = [zə̆p'ar] : [x] x > [z̆əpart'i]
      le gars part : le gars part-il = je pars : x x > je pars ti

   The Canadian French dialect in question forms yes/no questions by
1) rising intonation, 2) inversion, and 3) *ti* attachment. The coöccur-
rences of the three processes are shown in (39).[22]

		INT	INV	*ti* ATT
(39) a.	Tu vas?	+	-	-
b.	Vas-tu?	+	+	-
c.	Tu vas ti?	+	-	+

   A synchronic grammar therefore provides three specific transformations
(besides *WH* shift) for interrogatives. The diachronic problem is to
systemically relate *ti* attachment to any preceding stages in the grammar.
The other changes that were considered above fell into the dichotomy of
simplification-complication. None of these changes altered the basic

process of inversion. *ti* attachment is an entirely different process.

It could, however, be argued that *ti* is derived by a complicated intermingling of inversion and phonology. The argument would run as follows. An inversion transformation applies. A pronominalization rule converts the inverted NP into *i(l)* and normal phonological rules yield *verb + t + i*.

There are several problems with this conception. A non-formal one is that native speakers refuse to accept any identity between [i] in *il vient* [i vjɛ̃] and [i] in *Ta mère viendra ti?* A formal problem is that there would be no way to account for the *t* in

(40) Vous allez ti?

or in

(41) Nous sommes d'accord t'y pas?[23]

Example (41) shows a modification of the tag *n'est-ce pas?* The negative *pas* is retained and the interrogative marker *est-ce* is replaced by *ti*. Loss of *ne* as part of the negative is common.

The problem of the *t* might be solved by inserting *t* epenthetically before *il* when *il* is the pronominalized inverted pronoun of interrogatives. Additional *ad hoc* machinery could be introduced to delete the verbal element in the tag *t'y pas* of (41).

If each of these rules also had diachronic status, the evolution of *ti* would remain within the framework of generative diachrony. The generalization of *il* to all persons would be a simplification. The *t* would be a generalized element from the third person verb--a rule addition in the phonology could accomplish that. The verb deletion in *t'y pas* (41) could be a syntactic rule addition. However, *il* retains its traditional scope as masculine singular or indefinite pronoun. It is clearly distinct from *je, tu, elle(s), nous, vous* and *ils*. The diachronic relevance of the added rules in this scheme is vague and the whole operation is excessively complicated--especially in view of the notion of overall simplicity in grammars. There is no internal reason to prefer an inversion-epenthesis solution of *ti* over an attachment solution. The attachment solution consists of a simple statement that *ti* is attached to the (first) verb in the environment of *Q*.

If *t* were epenthetic and epenthesis were a separate rule added to the grammar, linguists would anticipate dialects (historical or present) in which *il* had been generalized but in which *t* epenthesis had not been introduced. Published accounts present only a uniform *ti*.[24] I therefore take *ti* attachment to be the correct formulation.

Diachronically, *ti* attachment represents a complete break with inversion. Modifications of structural descriptions or structural changes of rules do not disturb the integrity of a system: an inversion rule remains an inversion rule whether its output meets the conditions of pronominalization or not. Rule additions and rule loss form part of the accepted view of diachronic processes in a generative grammar. Changes in the specifications of sub-categories of lexical redundancies are already required. Reordering of rules is a necessary process.

It is not a necessary condition on rule additions that they be motivated by any internal factors of pre-existing grammars.[25] They may be added for various reasons beyond the scope of the formal linguistic structure. However, there are clear internal sources of the *ti* particle. An approach to language change which does not permit the expression of the relationship between source of change and the change itself is inadequate.

Traditional proportional analogy provides a means (see 38) of doing this for the *ti* particle. Generative reinterpretations of analogy must be able to accomplish the same connections if they are to successfully replace analogy in diachronic linguistics.

5. CONCLUSION

Given the generative approach to diachrony with reconstruction of optimal grammars, *ti* formulation has the following status. Generation A had an inversion transformation and generation B had an attachment transformation. The two transformations are unrelated except that they are both sensitive to Q.[26] As an added rule, *ti* attachment is an entirely independent phenomenon. It can have no reference to information supplied by inversion transformations.[27] There is no way, in a generative framework, to make reference to the possible origin of *ti*.

This limitation puts the historical linguist in the position of being unable to comment upon the relationship between two stages of a language. He is unable to describe the conditions under which the change took place. Grammars for two stages of a language are self-contained phenomena and the elements making up the respective grammars are unconnected. Only anecdotal statements about the relationships between two grammars are allowed. Even this is not possible in the case of the *ti* particle, since the conditions of change are unspecified. The facts (or possibilities, at least) are thus obscured or ignored. The linguist, before broaching the area of cause of change, must be able to delimit the conditions under which linguistic changes occur and define the difference between successive stages.

Generative diachrony must now develop a means of interpreting analogical changes which are not simplifications.

NOTES

1. I would like to thank Professors JoAnn Creore, Eugene Dorfman and Gary D. Prideaux for helpful comments and criticisms of earlier versions of this paper. I have also profited from discussions with Paul Fletcher, Bernard Rochet and other colleagues at the University of Alberta.

2. The ways in which the positions taken in this paper differ from those presented by R. Kayne and R. W. Langacker in this volume do not affect the basic problem.

3. Sturtevant (1947, Chapter 10) presents a classical treatment. Szemerenyi (1960:7-9) presents a typical example.

4. Lehmann (1962:181); King (1969:131-2), Kiparsky (1965, Chapter I·I); and Kiparsky (1967:88-9), all point out various aspects of these problems.

5. Kuryłowicz (1949) and Mańczak (1958) provide the most recent and specific attempts at formulating these notions. For a criticism of Kuryłowicz see Kiparsky (1965, Chapter II). For additional criticism of Kuryłowicz and remarks on Mańczak see Patterson (1971).

6. Kiparsky (1965, 1967, 1968b) and King (1969) present arguments to support this position. Patterson (1971) points out some instances, not treated here, in which this notion is inadequate.

7. King (1969:51 ff. and *passium*) presents discussion, examples and references for rule reorderings. Kiparsky (1968b) differentiates types or reorderings. Klima (1964) presents some syntactic examples. Closs (1965:405-8) discusses various types of change and implications for diachronic syntax. R. Lakoff (1968, Chapter 6) discusses some changes in the redundancy rules governing verbs and complementizers in Latin and Spanish.

8. Foulet (1921:246; 1930:308) provides a more detailed account of the conditions on inversion. In the latter work he provides detail on exceptions to the general rule.

Old French examples are translated and glossed in the following schema:
a. Old French (source)
b. Modern French--approximation
       English gloss

9. Ewert (1943:276) says in "Middle French".

10. Examples from Sandfeld (1965:14). Ewert (1943:276) lists *à peine* 'hardly', *peut-être* 'maybe', *en vain* 'vainly', *aussi* 'therefore', *toujours* 'nevertheless', as adverbs requiring inversion in literary French. That the inversion rule no longer applies in the environment of (left shifted) adverbs in popular French is not germane to the discussion at hand.

11. Example (10) was presented as an example of lexical complication in a paper presented to the L.S.A. Winter Meeting in San Francisco, December 1969, by S.G. Thomason.

12. Martinet (1952, 1955a) formulated the precursor of this idea as applied to phonology. Labov has gone a step further in requiring the incorporation of non-linguistic information into diachronic accounts.

13. Parents are not necessarily the direct source of data in language acquisition. Weinreich *et al.* (1968:144-6) state that peer-groups and slightly older children provide the main body of data for the child.

14. This section draws heavily on examples and information presented by Foulet (1921) and (1930:232-5). A more detailed generative account of the diachrony of French interrogatives will appear in my dissertation (1971). Price (1966) provides a more detailed analysis of pronouns as well as useful references.

15. *cil* is the masculine singular form of the demonstrative. *ce* (sometimes spelled ço) is the neuter form.

16. It is possible that the reduplicated pronoun derived from the application of a NP copying transformation and a subsequent and obligatory pronominalization of the copie NP. A NP deletion rule would then delete the original NP(d4 in 14). Langacker (1965) presents this solution for Modern French.

17. Many pertinent details are missing from this sketch. An attempt is made in my dissertation to specify some conditions on *c'est que* deletion. Also, the status of *est-ce que* with first person singular pronouns is discussed at length. The *ce* in *est-ce que* and a semantic problem it raises are also discussed.

It may be contended that *c'est que* does not appear in underlying re-presentations but is introduced transformationally under appropriate conditions. This problem is discussed in my dissertation. (Langacker 1965 derives *est-ce que* from underlying sources.) The choice between the two possibilities would not affect the basic argument of this paper. In the discussion of this construction below, "insertion" could be substituted for "deletion" without altering the interpretation of the changes.

18. The phenomenon described here is fairly widespread throughout France and Canada. Guiraud (1969) presents many examples (48-9) from what he calls (6-7) the 'language of the urban people'--i.e. the working class of Paris. The *ti* particle occurs in Normandy (Joret 1877) and Lyons (Rolland 1878), as well as most of the Provencal area. (See note 21). I have been unable to locate information which would delimit the geographical range of *ti*. Dates for all areas are uncertain.

One very interesting phenomenon is that although *ti* appears to be widespread in Canada, it does not occur at all in Louisiana French (cf. Juilland and Conwell).

19. The term 'dialect' is used loosely here. The variety of French specifically referred to is that spoken by a 19 year old female student at the University of Alberta who was born in Amos, Abitibi County, Québec, to parents who were born and raised in Saint Prosper, Comté Champlain (near Trois Rivières) Quebec and who emigrated, as adults, to Amos in 1914. This student has been in Alberta since October 1969 and maintains extensive contacts in the francophone community of Edmonton.

20. Some discussion of this point will appear in my dissertation. In brief, it should be noted here that the *ti* in modern Provencal dialects is probably a borrowing from northern dialects (Ronjat 1937:624).

21. In some varieties of Canadian French there has been an identi.al extension of *tu* [tsü] from the second person singular. Its precise role in these varieties is unclear because it co-exists with *ti*. The use of *tu* or *ti* is determined, in some cases, by stylistic criteria. In other cases the two are freely interchangeable.

22. Rolland's (1878) example *voulez-vous t'y?* shows a possibility not permitted in the Canadian data.

23. Example taken from Rolland (1878). The original orthography is preserved.

24. Joret (1876) found in Norman dialect that *ti* could not be used in second person interrogatives. This restriction is an internal constraint on the *ti* attachment transformation (diachronically and synchronically) and is not a counter-argument to the thesis of this paper.

25. The term "internal factors" is used in the sense of Laboy's (1963: 274) "structure", and is subject to the criticism in Labov (1968:282).

26. *Q* is used here as an abbreviatory device for whatever it is that triggers interrogative transformations. For recent discussion of the status of *Q* see Baker (1970), Langacker (1969a) and Langacker's paper in this volume.

27. Except, of course, indirectly, if the two transformations constitute a 'feeding order' (Kiparsky 1968b:197).

RONALD W. LANGACKER
UNIVERSITY OF CALIFORNIA, SAN DIEGO

FRENCH INTERROGATIVES REVISITED

The analysis of French interrogatives that I proposed earlier (Langacker: 1965 and 1966a) has recently been criticized in print by several writers, including Roulet (1969), Hirschbühler (1970), and Huddleston and Uren (1969).* No doubt there are other criticisms, published and unpublished, that I am not aware of. It is not surprising that my analysis has been called into question; in its essentials, it dates back to 1963, a rather remote era in the history of transformational grammar. I am only surprised that the criticisms have been so long coming and that there have not been more of them.

The analysis of French interrogatives is much more complex than one might initially expect, and it will be helpful to divide the discussion into several sections, each pertaining to one facet of my original analysis. My purpose is not to argue that I have been right all along and my critics misguided—on the contrary, many of their points are valid or potentially valid, and several aspects of the treatment of French questions are in serious doubt. Within each area, I will try to pose the major issues, summarize the arguments that have been presented, and make it clear just where we stand. In several cases, it will be seen that the analysis of French interrogatives is tied up with more general theoretical issues. This entails that a definitive solution is probably not now possible, but it also greatly enhances the interest of working towards such a solution.

1. WHAT MAKES THIS SENTENCE A QUESTION?

It should be apparent that French interrogatives are not formally marked in any consistent way. That is, there is no unique feature of surface structures that differentiates questions and non-questions in all instances. French questions are sometimes said to be marked by a special "question intonation", a rising intonation that contrasts with the final falling intonation of declarative sentences. While this may be true of "yes-no" questions (YNQ), such as (1), it is not in general true of "WH" questions (WHQ), such as (2).

(1)   Est-il là? 'Is he there?'

(2)   Qui voit-il? 'Who does he see?'

Nor is the presence of a special question word a consistent property of interrogatives; this is immediately apparent from YNQ like (1). The other possibility is special word order. In both (1) and (2), the subject pronoun follows the verb, while it precedes the verb in declaratives. However, not all questions display this inversion, and the inversion is not restricted to questions, as shown by (3)-(5).

(3)   Qui est là? 'Who is there?'

(4)   Il est là? 'Is he there?'

(5)   Peut-être y a-t-il encore de l'espoir. 'Perhaps there is
                                               still hope.'

Of course, it might be possible to define questions in terms of a disjunctive set of formal markings, but there would be little point in doing so; disjunctive conditions merely formalize the lack of a generalization.
    Another alternative is to define questions in terms of the application of certain syntactic transformations. This is the approach Chomsky takes for English in *Syntactic Structures*, in which a question is defined as a sentence which undergoes the rule of Subject-Auxiliary Inversion, as in derivation (6).

(6)   Spiro can bring us together. ====>

Can Spiro bring us together?

In retrospect, this approach is inadequate for both English and French. The French analog of Subject-Auxiliary Inversion does not apply in the derivation of (3) and (4), and it does apply in the derivation of the declarative sentence (5). Similar remarks hold for English sentences like (7) and (8).

(7)   Who is there?

(8)   Seldom has Spiro said anything profound.

It seems that there is no motivated syntactic rule that applies in the derivation of all interrogative sentences and no other sentences.
    If questions are not identified as such either in terms of their surface structures or in terms of their transformational derivation, they must be marked as questions in deep structure (if they are marked at all). Two basic alternatives are available for distinguishing questions and

non-questions in deep structure. One alternative is to insert a special marker--Q, WH, or both--in the deep structure of interrogatives. This is the approach adopted in Katz and Postal (1964) and in my early analysis of French questions. The other alternative is to postulate an abstract performative verb of questioning in the underlying representation of interrogatives; the performative clause is normally deleted (or always deleted, depending on one's analysis of performatives and their relation to less exotic lexical items).

Numerous variants of both approaches are conceivable, so I will simplify and consider the two approaches schematically. What is at issue is the choice between structures like PM1 and PM2 as the underlying representation of questions; sentence (2) will serve as a concrete illustration.

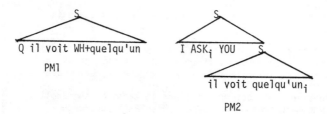

In PM1, Q identifies the structure as an interrogative one, and WH marks the constituent that is being questioned. Q has a semantic representation something like 'I ask you' (it is stated much more precisely in Katz and Postal, 1964). In PM2, the higher, performative clause I ASK YOU provides the semantic information conveyed by Q in the other structure. I wish to make no specific claim regarding the form of this higher clause-- I ASK YOU is only an ad hoc representation. The use of an index, written as a subscript in PM2, is intended more seriously. When a performative verb and an indefinite share the same index, i in PM2, this means that the indefinite is in the "scope" of the performative. An indexed indefinite is realized in surface structure as a question word through the insertion of WH and the proper phonological "spelling". The use of this index is for the most part equivalent to marking the questioned constituent with WH, but there is an important difference. If a sentence contains more than one governing verb and more than one question word, the indexing allows one to determine which question word is governed by which interrogative verb; it is only necessary to compare the indices and see which ones match. LeRoy Baker (1968 and 1970) has demonstrated the necessity for this indexing. (Indexing is possible with either analysis-- if abstract performative verbs are rejected, the index can be associated with Q.)

I have no intention of arguing for either structure here, and it is unlikely that I could convince anyone if I tried. It should be apparent that the choice between PM1 and PM2 is part and parcel of the much more general theoretical debate concerning the merit of abstract performative verbs. When that general debate is resolved, the more specific matter of choosing between PM1 and PM2 will also be resolved.

However, this indeterminacy does not prevent me from having a preference. For several reasons--note that I do not call them "arguments"--I prefer to analyze questions in terms of structures like PM2, with a governing performative verb that does not always surface. One reason is that the use of Q is totally ad hoc, as I have argued in a recent paper on English questions (1969), whereas the use of a performative verb promises to have some explanatory value. Secondly, structures like PM2 minimize the difference between direct and indirect questions. With a performative analysis, the underlying representations of sentences like (9)-(12) would be directly analogous.

(9)   Qui va venir? 'Who is going to come?'

(10) Dites-moi qui va venir. 'Tell me who is going to come.'

(11) Je vous demande qui va venir. 'I ask you who is going to come.'

(12) Il ne sait pas qui va venir. 'He doesn't know who is going to come.'

Under this analysis, the differences among (9)-(12) reside solely in the identity and deletability of the governing verb (and other elements in the main clause). Baker (1968 and 1970) has argued convincingly that direct and indirect questions are basically the same type of clause, and a performative analysis accounts for this automatically by treating direct questions as a special case of embedded questions.

Let us then adopt the performative analysis, at least for purposes of discussion, and return to the problem at hand: What makes a question a question? With respect to direct questions like (9), the answer is easy: a question is a sentence that derives from an underlying structure, like PM2, which contains a performative verb of questioning. However, it is not so easy to define the notion question in such a way that both direct and indirect questions are correctly characterized. I feel the definition must be semantically based, but an interrogative clause certainly cannot be defined as one that requests information. (12), for instance, contains an interrogative clause, but no request for information is involved.

Let me offer the following as a rough first approximation to the characterization of an interrogative clause. An interrogative clause is one that contains an underlying indefinite determiner (such as *quelque*) or disjunctive (such as *ou*) in the scope of a governing verb. (At the semantic level, 'some' and 'or' can probably be equated, but I will not try to argue for their relationship in this paper.) The relation between the governing verb and the embedded question clause involves the distribution of truth or falsity over the set of propositions the embedded clause consists of or abbreviates. In (13), for example, the speaker is asking the hearer to specify which of two propositions is true and which false; the two are given in (14) and (15).

(13) Je vous demande si Pierre est stupide ou non. 'I ask you whether Peter is stupid or not.'

(14) Pierre est stupide. 'Peter is stupid.'

(15) Pierre n'est pas stupide. 'Peter is not stupid.'

Similarly, (16) denies that Henry knows the distribution of truth values over the set of propositions of the form 'Woman$_x$ likes Peter', where each 'woman$_x$' belongs to the set of women under consideration.

(16) Henri ne sait pas quelle femme aime Pierre. 'Henry doesn't know which woman likes Peter.'

In summary, direct questions are easily characterized as sentences from which a performative clause of questioning has been deleted. However, the character of this performative clause has yet to be determined precisely. Direct questions are only a special case of the interrogative clause construction. Whereas direct questions always involve a request for information, this is not true of interrogative clauses in general. An interrogative clause is characterized, rather, by an indefinite or disjunctive element in the scope of a governing verb. The relation between the governing verb and the interrogative clause concerns the distribution of truth values over the propositions that the interrogative clause contains or abbreviates. This characterization is terribly vague and imprecise, but I feel that finding out what makes a question a question is basically a matter of refining and clarifying this definition.

2. QUESTION INTONATION?

The analysis of English question intonation proposed in Katz and Postal (1964) is noteworthy for the complicated way in which it expresses the lack of a generalization. To account for the fact that YNQ have rising intonation while WHQ have falling or "declarative" intonation, they let their question marker Q be interpreted phonologically as a high point in the intonation of a sentence. One rule moves Q to the end of a clause to produce, by the application of phonological rules, the desired rising intonation. To prevent WHQ from receiving rising intonation, they add a restriction to this rule that blocks its application when the clause contains WH. Finally, they give another rule that deletes Q sentence-initially. All this simply to say that YNQ have rising intonation.

I tried to improve on this for French questions in my dissertation and met with only partial success. The analysis was considerably simpler than Katz and Postal's, but it meets with numerous difficulties, including a clear set of counterexamples.

Instead of using a special element Q to mark interrogatives, I used WH; (1) thus had an underlying structure like (2), and (3) an underlying structure like (4).

(1)   Est-elle jolie? 'Is she pretty?'

(2)   WH elle est jolie

(3)   Qui vois-tu? 'Who do you see?'

(4)   WH tu vois quelqu'un

Following Katz and Postal, I assumed that this question marker WH was interpreted phonologically as an intonation high. Two rules are then needed: (a) WH can be attached to an indefinite to form a question word (as in the derivation of (3)); and (b) an unattached WH is moved to the end of the sentence. This accounts nicely for the rising intonation of (1) and the falling intonation of (3). Moreover, it correctly predicts the fact that *quoi* has higher pitch than *à* in (5).

(5)   À quoi pense-t-il? 'What is he thinking about?'

The analysis captures the generalization that rising intonation and a WH question word are mutually exclusive; it does so by deriving rising intonation from an unattached WH, and a question word from an attached WH. Furthermore, the analysis could be made even simpler by having WH in final rather than initial position in deep structure. So far so good.

Unfortunately, problems arise. First, the use of special question markers like Q and WH is, I believe, ad hoc and unmotivated, and I would prefer not to base an analysis on them. Secondly, the analysis makes false predictions. It predicts that sentences like (6), which I did not consider, should have rising intonation, since the WH formative comes on the last word of the sentence.

(6)   Elle aime qui? 'Who does she like?'

However, (6) has regular falling intonation. (I am excluding "echo" and "incredulity" questions from consideration, since they present special problems.) Finally, I have serious doubts that there is any such thing as question intonation in French.

In a recent paper on English question intonation (1970), I argued that the rising intonation characteristic of YNQ is nothing other than the suspended intonation of the first clause of either-or sentences, from which YNQ must be derived. Sentence (7), for example, can be analyzed as a truncated version of (8); (8) in turn can be regarded as the interrogative counterpart of the declarative either-or sentence (9).

(7)   Are you married?

(8)   Are you married, or aren't you married?

(9)   Either you are married, or you aren't married.

For my dialect of American English, no special rules at all are needed to account for the intonation of YNQ. The range of possible intonation contours for (7) matches the range possible with the first clause of (8) and (9). Whatever principle accounts for the intonation associated with conjoined structures will therefore automatically assign the proper intonation to YNQ. We are dealing, not with question intonation, but with the intonation of non-final conjoined clauses.

  I would like to suggest that a similar analysis may be appropriate for question intonation in French. I would postulate something like PM3 as the underlying representation of (1), for instance.

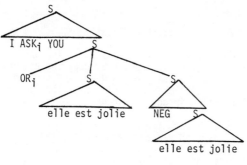

PM3

As the first clause of a conjoined structure, *elle est jolie* will receive rising or suspended final intonation, as it does in declaratives like (10).

(10)   Ou elle est jolie, ou elle n'est pas jolie.

      'Either she is pretty, or she isn't pretty.'

This suspended intonation is, I speculate, the same as the so-called "question intonation".

Let me close this section on a cautionary note. I do not CLAIM that question intonation is the same as that of non-final conjoined clauses, I only SPECULATE that this is the case. The judgments involved are subtle enough that I feel the matter would best be investigated by a native speaker. (Hirschbühler 1970:99-102 proposes something fairly similar.) Moreover, we are dealing here, not with a single intonation pattern, but rather with a whole range of possible patterns. The hypothesis does not assert that the intonation curve most frequently associated with YNQ is identical to the one most frequently associated with non-final conjuncts; it only asserts that the two constructions have the same range of intonational possibilities. Finally, the hypothesis is not necessarily an all-or-nothing affair. Even if the two constructions do not share precisely the same range of intonational possibilities, it is certainly the case that the ranges overlap considerably. I would still take the general non-falling character of YNQ intonation to be a reflection of the fact that YNQ derive from non-final conjuncts. If special rules of question intonation are needed, their function can probably be limited to specifying fine detail, and they can be triggered by the governing performative verb.

3. HOW DID I GET IN THIS POSITION?

An analysis of French interrogatives must somehow account for the inversion and reduplication illustrated in (1)-(3).

(1)   Est-elle maigre? 'Is she thin?'

(2)   Marie est-elle maigre? 'Is Mary thin?'

(3)   Que veut Marie? 'What does Mary want?'

In my 1965 paper, I proposed that three rules were responsible for reduplicating and inverting the subject. The first rule (RED) copies the subject NP after the verb when it is preceded by WH; the second rule (PRO) pronominalizes the reduplicated NP; and the third rule (DEL) deletes the original NP if it remains identical to the copy after pronominalization. (The problem of ensuring that the right rules apply in the right derivations will be dealt with in the next section.) The anticipated derivations of (1)-(3) are sketched below.

(1)   elle est maigre ====> elle est elle maigre ====> Est-elle maigre?
                (RED)   (DEL)

(2)   Marie est maigre ====> Marie est Marie maigre ====>
                (RED)   (PRO)
         Marie est-elle maigre?

(3)   que Marie veut ====> que Marie veut Marie ====>
                    (RED)   (DEL)
       Que veut Marie?

One criticism that has been directed at this analysis, though not in print to my knowledge, concerns the relation between these rules and the rule of dislocation (DISL). Assuming that it is indeed a rule (I have my doubts), DISL is the rule that derives (5) and (6) as variants of (4).

(4)   Je vois votre frère.   'I see your brother.'

(5)   Votre frère, je le vois.   'Your brother, I see him.'

(6)   Je le vois, votre frère.   'I see him, your brother.'

The criticism is simply that the reduplication in sentences like (2) exemplifies dislocation rather than a special reduplication rule that functions in question formation. Under this proposal, (2) would have the derivation given below; notice that only DISL and a special inversion rule (INV) are needed in this alternative analysis:

(2)   Marie est maigre ====> Marie elle est maigre ====>
                    (DISL)   (INV)
       Marie est-elle maigre?

Although DISL is the obvious diachronic source for questions like (2), I think there are good reasons for rejecting it as pertinent to the synchronic analysis of French interrogatives. I will suggest in sections 5 and 6 that the relation between synchronic and diachronic analysis is not terribly clear, and that certain kinds of arguments against synchronic analyses rest on rather shaky theoretical foundations. Nevertheless, in this case the evidence is clear enough and extensive enough to survive any but the most foolhardy skepticism.
    If DISL were the rule that accounted for the reduplication of the subject in questions like (2), the intonational difference between (2) and (7) would be unexplained.

(7)   Marie, est-elle maigre?   'Mary, is she thin?'

DISL typically introduces an intonation break between the dislocated NP and the main clause, but this intonation break is lacking in (2). It might be possible to counter by claiming that DISL only optionally introduces this intonation break; in fact, it may well be optional, since some speakers allow dislocated sentences like (8), with no special intonation.

(8)   Ton père il t'appelle. 'Your father is calling you.'

However, not all speakers accept such sentences, and there are numerous other difficulties in any case.

In WHQ, the difference between dislocation and question reduplication stands out much more clearly, since a dislocated NP precedes the question word while the subject of a reduplicated question follows it:

(9)   Marie, qui voit-elle?   'Mary, who does she see?'

(10) Qui Marie voit-elle?   'Who does Mary see?'

Another difficulty is that *ce* is possible as the copy of *cela* or a human noun under DISL, but not in reduplicated questions:

(11) Cela, c'est vrai.   'That's true.'

(12) Cela est-il vrai?   'Is that true?'

(13) *Cela est-ce vrai?   'Is that true?'

(14) Henri, c'est mon ami.   'Henry, he's my friend.'

(15) Henri est-il mon ami?   'Is Henry my friend?'

(16) *Henri est-ce mon ami?   'Is Henry my friend?'

An even more serious difficulty is that dislocation is only possible with definites, while reduplicated questions also work with indefinites:

(17) *Quelqu'un, il veut me voir.   'Someone, he wants to see me.'

(18) Quelqu'un veut-il me voir?   'Does someone want to see me?'

Finally, it is not clear that DISL is meaning preserving. In other words, (2) and (7) may not be synonymous.

For these reasons, I feel that the original three-rule analysis is definitely preferable to an analysis that incorporates DISL as part of question formation in French. However, my analysis is not itself without problems, and Hirschbühler has been kind enough to bring them to light (p. 40-43). According to my analysis, the same reduplication rule (RED) is responsible for copying both pronouns and full NP subjects after the verb. Unfortunately, pronouns and full NP's are positioned differently with respect to *pas* and past participles:

(19) Où n'ira pas Paul?   'Where won't Paul go?'

(20) Où Paul n'ira-t-il pas?   'Where won't Paul go?'

(21) Où a mangé Paul?   'Where did Paul eat?'

(22) Où Paul a-t-il mangé? 'Where did Paul eat?'

Wherever RED places the copy of the subject, the result is bound to be incorrect for either pronominal or non-pronominal subjects.
   The force of this criticism depends crucially on the assumption that the order of a reduplicated subject with respect to the elements of the verb group (including negation) is determined solely by the reduplication rule. However, this is not a necessary assumption, nor is it, in my opinion, a terribly plausible one. It is well known that the verb group in French is highly inflexible syntactically. The elements of the verb group, which include the main and auxiliary verb, negative elements, and subject and object pronouns, occur in a rigidly prescribed order and preclude, for the most part, the insertion of other constituents. Phonologically, subject and object pronouns are incorporated in the verb group, even though they are separate constituents at more abstract levels of representation. From all indications, therefore, the surface order of elements within the verb group is determined by rigid surface constraints that may well be presumed to override or control the placement of constituents by syntactic rules. In particular, subject pronouns, as distinct from non-pronominal subjects, must be incorporated phonologically as part of the verb group, and it does not seem at all unreasonable to maintain that this surface structure or phonological requirement accounts for the apparent discrepancy in the placement of the subject in (19)-(22). I do not claim to have proved this, nor do I pretend to understand in detail the nature of the constraints. However, I do believe that there are good grounds for doubting the force of Hirschbühler's criticisms (though they are perfectly valid given the somewhat antiquated and overly rigid theoretical framework of the standard transformational model).
   Because he found my analysis untenable (mistakenly, I hope), Hirschbühler proposed another set of rules to account for French questions involving inversion and reduplication:

(a)   A pronoun subject is adjoined as the left-most element of the verb group.

(b)   A non-pronominal subject is reduplicated as a pronoun that is attached as the left-most element of the verb group.

(c)   A pronoun attached as the left-most element of the verb group is permuted with the first following verbal element (the auxiliary or main verb).

(d)   A non-pronominal subject is transported and attached to the right of the main verb.

I will not examine this analysis in any great detail, since it was motivated mainly to avoid the order problem illustrated in (19)-(22), which I do not believe to be a real problem. The solution Hirschbühler offers is to give two different permutation rules, rule (c) for pronoun subjects and rule (d) for other subjects. In other words, he claims that there is no generalization at all to be made regarding the movement of interrogative subjects to post-verbal position. Consequently, his analysis is more complex than mine (in terms of the number of elementary transformational operations involved), even if we exclude (a) and (b) from the count.

Rules (a) and (b) are independently required in Hirschbühler's analysis. (a) is the rule, alluded to above, that attaches a subject pronoun to the verb group, at least for phonological purposes. Rule (b) accounts for the reduplication in sentences like (8), which Hirschbühler posits as an intermediate stage in the derivation of reduplicated questions, as illustrated in (23):

(23) ton père t'appelle ====> ton père il t'appelle (=8)
                    (b)
      ====> Ton père t'appelle-t-il? 'Is your father
      (c)   calling you?'

However, I would like to argue that rule (b) is incorrect and that sentences like (8) exemplify dislocation with optional omission of the usual intonation break. I would also like to argue that sentences like (8) are inappropriate as an intermediate stage in the derivation of reduplicated questions. For one thing, not all speakers accept sentences like (8), even among those for whom reduplicated questions are grammatical. Moreover, sentences like (8) are ungrammatical if the subject is indefinite, as in (24).

(24) *Quelqu'un il t'appelle. 'Someone is calling you.'

The corresponding reduplicated questions are, however, grammatical.

(25) Quelqu'un t'appelle-t-il? 'Is someone calling you?'

These facts are explained if sentences like (8) are treated as instances of dislocation and are not invoked as intermediate stages in the formation of reduplicated questions.

In summary, I have found no really persuasive argument to lead me to abandon this particular aspect of my analysis of French interrogatives. However, the problem posed by sentences like (19)-(22) has not yet been fully resolved, and a definitive resolution of this problem may have to await a much fuller understanding of the interaction between grammatical rules and surface patterns.

4. POURQUOI N'EST PAS CETTE PHRASE GRAMMATICALE?

The three rules discussed in the last section (RED, PRO, and DEL) generate ungrammatical strings as well as grammatical ones if allowed to apply without restrictions. The rules imply at least the following incorrect derivations:

(1)   WH+quelque chose tombe ====> *Que tombe? 'What falls?'
                           (PHON)

(2)   WH+quelque chose Henri voit ====> WH+quelque chose
                              (RED)
        Henri voit Henri ====> WH+quelque chose Henri voit
                (PRO)
        il ====> *Que Henri voit-il? 'What does Henry see?'
        (PHON)

(3)   WH+quelqu'un Henri voit ====> WH+quelqu'un Henri
                         (RED)
        voit Henri ====> WH+quelqu'un voit Henri ====>
        (DEL)   (PHON)
        *Qui voit Henri 'Who does Henry see?'

(4)   pour WH+quelque raison Paul mange ====>
                              (RED)
        pour WH+quelque raison Paul mange Paul ====>
                               (DEL)
        pour WH+quelque raison mange Paul ====>
                          (PHON)
        *Pourquoi mange Paul? 'Why does Paul eat?'

Note that none of the three rules can apply in (1). PRO and DEL depend on the prior occurrence of RED, and RED can only apply when WH precedes the subject NP: in (1), WH does not precede the subject NP, but rather is part of it.

    The only thing that is clear about the restrictions needed to block such derivations is that nobody has yet discovered a way to state them that is not ad hoc. There are numerous ways of stating the restrictions in a grammar, but no one has yet explained them or shown them to follow from more general principles. Consequently, there is little to discuss. If there is a neat solution, it awaits discovery. If there is not, determining the proper filtering mechanism to exclude the incorrect derivations is a matter of linguistic metatheory. The metatheoretical question of how to handle unexpected gaps in otherwise productive syntactic patterns is clearly beyond the purview of this paper.

    Three different filtering devices have been proposed, none very satisfactory. In my 1965 article, I employed a special "question word" transformation. All the restrictions were built into this rule as special conditions on its application. What the rule did was to change the gender of a pro form from feminine to masculine if the pro form happened to be in a structure from which a well formed question could derive. For instance, *chose* occurs in French as a feminine noun, but *que*, presumably from *WH+quelque chose*, is masculine. If the question word rule applies, *chose* is marked masculine, and *WH+quelque chose* is manifested phonologically as *que* or *quoi*. If it does not apply because the result would be ungrammatical, an interrogative with the feminine *quelle chose* 'What

thing?' is derived instead. I wish to disavow this solution. For one
thing, it runs into problems with rule ordering. For another, it depends
on an idiosyncrasy of gender in French and cannot possibly aspire to
universality.

In my dissertation, I used a slightly different approach. I used the
masculine pro forms, including *chose* and *personne,* to underlie question
words, negative words (e.g. *rien* 'nothing' and *personne* 'nobody'), and
also certain positive expressions, notably *quelque chose* and *quelqu'un.*
The occurrence of one of these masculine pro forms in a sentence was
taken to mark the sentence as deviant unless some special rule erased
the violation by changing the value of an ad hoc syntactic feature set up
for this purpose. With this approach, the filtering can be imposed by
formulating a rule that changes the value of this feature in exactly
those structures from which grammatical questions can be derived. The
analysis is very similar to the preceding one, but gender is not used
and some underlying structures are filtered out entirely. While I feel
that this represents an improvement over the first approach, it is no
less ad hoc and relies on the suspicious device of inventing syntactic
features just to mark violations.

Hirschbühler does not fare much better. He disagrees with the data,
claiming that sentences like *Qui voit Henri?* 'Who does Henri see?' are
grammatical. If so, the restrictions are simplified somewhat. However,
speakers differ on this point, some accepting such sentences and others
rejecting them. Be that as it may, his approach to imposing the necessary restrictions is equally ad hoc--he simply builds them in as special
conditions on various of his transformations.

Where do we stand? We know that some WHQ are ungrammatical even
though they would be expected to be grammatical by force of analogy. An
adequate linguistic description of French must somehow exclude these
sentences. Beyond that, nobody seems to have anything cogent to say.

5. QU'EST-CE QUE "QU'EST-CE QUE"?

In my 1965 analysis, the question formulas *qu'est-ce que, qui est-ce
que,* and so on were analyzed as the interrogative counterparts of "cleft
sentences". Thus the same rules that derive (b) from (a) in (1)-(3) will
also derive (b) from (a) in (4)-(8).

(1)   (a) C'est un loup. 'It's a wolf.'
       (b) Qu'est-ce? 'What is it?'

(2)   (a) C'est Pierre. 'It's Peter.'
       (b) Qui est-ce? 'Who is it?'

(3)   (a) C'est à Paris. 'It's in Paris.'
       (b) Où est-ce? 'Where is it?'

(4)   (a) C'est ceci que tu veux. 'It's this that you want.'

    (b) Qu'est-ce que tu veux? 'What do you want?'

(5) (a) C'est un loup qui court là-bas. 'It's a wolf that is
                                       running over there.'
    (b) Qu'est-ce qui court là-bas? 'What is running over there?'

(6) (a) C'est Pierre qu'elle voit. 'It's Peter that she sees.'
    (b) Qui est-ce qu'elle voit? 'Who does she see?'

(7) (a) C'est Pierre qui vient. 'It's Peter that is coming.'
    (b) Qui est-ce qui vient? 'Who is coming?'

(8) (a) C'est à Paris qu'il habite. 'It's in Paris that he lives.'
    (b) Où est-ce qu'il habite? 'Where does he live?'

Of course, it is not literally true that (b) derives from (a). More precisely, (b) derives from an underlying representation analogous to (a) except that it is marked as an interrogative and has an indefinite pro form, rather than a fully specified nominal, after *c'est*.

On the face of it, this analysis has several advantages. First of all, it is advantageous because it requires no special rules. The regular rules of question formation--the preposing of nominals marked with WH and pronoun inversion--automatically derive the various interrogative formulas *qu'est-ce que*, *où est-ce que*, etc. from the proposed underlying representations. These underlying representations exemplify a construction, the cleft sentence construction, that must be generated independently of any consideration of questions. Moreover, the distribution of *qui* and *que* is correctly predicted with no extra apparatus. *Qui* appears as the last element of the interrogative in exactly those cases where *qui* appears in the corresponding cleft sentence.

However, these advantages have not blinded critics, including myself, to certain problems. Some of the criticisms pertain to the derivation I proposed for the underlying cleft sentences, the (a) examples in (4)-(8). This derivation is little better than ad hoc and does violence to the semantic facts, but I wish to pass over the whole matter without comment. So far as the analysis of French interrogatives is concerned, the source of the cleft sentence construction is not crucial, only its existence. However it is to be derived, it is clear that this construction is in principle available to underlie *qu'est-ce que*-type interrogatives.

Another, more pertinent problem, which I myself pointed out, concerns the possibility of indefinite pro forms occurring in clefted position. (9), for instance, is the source of (10) when embedded to an interrogative verb, but the wellformedness of (9) is subject to some doubt (we are dealing with the cleft sentence interpretation of (9), not the relative clause interpretation).

(9) C'est quelque chose que tu vois. 'It's something that you see.'

(10) Qu'est-ce que tu vois? 'What do you see?'

So far as I have been able to determine by consulting with native speakers, sentences like (9) are well formed. The important requirement of the cleft sentence construction is that the clefted element have some contrastive value. *Quelque chose* is rather far down the scale so far as contrastive value is concerned, but it does contrast with *quelqu'un*. Moreover, even if sentences like (9) are judged ungrammatical, it is not clear that this militates against using them as the source for sentences like (10). The constraint that the clefted element after *c'est* must have contrastive value may apply only at the level of surface structure, in which case interrogatives like (10) would be exempt, WH movement having moved the clefted element out of the position of focus. Finally, the fact that sentences like (11) are grammatical in some dialects constitutes strong syntactic evidence that structures like (9) must be allowed to underlie questions.

(11) C'est quoi que tu vois? 'It's what that you see?'

Roulet (1969) offers an alternative analysis based on his analysis of YNQ beginning with *est-ce que*. He treats *est-ce que* as an unanalyzable particle (symbolized ESK) that is inserted transformationally and later permuted with a simple question word. He posits derivations roughly like (12).

(12) tu vois que ====> que tu vois ====> ESK que tu vois ====>
      que ESK tu vois = Qu'est-ce que tu vois?

I will not examine this analysis in detail, for Roulet offers no evidence in support of it. Nor does he provide any cogent criticisms of my proposed derivation; he was only concerned with simple sentences and for this reason sought derivations for *qu'est-ce que* and company that did not involve embedding. Moreover, his analysis has at least one obvious defect. If *est-ce que* is an unanalyzable particle, the interrogative formulas *qu'est-ce qui* and *qui est-ce qui* cannot be generated (except by ad hoc means). An analysis in which the choice between *qui* and *que* is correctly made on independent grounds is certainly to be preferred, other things being equal.

Huddleston and Uren (1969) give two arguments against the derivation I propose. First, they point out that questions like (13) are grammatical, even though the corresponding declaratives are deviant.

(13) Qui est-ce que c'est qu'il a vu? 'Who is it that he saw?'

(14) *C'est Pierre que c'est qu'il a vu. 'It's Peter that he saw.'

However, as Hirschbühler observes (p. 61), the ungrammaticality of (14) proves nothing by itself. There is no obvious sense in which (14) is

semantically ill formed. It is more likely that such sentences are filtered out by the syntax. In particular, one can posit a surface structure constraint that rejects sentences of the form *c'est (NP) que c'est
que X*. Because of subject inversion, (13) passes through this filter,
but (14) is screened out. The need for such a constraint is not a
liability of the analysis, since some special constraint must be invoked
to block sentences like (14) in any analysis. Moreover, the constraint
is independently motivated, since sentences like (15) are grammatical to
the exclusion of sentences like (16).

(15) C'est que Jean est stupide. 'John is stupid.'

(16) *C'est que c'est que Jean est stupide. 'John is stupid.'

Their second criticism is that questions like (10) are ambiguous between a cleft and a non-cleft reading, while the analysis does not predict any such ambiguity. (10), in other words, could be translated as
either 'What do you see?' or 'What is it that you see?'. Hirschbühler
disagrees (p. 71), claiming that only the non-cleft reading is possible
in his dialect.

This disagreement is not terribly surprising; most speakers of English,
myself included, would find it hard to describe the semantic difference,
if any, between 'What do you see?' and 'What is it that you see?'. The
source of the difficulty is not hard to discern. In declaratives, cleft
and non-cleft sentences have a clear presuppositional difference. (17),
for instance, presupposes that someone left; (18) does not presuppose
this--it asserts it.

(17) C'est Jean qui est parti. 'It's John that left.'

(18) Jean est parti. 'John left.'

(19) Qui est parti? 'Who left?'

Interrogatives have the same presupposition as cleft sentences; the presupposition associated with (19) is the same as the one associated with
(17). Consequently, simple questions and clefted questions do not differ
in any significant way in regard to their presuppositions. (20) makes
the same presupposition that (19) does, namely that someone left.

(20) Qui est-ce qui est parti? 'Who (is it that) left?'

This presupposition may be redundantly specified in (20)--once because
it is a cleft sentence and once because it is an interrogative--but I am
not terribly sure; too little is known about presupposition and about the
semantics of cleft sentences. However, I do not think that it has been
established conclusively that there is any semantic incompatibility
between *qu'est-ce que*-type questions and the underlying clefted structures.

Such a demonstration would have to involve some careful and quite subtle semantic analysis, and it might prove to be of considerable interest.

However, let us suppose the worst, namely that *qu'est-ce que*-type interrogatives are ambiguous, or that they are unambiguous with the wrong interpretation, the non-cleft interpretation. There are other difficulties as well with the derivation of such questions from clefted structures. For the most part, at least, the interrogative formulas are restricted to present tense, but this is not the case with cleft sentences:

(21) *Qu'était-ce qu'il voulait? 'What was it that he wanted?'

(22) C'était une femme qu'il voulait. 'It was a woman that he wanted.'

Furthermore, the question formulas do not tolerate negation, but cleft sentences do:

(23) *Qui n'est-ce pas qui est là? 'Who isn't it that is there?'

(24) Ce n'est pas Jeanne qui est là. 'It's not Jean who is there.'

Can the analysis be maintained in the face of these semantic and syntactic discrepancies?

I believe it can, but I also believe that a definitive decision is not possible at this time. First let me observe that the problems posed by (21)-(24) do not necessarily militate against the derivation I propose. At worst, ungrammatical sentences like (21) and (23) can be excluded by some ad hoc constraint. Now, ad hoc constraints are certainly undesirable, but the relevant consideration is that some such constraints are necessary in any obvious alternative analysis. Suppose, for instance, that *qu'est-ce que, où est-ce que*, etc. are treated as unanalyzable interrogative formulas inserted transformationally, and are not derived by productive rules from underlying cleft sentences. In this event, some special constraint or constraints will have to be added to the grammar in order to prevent the regular rules that function in the derivation of other questions from deriving (21) and (23) from (22) and (24) respectively (or from analogous underlying structures with indefinite pro forms). In short, the deviance of (21) and (23) is not a problem peculiar to my analysis of *qu'est-ce que*-type questions; it appears to be a problem for anybody.

Be that as it may, the actual or potential problems facing the derivation of *qu'est-ce que* etc. from cleft sentences are of two sorts. First, *qu'est-ce que*-type questions may not have quite the same semantic value as cleft sentences. Second, these interrogative formulas lack syntactic flexibility; they are restricted to present tense and cannot be negated, but declarative cleft sentences are not so restricted. Given the usual assumptions and forms of argumentation characteristic of generative syntax, these properties count as evidence against the analysis, however

weak the argument may be.   But I am not sure that the argument has any
force to it at all, primarily because I believe we may be dealing with
a widespread and perhaps crucially important phenomenon that contemporary
linguistic theory does not adequately handle, or even clearly recognize.
    Semantic specialization and lack of syntactic flexibility are both
characteristic of complex lexical items, such as nominalizations and
idoms.   To me this this suggests that *qu'est-ce que* and the other interrogative formulas have frozen to some degree into fixed, "lexical" patterns.
As a species of lexical item, they may be expected to display a certain
amount of syntactic and semantic idiosyncrasy.   But when I suggest that
qu'est-ce que, qui est-ce qui, and so on are lexical items, I do not wish
to imply that they are unanalyzable units, nor that they are inserted
transformationally into simple sentences.   In other words, I believe that
it is unwarranted to assume that the property of "being a lexical item
with syntactic and semantic peculiarities" and the property of "being
derived by productive syntactic rules" are incompatible.
    Contemporary linguistic theory and practice does make the assumption
that these two properties are incompatible, but this assumption is not a
necessary one, and to my knowledge no one has ever tried to substantiate
its validity.   The lexicalist hypothesis assumes that the dictionary
component of a grammar contains all lexical items that exemplify any
derivational pattern with which the slightest taint of irregularity or
non-productivity is associated.   Nouns like *swimmer* cannot be transformationally derived, since the agentive nominalization pattern is not fully
productive and some agentive nominals are not semantically regular; e.g.
a *professor* is not simply one who professes.   The transformationalist
hypothesis would preserve a transformational derivation for the regular
agentive nominals, but the irregular ones like *professor* would still be
incarcerated in the lexicon.   Generative semantics allows irregular lexical items to be derived transformationally so long as the irregularity
resides only in the presuppositional portion of the item; *professor* would
presumably still not be derived from *profess*.
    I do not know the proper derivation of *professor,* but I would like to
suggest that no existing version of transformational theory adequately
handles the intimate relationship between syntax and lexicon.   Current
transformational theory tries to make the lexicon the repository of all
irregularity, leaving only general statements in the syntax, but I do
not believe this kind of dichotomy is tenable.
    In particular, I would like to call attention to an important but
hitherto hardly recognized phenomenon that might be called "syntactic
metaphors" or "syntactic idioms".   Syntactic idioms are fully productive
syntactic constructions that become "lexicalized" in the sense that they
take on special semantic significance, sometimes with concomitant syntactic
peculiarities.   "Concealed questions" (Baker 1968) are a good example.
Concealed questions are simply embedded questions going incognito in the
disguise of regular noun phrases with relative clauses or prepositional
phrases; (25)-(27) are typical English examples, and (28) is an example
from French.

(25) I want to know the extent to which the work has been mismanaged.

(26) Tell me the nature of your difficulties.

(27) I never knew the plane which she was to arrive on.

(28) Dites-moi la quantité de vin que vous pouvez boire.
'Tell me the quantity of wine that you can drink.'

As another example, WHQ can sometimes be used as the equivalent of negative declaratives. For instance, (29) and (30) share a reading.

(29) Who's afraid of Liz Taylor?

(30) No one is afraid of Liz Taylor.

In French, as is well known, *que* cannot start an embedded question; *ce* plus a relative clause is used in its place, making sentences like (31) ambiguous between an interrogative and a declarative reading.

(31) Dites-moi ce qu'il sait. 'Tell me what he knows.'

This might be regarded as a special case of concealed questions.
    Clearly, sentences like these cannot be listed in the lexicon as lexical items; there are infinitely many sentences exemplifying each construction, and in any case the phenomena are fully productive, not "lexical" in the narrow sense of the term. What has become lexicalized is not a word or sequence of words, but SYNTACTIC CONSTRUCTIONS. The WHQ construction has acquired the meaning of negative declaratives, the *ce* plus relative clause construction has acquired the meaning of embedded questions, and so on. Moreover, there are concomitant syntactic peculiarities. For example, WHQ cannot be used as the equivalent of negative declaratives when they are embedded; (32) is not a paraphrase of (33).

(32) I know who's afraid of Liz Taylor.

(33) I know that no one is afraid of Liz Taylor.

But what does it mean for an entire construction to be lexicalized? Current theory does not allow one to talk in these terms. A construction cannot be put in the lexicon, nor can transformational rules, as normally conceived, account for the "irregular" use of these constructions in any natural way. Perhaps transderivational constraints are relevant, or maybe rules of "idiomaticization" that can apply at the level of semantic representation. Perhaps a wild new kind of semantic interpretation rule will do the job (if you still believe in semantic interpretation rules). In any event, syntactic idioms are important and pervasive in language, and they cast severe doubt, it seems to me, on certain tacit but fundamental assumptions of generative grammar. I am not prepared to offer a theory of syntactic idioms; for present purposes, it is sufficient to call attention to their existence and potential significance.

Let us return now to *qu'est-ce que*-type questions, and let us suppose the worst in regard to the proposal to derive these questions from cleft sentences--namely, that they do not have the meaning normally associated with cleft sentences and are subject to certain syntactic restrictions. Does this mean that they are not to be derived from cleft sentences by means of the regular question rules? Given the existence of syntactic metaphors, such a conclusion simply does not follow. Regardless of their semantic value, syntactic metaphor sentences function syntactically as sentences of the type they mimic. Syntactically, (29) is a question, and (31) contains a relative clause; unless they are derived by the regular rules of question formation and relativization, significant generalizations will be lost. By the same token, *qu'est-ce que*-type questions are syntactically the interrogative forms of cleft sentences, and important generalizations will be lost if they are not so derived.

For example, *qu'est-ce que, qui est-ce qui,* etc. are only special cases of a far more general construction including such formulas as *quand est-ce que, quelle femme est-ce que* and so on; clearly, this construction is productive and open-ended. These formulas cannot all be stored in the dictionary. And if only the more common ones like *qu'est-ce que* are listed in the dictionary as special lexical items (the others being derived from cleft sentences by regular question rules), ad hoc restrictions will have to be imposed to PREVENT these same formulas from being derived from regular underlying representations by means of the same question rules that derive all the others. If *est-ce que* is extracted from these formulas and listed as a special lexical item that is inserted transformationally, ad hoc apparatus will presumably be required to account for *qu'est-ce qui, qui est-ce qui, quelle femme est-ce qui,* and so on. Unless the *qu'est-ce que* formulas are derived by the question-formation rules from underlying cleft sentences, there will be no natural way to account for variant forms such as (34) and (35), which are grammatical for many speakers.

(34) C'est quoi qu'il veut? 'What does he want?'

(35) Qui c'est qui est là? 'Who is there'?

To summarize, I think the preponderance of evidence clearly favors the derivation of *qu'est-ce que*-type questions from underlying cleft sentences. No special rules or underlying representations are required, and in fact regular rules and derivations would have to be blocked in some ad hoc way in order to prevent the derivations I proposed as the correct ones from going through. There are certain syntactic restrictions on *qu'est-ce que*-type questions that are not imposed on the corresponding clefted declaratives, but I showed earlier that these restrictions are a problem in any obvious alternative analysis. It is possible that *qu'est-ce que*-type questions do not have precisely the semantic value that one would expect given their putative source, but I do not believe that this has been established. Even if the semantic difficulty is granted as a real one, this does not in itself invalidate the proposed analysis. I hope to have shown that it is not at all uncommon for one syntactic construction to be used metaphorically or idiomatically with the semantic force of another, and at worst I would have to claim that clefted questions are used in French with the semantic value of non-clefted interrogatives. In this event, *qu'est-ce que*-type questions are still derived syntactically by regular question rules from cleft sentences, just as (29) is syntactically a question in English and (31) syntactically involves a relative clause in French. However, the construction, having been idiomaticized, has lost its pristine semantic value and picked up a few syntactic peculiarities.

Current linguistic theory has nothing of substance to say about syntactic idioms. For this reason, the book on *qu'est-ce que* and company cannot yet be closed. I do believe that this construction is derived syntactically from cleft sentences, but I am not fully sure of the implications of this claim. *Qu'est-ce que* and company are still problematic, but it is important to realize the nature of the problem they pose. They raise the whole issue of the relation between syntax and lexicon, an issue that no one has yet resolved satisfactorily. I think that this is perhaps the most important issue in linguistic theory today, one whose magnitude is not fully appreciated, and one that will prove to be crucial in developing a theory of syntactic change.

6. QU'EST-CE QUE "EST-CE QUE"?

In 1965, I proposed that *est-ce que* questions are merely the interrogative counterparts of statements in *c'est que*. (1), for example, derives from (2) by the regular rules that invert the subject and verb in French interrogatives.

(1) Est-ce que la mort est certaine? 'Is death certain?'

(2) C'est que la mort est certaine. 'Death is certain.'

At the time, I failed to distinguish clearly between the "causal" and non-causal sense of *c'est que*. On the causal reading, (2) means something like (3).

(3) C'est parce que la mort est certaine. 'It's because death is
                                            certain.'

This is the most common reading, but for many speakers (2) can also be a simple emphatic, with no causal sense at all. For instance, in an

argument in which one person denies that death is inevitable, the other
could challenge his claim by uttering (2). The causal sense of (2) is of
no relevance to the present discussion; *est-ce que* questions are claimed
to derive from the non-causal or emphatic *c'est que* construction.

Moreover, the grammatical source of this emphatic construction is not
at issue. I would propose something like PM4 as the proper underlying
structure, the surface form being derived by extraposition and the *ce*
insertion that regularly accompanies it; sentences like (4) and (5) add
syntactic and semantic plausibility to this analysis, marginal though
they are.

(4)   Votre père est mort. Cela est--vous ne pouvez pas le changer.
      'Your father is dead. That just is--you cannot change it.'

(5)   Dieu est. 'God exists.'

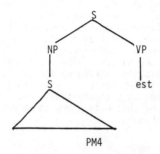

PM4

Be that as it may, the appropriateness of *c'est que* sentences as the
source of *est-ce que* interrogatives is what is at issue, not their
provenience.

Roulet (1969:150) criticizes this analysis as counter-intuitive, but
I do not believe this criticism has any force to it. It is not clear
that this putative relationship should be expected to be subject to
introspection, nor is it clear that Roulet is not repeating my error and
confusing the causal and non-causal *c'est que* constructions. Huddleston
and Uren (1969:12) object that the emphatic *c'est que* construction is
used too infrequently to underlie *est-ce que*, but it remains to be shown
that frequency of use has any bearing on the appropriateness of derivations.
They also object that the analysis must be wrong because (6) is grammatical
while its putative source, (7), is not.

(6)   Est-ce que c'est qu'il vient plus tard? 'Is it the case that he
                                       is coming later?'

(7)   *C'est que c'est qu'il vient plus tard. 'It's the case that he
                                       is coming later.'

However, (7) can be blocked by a surface structure constraint having independent motivation, as we saw in the previous section.

There are indeed problems with the analysis, but I believe they are comparable to the ones that arise in the derivation of *qu'est-ce que* etc. and can be handled in a similar manner. Hirschbühler (1970:62-66) has been thoughtful enough to point most of them out. For one thing, *c'est que* sentences sometimes have a special nuance of flattery lacking in *est-ce que* questions, as exemplified in (8).

(8) C'est qu'il est intelligent, ce petit. 'This kid's smart!'

However, this is by no means always true, and I do not take it to be a serious argument, particularly in light of the preceding discussion. More serious is the objection that sentences in *c'est que* or *ce n'est pas que* cannot be used as answers to *est-ce que* questions, although they should be possible, if not probable, given the analysis This may be because the *est-ce que* questions have been idiomaticized; it is perfectly conceivable that they derive from the emphatic *c'est que* construction syntactically, though they lack the emphatic force of this construction as it is manifested in declaratives. If the relation between questions and their possible answers is specified at the level of semantic representation, the fact that *est-ce que* questions are not answered by *c'est que* declaratives is explained.

Hirschbühler also points out that *est-ce que* is fixed in form; it cannot occur in other tenses, and I might add that inversion of *ce* and *est* is obligatory, though question inversion is sometimes optional in French. On intuitive grounds as well, it is clear that *est-ce que* has frozen into a fixed lexical unit. However, I hope to have shown that the lexical status of *est-ce que* is not necessarily incompatible with the claim that it derives by question inversion from *c'est que*. The difference in status between *qu'est-ce que* and *est-ce que* is only one of degree, and in the former case the grounds for maintaining the proposed syntactic derivation are, in my opinion at least, compelling.

Of course, *est-ce que* is on its way to becoming an unanalyzable question marker (this may have happened already in some or many dialects), but there are grounds for believing that this has no yet happened in the standard language. If *est-ce que* is simply inserted transformationally, some ad hoc restriction will have to be placed on the regular question inversion rule to prevent it from applying to the emphatic *c'est que* construction and deriving *est-ce que* questions from it. Moreover, it would not suffice to have just one question marker, ESK; the negative *n'est-ce pas que* would have to be stored in the lexicon alongside it, but this form is fully regular in terms of the analysis I propose. To be sure, the case is not so compelling as it was for *qu'est-ce que*-type questions, since we are dealing with only one or two formulas, not an open-ended set. But I think the difference is only one of degree. I do not claim with full certainty that *est-ce que* must still derive from *c'est que.* However, I do believe that one can reject this analysis only by making certain assumptions about the interaction between syntax and lexicon that have not as yet been clearly spelled out and convincingly defended. The matter is still an open one, and a definitive solution is intimately connected with a much broader and more significant theoretical question.

One final matter. What is the source of *est-ce que* in those dialects that lack the emphatic *c'est que* construction? Since I have already stretched your credence to the breaking point, if not far beyond, I may as well follow my instincts to their logical conclusion and close with the following non-answer: If *c'est que* did not exist, linguists would have to invent it.

NOTE

*I would like to express my appreciation to S.-Y. Kuroda for his helpful comments on a draft of this paper, and also to the various native speakers of French who have lent me their intuitions.

APPENDIX

When this paper was written, I did not have access to the paper by Richard Kayne that appears elsewhere in this volume. Kayne's arguments call into serious doubt the analysis of question inversion that I defended in section 3. His arguments are well made and reasonably convincing, and I am inclined to accept his formulation of question inversion in preference to the one I proposed in 1965. However, his arguments depend crucially on a handful of assumptions, some of which have been implicit in generative grammar since its inception but have never been adequately scrutinized and defended. Consequently, I feel the whole matter is still very much open to discussion, and it is quite important that the underlying theoretical questions be made explicit. Let me therefore offer the following, not in defense of my original analysis (for I think Kayne's is probably correct), but rather to make it clear just what is at issue.

The basic tenets of Kayne's analysis of question inversion are these: (A) The inversions of clitic and non-clitic NP's reflect the operation of two different rules, the latter to be equated with subject-postposing in relatives and other subordinate clauses. (B) The same rule should be responsible for inversion of simple clitic subjects and for the clitic placement in questions displaying "complex inversion". (C) Clitic inversion cannot be a copying-plus-deletion operation; rather, clitic insertion (for non-clitic subjects) followed by permutation must be postulated. I will first discuss (B) and (C), returning to (A) afterwards.

Claim (B) is non-controversial. Kayne and I both use a single sequence of rules to account for the post-verbal clitics in (1) and (2):

(1) Est-il là? 'Is he there?'

(2) Pierre est-il là? 'Is Peter there?'

However, we propose slightly different derivations, and this is where claim (C) enters the picture. The derivations I suggested are as follows:

(1) il est là ====> il est il là ====> Est-il là?
         (RED)   (DEL)

(2) Pierre est là ====> Pierre est Pierre là ====>
          (RED)   (PRO)
     Pierre est-il là?

Kayne, on the other hand, proposes the rules of clitic insertion (INS) and clitic inversion (INV), as in these derivations:

(1) il est là ====> Est-il là?
         (INV)

(2) Pierre est là ====> Pierre il est là ====>
          (INS)   (INV)

Pierre est-il là?

The differences between the two analyses are certainly not radical, especially when one realizes that inversion in a transformational grammar
consists formally in copying plus deletion.
 Nevertheless, the analyses are different, and Kayne presents arguments
for his solution. The first argument concerns questions with *ce* as
subject, and it runs something like this: A distinction must be made
between subjects that are NP's (e.g. *cela* and *Pierre*) and subjects that
are not NP's, but only clitics (e.g. *ce, il*). The copying rule (equivalent to my RED and PRO) would have to be formulated so as to apply only
to NP's, not clitics; this restriction accounts for the deviance of (3)
alongside the grammaticality of (4).

(3)   *C'est-il faux? 'Is it false?'

(4)   Cela est-il faux? 'Is that false?'

(3) would be derived by COPY (which copies all third person masculine
singular nominals as *il*) if COPY could apply to clitics, but it will be
correctly blocked if COPY cannot apply to clitics. (For Kayne, (1) in a
copying analysis would have the derivation *lui est là* ====> *lui est-il
là* ====> *Est-il là?*.) But if COPY cannot apply to clitics, how can
sentences like (5) be derived?

(5)   Est-ce vrai? 'Is it true?'

In a copying-plus-deletion analysis, copying itself is responsible for
clitic positioning.
 Kayne's argument hinges on the assumption that the reduplicated form
of *ce*, like that of *cela*, would have to be *il*, but this is not a necessary assumption. The clitic copy of a non-clitic NP must necessarily
be different from the original, but there is no a priori reason to expect
the clitic copy of a clitic to be anything but the clitic itself. Thus
one could counter by claiming that the copying rule should be formulated
instead as follows: A subject nominal is copied after the following
inflected verbal element and then reduced to clitic form. It must further
be agreed by convention that the clitic form of a clitic is the clitic
itself, so that *ce* is copied as *ce* rather than *il*. (4) and (5) then have
these derivations (COPY combines the properties of my rules RED and PRO):

(4)   cela est faux ====> Cela est-il faux?
            (COPY)

(5)   ce est vrai ====> ce est ce vrai ====> Est-ce vrai?
            (COPY)   (DEL)

The crucial point here is the convention that the clitic form of a clitic is the clitic itself, a convention for which I am not prepared to argue on independent grounds, but which is in no way implausible. The opposite convention would seem to me to be the one that required justification, though in a sense it follows from the usual transformational format.

Kayne's argument also assumes that in a copying-plus-deletion analysis the copying of a non-clitic subject as a clitic would consist in a single rule rather than in two separate but related rules. In my analysis, I make the opposite claim; RED and PRO are separate rules. Hence the argument can be refuted even if the clitic form of the clitic *ce* is taken to be *il* rather than *ce* itself. RED can be made to apply to any subject NP, but the following reduction rule, PRO, can be restricted to non-clitics (Kayne also assumes that rules can refer to non-clitics); hence *ce* would not be pronominalized to *il*. We thus uncover another crucial hidden assumption, this one pertaining to the way simple transformational operations are grouped into rules.

I cannot evaluate the other argument fully, since Kayne alludes to an analysis involving *on* that he does not present. The argument concerns sentences like (6).

(6)   Pourquoi Jean et moi ne devrait-on pas partir tout de suite?
      'Why shouldn't John and I leave right away?'

To derive such sentences in terms of my analysis, it would apparently be necessary to allow a conjoined subject to be copied after the verb as the grammatically singular clitic *on*. Kayne claims to have an analysis of *on* that precludes this sort of derivation; if so, his formulation must be correct. In the text, however, he bases this argument on subject-verb agreement. (Analogous arguments and counterarguments can be made in terms of reflexivization.) Since the verb agrees with the copy *on*, my analysis entails a complication of the subject-verb agreement rule; normally, the verb agrees with the NP that precedes it, but in this particular type of sentence, it must agree with *on*, which follows it and does not precede it at any point in the derivation.

The crucial assumption here, of course, is that subject-verb agreement is correctly formulated as a transformation that makes a verb agree with the nominal that precedes it in the linear order of a string. This is the way subject-verb agreement is normally conceived in generative syntax; under standard operating procedures, it is not even possible to refer to the notion "subject" in a transformational rule. However, this modus operandi has never really been justified on empirical grounds--the whole approach is an artifact of the history of transformational grammar, a very suspicious one at that. If one assumes that subject-verb agreement is just that, agreement between a verb and its subject (regardless of linear order), the force of Kayne's argument disappears. I emphasize that I have not refuted his argument; I merely wish to point out that it depends on an implicit assumption with rather shaky empirical foundations.

Incidentally, the fact that *on* functions as the superficial subject of *devrait* in (6) suggests that a reanalysis of French in terms of under-lying verb-initial order might be appropriate. Copying rules normally involve pronominalization of the original NP, not the newly inserted copy, and (as a corollary) the pronominal element of the pair is normally the one that functions syntactically in the slot of the original NP. This is true in dislocated sentences like (7), for instance.

(7)   Pierre, il travaille toujours.   'Peter, he always works.'

These generalizations will be preserved if the "inverted" pronouns in sentences like (6) and (4) reflect the underlying position of the subject NP, with pre-verbal NP's being created by a copying rule that may or may not be followed by deletion of the original. The whole matter of question inversion in French might profitably be reexamined in this light.

To summarize, Kayne's analysis and mine agree with respect to claim (B), but they disagree in regard to claim (C). If Kayne's arguments concerning point (C) are correct, his analysis is to be preferred. These arguments, however, depend crucially on the correctness of certain assump-tions that have not conclusively been established as correct: the assump-tion that *il* is to be expected as the clitic form of the clitic *ce* because it is the clitic form of *cela*; the assumption that copying-as-a-clitic must consist in one rule, not separate copying and reduction rules; and the assumption that subject-verb agreement is a transformation that does not refer to the notion "subject", but rather to the notion "NP that precedes the verb in linear order".

If these assumptions should prove false, this would not in itself constitute grounds for preferring my analysis; further considerations would have to be brought to bear on the matter before one could choose between the analyses on a principled basis. Two considerations come to mind that favor my analysis, but I am not sure how much force they have. For one thing, my proposed analysis involves fewer elementary transforma-tional operations than Kayne's. I posit rules that copy a subject nominal after the verb (one operation), pronominalize it (one operation), and then delete the original under identity (one operation)--a total of three operations. Kayne's analysis, on the other hand, involves four operations; his insertion rule copies and pronominalizes a non-clitic NP (two operations), and his inversion rule copies a clitic NP after the verb and deletes the original (two operations). (In either analysis, clitic insertion could involve simply feature copying rather than NP copying plus pronominaliza-tion.) I am inclined to give more weight to the number of elementary operations an analysis requires than to the number of transformations into which they are grouped, but I do not know whether all this numerology should be taken too seriously, especially since the counting itself involves some rather shaky assumptions.

The second consideration concerns dialects or styles in which clitic inversion is optional, allowing sentences like (8).

(8)   Où elle est? 'Where is she?'

In Kayne's analysis, but not mine, the derivation of (9) has (10) as an intermediate stage, so one might expect (10) to be grammatical in these dialects.

(9) Où Marie est-elle? 'Where is Mary?'

(10) *Où Marie elle est? 'Where is Mary?'

The ungrammaticality of (10) might tend to support my analysis, but it is also possible that (10) can be prevented by some independently required surface constraint.

Let us turn now to claim (A), the claim that entirely different rules are responsible for the inversion in (11) and (12).

(11) Quand partira ce garçon? 'When will this boy leave?'

(12) Quand partira-t-il? 'When will he leave?'

Kayne amasses an impressive array of evidence to support this claim. Nevertheless, the arguments depend crucially on certain implicit assumptions of generative grammar that are not necessarily immune to skepticism.

Kayne argues that the inversion of non-clitic NP's, as in the derivation of (11), is effected by a rule sensitive to WH, the same rule that postposes the subject in relative clauses, as in (13).

(13) la femme qu'a vue le garçon 'the woman that the boy saw'

Clitic inversion is not sensitive to WH, but rather to the "question-hood" of the clause of which the clitic is the subject.

One argument for distinguishing clitic and non-clitic inversion is that inverted clitic and non-clitic NP's sometimes have different surface structure positions:

(14) Que voulait manger ce jeune homme? 'What did this young man want to eat?'

(15) Que voulait-il manger? 'What did he want to eat?'

This problem was discussed briefly in section 3 of the text. The force of the argument depends on the assumption that the inversion rule alone is responsible for the surface placement of the inverted subject in the predicate, but this is not a necessary assumption, particularly when it is realized how little we really know about the interaction between surface patterns and transformational derivations.

A second argument for distinguishing clitic and non-clitic inversion is that only the latter can apply in embedded questions.

(16) Je sais très bien à quelle heure partira ce garçon.
      'I know very well when this boy will leave.'

(17) *Je sais très bien à quelle heure partira-t-il.
      'I know very well when he will leave.'

Moreover, non-clitic inversion is applicable to relative clauses as well
as direct and embedded questions, and the placement of the postposed NP
obeys the same restrictions in the three constructions; clitic inversion
is restricted to direct questions. These would seem to be strong grounds
for separating the two rules, and indeed, I think Kayne is probably right
in distinguishing them.
     Still, the matter is not perfectly cut-and-dried. An alternative
analysis, quite compatible with my original one, might run as follows.
A distinction must be made between the inversion in direct questions
(both clitic and non-clitic) and the inversion in embedded questions,
relatives, and other constructions. My three-rule analysis (RED,PRO,
DEL) accounts for the former, and a separate rule, similar to Kayne's
"stylistic inversion" rule, accounts for the latter, which is restricted
to non-clitic subject nominals. The independently needed restriction
of stylistic inversion to non-clitic subjects accounts for the fact that
(16), but not (17), is grammatical. Moreover, postposed subjects in
embedded questions, relative clauses, and other constructions are subject
to the same restrictions because the same rule postposes them all.
     However, it is still necessary to explain why the postposed non-clitic
subjects obey the same restrictions in direct questions and in those
constructions to which stylistic inversion applies; (18) and (19), for
instance, are apparently ungrammatical for the same reasons, but they
are claimed to be derived by different rules.

(18) *Depuis quand est ton ami malade? 'How long has your
                                          friend been sick?'

(19) *à l'époque où était ton ami malade 'at the time when
                                            your friend was sick'

Unless they are derived by the same rule, there is no reason to expect
the positioning of the postposed subject to obey the same restrictions
in the two constructions.
     The crucial assumption is hidden in this last sentence. Kayne's
argument implicity assumes that the surface position of a postposed
nominal is fully determined by the postposing rule itself, and that two
different postposing rules cannot both feed the same set of restrictions
that determine the precise location of the postposed nominal in surface
structure (or specify the ungrammaticality of a sentence in which postposing has occurred but where no postposed subject is possible in any
position). This assumption is part and parcel of transformational

practice, but once again it is necessary to point out that it is not a necessary assumption, nor is it one that has been motivated explicitly by generative grammarians.

In particular, it might be maintained that the rule which postposes the subject in direct questions simply specifies that the subject is placed somewhere after the inflected verb. Where precisely a postposed subject will surface can be determined by rules that can, at least in principle, be conceived as distinct entities. One rule might specify that a postposed clitic subject is suffixed to the inflected verb. Another would specify the location of a non-clitic postposed subject, and this latter rule could effect the situation of the output of both question inversion and stylistic inversion. This analysis captures the same generalizations as Kayne's, but at the expense of breaking up question inversion into two parts--the part that stipulates that subject postposing occurs, and the part that says where the postposed subject is to surface. In the case of non-clitic subjects, the second part applies to the output of both question inversion and stylistic inversion.

This proposal is terribly vague and stands in need of much clarification and independent support, and I would not suggest it as a serious alternative to Kayne's analysis, at least not for the time being. However, I do not regard it as totally implausible, and I think it is important to make implicit assumptions explicit. The standard transformational theory does not allow one to write a rule that postposes a nominal without saying in the rule itself precisely where it goes. Nor does it allow one to state a generalization to the effect that postposed subject nominals obey certain restrictions regardless of what rule postposes them. Kayne's argument depends on these features of transformational theory, features that have not really been justified. We are only beginning to come to grips with the problem of how surface patterns interact with transformational derivations, and for this reason it would be premature to discard my proposal because of its vagueness alone.

Kayne's final argument pertains to YNQ. His stylistic inversion rule applies to non-clitic subjects in direct and indirect questions, in relative clauses, and in certain other constructions. This rule applies only when WH precedes the subject. He claims that *si* is not a WH word, which explains the ungrammaticality of (20).

(20)   *Il se demande si vont chanter les oiseaux.
       'He wonders if the birds are going to sing.'

Now consider (21)-(22).

(21)   *Chantent les oiseaux? 'Are the birds singing?'

(22)   Chantent-ils? 'Are they singing?'

Clitic inversion is possible in direct YNQ, but non-clitic inversion is blocked. His analysis accounts for this as follows: Non-clitic or

stylistic inversion is triggered by WH, but WH is not present in (20) or
(21), which are consequently ungrammatical, having undergone inversion.
(22) is acceptable because clitic inversion is sensitive, not to WH, but
to the question-hood of the clause. Since WH triggers one inversion but
not the other, they must be different rules.

There is at least one difficulty with this argument. Namely, the question-hood of a clause is not sufficient to trigger clitic inversion; the
presence of WH before the subject is also required, as shown by (23)-
(25).

(23) Elle aime qui? 'Who does she like?'

(24) *Aime-t-elle qui? 'Who does she like?'

(25) Qui aime-t-elle? 'Who does she like?'

For this reason, a WH constituent analogous to English *whether* must
presumably occur in the underlying structure of (21) and (22), though
it does not surface (at least in direct questions). However, Kayne
can still account for (20)-(22) by means of rule ordering. Clitic inversion applies first, triggered by WH, and the WH element is subsequently
deleted in YNQ. Following this deletion, stylistic inversion applies.
It cannot apply in YNQ, since WH has been elided in these, but it can in
WHQ, where it is retained. Inversion is correctly blocked in (20) and
(21).

This means of blocking (21) is not available in my analysis, since I
claim that the same rule, RED, postposes both clitics and non-clitics;
since (22) is grammatical, there is no principled reason why (21) should
not also be. I am forced to rule out (21) by means of an ad hoc constraint
like the ones discussed in section 4 that are needed to preclude such
questions as (26)-(28).

(26) *Que tombe? 'What falls?'

(27) *Que Pierre veut-il? 'What does Peter want?'

(28) *Pourquoi mange Paul? 'Why does Paul eat?'

However, I am not sure that I should be bothered too much by the necessity
to impose such a restriction, since some restrictions of this character
are apparently needed anyway. Moreover, Kayne's solution depends on
claims that merit closer scrutiny, interesting though they are. Among
these are the claim that the rules are ordered as stated above; that *si*
is not a WH word; that cleft sentences involve a relative clause marker;
that *quand* is not a WH word in (29); and so on.

(29) *Quand a crié l'enfant, je suis rentré.
      'When the child cried out, I went back.'

In short, I find this argument, like the others, less than overwhelming. At least one consideration suggests that the inversion of non-clitic subjects in direct questions should be grouped with clitic inversion rather than with the stylistic inversion that also applies in relative clauses. In relatives, subject postposing is an optional stylistic rule; (30) and (13) are equally grammatical.

(30) la femme que le garçon a vue 'the woman that the boy saw'

However, this is not so in direct questions (excluding dialects that permit sentences like (8)). Here inversion is necessary, both for clitic and non-clitic subjects:

(31) *Quand Pierre travaille? 'When does Peter work?'

(32) *Quand il travaille? 'When does he work?'

To summarize, none of Kayne's arguments is totally beyond the reach of fanatic skepticism, though they are certainly good arguments if all the assumptions characteristic of generative grammar are accepted at face value. On balance, his analysis of question inversion seems more likely to prove correct than mine, and I would no doubt be more fully convinced if I did not have a stake in the matter. In questioning his arguments, I hope to have raised some interesting theoretical issues on which a careful analysis of French interrogatives may have some bearing, issues that might otherwise have remained obscure.

RICHARD S. KAYNE
UNIVERSITÉ DE PARIS VIII/ VINCENNES

SUBJECT INVERSION IN FRENCH INTERROGATIVES

CONTENTS

Section I: The inversion of subject NP and that of subject clitic must be described by means of two distinct transformations. Section II: The 'complex inversion' construction must be described in terms of an inversion transformation, the same as that pertinent to the simple inversion of the subject clitic, rather than in terms of a pronominal copy transformation. Section III: The origin and subsequent displacement of subject clitics; the unity of 'ce' and 'ça'; the formalization of subject clitic inversion; notes on subject clitics and coreference.

SECTION I

Although pairs of sentences such as the following:

(1)   a. Quand partira ce garçon?
       b. Quand partira-t-il?

might lead one to think in terms of a unique subject-verb inversion transformation for direct questions, there are many well-known differences between the inversion of pronominal subjects and that of NP subjects. For example, only the pronominal subject may be inverted in yes-no questions:

(2)   *Partira ce garçon?
     . Partira-t-il?

Furthermore, there is a clear difference in status between the two constructions in questions introduced by the word "pourquoi":

(3)   ?Pourquoi part ce garçon?
      Pourquoi part-il?

In addition, for most speakers, the productivity of the NP-inversion,
but not that of the pronominal inversion, is affected by the presence
of certain types of post-verbal complements and modifiers:[1]

(4)　　*Quand deviendra ce comédien célèbre?
　　　　Quand deviendra-t-il célèbre?

　　　　*A quelle heure changera cette fille d'avis?
　　　　A quelle heure changera-t-elle d'avis?

　　　　*Depuis combien de temps en veut cet étudiant à ses professeurs?
　　　　Depuis combien de temps en veut-il à ses professeurs?

　　　　*A quoi joue cet homme mieux que toi?
　　　　A quoi joue-t-il mieux que toi?

　　　　*De quel oeil voit ton ami double?
　　　　De quel oeil voit-il double?

　　　　*De quel droit prétend ce charlatan que tout va bien?
　　　　De quel droit prétend-il que tout va bien?

　　　　*Depuis quand se connaît cette personne en histoire?
　　　　Depuis quand se connaît-elle en histoire?

　　　　*Où tient votre petite fille à ce que j'aille?
　　　　Où tenez-vous à ce que j'aille?

　　The existence of restrictions such as those shown in (2)-(4) would
force one to impose an ugly series of conditions on any single transformation postulated to account for both of the sentences in (1). Moreover,
it is clear that the required conditions would amount to no more than an
uninteresting restatement of the data and would contribute in no way to
an understanding of the above paradigms.
　　We shall instead consider examples (2)-(4) as evidence in favor of
the hypothesis that the subject inversion in sentences (1a) and (1b) is to
be accounted for by means of two distinct transformations, one of which
will apply only to subject pronouns; the other will apply to subject NP's,
but not to subject pronouns. Let us call the former "subject clitic inversion" (SUBJ - CL - INV), and the latter "stylistic inversion" (STYL-
INV), for reasons which will become more evident below.
　　The need for two separate transformations is made particularly clear
by the fact that the surface structure position of the inverted subject
pronoun is in general not identical to that of the inverted subject NP:

(5)　　Que voulait manger ce jeune homme?
　　　　*Que voulait manger-il?

*Que voulait ce jeune homme manger?
Que voulait-il manger?

Qu'a fait cette femme?
*Qu'a fait-elle?

*Qu'a cette femme fait?
Qu'a-t-elle fait?

We note that these examples suggest that the inversion of the subject
pronoun be construed as a simple interchange of the pronoun and the verbal
form with which it is in contact, a position consistent also with the
facts of (1)-(4). On the other hand, the above examples suggest a rather
different characterization of the "inversion" of the subject NP, which
could more readily be interpreted as a displacement of the subject NP to
the end of the sentence.

Such a formulation of the transformation STYL - INV would immediately
account for the ungrammaticality of the starred sentences in (4), which
would simply not be generable. Rather, postposing the subject NP to the
end of the sentence would yield:

(6)   ?Quand deviendra célèbre ce comédien?
        ?A quelle heure changera d'avis cette fille?
        ?Depuis combien de temps en veut à ses professeurs cet étudiant?
       *?A quoi joue mieux que toi cet homme?
        ?De quel oeil voit double ton ami?
       *De quel droit prétend que tout va bien ce charlatan?
        ?Depuis quand se connaît en histoire cette personne?
       *Où tient à ce que j'aille votre petite fille?

Compared to (4), which illustrated the simple inversion of subject NP and
verb, the sentences in (6), which illustrate the placing of the subject
in sentence-final position, are for the most part decidedly better, and
in any case never worse. In fact, several of the examples in (6) can be
made perfectly grammatical by increasing the length of the subject NP:

(7)   Quand deviendra célèbre le comédien que nous avons vu si bien
        jouer l'autre jour à la télévision?
        A quelle heure changera d'avis le prisonnier auquel la police
        est en train de faire subir des tortures inimaginables?
        De quel oeil voit double celui de tes amis qui a failli se tuer
        dans un accident de moto?
       ?De quel droit prétend que tout va bien le charlatan qui vient
        d'etre arreté par la police?

The sentences in (4), however, are not improved if the constituent
following the inverted subject NP is lengthened:

(8) *Quand deviendra ce comédien aussi célèbre que celui qui se pros-
titue à tourner des films de publicité?
*A quoi joue cet homme dix fois mieux que les joueurs professionnels?
*Où tient votre petite fille à ce que j'aille l'année prochaine
pendant les vacances de Noel?

This suggests that the acceptability of the output of STYL - INV, which
will be formulated as a rule moving the subject to sentence final-posi-
tion, thereby accounting for the contrast between (7) and (8), as well as
that between (4) and (6), is determined in part by considerations of
length.[2] Such 'stylistic' considerations, however, do not seem to play
a role in cases like (5).[3]
   The precise formulation of STYL - INV raises a number of difficult
questions; for example, not all complements lead to contrasts as clear-
cut as those in (4). Although there are numerous verb-complement combinations which cannot be broken up by STYL - INV,[4] there are others for
which that is less clearly true:

(9) ??Quand écrira ton frère à sa petite amie?
?Qu'écrira ton frère à sa petite amie?
Que dira ton frère à sa petite amie?

In addition, as evidenced by the sentences with 'écrire', the choice of
question word may play some role, although interrogative 'que' certainly
does not always allow placement of the subject NP directly to the right
of the verb:

(10) *Que veut votre femme que vous fassiez?

Examples of perfectly grammatical sentences where STYL - INV appears to
have put the subject NP to the left of a complement are:

(11) Où est allé votre ami pour trouver la paix?
A quoi s'intéressait cette personne en 1968?

These contrast with:

(12) *Dans quelle élection a voté votre ami pour Nixon?
*Depuis quand se connaît cette personne en histoire?

Such data cast doubt on the feasibility of maintaining the characterization
of STYL - INV as a transformation which throws subject NP's to sentence-
final position, since in (11) and (9), the postposed subject is not
sentence-final. On the other hand, (12), (10) and (4) continue to suggest
that STYL - INV may not be considered to invert subject and verb. An
ideal solution would consist of showing that those complements which can
follow the postposed subject, as in (11) and (9), are exactly those not
dominated by some intermediate node, call it VP; this would permit stating

STYL - INV as A - NP - VP - X → A - VP - NP - X where A stands for the
interrogative word and X for a variable. Unfortunately it is far from
clear that this approach is the optimal one. On the one hand, the question
of the justification and constituency of the node VP in French has been
little studied.[5] On the other hand, the complement in 'à' of 'dire' (v.
(9)) is an unlikely candidate for non-VPhood. Worse, there are some speakers
who accept some of the starred sentences in (4), and it would be surprising
to find such ideolectal differences attributable to differences in VP-
structure. Nor do the facts concerning 'quand' vs. 'que' lend themselves
to that approach (the special status of 'que', if that's what is relevant,
may be related to its atonic character). There is no doubt something here
that does depend on the degree of closeness between verb and complement,
but it remains to be seen if such a notion can be made precise.[6] In any
case, none of the above would suggest abandoning the original hypothesis
as to the postulation of two distinct transformations for the sentences
in (1).

An additional argument in favor of this distinction comes from consideration of embedded questions, in which the inversion of the subject NP
but not that of the subject pronoun is possible:

(13) Je sais très bien à quelle heure partira ce garçon.
      *Je sais très bien à quelle heure partira-t-il.

With respect to STYL - INV, we find in embedded questions restrictions
similar to those discussed earlier:[7]

(14) *Il voudrait savoir depuis quand est cette fille malade.
      *Dites-moi à quel moment a changé Marie d'avis.
      *Je me demande à quelle heure téléphonera ce garcon à ses parents.
      *On ne sait pas ce que veut Jean qu'on fasse.

Again, the positioning of the subject NP is as in direct questions
(cf. (5)):

(15) Je ne me rappelle pas à quelle heure devait partir mon ami.
      *Je ne me rappelle pas à quelle heure devait mon ami partir.

      On se demande ce qu'a dit le président.
      *On se demande ce qu'a le président dit.

Similarly, the construction is less satisfying with "pourquoi" (cf. (3)):

(16) ?Je ne me rappelle pas pourquoi devait partir mon ami.
      ??Il tient à savoir pourquoi est partie la fille.

Finally, the inapplicability of STYL - INV in yes-no questions (cf. (2))
is mirrored in the corresponding embedded question with "si":[8]

(17) *Tu sauras bientôt si va venir ta femme.
      *On ne sait pas si partira ce garçon.

Although the different behavior of STYL - INV and SUBJ - CL - INV in
embedded questions is certainly a clear indication that we are dealing
with distinct rules, this particular argument could be made much more
compelling by showing that the two-rule analysis can actually explain
why SUBJ - CL - INV, but not STYL - INV, should be limited to non-embedded
sentences.[9] We return to this question below.

Another important property of STYL - INV which distinguishes it
from SUBJ - CL - INV is that it is applicable in relative clauses:

(18) La maison où habite cet homme est très jolie.
      L'homme qu'a rencontré cette femme est bien connu.
      Le problème auquel réfléchit le savant est trivial.
      Ce dont parlera le conférencier, c'est ceci.

The positioning of the subject NP is as in interrogatives:[10]

(19) Au moment où voulait partir son amie . . .
      *Au moment où voulait son amie partir . . .

      Ce qu'a fait son père . . .
      *Ce qu'a son père fait . . .

As in interrogatives, the postposed subject may not appear between the
verb and certain types of verbal complements:

(20) *à l'époque où était cette fille malade
      *au moment où changeait Marie d'avis
      *la fille que croit Jean que tu aimes
      *celui à qui a donné ce garçon des bouquins
      *la femme avec laquelle tient son enfant à ce qu'il se marie

Again, in many cases, the order complement - subject NP is possible
especially if the subject NP is long:[11]

(21) à l'époque où était malade la fille dont on a parlé hier
      au moment où changeait d'avis le prisonnier que la police était
      en train de torturer

and, as in interrogatives, the examples in (20) are not improved by the
presence of a long complement:

(22) *à l'époque où était cette fille encore plus malade qu'elle ne
      l'est maintenant
      *celui à qui a donné ce garçon les bouquins qu'on lui avait offerts
      il y a deux mois

Once more the distinction between STYL - INV   and SUBJ - CL - INV is
justified by the observation that the latter is never applicable in
relatives:

(23) *La maison où habite-t-il est très jolie.
      *L'homme qu'a-t-elle rencontré est bien connu.
      *Ce dont parlera-t-il, c'est ceci.
      *Le problème auquel réfléchit-il est trivial.

Returning to the problem of the formulation of STYL - INV, we note that its applicability in both interrogatives and relatives suggests that it should be made sensitive to some characteristic common to these two constructions. A natural proposal would be to have STYL - INV depend on the presence of a clause-initial WH-element:[12]

e.g. $:\Big[_{S} \begin{matrix} A \ NP \ X \\ +WH \end{matrix} \Big] \rightarrow \Big[_{S} \begin{matrix} A \ X \ NP \\ +WH \end{matrix} \Big]$ (but v. fn. 6)

For the purposes of determining what counts as an initial WH-element, a distinction must be made between relative "que" and the conjunction, or complementizer "que":

(24)   Je connais la fille qu'a rencontrée Jean.
        *On sait qu'a pleuré Jean.

        Le fait que t'a communiqué cette fille ne nous intéresse pas.
        *Le fait que t'a parlé cette fille ne nous intéresse pas.

This would present no problem if relative 'que', but not the other, had been marked +WH (we. are taking +WH to be a marker assigned to those constituents which are to undergo WH-movement -v. Chomsky (1971)). Actually, there is a fair amount of evidence (v. Kayne (forthcoming - b)) that 'que' should not be considered a relative pronoun at all, and that the derivation of relative clauses with 'que' involve the deletion of a preposed relative element, schematically 'la table laquelle qu'il a cassée'→'la table qu'il a cassée'. If this is true, then in (24) the 'A' of the structural description of STYL - INV corresponds to this ultimately deleted relative element, rather than to 'que'. Given this analysis of relative pronouns, STYL - INV must be ordered before the deletion rule in question. If 'que', now considered a kind of clause-introducing element, is in the tree at the time of STYL - INV (rather than inserted under the appropriate conditions by a subsequent rule), STYL - INV must be reformulated as:[13]

$$_{S}\Big[\begin{matrix} A \ (que) \ NP \ X \\ +WH \end{matrix} \Big]_{S} \rightarrow {}_{S}\Big[\begin{matrix} A \ (que) \ X \ NP \\ +WH \end{matrix} \Big]_{S}$$

We note that this formulation of STYL - INV correctly predicts that if the initial WH-element is itself the subject, the inversion will not take place:

(25) Qui a crié?
Combien d'enfants voudraient le lire?
Elle sait laquelle lui plaît.

(26) *A crié qui?
*Voudraient le lire combien d'enfants?
*Elle sait lui plaît laquelle.

The statement of STYL - INV in terms of an initial WH-element, we recall, was motivated by its applying both in interrogatives and in relatives. The fact that SUBJ - CL - INV does not apply in relatives must consequently be considered evidence that it not be formulated in the same way. We have already seen a number of environments, in embedded sentences, where STYL - INV, but not SUBJ - CL - INV, was applicable. If SUBJ - CL - INV is not in general triggered by the presence of an initial WH-element, then we might expect to find cases of the applicability of STYL - INV but not SUBJ - CL - INV even in nonembedded sentences. Exclamatory sentences not containing a negative particle (v. Nø jgaard (1967)) and introduced by a NP containing the word "quel" seem to be just such a case:[14]

(27) Quels beaux visages ont ces jeunes femmes!
Quel plaisir m 'a fait son discours!

*?Quels beaux visages ont-elles!
*?Quel plaisir m 'a-t-il fait!

Since it is as we see not possible to use the presence of an initial WH-element as the trigger for SUBJ - CL - INV, we are led to stating the rule directly in terms of the environment "question". Formally, one way this could be accomplished would be by the use of a special interrogation marker (Q).[15] In any case, this approach correctly accounts for the fact that SUBJ - CL - INV is applicable in non-embedded yes-no questions as well as WH-element introduced questions.

Most importantly, this characterization of SUBJ - CL - INV, combined with the formulation of STYL - INV as a rule sensitive to the presence of an initial WH-element, is able to explain the assymetry with respect to the inversion of the subject found in yes-no questions (v. (2)). The fact that in yes-no questions, a subject NP may not be inverted:

(28) *Chantent les oiseaux?

will follow from the fact that the transformation moving subject NP's, STYL - INV, is sensitive to the presence of an initial WH-element, lacking in (28), rather than to the questionhood of the sentence. Looked at from this angle, the contrast between (28) and WH-questions:

(29) Depuis quand chantent les oiseaux?

loses its superficially anomalous character. Conversely, the contrast between (28) and:

(30) Chantent-ils?

is now seen to follow from the fundamentally distinct character of the rules inverting on the one hand, subject NP's (STYL - INV) and on the other hand, subject clitic pronouns (SUBJ - CL - INV).

We note that the contrast between (28) and (29) is mirrored in embedded questions:

(31) Il se demande à quelle heure son ami partira.
      Il se demande si son ami partira.

      Il se demande à quelle heure partira son ami.
      *Il se demande si partira son ami.

The absence of inversion with 'si' implies that "si" is not to be considered a WH-element.[16] This would seem to correlate with the fact that "si" lacks a plausible source compared to "où", "qui", "quoi", etc. Thus one could envision an analysis in which the latter three interrogative pronouns are derived from, respectively, WH + là, WH + quelqu'un, WH + quelque chose, but it is difficult to see what element X could be claimed to underlie "si" if "si" equalled WH + X.[17] More likely, "si" should be considered a word whose derivational history does not include any movement due to the rule of WH-preposing.[18]

The postulation of two distinct inversion rules thus permits an insightful account of the superficially anomalous behavior of the yes-no questions. We shall now attempt to account for the assymmetry between NP and pronoun inversion in embedded sentences:

(32) Elle te dira où habite son père.
      *Elle te dira où habite-t-il. (cf. (13))

With respect to this particular problem, the postulation of two distinct rules would not be much of an improvement over the original possibility (given just one rule) of ad-hocly restricting the inversion in embedded questions to just NP's, if it were still necessary to add an ad-hoc condition to SUBJ - CL - INV to the same effect (i.e., to prevent it from applying in embedded sentences).

We note, however, that, as a rule applying in all types of non-embedded questions, and not subject to any restrictions imposed by following complements, SUBJ - CL - INV (but not STYL - INV) bears a significant resemblance to subject-auxiliary inversion in English, which is likewise limited to application in non-embedded sentences. (The same appears to be true of the question inversion rule in Swedish, which involves inversion of subject and simple verb, rather than auxiliary.) This suggests that the above restriction on SUBJ - CL - INV is not to be considered an

accidental fact about French, but should formally be related to the corresponding facts in English (and Swedish). Such an approach would permit a
non ad-hoc solution to the lack of parallelism between the inversion of the
NP and that of the subject pronoun, insofar as only the rule moving the
latter is formally a simple inversion of subject and verb (or auxiliary)
conditioned by the environment "question".[19]

Moreover, it is possible that one can do more than simply reduce the
language particularity of the problem. Emonds (1969) has proposed a theory
of formal constraints on transformations which would provide a motivated
explanation for the restriction of certain types of transformations
(including SUBJ - CL - INV) to non-embedded sentences.[20]

The applicability of STYL - INV in embedded sentences, on the other hand,
seems to be related to the similar behavior of the rule of "length-inversion"
mentioned earlier (v. fn. 6). Although this result does not follow directly
from Emonds theory, it does not seem to be incompatible with it; one might
hope that such rules form a separate, but tightly constrained class not
subject to the structure-preserving constraint. We emphasize that the
possibility of an explanation along these lines depends on the existence
of two distinct transformations, STYL - INV and SUBJ - CL - INV, for pairs
such as (1).

We thus have two transformations, one of which applies to subject pronouns and the other to subject NP's. Stated in another way, SUBJ - CL -
INV is inapplicable to NP's:[21]

(33)　*Partira Jean?
　　　　*Quand est Jean parti?
　　　　*Où voulait Jean aller?
　　　　*A quoi est cette fille sensible?

vs.

　　　　Partira-t-il?
　　　　Quand est-il parti?
　　　　Où voulait-il aller?
　　　　A quoi est-elle sensible?

and STYL - INV is inapplicable to subject pronouns:

(34)　*Quelle belle femme a-t-il!
　　　　*Ce que disait-il, c'est ceci.
　　　　*Je sais très bien quand reviendront-ils.
　　　　*C'est à trois heures qu'arrivera-t-il.
　　　　*Qu'a fait-il?

vs.

　　　　Quelle belle femme a ce garçon minable!
　　　　Ce que disait Jean, c'est ceci.
　　　　Je sais très bien quand reviendront ses enfants.
　　　　C'est à trois heures qu'arrivera le prince.
　　　　Qu'a fait Jean-Jacques?

The facts of (33) and (34) indicate that subject (clitic) pronouns[22] in French are not NP's (at least at the point of application of STYL - INV and SUBJ - CL - INV). This correlates with the following paradigm:[23]

(35) *C'est il.
      *Il, souvent, va au cinéma.
      *Il seul est capable de le faire.
      *Il, qui est mon ami, voudrait te voir.

In particular, when pronouns are in NP position, they may be 'modified' and conjoined:

(36) Il a parlé de nous autres.
      Elle pense à eux deux.
      Elle ne connaît que toi et moi.
      Il aime bien tout ça.
Compare:
(37) *Avons-nous autres perdu?
      *Ils deux sont fous.
      *Tu et je partirons demain.
      *Tout ce n'est pas important.[24]

Given the formulation of STYL - INV we proposed earlier, the ungrammatical sentences of (34) cannot be generated if the subject clitic pronouns are not dominated by the node NP.[25] The formalization we shall propose in Section III for SUBJ - CL - INV will distinguish the grammatical from the ungrammatical sentences of (33).

SECTION II

French contains another interrogative construction, which we shall refer to as 'complex inversion.' This construction has a great deal in common with SUBJ - CL - INV. Like SUBJ - CL - INV (but unlike STYL - INV), this construction occurs in yes-no questions:

(38) Ton ami partira-t-il?
      Cela est-il vrai?

is always grammatical with 'pourquoi':

(39) Pourquoi cette fille a-t-elle fait cela?

is not affected by following complements:

(40) Depuis quand ce garçon est-il malade?
      A qui ce garçon offrira-t-il ce livre?
      A quelle heure le prisonnier changera-t-il d'avis?
      Où cette fille veut-elle que tu ailles?

positions the subject pronoun as in SUBJ - CL - INV:

(41) Où Jean voulait-il aller?
      Pourquoi Jean a-t-il fait cela?

      *Où Jean voulait aller-il?
      *Pourquoi Jean a fait-il cela?

is impossible in embedded questions (as well as in relatives and clefts):

(42) *Je ne comprends pas pourquoi la maison s'est-elle écroulée.
      *Dis-moi si ton amie va-t-elle venir.
      *Il sait très bien où cette fille habite-t-elle.
      *Ce que Jean dira-t-il, c'est ceci.
      *C'est à Paris que Marie-Yvonne habite-t-elle.

and in the exclamations introduced by 'quel' discussed earlier:

(43) *?Quels jolis visages ces filles ont-elles!

The extensive parallelism between 'complex inversion' and SUBJ - CL - INV suggests that they be considered one and the same construction.[26] This decision is supported by the observation that in every case in which one finds 'complex inversion', SUBJ - CL - INV is also possible. Thus in addition to questions, we have:

(44) A peine Jean était-il parti que...
      A peine était-il parti que...

      Sans doute cette fille reviendra-t-elle.
      Sans doute reviendra-t-elle.

(45) a. Cette fille reviendrait-elle que je ne
          serais toujours pas content.

      b. Reviendrait-elle que je ne serais toujours
          pas content.[27]

Given the desirability of reducing 'complex inversion' and SUBJ - CL - INV to a single rule, we can ask how that reduction can be accomplished. Since 'complex inversion' superficially resembles a copying operation, e.g., 'Quand Jean partira'---'Quand Jean partira-t-il', one might try to rework SUBJ - CL - INV in terms of a copying rule. Alternatively, since SUBJ - CL - INV seems to be a pure inversion, one might try to incorporate a true inversion into the 'complex' construction, e.g., 'Quand Jean partira-t-il' would be derived from 'Quand Jean il partira'. The important point is that the placement of the subject pronoun in post-verbal position not be accomplished by two entirely distinct rules; if it were, the fact that the 'complex' construction exists only alongside the simple would be accidental, as would be the very fact that the pronoun is positioned in the same way in the two constructions.

Before considering the two alternatives alluded to above, we point out that the 'complex inversion' construction is not equivalent to that with 'detachment'. The detachment construction is not possible with NP's such as 'quelqu'un': (v. Gross (1968))

(46) *Quelqu'un, depuis quand m'attend-il?
*Depuis quand m'attend-il, quelqu'un?
Depuis quand quelqu'un m'attend-il?

Furthermore, complex inversion differs from detachment with respect to the possible NP-pronoun combinations, in which way complex inversion also differs significantly from the usual coreference environments; i.e., the relationship between the pre-verbal NP and the post-verbal subject pronoun is not the normal pronominalization relationship:

(47) Pourquoi cela est-il faux?
Pourquoi ce que je dis te déplaît-il?

*Cela$_i$ est faux parce qu'il$_i$ ne correspond pas à la vérité.

*Ce$_i$ qu'elle dit ne vous intéresse pas et il$_i$ ne m'intéresse pas,

moi non plus.

As we see, NP's of the type 'cela', 'ce que je dis' are not possible coreferents for the pronoun 'il', except in complex inversion. The same is true of sentential NP's:

(48) Que Jacques ait dit cela ne vous intéresse-t-il pas?
*Que$_i$ Jacques ait dit cela ne vous intéresse sûrement pas,
et il$_i$ ne m'intéresse pas, moi non plus.

Similarly, the indefinite pronouns 'rien' and 'tout' can, in the complex inversion construction be associated with 'il', otherwise not:

(49) Pourquoi rien n'est-il tombé?
Depuis quand tout est-il en ordre?

(50) *Rien$_i$ n'est tombé parce qu'il$_i$(n')était (pas)
soutenu par des clous.
*Tout$_i$ est en ordre aujourd'hui mais demain il$_i$
sera en désordre.

The nominal components of certain idioms behave in much the same way:[28]

(51) Pourquoi assistance a-t-elle été pretée à une personne si méchante?

 *Assistance$_i$ a été prêtée à cette personne-ci bien qu'elle$_i$ n'ait
 pas été prêtée à celle-là.

Predicate nominals in subject position provide a parallel argument:

(52) Depuis quand ton meilleur ami est-il Jean-Jacques?
 Pourquoi ta meilleure amie est-elle Anne-Marie?

 *Son meilleur ami$_i$ est maintenant Jean-Jacques, mais il y a
 trois ans il$_i$ était Michel.
 *On sait que ta meilleure amie$_i$ est Anne-Marie, mais à notre
 avis elle$_i$ devrait être Jacqueline.

Conversely, there exist cases in which NP's otherwise associable with a
certain pronoun cannot co-occur with it in complex inversion; these all
involve the pronoun 'ce':

(53) C'est faux, cela.
 Cela m'intéresse bien que ce soit faux.
 Ce que tu dis n'intéresse personne parce que c'est insensé.
 C'est marrant, les enfants.
 C'est un garçon intelligent, ton ami.
 Son ami a l'air bête bien que ce soit un garçon malin.

 *Pourquoi cela est-ce faux?
 *En quoi ce qu'il dit est-ce insensé?
 *De quelle façon les enfants est-ce marrant?
 *Pourquoi ce garçon n'est-ce pas un bon élève?

    Returning now to the question of the derivation of complex inversion, let
us assume that the appearance of the subject pronoun is to be accounted for
by means of a rule placing a pronominal copy of the subject into post-verbal
position: 'Tout est en ordre' → 'Tout est-il en ordre.' It is clear from
the above example that this copying rule must be distinct from whatever
rules are to handle pronominalization in general (this follows trivially if
pronouns are to be generated in the base). The nature of the above examples,
moreover, suggests that the copying rule in question best be considered a
simple reduplication of the features of person, gender, and number (although
the latter plays no overt role, since the plural 's' of the post-verbal
subject pronoun is never pronounced) of the subject NP. Thus all third-person,
singular, masculine NP's will be reduplicated as 'il'; their indefinite or
demonstrative character (rien, tout, cela, etc.) will have no effect on the
operation of such a rule. (One would also have to require that the spelling
out of a pronoun marked only as third person, masculine, singular be 'il' -
this might then be related to the appearance of 'il' as the 'dummy' pronoun
in 'il fait beau', 'il semble que', 'il faut que', 'il y a Jean qui veut te
poser une question', etc.) The non-appearance of 'ce' in this construction
suggests that 'ce' could not represent the spelling out of such a limited
set of features.

This copying rule would then be stated so as to apply in questions, and with certain adverbs, and so as to place the copied pronoun directly after the tensed verbal element. To avoid the extremely undesirable position of having a totally distinct inversion rule applying in the same environments and placing the pronoun in the same position, in sentences like 'Est-il là?', one would need to claim that such sentences are in fact derived through copying, with subsequent deletion of the subject NP: 'Lui est là' --- 'Lui est-il là' --- 'Est-il là?'.[29]

We shall now proceed to argue that the description of complex inversion in terms of a rule placing a pronominal copy of the subject into post-verbal position is incorrect. Consider the following sentences:

(54) a. Pourquoi Jean et moi ne devrions-nous pas partir tout de suite?
b. Pourquoi Jean et moi ne devrait-on pas partir tout de suite?

If the subject NP is 'Jean et moi', the 'copied' pronoun can be either 'nous' or 'on'.[30] It is difficult to see how a rule copying the grammatical features of an NP can account for such a dual possibility. Such a rule might be expected to yield 'nous', but not 'on', since in other respects conjoined NP's like 'Jean et moi' act like first-person NP's:

(55) Jean et moi devrions partir tout de suite.
*Jean et moi devraient partir tout de suite.

Even worse, 'on' is grammatically singular:

(56) On doit partir.
*On doivent partir.

where its putative source is plural. A copying rule could be maintained in the face of these examples, however, if one postulated a rule deriving 'on' from 'nous' here, and if that rule applied after the copying transformation. However, we argue elsewhere[31] that the 'nous'/'on' alternation is best described otherwise. If this conclusion is correct, sentences (54) constitute a serious problem for the copying rule.

Even assuming that a 'nous' → 'on' rule could be justified, however, sentence (54b) still poses a difficult problem. The verb agreement in that sentence is with respect to 'on', not to 'Jean et moi':

(57) *Pourquoi Jean et moi ne devrions-on pas partir tout de suite?

This means that the agreement rule will have to be unnecessarily complicated to work (in this case only) with respect to a following, rather than preceding, subject, since, under the copying hypothesis, there is no point in the derivation of (54b) at which 'on' precedes the verb.

Considering for a moment a more general question about verb agreement in French, we note that there is a sense in which sentences with complex inversion actually contain two subjects, one NP subject and one clitic subject, the two usually agreeing in number and person. Sentence (54b) shows that in the one case where they do not agree, the verb agreement[32] is made with respect to the clitic subject (which, in the analysis we shall propose below, originates to the left of the verb). This dual character of the notion 'subject' in French bears, moreover, on the question as to whether transformations should be allowed to refer to relational notions, such as 'subject', or whether they should be restricted to referring to syntactic categories, such as NP. In fact, if we are correct in postulating the two transformations, STYL - INV and SUBJ - CL - INV, then our analysis constitutes a strong argument in favor of the claim made by the theory of transformational grammar that the 'notion' subject should not be relevant to the formulation of transformations. On the one hand, these two transformations use syntactic categories to distinguish between two syntactically different kinds of subjects. On the other hand, if transformations could refer to 'subject', we should be able to formulate a rule such as: "in questions, invert subject and verb", in which case the existence of 'Partira-t-il?' would lead us, incorrectly, to expect '*Partira Jean?' to be grammatical. In analogous fashion, the contrast: 'Elle sait très bien à quelle heure partira son amie.' vs. '*Elle sait très bien à quelle heure partira-t-il. 'would be inexplicable.[33]

The distinction between NP subjects and clitic subjects allows us to account for a couple of striking contrasts within the complex inversion paradigm too. Assume that we have a rule inserting a pronominal copy of the subject in post-verbal position. In the general case this rule will apply to subject NP's; we thus predict that it will not apply to subject clitics, i.e., that it will not be possible to have a clitic subject before the verb and a pronominal copy of it after. The following paradigm illustrates this fact:

(58)   Cela est-il vrai?
        Ceci est-il faux?
        Ça tiendra-t-il?

(59)   *C'est-il faux?
        *Ce ne serait-il pas vrai?

As subjects, 'cela', 'ceci', and 'ça' can be 'copied' onto the verb as 'il' in the complex inversion construction, but 'ce' cannot.[34] 'Ce' differs from the others precisely in that only it is a clitic:[35]

(60)   Est-ce vrai? *Est cela vrai? *Tiendra ça?

        *Ce, à mon avis, doit être faux.
        Cela, à mon avis, doit être faux.

        *Tout ce sera bientôt prouvé.
        Tout ça sera bientôt prouvé.

*C'est vrai, ce.
C'est vrai, ça.

Similarly, 'quelqu 'un' and 'on' can be semantically rather alike
(not exactly), yet still differ with respect to complex inversion:

(61)   Quelqu'un nous attend.
       On nous attend.

(62)   Quelqu'un nous attend-il?
       *On nous attend-il?

The reason is that 'on', but not 'quelqu'un', is a clitic:

(63)   Nous attend-on?
       *Nous attend quelqu'un?

       *On, à mon avis, nous attend.
       Quelqu'un, à mon avis, nous attend.

       *On de très important nous attend.
       Quelqu'un de très important nous attend.

Again, if syntactic processes applied to 'subjects' rather than to syntactic categories, it would be difficult to understand the assymmetry of
(58-9) and (62).
    Let us now return to the question of the derivation of the 'complex
inversion' construction. We have been considering the possibility that
the pronoun in sentences like 'Cela est-il vrai?' is introduced by means
of a transformation that places a pronominal copy of the subject to the
right of the tensed verb; we have called this the copying hypothesis.
We argued subsequently that the 'on' of sentences like (54b) did not lend
itself to such a description, and created a problem for the rule of subject-
verb agreement. We shall now take up additional arguments against the
copying hypothesis.
    The 'on' of (61) is semantically akin to indefinite pronouns, e.g.,
'quelqu'un'. In the complex inversion construction, 'quelqu'un' is copied
as 'il'; 'on' is not a possible 'copy' of an indefinite pronoun:

(64)   Quelqu'un nous attend-il?
       *Quelqu'un nous attend-on?

This correlates with our description of the copying rule as reproducing
the barest grammatical features of the subject NP. The problem, then,
is how to account for the appearance of this 'on' in post-verbal position
in sentences like 'Nous attend-on?'. We recall that in order to capture,
under the copying hypothesis, the systematic similarity between the complex
inversion construction and the simple inversion of the subject clitic, we

need to derive sentences like: 'Part-il?' from '*Lui part-il' with subsequent deletion of 'lui'. Thus, to derive 'Nous attend-on', we must
find a Pro_x such that the copying transformation applied to 'Pro_x nous
attend' will yield 'Pro_x nous attend-on'; the Pro_x could then be deleted.
In light of (64) though, it is difficult to see what such a Pro_x could be;
unless we propose some ad-hoc complication to the copying transformation,
the result of its application to any third person singular, masculine
pronoun will be 'il'.
  This type of difficulty is even more striking with respect to 'ce':

(65) Est-ce vrai?
      Est-ce vraiment un homme intelligent, ton ami?
      Est-ce vraiment aussi malin que ça, les enfants?
      Est-ce à Paris que tu habites?

Again, the question is how to account for the post-verbal position of 'ce'.
We saw above (v. (53)) that the potential copying rule had to be designed
so as never to produce the pronoun 'ce' as the copy of the subject NP,
even in the case of NP's closely related to 'ce' such as 'cela', 'ceci',
'ce qu'il dit'. But this means that the 'ce' in (65) can not be the result
of the copying rule; i.e., there is no Pro_y such that the result of the
copying rule's applying to it will be 'ce'.
  The sentences in (65), as well as

(66) Nous attend-on?

could, on the other hand, be derived in a natural way by means of a simple
inversion rule (SUBJ - CL - INV) from the corresponding declaratives:

(67) C'est vrai.
      C'est vraiment un homme intelligent, ton ami.
      C'est très malin, les enfants.
      C'est à Paris que tu habites.

(68) On nous attend.

Thus even if one postulates a copying rule for sentences with complex
inversion, there remain the cases of post-verbal 'ce' and indefinite 'on'
which are best derived via a simple inversion rule. But this would mean
a return to the undesirable situation of having two distinct rules, the
copying rule and SUBJ - CL - INV, which place a pronoun in the same post-
verbal position and apply in exactly the same environments.[36] This dupli-
cation could be avoided if the derivation of the complex inversion construction itself involved an inversion rule. Thus, the grammatical sentence of (64)
would be derived from an intermediate stage: 'Quelqu'un il nous attend'. This approach
would also avoid the agreement problem (v. (57)), if the agreement rule preceded
the inversion rule. Before exploring the consequences of such an analysis,

we shall offer one additional argument against the copying hypothesis.
  The pronominal 'copy' of the subject NP in the complex inversion
construction occurs in the form of a clitic pronoun, and not as the strong
form of a pronoun:

  (69)   Pourquoi cet enfant pleure-t-il?
         *Pourquoi cet enfant pleure lui?

         De quoi vos amis ont-ils parlé hier soir?
         *De quoi vos amis ont eux parlé hier soir?

Under the copying hypothesis, this fact could no doubt be described by
specifying that the copied pronoun be attached to the finite verb. One
might, however, ask a more difficult question, namely: why is it that
the copied pronoun is attached to the finite verb? Given the decision to
use a copying transformation, it would be just as easy formally to have
the pronoun placed next to the verb, as in the starred sentences of (69),
as to have it attached to it. In other words, a language exhibiting a
reduplicated clitic pronoun would be as easily describable, in the context
of the copying hypothesis, as a language exhibiting a reduplicated non-
clitic pronoun. Unfortunately, this predicted equality does not seem to
correspond to the facts, at least in the case of the Romance languages.
Those Romance languages which do not have subject clitic pronouns do not
have a 'complex inversion' construction. More strikingly, French developed
the complex inversion construction only after the subject pronouns acquired
clitic status.[37] This suggests that there might be a significant generalization between the existence of subject clitics and that of the complex
inversion construction. Thus we might speculate that in any language
exhibiting a complex inversion construction, the 'reduplicated' or 'inverted'
pronoun will be a clitic (where we might take clitic here to mean 'dominated by the node V'). If this is in fact a valid generalization, then
it is one which is not explained under the copying hypothesis.
  Let us therefore reconsider this problem in the light of what we shall
call the inversion bypothesis. Under this hypothesis, the common properties of the complex inversion construction and that involving the
simple inversion of the clitic subject, e.g., 'Partira-t-il?', will be
described by attributing the position of the post-verbal clitic pronoun
in both constructions to the effect of the rule discussed in Section I,
i.e., SUBJ - CL - INV. Just as 'Partira-t-il?' is derived from 'Il
partira' via the rule of SUBJ - CL - INV, a sentence such as 'Cela est-il
vrai?' will be derived from the intermediate structure: '*Cela il est
vrai' via application of the very same rule. How then does this hypothesis
permit a more insightful account of the correlation between 'complex inversion' and clitics? Notice first that in surface structure at least,
there are really two distinct subject positions in French. In sentences
with NP subjects, the subject is dominated by the node S:

In sentences with clitic subjects, on the other hand, the subject will end up dominated by the node V:[38] $\underset{Pro}{\overset{V}{\diagup}}$. Although there do not seem to be any cases of two subject positions being filled in any one surface structure,[39] it would not be implausible to claim that two could be filled at some intermediate stage of the derivation. Such an intermediate stage could then serve as a source for the complex inversion construction, via the rule of SUBJ - CL - INV.

Interestingly, the inversion hypothesis could not be naturally extended to generate the ungrammatical sentences of (69). In order to generate a sentence like '*Pourquoi ces enfants pleurent eux?' via an inversion rule, it would be necessary to pass through an intermediate: '*Pourquoi ces enfants eux pleurent?', a structure which would contain two NP subjects. But there is no need in French to talk of two distinct subject NP positions, i.e., an intermediate structure with two NP subjects cannot be justified in the same way that a structure with one NP subject and one clitic subject can. What this means is that the correlation between complex inversion and clitics is better accounted for under the inversion hypothesis than under the copying hypothesis.[40]

In fact, if it is correct that no language can have a complex inversion construction[41] unless it also has subject clitics, then not only is the copying hypothesis wrong for French, but the theory of grammar must be constrained so as to disallow the formulation of a transformation placing a pronominal copy of the subject to the right of the verb. If such a rule could be formulated, the theory would be too powerful in that it would permit the description of impossible languages. One straightforward way of restricting the theory to this end would be to prohibit the formulation of any transformation creating a pronominal copy of any constituent. This approach would also sucessfully eliminate the possibility of deriving '*Pourquoi ces enfants pleurent eux?' by placing a copy of the subject in between it and the verb: '*Pourquoi ces enfants eux pleurent?' and then inverting the copied pronoun and the verb.[42] Formally speaking, 'creating a pronominal copy of the subject' would not be an elementary transformation, but would rather involve copying the subject NP and then pronominalizing the copy. This means that pronominal copy transformations would automatically be excluded if pronominalization transformations in general did not exist. In other words, the copying hypothesis for the complex inversion construction in French depends crucially on the existence of a transformational solution to the pronominalization controversy, as opposed to an interpretive solution.[43]

If the suggestion that pronominal copy transformations be excluded from the theory of grammar, perhaps by excluding pronominalization transformations in general, is correct,[44] then the question arises how to generate the complex inversion construction under the inversion hypothesis. Deriving 'Cela est-il faux' from 'Cela il est faux' may very well have the advantage of relating the presence of the two subjects in the former sentence to the existence of two kinds of preverbal subjects in French, but the origin of the postulated intermediate stage 'Cela il est faux' needs to be made

precise. In particular, to be consistent, we may not derive the latter
from 'Cela est faux' by means of a pronominal copy transformation.

SECTION III

We propose the following analysis: All NP's in French will be introduced in the base along with a subject clitic. Rather than having, for
example, a phrase structure rule: NP → Det - N - COMP, we would have instead: NP → NP' - SCL, NP' → Det - N - COMP,[45] where SCL = subject clitic.
With third person NP's, SCL would be spelled out as 'il', 'elle', 'ils',
'elles' depending only on the syntactic features of number and gender of
the NP. The actual agreement between NP and SCL could be accomplished
either by transformation or interpretive rule. Outside of the features
of number and gender, the internal characteristics of a NP would play no
role; 'il' could be the SCL corresponding to NP's as diverse as 'quelqu'un',
'cela', 'que + S', 'tout' and 'son meilleur ami', and a SCL will occur
with the nominal components of idioms, e.g., 'assistance' - 'elle' (v.
(46)-(52)).

The distribution of subject clitics in surface structure is limited:
they occur post-verbally as a result of the application of SUBJ - CL - INV:

(70) Cela est-il vrai?
      Pourquoi sont-ils partis?

and they occur pre-verbally in the absence of a subject NP:[46]

(71) Il est malin.
      Ils sont partis.

(72) *Cela il est vrai.
      *Tout il est en ordre.

We shall consequently propose a rule of subject clitic deletion (SUBJ -
CL - DEL) which will apply after SUBJ - CL - INV to those subject clitics
still preceded by their associated NP. The derivation of 'Cela est vrai'
will thus be: 'Cela + il est vrai' → SUBJ - CL - INV (inapplicable) →
SUBJ - CL - DEL → 'Cela + $\emptyset$ est vrai'. The derivation of 'Cela est-il
vrai?' will be: 'Cela + il est vrai" → SUBJ - CL - INV › 'Cela est + il
vrai' → SUBJ - CL - DEL (inapplicable).

The rule of SUBJ - CL - DEL will be stated: [NP' - SCL] → [NP' - $\emptyset$].
                                                      NP   NP
In order not to incorrectly delete the subject clitics in (71), SUBJ -
CL - DEL must apply after the deletion of the strong form of the pronoun,
i.e., we take the deep structures for (71) to be approximately: 'Lui + il
est malin', 'Eux + ils sont partis'[47], and postulate a rule deleting non-
clitic subject pronouns. Let us call this rule STR - FRM - DEL (strong
form deletion). The derivation of 'il est malin' will be then: 'Lui + il
est malin' → STR - FRM - DEL → '$\emptyset$ + il est malin → SUBJ - CL - DEL

(inapplicable). With third person pronouns, STR - FRM - DEL may fail to
apply in emphatic environments:[48] 'Lúi est parti', in which case SUBJ -
CL - DEL becomes applicable. We shall very tentatively state STR - FRM -
DEL as:[49] [Pro - SCL] - V → [∅ - SCL] - V.
      NP   NP

   Finally, we postulate a rule of subject clitic adjunction (SUBJ - Cl -
ADJ), which will adjoin to the verb any subject clitic that has neither
been attached post-verbally by SUBJ - CL - INV nor deleted by SUBJ - CL -
DEL. The rule of SUBJ - CL - ADJ can be stated as follows:[50] [X - SCL] -
                                                        NP
V →[X] - SCL + V. We leave open the question of exactly what type of
NP
adjunction is involved. The derivation of 'Il est malin' will now be:
'Lui + il est malin' → STR - FRM - DEL → '∅ + il est malin' → SUBJ - CL -
DEL (inapplicable) → SUBJ - CL - ADJ → '∅ ´il + est malin'. Neither the
derivation of 'Est-il malin?' nor that of 'Cela est vrai' will involve
application of SUBJ - CL - ADJ. For example, the derivation of the former
will be: 'Lui + il est malin?' → STR - FRM - DEL → '∅ + il est malin?' →
SUBJ - CL - INV → '∅ est + il malin?' → SUBJ - CL - DEL, SUBJ - CL - ADJ
(both inapplicable).
   Before turning to the precise formulation of SUBJ - CL - INV, we shall
reconsider the derivation of the subject clitics 'ce' and 'on' in the
light of the above analysis. We argued earlier against the copying hypothesis by noting that post-verbal 'ce' and 'on' did not lend themselves to
a description in terms of a pronominal copy rule. [The facts supporting
that argument (v. (53)-(57) and (64)-(68)) can equally well be taken to
indicate that 'ce' and 'on' should likewise be treated differently from the
other subject clitics under the inversion hypothesis.] The problem with
the copying hypothesis was, specifically, that one needed more than one
rule to get all the subject clitics to post-verbal position. Under the
inversion hypothesis, once 'ce' and 'on' are introduced into pre-verbal
subject clitic position in the manner to be described below, a single
rule (SUBJ - CL - INV) will move all subject clitics to post-verbal clitic
position under the appropriate conditions. We note, moreover, that the
problem of getting 'ce' and 'on' to pre-verbal position is shared by both
hypotheses, since 'ce' and 'on' exhibit clitic behavior in pre-verbal
position (v. (58)-(63)). The need for but one post-verbal positioning
rule is thus a decisive advantage for the inversion hypothesis.
   As a subject clitic, 'ce' has an extremely limited distribution; it
occurs primarily with the verb 'être':

   (73) C'était vrai.
           Ce n'est pas faux.
           Ce sera Jean qui gagnera.
           Il ne faut pas que ce soit mal fait.
           Ce sont des filles intelligentes.

With most verbs, it is not a possible subject:

(74)   *Ce correspond très bien à ce qu'il a dit.
       *Ce compte énormément.
       *Ce va embêter tout le monde.
       *Ce ne veut rien dire.
       *C'évoque les années 30.

What is possible here is 'ça':

(75)   Ça correspond très bien à ce qu'il a dit.
       Ça compte énormément.
       Ça va embêter tout le monde.
       Ça ne veut rien dire.
       Ça évoque les années 30.

There is moreover an odd gap in the distribution of 'ça'; 'ça' cannot occur directly before 'est' (or 'était'):

(76)   *Ça est faux.
       *Ça est Jean qui me l'a dit.
       *Ça est un type intelligent.
       *Ça était excellent.

Compare:

(77)   Ça ne lui était pas inconnu.
       Ça va être Jean qu'on choisira.
       Ça m'a l'air d'être un type intelligent.

The ungrammaticality of (76) is not entirely attributable to the vowel following 'ça':

(78)   Ça intéresse tout le monde.
       Ça amuse pas mal ton copain.
       Ça évitera de tout refaire.

The fact that a gap in the paradigm of 'ça' is found precisely with the verb which allows 'ce' suggests that 'ce' and 'ça' be considered realizations of the same underlying element. This decision is supported by the occurrence of 'ce' and 'ça' alone (even to the exclusion of 'cela') in two rather particular constructions. One is the cleft-sentence construction:[51]

(79)   Ce sera Jean qui gagnera.
       C'est toi qui l'as dit.

       Ça va être Jean qu'on choisira.
       Ça pourra être Jean qui gagnera.

*Cela sera Jean qui gagnera.
*Cela va être Jean qu'on choisira.

The other is a construction in which 'ce' (or 'ça') has a specific human
referent; this is possible in sentences with predicate nominals such as
the following:

(80)   C'est un garçon intelligent, ton ami.
       Ça m'a l'air d'être un garçon intelligent, ton ami.

       *Cela est un garçon intelligent, ton ami.
       *Cela m'a l'air d'être un garçon intelligent, ton ami.

Most strikingly, both 'ce' and 'ça' occur, in this construction, along
with the word 'tous' (morphologically a plural):

(81)   C'est tous des salauds.
       Ça m'a l'air d'être tous des salauds.[52]

Compare:

(82)   *Cela est tous des salauds.
       *Cela m'a l'air d'être tous des salauds.
       *Ce groupe partira tous demain.
       *Sa famille aime toutes Jean-Jacques.

If one postulates a rule replacing a third person pronoun by a demonstrative in the predicate nominal construction to account for the
appearance of 'tous', then the rule need mention only a single 'replacing
element' if 'ce' and 'ça' are ultimately the same.

We consequently propose the following analysis for 'ça'/'ce': the two
are realizations of an underlying element, call it 'C,' which is introduced as a NP. The phrase structure rules given above will introduce an
adjacent subject clitic node which could subsequently show up as 'il'.
Thus we would have, schematically: [[C,] - [il]]. We now postulate
                                    NP   NP'   SCL
a transformation, which shall be called CE - CL ('ce' - cliticization),
stated as follows:[53]

CE - CL: [C, - [X]] - 'être' → [∅ - [C,]] - être'
         NP   SCL   NP   SCL

In other words, 'C,' is inserted into subject clitic position when followed
by 'être'. The rule CE - CL will precede both SUBJ - CL - INV[54] and SUBJ -
CL - ADJ. [The rule SUBJ - CL - DEL, which, since it follows SUBJ - CL -
INV, must follow CE - CL, will never be applicable to 'ce'; when 'ce' is
in clitic position, the NP' position to its left is necessarily empty.]
When in subject clitic position, 'C,' will be spelled out as 'ce';[55]

when in NP position, it will be spelled out as 'ça', except if followed
by a complement (dominated by the node S) such as the following:

(83) Elle apprécie tout ce que tu fais.
      Ce à quoi elle pense, c'est ceci.

(Notice that in NP position the 'e' of 'ce' is not subject to elision:
'*Ç'a quoi...').

(84) Elle tient à ce que tu t'en ailles.
      Ce qu'il est bête!

In standard French at least, the 'ce' of (83)-(84) is not replaceable by
'ça'.[56]
     The preceding analysis accounts for the fact that 'ce' does not co-
occur with 'il' in the complex inversion construction,(v. (59)). In
addition, if the only source of subject clitic 'ce' is the rule CE - CL,
as we would claim, then we have successfully accounted for the fact that
'ce' never appears as the inverted element in the complex inversion
construction (v. (53)).
     The fact that, in our analysis, the rule CE - CL is the only source of
subject clitic 'ce', implies, moreover, that 'ce' may not be introduced
by the rule(s) which account for the appearance of the other subject
clitics. For example, if the node SCL is expanded in the base as a complex
of features, including only whatever features are necessary to describe
the different persons, plus the features $\pm$ masculine, $\pm$ singular (if these
features are fully specified, i.e., with either '+' or '-', then there must
be a filtering mechanism to insure that NP' and SCL match correctly, e.g.,
'*le garçon-elle'), then the set of subject clitics 'il(s)', 'elle(s)',
'je', 'tu', 'nous', 'vous' represent the spelling out of the various combinations of different values of these features. In the third person,
'+ masculine' will yield 'il(s)', '-masculine', 'elle(s)'. No combination
of these features will be realizable as 'ce'.
     Interestingly, this lack of parallelism between 'ce' and the other
subject clitics is mirrored elsewhere in the grammar of modern French.
'Il(s)', 'elle(s)', 'je', 'tu', 'nous', 'vous' are paralleled by the strong
 form 'personal pronouns', which are all subject to the rule of clitic
placement and to the rule involved in the derivation of possessive pronouns
(cf. fn. 49):

(85) Jean le(s)/la/me/te/nous/vous connaît.
     *Jean connaît lui/eux/elle(s)/moi/toi/nous/vous.

      son/leur/mon/ton/notre/votre livre.

'Ça'/'ce' do not fall into this class:

(86) *Jean ça/ce comprend. Jean comprend ça.

That is, 'ça' is not subject to clitic placement. Nor does it have a
possessive form; there is no form which is to 'la description de ça' as
'ton portrait' is to 'le portrait de toi' (clearly 'cette description'
is not a possessive corresponding to 'la description de 'ça').

The subject clitic 'on' might seem to be more like the personal pronouns than is 'ça'/'ce', semantically (and hence informally) speaking.
In one of its uses, 'on' is interchangeable with the subject clitic 'nous'.
There is no obvious difference in meaning between 'Nous sommes tous là'
and 'On est tous là'.[57] In another of its uses, 'on' is similar (not
identical) to the indefinite use of the subject clitic 'ils': 'Ils m'ont
dit de ne plus revenir', 'On m'a dit de ne plus revenir.' Furthermore,
unlike 'ce', and like the other subject clitics, 'on' is not severely
constrained with respect to the range of verbs with which it may occur.

In the analysis we have proposed, the subject clitics 'il(s)', 'elle(s)',
'je', 'tu', 'nous', 'vous' can be considered to play no semantic role.
In a sentence like 'Tu es bien', which will be derived from 'Toi-tu es
bien', the semantic content of the subject can be attributed to the NP-
like pronoun 'toi'. In at least two of its uses, however, 'on' does not
lend itself to this type of description, i.e., there does not seem to be
any NP-like pronoun to which one could attribute the semantic content of
the 'on' in the sentence: 'On ne nous aime plus'. Nor is there an
acceptable NP-like counterpart to the 'on' of: 'Quand on ne boit pas assez,
on tombe malade.'[58]

We propose, then, that 'on' be the only meaning-bearing element introduced in the base under the node SCL. The deep structure of the two
sentences in the preceding paragraph will contain a subject NP of the
form: $[\emptyset$ -[on]].[59] In sentences such as 'On est tous là', the subject
SCL
NP in deep structure will be: [[nous] - [on]] (thereby accounting for
NP' SCL
the appearance of 'tous'). 'On' will be specified as being compatible
with a first person plural NP', but no others.[60] One could think of these
conditions as subcategorization features. The deep structure of sentence
(54b) - 'Pourquoi Jean et moi ne devrait-on pas partir tout de suite' will
contain a subject NP of the form [[Jean et moi] - [on]].[61] The derivation
NP' SCL
of sentence (54b) will subsequently involve application of the transformation SUBJ - CL - INV.

Let us now turn to the formal statement of this transformation. We
recall that SUBJ - CL - INV is triggered by the environment 'question'
rather than by the presence of an initial WH-word. Let us assume that
there is a marker '+Q' associated with the initial question word: 'Où...?'
+Q
Since interrogative words also serve other purposes e.g., 'qui', 'quoi',
'lequel', 'où' are also possible relative pronouns, and since there is
no overt interrogative element in yes-no questions, the marker '+Q' will
be considered to have originated in sentence-initial position.[62]

An apparent problem for this analysis is posed by the fact that SUBJ - CL - INV does not apply in questions not exhibiting WH-movement:[63]

(87)   Tu habites où?
       Elle a dit quoi?

While the sentences in (87) can be interpreted as simple requests for information, the following can only be interpreted as echo questions:

(88)   Habite-t-il où?
       A-t-elle dit quoi?

The sentences of (88) imply a previously asked question of the form:

(89)   Habite-t-il à Paris?
       A-t-elle dit qu'elle va se suicider?

The sentences of (87) can have this kind of interpretation, i.e., as follow-ups to:

(90)   J'habite à Paris.
       Elle a dit qu'elle est malade.

but do not need to. The problem is that if (87) contains the marker '+Q', then SUBJ - CL - INV will apply and we would expect (88) to be possible as requests for information.
    However, it is not clear that one must assume the existence of the same marker in (87) as in questions with WH-movement:

(91)   Où habites-tu?
       Qu'a-t-elle dit?

To do so would amount to saying that WH-movement was optional in questions, although obligatory in relatives and exclamations:[64]

(92)   La fille avec qui il est sorti est là.
       Quelle belle voiture vous avez!

       *La fille (qu')il est sorti avec qui est là.
       *Vous avez quelle belle voiture!

A funny coincidence would then be left unexplained, namely, of the three WH-constructions, the only one that need be specified as undergoing optional movement is precisely the one which has a corresponding 'echo' construction (there do not seem to exist echo relatives or exclamatives).
    This suggests that (87) might be derived as echo questions, even in their use as requests for information. In other words, (87) would not be syntactically ambiguous, but would derive from a single deep structure

(not containing the marker '+Q'). The semantic component would then assign such sentences two distinct 'meanings'. If this is correct, we might expect to find syntactic differences between (87) and (91) which are not explainable simply in terms of difference in position of the WH-word. There are several such differences. First, there are no embedded questions corresponding to (87):

(93)   Elle sait très bien où tu habites (corresponds to (91)).

(94)   *Elle sait très bien tu habites où.
       *Elle sait très bien si tu habites où.

Second, there is a difference in certain impersonal constructions:

(95)   *Lesquelles a-t-il été mangé?

(96)   ?Il a été mange lesquelles?

Third, we have the contrasts;

(97)   Comment ça se fait que tu n'étais pas là?

(98)   *Ça se fait que tu n'étais pas là comment?
       *Ça se fait comment que tu n'étais pas là?

(99)   Comment est-il possible que tu partes déjà?

(100) *Il est possible comment que tu partes déjà?
       *Il est possible que tu partes déjà comment?

Fourth, based on the word 'diable':[65]

(101) Où diable est-il allé?
       Que diable a-t-il laissé dans le four?

(102) *Il est allé où diable?
       *Il a laissé quoi diable dans le four?

The crucial point is that the ungrammaticality of (94), (98), (100) and (102) and the grammaticality of (96) are independent of the meaning, i.e., independent of whether the interpretation is as a request for information or as an echo question. We conclude that questions in which WH-movement has not applied should be treated parallel to echo questions, and that there is no marker '+Q' in their deep structure.[66]

The formal statement of the transformation SUBJ - CL$_X$ - INV will therefore include a term representing the interrogative element: $\frac{X}{+Q}$ (X can be null in the case of yes-no questions in which case the marker is unattached.)

Since in the general case, the interrogative element is not the (subject) NP which contains the subject clitic to be inverted we must have a term: [Y SCL]. Let us then write:

$$\begin{array}{cccc} \text{NP} & & & \\ \text{X} & \text{[Y SCL]} & \text{V} \rightarrow \text{X} & \text{[Y]} & \text{V + SCL} \\ \text{+Q} & \text{NP} & & \text{+Q NP} \end{array}$$

Y is a variable[67] and V a verb, in particular the verbal element adjacent to the subject (i.e., the finite verb). Y can be null, e.g., as in the case of 'ce'. The string V + SCL will be dominated by the node V in derived structure (cf. fn. 38). The derivation of 'Cela est-il vrai' will now be: '+Q [Cela-il] est vrai' → SUBJ - CL - INV → '+Q Cela est + il vrai?' The derivation of 'Est-ce vrai?' will be: '+Q[C, - il] est vrai' → CE - CL → '+Q [∅ - C,] est vrai' → SUBJ - CL - INV → '+Q[∅] est + C, vrai' → morphophonemics → 'est-ce vrai?'

The formulation of SUBJ - CL - INV given above predicts, correctly, that if the questioned element is itself the subject NP, then the rule will be inapplicable; i.e., the structural description will not be met if the marker '+Q' is attached to the only NP preceding the verb. The SCL contained in the questioned subject will therefore not be attached to the verb and will subsequently be deleted by the rule of SUBJ - CL - DEL. Thus we will have:

(103)   Qui vous a offert ce livre?
          Lesquelles te plaisent le plus?
          Quelle femme t'a dit cela?

and not:[68]

(104)   *Qui vous a-t-il offert ce livre?
          *Lesquelles te plaisent-elles le plus?
          *Quelle femme t'a-t-elle dit cela?

In non-colloquial French, the rule of SUBJ - CL - INV is obligatory. The following sentences are only possible in colloquial French:

(105)   Où tu vas?
          Pourquoi il pleure?

The same holds true with complex inversion. Only in colloquial French may we have:

(106)   Quand ton ami va venir?
          Pourquoi ton fils a fait ça?

In non-colloquial French, we thus get:

(107)   Où vas-tu?
          Pourquoi pleure-t-il?

Quand ton ami va-t-il venir?
Pourquoi ton fils a-t-il fait ça?

Sentences such as (106), however, raise the further question of the interaction between SUBJ - CL - INV and the transformation discussed in Section I, STYL - INV, since one also gets:

(108) Quand va venir ton ami?

An important observation is that STYL - INV may not apply if SUBJ - CL - INV has previously applied. For example, if SUBJ - CL - INV applies as in (107) to yield 'Quand ton ami va-t-il venir?', STYL - INV may not then apply to produce:

(109) *Quand va-t-il venir ton ami?

A sentence like (109) is only possible as an instance of detachment. This is clearly shown by the following, where confusion with detachment is impossible (cf. *Il est faux, cela - v.(47)):[69]

(110) Depuis quand tout cela t'amuse-t-il?
       A quoi tout cela vous a-t-il fait penser?

(111) *Depuis quand t'amuse-t-il tout cela?
       *A quoi vous a-t-il fait penser tout cela?

In the same vein, STYL - INV may apply to an intermediate '*Que tout cela veut dire' to yield:

(112) Que veut dire tout cela?

but it may not apply to an intermediate '*Que tout cela veut-il dire' to yield:[70]

(113) *Que veut-il dire tout cela?

The above facts would follow naturally if STYL - INV were ordered before SUBJ - CL - INV; this ordering would immediately exclude (109), (111), and (113). In the derivation of (108), STYL - INV would apply first, after which SUBJ - CL - INV would be inapplicable. The ordering of STYL - INV before SUBJ - CL - INV (which one might attempt to relate to the latter's applying only in non-embedded sentences) has, moreover, an additional desirable consequence. Consider the following:

(114) A quelle heure le concert va commencer?

(115) Elle sait tres bien à quelle heure le concert va commencer.
       L'heure à laquelle le concert va commencer ....

In both (114) and (115), STYL - INV could have applied:

(116) A quelle heure va commencer le concert?

(117) Elle sait très bien à quelle heure va commencer le concert.
       l'heure à laquelle va commencer le concert ...

but didn't. The problem is that (114) is grammatical only in colloquial
French, whereas (115) is possible in both colloquial and non-colloquial.
This might seem to indicate that in non-colloquial French, STYL - INV
need be specified as optional in embedded sentences but obligatory in
non-embedded sentences.
     The ordering of STYL - INV before SUBJ - CL - INV, however, permits
us to regard STYL - INV as uniformly optional, i.e., both in embedded
and non-embedded structures, even in non-colloquial French. Recall that
in non-colloquial French, SUBJ - CL - INV is obligatory (cf. (105)).
Consider now the derivation of (114), with STYL - INV everywhere optional.
First, STYL - INV may or may not apply. If it does apply, we get (116).
If it does not apply, we move on to SUBJ - CL - INV. In colloquial
French, SUBJ - CL - INV need not apply and we derive (114). In non-
colloquial style, SUBJ - CL - INV is obligatory and therefore must apply,
yielding:

(118) A quelle heure le concert va-t-il commencer?

Sentence (114) is not generable in non-colloquial French because SUBJ -
CL - INV is obligatory there; STYL - INV may therefore be considered
uniformly optional.
     The ordering of STYL - INV before SUBJ - CL - INV, combined with the
ordering, suggested earlier, of SUBJ - CL - INV before SUBJ - CL - ADJ,
implies that STYL - INV will invariably apply at a point at which the
subject clitics have not yet been moved out from their original NP.[71]
The latter part of the derivation of (116) is, then: 'A quelle heure
[le concert-il] va commencer' → STYL - INV → A quelle heure va commencer
[le concert-il] → SUBJ - CL - INV (inapplicable) → SUBJ - CL - DEL → A
quelle heure va commencer [le concert - ∅]'.
     The grammar of French will thus contain two distinct "subject-inversion"
transformations, STYL - INV and SUBJ - CL - INV, applying in that order.
In addition we have postulated a number of other transformations related
to the syntax of subject clitics: STR - FRM - DEL, SUBJ - CL - DEL, SUBJ -
CL - ADJ and CE - CL (See Appendix), and proposed that subject clitics
originate as a kind of NP affix. We shall at present turn to a brief
discussion of some issues related to this proposal.
     One of the considerations that motivated our analysis of subject
clitics was the impossibility of a complex inversion construction of the
form '*Pourquoi cet enfant pleure lui?' (v. (69)). The analysis given
here could not readily be extended to describe such a construction without allowing NP-like pronouns to be generated as affixes on NP's. Insofar

as the generation of clitics as affixes is far more natural than the
generation of NP's as affixes, we can claim to have explained, e.g.,
why French, a language with subject clitics, is the only Romance language
to have a complex inversion construction.

The interaction of subject clitics and the problem of coreference may
turn out to provide additional support for the present analysis. Given
that the deep structure of 'il est là' will contain a NP of the form
[[lui] - [il]], there is no longer any reason to have such subject clitics
   NP'   SCL
involved in coreference relationships. For example, the possible coreference between 'Jean' and 'il' in 'Jean croit qu'il est malade' could
be described in terms of coreference between 'Jean' and the ultimately
deleted 'lui': 'Jean$_i$ croit que lui$_i$ -il est malade'. [The term 'coreference' would then be inappropriate for the relationship between 'lui'
and 'il' here, or between 'cela' and 'il' in 'Cela est-il faux?'].

This may in fact provide an explanation for the facts of (47), (48)
and (50), i.e., the impossibility of establishing a true coreference
relationship between 'il' and 'cela', 'ce qu'il a dit', 'que + S', 'tout',
'rien'. This would follow, under the hypothesis that coreference is
determined by 'lui' rather than 'il', from the impossibility of coreference
between 'lui' and the NP's in question:

(119) *Cela$_i$ m'intéresse parce que tu as parlé de lui$_i$.

    *Ce$_i$ qu'elle a dit, je pense souvent à lui$_i$.

    *Que$_i$ tu sois malin n'intéresse personne; on ne pense plus à lui$_i$.

    *Tout$_i$ est tombé parce qu'elle s'est appuyée sur lui$_i$.

    *Rien$_i$ n'est tombé parce qu'elle (ne) s'est (pas) appuyée sur lui$_i$.

The ungrammaticality of (119) might in turn be explained by the absence
of a head noun in any of the relevant NP's,[72] if the rule determining
the possibility of coreference with 'lui' depends on the presence of a
head noun.

One apparent difficulty with the above proposal is that 'cela', 'ce
que tu dis', and 'que S' can sometimes be referred to by 'le' (although
never by the dative clitic 'lui'). It would consequently be necessary
to analyze such instances of 'le' as a kind of special neuter pronoun not
derived from 'lui'. This in turn might be linked to the existence of a
pro-predicate 'le', as in 'Malin, tu ne l'es pas'.

There is also a problem with 'lui' referring to inanimates:

(120) ?Je n'aime pas ce livre$_i$ parce que tu m'as trop parlé de lui$_i$.

For many speakers, sentences like (120) are not possible, despite the presence of the head noun 'livre'. If we are correct in our account of the ungrammaticality of (119), then the ungrammaticality of (120) must be due to some additional mechanism, perhaps one that imposes an animate interpretation on overt occurrences of the strong form pronouns. The difference in explanation between (119) and (120) would then correlate with the fact that judgments about (120), but not (119), vary greatly from speaker to speaker (some accept (120)) and even seem to depend on the choice of verb. Such an analysis would also be consistent with the fact that 'il' can refer readily to inanimates: 'Ce livre$_i$ te plaît parce qu'il$_i$ n'est pas long' (as can dative 'lui', with certain verbs).[73]

Finally, the special status of subject clitics, combined with the assumption that coreference involving 'lui' depends on the presence of a head noun, would suffice to explain the fact that 'on' (a subject clitic) cannot enter into a coreference relationship with 'lui', 'il', 'le':

(121) *On$_i$ m'a dit de lui$_i$ envoyer ce colis.
*On$_i$ m'a demandé de l$_i$ 'aider.
*On$_i$ m'a dit qu'il$_i$ était triste.
*On$_i$ m'a longuement parlé de lui$_i$(-même).

The above are instances of 'on' meaning approximately some unspecified person. The same paradigm holds for generic 'on':[74]

(122) *Quand on$_i$ croit qu'il$_i$ est malade, ...
*Quand on$_i$ parle trop souvent de lui$_i$(-même) ...
etc.

and for the 'on' associated with 'nous'.

APPENDIX

For convenience, we repeat the formulation of the various transformations given in the text:

STR - FRM - DEL (deletion of the strong form subject pronoun):[75]

$$[Pro - SCL] - V \rightarrow [\emptyset - SCL] - V$$
$$NP \qquad\qquad NP$$

STYL - INV (stylistic inversion):

$$[\ A\ (que)\ NP\ X] \rightarrow [A\ (que)\ X\ NP]$$
$$S\ +WH \qquad\qquad S\ S \qquad\qquad S$$

SUBJ - CL - INV (subject clitic inversion):[76]

$$X \quad [Y \; SCL]V \rightarrow X \quad [Y] \; V + SCL$$
$$+Q \; NP \qquad\qquad +Q \; NP$$

SUBJ - CL - DEL (subject clitic deletion):[77]

$$[NP' - SCL] \rightarrow [NP' - \emptyset]$$
$$NP \qquad\qquad NP$$

SUBJ - CL - ADJ (subject clitic adjunction):

$$[Y \; SCL] - V \rightarrow [Y] - SCL + V$$
$$NP \qquad\qquad NP$$

CE - CL ('ce' - cliticization):

$$[C, - \quad [X]] - \text{'être'} \rightarrow [\emptyset - [C,]] - \text{être}$$
$$NP \quad SCL \qquad\qquad NP \quad SCL$$

Except for CE - CL, the rules will apply in the order given (see text for relevant discussion), i.e.:

STR - FRM - DEL
STYL - INV

CE - CL

SUBJ - CL - INV
SUBJ - CL - DEL
SUBJ - CL - ADJ

CE - CL must apply before SUBJ - CL - INV, but its ordering with respect to the first two of the above is unclear.

NOTES

1. An example of this type, using the expression 'monter à cheval' is given by Renchon (1967:74).
2. There are other factors involved. The sentence:

(a)   ?De quel oeil voit double celle-ci?

is better if 'celle-ci' refers to someone being pointed out ('this one here') than if it refers to someone previously mentioned in the conversation ('the latter'). Comparable distinctions may play a role in sentences like 'Il est arrivé ceci'.

3. Counterparts (with respect to the linear sequence of constituents) to many of the examples of (4) can be found which are grammatical:

(b)   On n'arrive pas à faire changer cette fille d'avis.
      Cela va faire devenir ce comédien célèbre.
      Il connaît sa femme mieux que toi.
      Tu devrais prévenir ce charlatan que tout risque d'aller de moins en moins bien pour lui.

so that there is no hope of accounting for (4) in terms of "unlikely sequences" of constituents. (In fact it is rather the sequence "subject pronoun plus complement" which is "unlikely", since it occurs only as a result of SUBJ - CL - INV!)
    In particular the first two of the above sentences show that there is another rule in French (v. Kayne (forthcoming-d) which can 'break up' expressions like 'changer d'avis', and the sequence 'devenir' plus adjective, even though STYL - INV cannot (since STYL - INV is not a subject-verb inversion rule). Furthermore, no insight would be gained into the ungrammaticality of sentences such as:

(c)   *Où voulait ton ami aller?
      *Que va Jean faire?

by invoking the fact that "vouloir" and "aller" can otherwise not be separated from the following infinitive by a NP (which would still not explain why they cannot be in this construction - cf. English "Does your friend want to leave?", although "do" and a following verb are normally not separable via an intervening NP), especially in light of the following examples:

(d)   Que laissera tomber Jean?
      *Que laissera Jean tomber?

(e)   Quand laissera-t-il partir sa fille?
      *Quand laissera Jean partir sa fille?

Even though the verb 'laisser' can occur separated from a following infinitive by a NP in sentences such as:

(f)   Marie a laissé Jean tomber.
      On a accepté de laisser Jean partir.

STYL - INV may still not place the subject of 'laisser' in between 'laisser' and the infinitive in (d) and (e). As expected, SUBJ - CL - INV acts differently, as shown by the first sentence in (e), as well as by:

(g)   Que laissera-t-il tomber?

4. The opinions of various grammarians seem to bear out this observation; v. Cledat (1928), Renchon (1967). For many examples bearing on
the question of exactly which complements exhibit what behavior, see
Engwer (1933, 1935) and especially Strohmeyer (1935).
5. The question of VP constituency in English is considered in Chomsky
(1965), Lakoff and Ross (1966), and Michelson (1969).
6. If STYL - INV is maintained as a rule moving subject NP's to sentence-final position, then the derivation of (11) must involve some subsequent reordering rule to place the complement in final position. The
nature of such a rule is unclear; in particular, pairs such as:

(h)   Quand écrira à Jean la fille dont nous avons parlé l'autre jour?
      *Quand écrira la fille au garçon dont vous avez parlé l'autre jour?

(for those speakers who reject (9) with 'quand') show (as does (8)) that
the rule of "length-inversion" (v. Gross (1968)):

(i)   ?On donnera à ce garçon ce livre.
      On donnera à ce garçon le livre qu'on a trouvé chez toi.

may not apply to the result of STYL - INV. This could be accounted for
by ordering STYL - INV after "length-inversion", or perhaps, noting that
the two rules have certain formal similarities, e.g., difference in acceptability due to factors of length, by claiming that such rules are to be
interpreted as a disjunctive block. The type of reordering shown in
(i) need not throw things to sentence-final position:

(j)   ?Il a fait porter à sa femme des livres.
      Il a fait porter à sa femme des livres par son domestique.

Direct objects act like the complements in (4):

(k)   *Où mettra cette fille ses livres?
      Où mettra-t-elle ses livres?

      *Où mettra ses livres cette fille?

but a long subject increases acceptability but little:

(1)   *?Où mettra ses livres la fille qui est entrée en retard?

If the object is the nominal part of an idiom, the sentence is improved
(cf. below with respect to relative clauses):

(m)   A quelle heure aura lieu la manifestation qui a été interdite
      par le gouvernement?

Whether or not the result is perfect may depend on the idiom (v. Renchon (1967:69)).

7. Those speakers who accept certain of the sentences in (4) will accept the corresponding embedded questions (and relatives - v. below). In embedded questions, STYL - INV is optional:

(n)   Tu sais très bien à quelle heure arrivera ton amie.
        Tu sais très bien à quelle heure ton amie arrivera.
        Il voudrait savoir depuis quand cette fille est malade.

We shall take up in Section III the question of whether STYL - INV is to be considered optional or obligatory in non-embedded questions.

8. For some discussion of the embedded counterpart of yes-no questions, see Katz and Postal (1964).

For some speakers, the inversion in embedded questions is more acceptable than in direct questions in the presence of a pronominal object:

(o)   ?Dites-nous quand les lira votre fils.
        ??Quand les lira votre fils?

If the object is attached to an embedded infinitive, we have:

(p)   Dites-nous quand voudrait les lire votre fils.
        ?Quand voudrait les lire votre fils?

The facts concerning such sentences are on the whole extremely unclear. There are no such "restrictions" on SUBJ - CL - INV:

(q)   Quand les lira-t-il?

9. SUBJ - CL - INV seems to be able to apply in embedded sentences in the case of "est-ce que":

(r)   Je ne savais pas pourquoi est-ce qu'il était parti.
        Vous saurez bientôt quand est-ce qu'il va rentrer.
        Tu te rappelles parfaitement bien où est-ce que tu as mis les billes.

This is not a general fact about the combination "ce est":

(s)   *Tu sauras bientôt pourquoi est-ce important.
        *Il ne comprend pas pourquoi est-ce à Paris qu'il doit aller.

More striking, it is not true of embedded yes-no questions:

(t)   *Tu sauras bientôt (si) est-ce qu'il va rentrer.
        *Je ne savais pas (si) est-ce que je devais partir ou non.
        *Il ne sait pas (si) est-ce qu'il peut se permettre cela.

The special behavior of 'est-ce que' here is certainly related to its semi-frozen character (v. Langacker (this volume)). In embedded questions, another reflection of this semi-frozenness lies in the fact that only with 'est-ce que' is interrogative 'que' (rather than 'ce que') permitted:

(u)   Tu sais très bien ce qu'il a fait.
       *Tu sais très bien qu'il a fait.

       Tu sais très bien qu'est-ce qu'il a fait.

10. This is true even of NP's which can otherwise occur between the finite verb and the infinitive or past participle (cf. fn. 3):

(v)   Il voulait presque tout remettre en cause.
       Il a presque tout fait par lui-même.

(w)   ?Au moment où allait tomber presque tout
       *Au moment où allait presque tout tomber

       ?Le fils a qui a été laissé presque tout
       *Le fils a qui a été presque tout laissé

These examples further indicate that STYL - INV is ordered after the rule moving "tout" / "tous" to the left (v. Kayne (forthcoming-d)).
11. Sentences such as (21) are more readily accepted than the corresponding interrogatives. Correspondingly, it is somewhat easier to find examples of STYL - INV applying even in the presence of an object, in particular in the case of idioms:

(x)   le jour où a pris fin la guerre de trente ans

See Le Bidois (1952:265) and Lerch (1934:388) for additional examples. Especially interesting in the light of the analysis proposed in the text is the fact that of the literary examples found by Le Bidois in which STYL - INV has applied despite the presence of a true direct object, all exhibit the order object-subject, e.g.(p. 266):

"Les plaisirs...auxquels dans sa mémoire avaient donné leur forme ces canapés sur lesquels..."

rather than the order subject-object.
12. The linguistic significance of the generalization concerning clauses introduced by a WH-element is supported by the parallelism in the historical development of subject NP inversion in relatives and embedded interrogatives; see Orlopp (1888:27-8), Koopman (1910:103ff), Foulet (1921:246-7) and Philippsthal (1886:23).
13. STYL - INV is also applicable in cleft sentences. The logic of the argument in the text leads to the conclusion that at that point in the

derivation of sentences such as:

   (y)   C'est à Paris qu'habite ce garçon.

at which STYL - INV applies there be a relative element to the left of
"que". That clefts and relatives have something in common is suggested
by the existence of sentences like:

   (z)   C'est ce garçon-là dont a parlé ton frère.

(cf. *C'est à Jean à qui il a parlé, which was possible in earlier
stages of French). For a detailed comparison of differing analyses of
cleft sentences, see Moreau (1970).
   Not surprisingly, SUBJ - CL - INV is inapplicable in clefts:

   (a')   *C'est à Paris qu'habite-t-il
          *C'est alors qu'a-t-elle éclaté.

For many speakers, STYL - INV is not applicable in sentences of the
following type (although such sentences are often found in journalistic
prose):

   (b')   ?Quand a crié l'enfant, tout le monde s'est affolé.
          ?Tu changeras d'avis quand rentrera ta femme.
          ?Alors que chantait Marie, une bombe a éclaté.

Compare:

   (c')   Je ne sais pas quand a crié l'enfant.
          C'est alors qu'a éclaté la bombe.

The clear difference in status between (b') and (c') suggests that the
derivation of such time-adverbial subordinate clauses does not involve
the rule of WH-preposing, i.e., that they are not to be assimilated to
relative clauses.
   Such adverbial clauses also differ from constructions involving
WH-preposing in that the former, but not the latter, are subject to a
rule replacing the 'adverbial word' by 'que' in conjoined structures
(v. Kayne (forthcoming-b)):

   (d')   Quand il viendra et qu'il verra ce qui s'est passé, il se fâchera.

   (e')   *Elle sait quand il viendra et qu'il verra ce qui s'est passé.

One might wonder whether, for those speakers who accept (b'), the
inversion there should be handled by some extension of STYL - INV. A
similar question arises with the following constructions:

(f')   Demain reviendront les deux mêmes personnes.
        Ici passera la nouvelle autoroute.
        A Jean correspond Paul.

The inversion triggered by certain preposed adverbials and prepositional
complements, as in (f'), resembles that of STYL - INV in the placement
of the subject:

(g')   Demain vont venir les deux mêmes personnes.
        *Demain vont les deux mêmes personnes venir.

and in its not taking place with subject pronouns:

(h')   *Demain reviendront-elles.
        *Ici passera-t-elle.
        *A Jean correspond-il.

cf.   *Quand a-t-il crié, tout le monde s'est affolé.

Since there is no preposed WH-element in these cases, the formulation
of STYL - INV given in the text could not account for the inversion.
Since it is not clear how to characterize the class of complements that
can trigger inversion as in (f'), and since even there complete homo-
geneity is lacking:

(i')   Demain les deux mêmes personnes reviendront.
        *A Jean Paul correspond.

we shall leave open the question of whether it is (some extension of)
STYL - INV itself that is to account for these cases.
    For discussion of the marginal:

(j')   Viendront ensuite celles dont je vous ai parlé hier.

and related constructions, see Spitzer (1941).
    14. This judgment accords with that of Nø jgaard (1967), Lerch (1934:
409), Le Bidois (1952), Papić (1970), and Clédat (1928:88).
    15. For discussion of this Q-marker, see Katz and Postal (1964) and
Baker (1970). 'Q' might be reformulable as a feature attached to a
COMPlementizer node - v. Chomsky (1971) and Bresnan (1970).
    16. One might argue that the derivation of direct questions involves a
deletion of "si", in which case the explanation for (28) would rather be
like that for (31), but only if it is assumed that the deletion of "si"
follows STYL - INV.
    Equally plausible would be the assertion that 'si' is inserted in non-
embedded questions lacking a WH-element, in which case the starred sentence in (31) would be excluded parallel to (28), if the insertion of

'si' followed STYL - INV. If it preceded STYL - INV, there would still be no problem, since an inserted 'si' is clearly not an element subject to WH-preposing.

We recall that "si" acts differently from the true WH-words with respect to the appearance of "est-ce que" in embedded questions, (v. fn. 9) although it is unclear how to relate that fact to the present discussion.

17. 'Si' corresponds much more closely to English 'if' than to 'whether'; the latter may be a WH-word synchronically, and apparently was definitely one in earlier stages of English (v. Klima (1965)):

(k')   He doesn't know whether (*if) to leave.
       *Il ne sait pas si partir.

(l')   He doesn't know whether (*if) or not he should leave.
       *Il ne sait pas si ou non il doit partir.

What is possible for (l') is: 'Il ne sait pas s'il doit partir ou non' and 'Il ne sait pas si, oui ou non, il doit partir.' The sentences in (k') are particularly revealing in that WH-words usually are possible with infinitives (for some discussion of 'pourquoi' - 'why' in this regard, see below): 'Il ne sait pas quand partir, à quelle heure partir, où aller, laquelle choisir.'

In fact, there is no one word in French that corresponds to 'whether':

(m')   He'll stay, whether or not you leave.
       Il restera, que tu partes ou non.

This would seem to be significantly related to the absence of a true equivalent of 'either' (as well as 'neither' and 'both'):

(n')   Either John or Mary   Ou Jean ou Marie
       Neither John nor Mary   Ni Jean ni Marie
       Both John and Mary   Et Jean et Marie

(o')   Either one   L'un ou l'autre
       Neither one   Ni l'un ni l'autre
       Both (of them)   (Tous) les deux

18. Perhaps the 'si' of embedded questions should be related to that in:

(p')   Si Marie vient, dis-lui d'attendre.

which, notably, does not allow STYL - INV:

(q')   *Si vient Marie, dis-lui d'attendre.

The absence of infinitivization in (k') might then be related to:

(r')   Tu arriveras en retard si tu pars à cinq heures.
       *Tu arriveras en retard si partir à cinq heures.

The two 'si' differ, however, parallel to (d') and (e') with respect to
'replacement' by 'que':

(s')   S'il vient en retard et qu'il se conduise mal, engueule-le.
       *Elle se demande s'il viendra en retard et qu'il se conduise mal.

19. STYL - INV is formally unlike subject-auxiliary inversion in
English in that it is not a simple inversion of subject and verbal element, as shown by (4) and (5), and in that it is not triggered by the
environment 'question', as shown by (2) and (3), as well as by its being
optimally statable in terms of a preposed WH-element. In this regard,
the grammatical sentences of (27) contrast with: What a fool he's been!
*What a fool has he been! How very right you are! *How very right are
you!
     Both subject-auxiliary inversion in English and SUBJ - CL - INV in
French occur with certain preposed elements, such as:

(t')   Not once did he apologize
       Peut-être viendra-t-il.

The classes of such elements are different in the two languages. In
neither are they the same as those discussed in fn. 13 (f').
     20. It is clear that in Emonds' framework SUBJ - CL - INV cannot be
"structure preserving", but it is also necessary that it not fit the
description of a "minor movement rule". This will be true by virtue of
the formal properties of such rules if SUBJ - CL - INV is construed as
attaching the clitic to the verb (v. Section III).
     Relevant to this problem is the observation that in Middle French, the
second half of a conjoined structure could act like an embedded sentence
with respect to SUBJ - CL - INV: "est-ce vrai ou (si) c'est faux?" as
well as with respect to the formally similar rule of clitic inversion in
imperatives: "fais-le cuire et le mange ensuite" (v. Haase (1969)) and
Orlopp (1888:21).
     21. Similarly, in environments other than questions in which SUBJ -
CL - INV is applicable, e.g.:

(u')   Peut-être est-il parti.
       Sans doute reviendra-t-elle.

we have:

(v')   *Peut-être est Jean parti
       *Peut-être est parti Jean
       *Sans doute reviendra cette fille.

22. By subject clitic pronouns, we mean those pronouns subject to
SUBJ - CL - INV. These exhibit clitic-like behavior (see text) and in
this way share significant properties with the object clitic pronouns:
'Jean *la* connait'. Under certain circumstances, the non-clitic strong
forms may be used as subjects: 'Toi seul aimes Marie'. (There is some
morphological overlap between clitics and strong forms, e.g. 'nous',
'vous': 'Connaissez-vous Jean', 'Vous seul connaissez Jean', cf.
'Jean vous connaît', 'Jean ne connaît que vous.') As NP's, the strong
forms, when used as subjects, might be expected to undergo STYL - INV,
but we have:

(w') *Quand partira lui?
      *Ce que dirai moi, c'est ceci.
      *C'est Jean que préfères toi.

In other cases, NP's with a coreferential function are subject to STYL -
INV:

(x') Un homme est entré. Que dira cet homme?
      Voilà ce que dira cet homme.

The ungrammaticality of (w') is to be related to the impossibility of:

(y') *Moi dirai ceci.
      *Toi préfères Jean.

and to the fact that "Lui partira" is only possible with very special
intonation. Evidence that this is the correct approach is constituted
by the following paradigm:

(z') *Quand partirai moi-même?
      *Que direz vous autres?
      *Ce que ferons nous deux, c'est ceci.

(a") *Moi-même partirai.
      *Vous autres direz cela
      *Nous deux ferons ceci.

although for some speakers (a'') is slightly better than (z') (cf. what was
said above about 'lui').
   As expected, application of SUBJ - CL - INV to the strong forms is
totally impossible: **Quand est lui parti? **Partira lui? (cf. **Ce
que dira-t-il, c'est ceci.), and distinctly worse than: *Ce que dira
lui, c'est ceci.
   23. For more detailed discussion and additional arguments in favor of
the non-NP status of subject clitic pronouns, see Kayne (forthcoming-c),
and especially Kayne (forthcoming - d).

24. As a subject pronoun, 'ce' is a clitic and so cannot be modified.
In non-verbal environments (where it could not be a clitic), 'ce' has a
very limited distribution, but when possible, it can as expected be modified: 'Il a écouté tout ce qu'elle a dit.' (NB 'ce' here is in an NP
position: il a écouté l'histoire qu'elle a racontée.)
     Possessive pronouns, whether in article position or not, cannot be
modified or conjoined:

> (b") *Le nôtre autre est meilleur que celui de Jean.
>   *Leur deux livre est mauvais.
>   *Mon et ton professeur est très bon.

Significantly,   possessive pronouns occupy a position in which NP's are
impossible:

> (c") *Le cette fille est meilleur que celui de Jean.
>   *Jean livre est mauvais.
>   *Mes amis professeur est très bon.

For some additional discussion of possessives, see Kayne (forthcoming -
d).
     25. We have as yet no explanation for the fact that STYL - INV is
dubious if the WH-word is 'pourquoi' (v. (3) and (16)). Rather than
codify our inability to find a solution to this problem by imposing an
ad-hoc constraint on the rule, we prefer to leave the question open
(after mentioning a number of considerations which may be relevant).
     First, one must ask why it is STYL - INV, rather than SUBJ - CL - INV,
which exhibits this (superficial) anomaly. Second, one must ask why it
is 'pourquoi' (rather than 'où', or 'de quoi', or 'depuis quand') which
is singled out. A number of grammarians (v. Renchon (1967), Lerch (1934),
Koopman (1910))have suggested that one factor may be that 'pourquoi' is not
closely linked to the verb. Clédat (1928) states that 'en vue de quoi'
acts like 'pourquoi'. Several informants find that inversion of the NP
with 'pour quelle raison' is distinctly better than with 'pourquoi'.
Complements of place and time permit inversion. Adnominal complements
are rather unclear: *?la table dont a cassé le pied; le livre dont ont
été critiqués les 2 premiers chapitres.
     'Pourquoi' differs from other interrogative words with respect to in-
finitives: Dis-moi où aller, qui voir, avec qui parler, ??pourquoi
partir (cf. Pourquoi partir?). Compare the English: tell me where to
go, who to see, ?? why to leave; *Where go? *Who see? Why leave? and
negation: 'Pourquoi pas?' *Quand pas? Perhaps most pertinently,
'pourquoi' can sometimes be replaced by 'que', unlike other interrogatives :
'Je me demande pourquoi il peut rester et que moi, je dois partir' (cf.
fn. 13 - (e')).
     26. 'Complex inversion' is not possible with 'que', although SUBJ -
CL - INV alone is (so is STYL - INV):

(d'') *Que cet enfant a-t-il fait?

      Qu'a-t-il fait?
      Qu'a fait cet enfant?

We would attribute this fact not to a restriction on the rules producing the complex inversion construction, but to the very special status of 'que', and would relate it to the following:

(e'') *Que, à votre avis, a-t-il fait?

      Où, à votre avis, est-il allé?
      Quand, à votre avis, est-il parti?

Notice that in both cases, addition of 'diable' results in an improvement:

(f'') Que diable cet enfant a-t-il fait?
      Que diable, à votre avis, a-t-il fait?

For more detailed discussion of this question, see Kayne (forthcoming-b), where we, in addition, propose an explanation for the impossibility of 'que' as subject:

(g'') *Que tombera?
      *Qu'a été fait par cet enfant?

This explanation is not exactly the same as that for (d''), cf. *Que diable tombera? but is rather related to the behavior of 'que' in relatives:

(h'') Ce que cet enfant a fait, *ce que tombera

   At present, we have no explanation for the following facts concerning 'quel', which, at least superficially, resemble those of (d''):

(i'') Quel est-il? Quel est cet argument?

      *Quel cet argument est-il?
      *Quel, à votre avis, est-il?

Compare also:

(j'') Je me demande quelle peut en être la raison
      *Je me demande quelle la raison peut en être.

These paradigms may be related to the existence of the alternation 'quel'/ 'lequel'.

27. STYL - INV is impossible in this construction:

(k'') *Reviendrait cette fille que je ne serais toujours pas content.

There is one case in which inversion of the subject pronoun occurs, while 'complex inversion' does not:

(1'')   Cela, a-t-il dit, est faux.
        *Cela, Jean a-t-il dit, est faux.

One possibility would be to claim that 'complex inversion' is impossible in these 'incises' because there is some kind of constraint requiring that the verb not be preceded by a NP:

(m'')   Cela, a dit Jean, est faux.
        *Cela, Jean a dit, est faux.

If (m'') were an instance of STYL - INV, which is doubtful (v. Strohmeyer 1935)), then it would be one case in which that rule is obligatory. We note that the 'incise' construction has been exceptional in many ways throughout the history of the language (v. Franzén (1939) and Buscher-bruck (1941)). Specifically relevant here is the fact that in Old French, there was a rule postposing object clitics from sentence-initial position. Normally a complement moved to sentence-initial position blocked the postposition of the clitics. Significantly, the rule was not blocked in the 'incise' construction. Thus even if the inversion of footnote 13 were ultimately to be incorporated into the realm of STYL - INV, (m'') might still remain apart. Moreover, while the environments for the inversion of the subject clitic in (44) and (45) may turn out to have something in common with questions (e.g. (45) is paraphrasable with 'même si', recalling the 'si' of embedded questions), it is much less obvious what common property could be found between questions and (1"). More likely, the inversion in (1") and (m") should be accomplished by a single rule specific to the 'incise' construction.
28. These last two cases are even more striking than the previous ones, in that 'tout', 'rien', and 'assistance' cannot be associated with 'le' ('la') either (although 'cela', 'ce que je dis' and 'que S' often can):

(n")   *Rien n'est tombé parce qu'on (ne) l'avait (pas) collé au mur.
       *Bien que tout soit tombé, je ne compte pas le ramasser.
       *Assistance a été prêtée à cette personne-ci mais on ne la
        prêtera pas à l'autre.

29. Since in the general case the copying rule would have to be stated with respect to subject NP's, it would not be possible to have the following derivation: il est la --> il est-il la --> est-il la?, since 'il' is not a NP.

30. It would be difficult to claim that (54b) is an instance of detachment, rather than copying, since a 'detached' (v. Gross (1968)) NP is not readily placeable in between interrogative word and verb: 'Pourquoi est-ce mauvais, l'argent?'; ??Pourquoi, l'argent, est-ce mauvais? In particular, there are speakers who find (54b) perfectly grammatical while rejecting outright all examples with interrogative word followed by detached NP (cf. also the clear difference between (54b) and the starred sentences of (53)).

31. See Kayne (forthcoming - c).

32. The reflexive clitic likewise 'agrees' with the clitic subject:

(o")   Pourquoi Jean et moi ne s'amuserait-on pas à la soirée?
    *Pourquoi Jean et moi ne nous amuserait-on pas à la soirée?

Both verb agreement and reflexive clitic 'agreement' are 'internal' to the verb group. Agreement outside the verb group is rather with the NP subject:

(p")   Pourquoi Jean et moi ne devrait-on pas aller voir notre professeur?
    *Pourquoi Jean et moi$_i$ ne devrait-on pas aller voir son$_i$ professeur?

For further discussion, see Kayne (forthcoming - c).

33. In addition, we would claim that looking at syntactic processes in the light of transformations formulated in terms of syntactic categories allows one to understand the disappearance, around the fifteenth century, of the construction "Partira ce garçon?' (grammatical in Old French), an historical development which has long puzzled philologists; see Kayne (forthcoming - a).

34. Sentences like "C'est-y faux?' are possible in popular French, which uses an interrogative particle 'ti'. This particle is independent of the subject: Marie aime-ti Paul? J'suis-ti comme elle?

35. 'Ce' is not a clitic in certain other environments (v. fn. 24). See also below.

36. The apparent exception to the word 'exactly' (namely, the 'incise' construction) would disappear if the inversion of the subject pronoun there were not accomplished by SUBJ - CL - INV; see fn. 27.

37. For further discussion of the historical development of the transformations discussed in this paper, see Kayne (forthcoming - a).

38. We argued earlier that subject clitics were not NP's. This does not immediately imply that they are dominated by the node V. An argument that they are so dominated can be constructed on the basis of their similarity to object clitics, which in turn can be shown to be dominated by V (v. Kayne (forthcoming - d)). A related argument can be based on the contrast:

(q")   *On boira du bon vin et mangera de la bonne viande.
    On a bu bon vin et mangé de la bonne viande.

Although there is no rule deleting a second 'on' in conjoined structures, the second of two 'on' can be deleted via a rule of auxiliary-deletion; i.e., 'on' can 'fall' with the auxiliary since it is attached to it. For more detailed discussion of the problem of subject clitics in conjoined structures, see Kayne (forthcoming - c).

39. It is unlikely that 'celui-là' in sentences like:

(r") Celui-là, il est dingue.

is in subject position at all, although it is not clear exactly what structural configuration these 'detached' NP's are in. Note that they also occur sentence-final (though not under the same conditions), and can coexist with actually occurring subjects:

(s") Il est dingue, celui-là.
Celui-là, tout le monde l'aime beaucoup.

40. One possible formulation of the copying hypothesis is given in Langacker (1965).

41. We recall that complex inversion must be distinguished from 'detachment'. Thus sentences like 'Cela est-ce vrai?' are instances of the latter. The detachment construction does not in general depend on clitics: it exists, for example, in spoken English:

(t") That friend of yours we were talking about, is he really all that smart?

and can occur in French with non-clitic pronouns (the same is not true of detachment to the right):

(u") Celui-là, tout le monde a peur de lui.

42. Since the complex inversion construction only occurs in non-embedded sentences, and in Emonds (1969) framework would thus involve the application of a root tranformation, one might ask whether Emonds' characterization of such transformations would not be pertinent to the problem at hand. However, as far as we can see, nothing specific to Emonds' theory would prohibit inserting, in root sentences, a copy of the subject to the right of the subject and then inverting it with the verb. Emonds' theory would not allow placing a copy of the subject to the right of the verb, given the node VP in French, if he were correct in claiming that root transformations only attach material to the node S. This restriction seems to be violated, though, by SUBJ - CL - INV, a root transformation which nonetheless attaches material inside the verb group. Furthermore, it appears that in Swedish, adverbs (of all kinds) can occur in between verb and object only in root sentences (and in between subject and verb only in embedded sentences), suggesting, within Emonds' framework, that

there is a root transformation placing adverbs in between verb and object, i.e., not attached to the node S (assuming the node VP in Swedish).

43. For an argument against a pronominalization transformation in French, see Kayne (1971). For further discussion of the pronominalization controversy, see Kuroda (1971) and the references cited therein, as well as those cited in Kayne (1971).

44. Note that placing a pronominal copy of some constituent somewhere else in the sentence is formally similar to a transformation which would "move a constituent, leaving a pronominal copy behind." In the latter case, a constituent would be copied and the original then pronominalized. For example, the detachment construction might be derived as follows: 'Celui-là est bête' → 'Celui-là est bête, celui-là' → 'Il est bête, celui-là'. If the suggestion in the text is correct, then such an analysis is impossible, and detachment would have to be derived otherwise, perhaps by an extension of the base plus new interpretive mechanisms, perhaps by reduction from conjoined structures.

45. The use of the nodes NP, NP' would not appear ad-hoc in the context of the theory of base rules proposed by Chomsky (1970b); in Chomsky's notation, one might have, e.g., $\bar{\bar{N}}$, $\bar{N}$.

46. In standard French, sentences such as:

(v'') Celui-là, il est bête.

can only be instances of detachment. NP's which are incompatible with detachment to the left cannot appear as in (v'') even if under other conditions they can be 'coreferential' with 'il':

(w'') Quelqu'un d'autre$_i$ m'a dit qu'il$_i$ était malheureux.
  *Quelqu'un d'autre, il est malheureux.

The contrast between 'celui-là' and 'quelqu'un d'autre' is mirrored, as expected, in 'detached' sentences having nothing to do with subject clitics:

(x'') Celui-là, tout le monde l'aime beaucoup.
  *Quelqu'un d'autre, tout le monde l'aime beaucoup.

In popular French, sentences such as (v'') are not necessarily instances of detachment. The significant relation between the popular construction and the standard French complex inversion was noticed by Damourette et Pichon (1934:464).

47. A number of arguments to the effect that 'lui', 'eux' must be postulated as deep structure subject NP's are given in Gross (1968).

48. Some speakers do not accept such sentences. For all speakers, the corresponding sentences with 'moi' and 'toi' are impossible: '*Moi n'aime pas ça.', '*Toi aurais dû le faire.' Possible is: 'Toi seul es fou'.

49.   If STR - FRM - DEL applies prior to the rule of STYL - INV, the
sentences of (w') - fn.22 will be excluded. One problem with the
formulation given in the text is that it does not exclude (a'') (nor, consequently, (z')) - fn. 22.   We would like to be able to say that sentences
such as '*Moi-meme partirai' are impossible for the same reason as
'*Moi partirai'. If STR - FRM - DEL were obligatory (with certain exceptions - v. fn. 48) and if its structural description were met by the
'moi' of 'moi-même', then (a'') would simply be a case of having failed
to apply an obligatory rule. (Applying the rule would not yield a grammatical sentence either, presumably because its application would violate
constraints of the type discussed in Chomsky (1971)). Similar facts can
be found with respect to the rule of clitic placement (v. Kayne (forthcoming - d)):

  (y'') *Il connaît moi-même.
         *Elle a vu vous autres hier soir.
         *Il voudrait tuer nous deux.

   Another problem common to STR - FRM - DEL and clitic placement (and
also, in this case, to the rule placing pronouns in article position in
possessives - v. fn. 24) is how to formally characterize the class of
elements to which the rule is applicable - the label 'Pro' needs close
examination.
   50.   One might explore the possibility of replacing SUBJ - CL - ADJ
by a convention on the placement of affixes (v. Emonds (1969)).
   SUBJ - CL - ADJ must precede the rule of auxiliary deletion (v. fn.
38).
   51.   This construction was referred to in fn. 13.
   52.   We do not have:

  (z'') *Ça m'a tous l'air d'être des salauds.

This would follow if the rule taking 'lui' - 'eux' - 'elle(s)' to 'ça/ce'
applied in (z'') before the rule of subject-raising discussed by Ruwet
(1970) did, and did not apply to any but a bare pronoun, i.e., 'tous +
eux' ≠ '*tous ça'. The 'tous' of (81) would have been moved off the
subject prior to the introduction of 'ça' (and therefore prior to subject-
raising).
   53.   CE - CL is optional in certain cases (cf. (76)):

  (a''') Ça/ce serait mieux.
          Ça/ce sera merveilleux.
          Est-ce qu'il faut que ça/ce soit comme ça.

As an auxiliary, 'être' permits 'ce':

  (b''') C'est devenu inutile.
          C'est resté incompréhensible.

If 'être' is preceded by an auxiliary, 'ce' is questionable:

(c''')   ?Ç'aurait été mieux. cf. Ça aurait été mieux.
       *?Ç'a été mal fait.

       *Ce n'aurait pas été bon.
       *Ce n'a pas été mal fait.

The presence of 'ne' is not usually incompatible with CE - CL:

(d''')   Ce ne sera pas merveilleux.
        Ce n'est pas bon.
        Ce n'était pas mauvais.

If 'être' is preceded by a 'subject-raising' verb (v. Ruwet (1970)), 'ce' is generally not possible:

(e''')   *Ce va être bon.
       *Ce vient d'être approuvé.
       *Ce commence à m'ennuyer.
      *?Ce pourrait être Jean qui sonne.
       *Ce parait être juste.
       *Ce semble être illégal.
      *?Ce devrait être plus long.
but:
(f''')   Ce doit être vrai. cf. *Ce doit embêter tout le monde.

This suggests that CE - CL be ordered after 'subject raising'. Sentence (f''') could be generated either by allowing for an optional 'devoir' before 'être' in the structural description of CE - CL or by considering (f''') to be a partially frozen expression. In this regard, we note that SUBJ - CL - INV may not apply to 'ce doit': '*Pourquoi doit-ce être vrai?' (cf. fn. 54), although 'devrait-ce', 'pourrait-ce' seem possible - cf. (g''').

The sentences of (d''') suggest either that CE - CL be complicated to allow for an intervening 'ne': [C, - [X]] - (ne) - être or that 'ne'
                          SCL
has not yet been placed in pre-verbal position at the point of application of CE - CL. A related fact, valid for at least some speakers, is that CE - CL is obligatory with 'est' and 'était' (v. (76)) even in the presence of 'ne': '*Ça n'est pas vrai' vs. 'Ce n'est pas vrai' (for these speakers).

The non-negative sentences of (c'''), if perfectly grammatical, would require allowing for an intervening 'avoir': [C, - [X]] - (ne) - (avoir) -
                                     SCL
être thereby making the wrong prediction for the second half of (c'''), and necessitating some kind of filtering device, the need for which might be further indicated by the following paradigm:

(g''')　Ça (*ce) m'est égal.　C'est égal.
　　　　Ça (*ce) m'est resté indifférent.
　　　　Ça (*ce) lui est inconnu.

(but: C'en est l'auteur. C'en est un.)

　　　　Lui est-ce vraiment inconnu?
　　　　T'est-ce vraiment égal?

'Ce' is not possible with dative clitics unless post-verbal. This suggests
that CE - CL applies regardless of intervening clitics (necessarily the
case, without special statement, if CE - CL precedes clitic placement)
and that one filter out, subsequent to SUBJ - CL - INV, sequences of the
form ''ce' + ('ne') + dative'. Before the existence of such filtering
mechanisms can be countenanced as being the most insightful means of
describing the facts under discussion, much more study is required, both
of the general form of potential filters and of the syntax of 'ça'/'ce'
(e.g., with other clitics: 'Ça y est', 'Ça l'est', etc.).
　　The paradigm for reflexive clitics with true verbs is slightly different
from that of (g'''):

(h''')　Ça (*ce) s'est mal passé.
　　　　*S'est-ce mal passé?

This would follow if 'être' with reflexives was derived from 'avoir' and
if that change took place after CE - CL.
　　54.　The application of SUBJ - CL - INV to the output of CE - CL will
yield:

(i''')　　Est-ce Jean qui pleure?
　　　　　N'est-ce pas important?
　　　　　Etait-ce vraiment comme cela?

In other cases, a somewhat unnatural sentence results:

(j''')　　?Sera-ce mieux?
　　　　　?Sont-ce des garçons intelligents?
　　55.　The fact that there exists a rule of CE - CL (it would be surprising to find a rule inserting 'la liberté' into SCL position) should no
doubt be attributed to the relationship between 'ca'/'ce' and the demonstrative article 'ce'/'cette'/'ces'. One might speculate, for example, that
$[ça] = \begin{bmatrix} [C,] & - & [\emptyset] \end{bmatrix}$. 'Cela' and 'ceci' might then be $\begin{bmatrix} [C,] & - & [\emptyset] & - & \begin{Bmatrix} -là \\ -ci \end{Bmatrix} \end{bmatrix}$
$\underset{NP'}{}$ $\underset{Art \quad N}{}$ $\underset{NP'}{}$ $\underset{Art \quad N}{}$

and therein might lie the incompatibility (due to the absence of a head
noun) between 'cela' and 'lui' with respect to coreference (see below and
(47)). The underlying article character of 'C,' would allow its being

substituted, under Emonds' structure preserving hypothesis, for a subject clitic pronoun, if the latter had something in common with articles.
For discussion relevant to this footnote, see Gross (forthcoming).
   56.   There is an important difference between 'ce' and 'ça' that we
have not yet mentioned. In the predicate nominal construction discussed
in the text (v. (80)-(81)), the verb may agree either with 'ce' or with
the plural predicate nominal:

   (k''')   C'est tous des salauds.
             Ce sont tous des salauds.

With 'ça', plural agreement is not possible:

   (l''')   *Ça sont des salauds.

These facts may be described by postulating a rule in effect marking the
verb (or perhaps 'ce') as plural in the presence of a plural predicate
nominal. If this rule follows CE - CL, then (k''') and (l''') can be
distinguished; e.g., if the rule applied in the environment: [C,] - être-
NP.   SCL
   57.   We have so far been unable to find any clear counterexamples to
this claim. See Kayne (forthcoming - c) for further discussion.
   58.   Although a possible coreferent for generic 'on', 'soi' does not
fill the bill; it is not a possible subject of a verb, even in conjoined
structures, and is a possible coreferent for NP's (e.g., 'chacun') which
are not possible coreferents for 'on' (any coreferent of 'lui', on the
other hand, is a possible coreferent of 'il'). In addition, 'soi' may
be semantically inappropriate.
   59.   Rather than '∅', one might think in terms of a dummy pronoun. We
leave this question open.
   60.   This will exclude the ungrammatical sentence of (64).
   61.   For a viable analysis of conjoined NP's compatible with the base
generation of 'Jean et moi', see Dougherty (1970,1971).
   The rule of SUBJ - CL - DEL may not apply to such NP's:

   (m''')   *Jean et moi devrait partir tout de suite.

More precisely, the rule must apply (since it is obligatory), but when it
does it violates the principle of recoverability of deletion (v. Chomsky
(1965)), thus yielding an ungrammatical result.
   The deletion of 'nous' from the structure [nous-on] would probably
not violate that condition if the rule deleting it (STR - FRM - DEL)
referred to a specified set of elements rather than a syntactic category
(cf. fn. 49).
   For more detailed discussion of the entire question of 'on', see Kayne
(forthcoming - c).
   62.   This was proposed in Katz and Postal (1964). The feature '+Q'
(cf. fn. 15) might be considered to be attached to a node COMP (v. Bresnan
(1970)).

On the other hand, whatever feature it is that triggers SUBJ - CL - INV with adverbs like 'à peine' would seem to come to sentence-initial position along with the adverb:

(n''')   Sans doute est-il déjà parti.
         Peut-être cette fille reviendra-t-elle demain.

         *Est-il sans doute déjà parti.
         *Cette fille reviendra-t-elle peut-être demain.

63.   The relevance of these facts to our analysis is pointed out by Langacker (this volume).
64.   Movement in relatives and exclamations is not always obligatory:

(o''')   La fille qu'il est sorti avec elle est là (popular)
         Vous avez une si belle voiture!

but in such constructions, there is no WH-word, although there is in (87), so the assymmetry would remain.
65.   With 'donc', we have:

(p''')   Où donc est-il allé?
         *Il est allé où donc?

although some may accept, with an intonation break:

(q''')   Il est allé où, donc?

Also:

(r''')   Quand part-il donc?
         *Il part donc quand?

66.   Echo questions must therefore have no such marker in their deep structure. We note that rather than considering sentences like (87) as semantically ambiguous, one might think in terms of a single construction being 'used' in different ways. Unfortunately, we have no clear idea as to the derivation of echo questions. The arguments in the text would be strengthened if an explanation were found, consistent with our hypothesis, for the observed contrasts. For example,'echoes' seem natural only upon the heels of a specific statement. If someone says 'I ate three apples', one can reply, incredulously, 'You ate how many apples?', but not if he had said 'I ate some apples'. The contrast between (100) and 'Tu l'as fait comment?' might be related to the possibility of 'Je l'ai fait de la façon suivante.' vs. '*Il est possible de la façon suivante que je parte.' It goes without saying that we have but scratched the surface of this topic.

67.   For clarity, we omit the end variables: W X [Y SCL] V Z
                                             — +Q   —

68.   In fact, given our claim that subject clitics originate as a
kind of NP affix, plus the use of a marker attached to the preposed interrogative element, if any, there is no way to write a single transformation
that would move the clitics off the NP's both in (104) and in the general
case of complex inversion. One could, however, conceive of a new formalism
                          [Y SCL] V   [Y] V + SCL
which would permit this: NP   X →   X   i.e., if one
                                +Q   +Q
allowed a double structural description with the interpretation that the
string in question must satisfy both halves separately. The ungrammaticality of (104) could then be taken as an argument in favor of the standard
formalism, with a single, linear structural description.
   Some speakers accept sentences like:

(s''') ??Combien de familles françaises ont-elles plus de deux voitures?

although not those in (104). Such speakers might be analyzing (s''') as:
interrogative element = 'combien', NP = 'de familles francaises' rather
than the expected: interrogative element = 'combien de familles francaises',
NP = ∅. This in turn might be related to the possibility of having 'combien'
separated from an 'associated' complement: 'Combien connaît-il de familles
françaises?'
69.   In some cases, there may be overlapping with a kind of extraposition. Thus, 'Pourquoi quelque chose d'effroyable est-il arrivé?' is
the complex inversion corresponding to 'Qqch. d'effroyable est arrivé'.
The sentence 'Pourquoi est-il arrivé qqch. d'effroyable?' is not an instance
of STYL - INV, but rather of SUBJ - CL - INV applied to the extraposed
form: 'Il est arrivé qqch. d'effroyable'.
70.   Sentence (113) contrasts with: 'Que voulait lui dire sa petite
soeur?' Compare also fn. 8.
71.   This accounts for the fact that STYL - INV cannot leave a subject
clitic behind:

(t''') *Qu'il veut dire tout cela?
        *Ce qu'il veut dire tout cela, c'est...
        *Elle sait très bien à quoi il vous fait penser tout cela.

since the subject clitic will be moved along as part of the subject NP.
   Notice that this means that the explanation proposed earlier (v. (34))
for the inapplicability of STYL - INV to subject clitics is not quite
correct, although it is still true that subject clitics are not NP's.
The problem is how to exclude, e.g., '*Ce que dit-il, c'est ceci' as
opposed to 'Ce que dit Jean'. (Actually, the hyphens in (34) are misleading; we would not at all expect STYL - INV to attach the clitic to
the verb.) We suggested in fn. 49 that STR - FRM - DEL precede STYL -

INV. If this is correct, then at the point of application of STYL - INV, we will have 'Ce que [$\emptyset$ -il] dit'. Although 'il' is not a NP, it is
NP
contained in a larger NP which should apparently be sujbect to STYL - INV: 'Ce que dit [$\emptyset$ -il]'. One possibility for excluding such a derivation
NP
would be (cf.fn. 77) in terms of a convention filtering out surface structures containing 'affixes' not in clitic position. (Since STYL - INV must itself follow (object) clitic placement (cf. fn. 10 and the ordering of 'tout'-movement after clitic placement given in Kayne (forthcoming-d)), the 'il' could not be attached to any verb form by clitic placement (even assuming the latter to be formulated in such a way as to make the question of ordering meaningful). The alternative of a filtering convention might find support in a study of 'en' and 'y', which lack corresponding strong forms. We leave this question open.

    72.   See fn. 55. We are analyzing 'tout' as   [[tout] - $\emptyset$], where Q
NP Q
equals whatever node dominates 'tout' in 'tout le gateau'. The correctness of such an analysis for 'rien' is less obvious. We note, however, that 'rien' is subject to the transformation moving 'tout', 'tous', 'chacun' to the left, all of which are quantifiers (v. Kayne (forthcoming-d)).

    73.   The 'il' of 'Il est arrivé trois enfants','Il pleut','Il est important qu'elle parte', need not have anything to do with 'lui'. If such 'il' are inserted transformationally into a vacant subject position, the rule could be stated so as to insert 'il' directly into subject clitic position, leaving the NP' position empty. The absence of 'lui' might then play a role in an explanation for the failure of this 'il' to show up as an accusative:

    (u''') *Je l'entends pleuvoir.
          *On l'a vu arriver trois enfants.
          *Tout le monde le croit important qu'elle parte.

An adequately detailed study of the interaction of (object) clitic placement and subject clitics is beyond the scope of this article.

    74.   Generic 'on' can be coreferential with 'soi' and with a possessive pronoun derived from 'soi': 'Quand on$_i$ aime son$_i$ travail,...' Possessive pronouns derived from 'lui' cannot be coreferential with 'on', 'cela', 'que S', etc.

    The notion 'head noun' used here is in need of further study. The following can be coreferential with il(s)': 'quelqu'un', 'chacun', 'ces deux-la', and 'lui' itself. Thus 'lui' might be considered a pro-noun (v. Gross (forthcoming)), 'ce deux-là' an instance of a deleted 'eux', and 'un' a (pro-) noun (cf. 'les uns'). Forms such as 'celui-là' provide further support for the fundamental distinction claimed earlier between 'ce' and the personal pronouns.

    75.   See fn. 49. The symbol '$\emptyset$', the null element, indicates deletion The verb probably does not have to be specified as finite since there may not be any cases of strong form pronoun before non-finite verb at the point of application of the rule.

Alternatively, we could use the more usual number notation:
[Pro - SCL] - V → Ø 2 3
　1　　 2　　 3

76.　　As mentioned earlier, the clitic will be attached to the finite
verb, rather than the past participle, by virtue of the former's adjacency
to the NP. There is no question in French of 'auxiliary + past participle'
being dominated by the node V: 'Ils *ont* sans doute presque tous presque
tout très bien *compris*'.

As stated, SUBJ - CL - INV does not allow for material intervening
between the subject NP and the verb. The derivation of sentences like:
'Le connais-tu?', 'Pourquoi Jean t'en voulait-il?', with intervening
object clitics, will in fact proceed correctly if the sequence 'object
clitic(s) + verb' is itself dominated by the node V (as argued in Kayne
(forthcoming - d)). The same will be true of 'ne': 'Ne le fera-t-il pas?'
if 'ne' is dominated by the node V with finite verbs. Adverbial elements
can intervene between subject NP and verb in French only if flanked by
pauses; in the absence of a theory of syntactic pauses, it is difficult
to say whether sentences like: 'Pourquoi tout cela, à votre avis, est-il
important?' bear on the formulation of SUBJ - CL - INV. Of course, if elements
like 'à votre avis' are placed between subject NP and verb after SUBJ -
CL - INV, the answer is necessarily negative.

77.　　Given context-free base rules, subject clitics will be generated
as part of NP's occupying deep structure positions other than that of
subject. This is moreover a necessary fact, insofar as subject clitics may
occur overtly corresponding to deep structure objects: 'Pourquoi ce
garçon sera-t-il fusillé?', 'As-tu été mis à la porte?'. SUBJ - CL - DEL
will consequently apply in surface object NP's: 'Elle aime bien [ce
garçon - il]' → SUBJ - CL - DEL → 'Elle aime bien [ce garçon - Ø],' as
well as in deep structure subjects moved out of subject position by transformation: 'La police - elle fusillera ce garçon - il' → Passive →
→ 'Ce garçon - il sera fusillé par la police - elle → SUBJ - CL - DEL →
'Ce garçon - Ø sera fusillé par la police - Ø.' If a NP of the form
[Ø - on] (see text) is in an object position in surface structure, the
derivation will block (SUBJ - CL - DEL will be inapplicable), perhaps by
virtue of the filtering mechanism suggested in footnote 71.

The decision to generate NP's of the form [cette fille-elle] in the base
is independent of the set of transformations given in the text. An alternative analysis compatible with all the transformations proposed would
retain the PS-rules as in the text but would have the node SCL unfilled
in the base except in the case of 'on' ('ce' would continue to be introduced
via CE - CL). There would then be a kind of agreement transformation
introducing the grammatical features of NP' under the empty SCL node: such
a transformation could be ordered after rules such as Passive and subject-
raising and stated so as to apply only in (derived) subject NP's. This
proposal might be empirically distinguishable from the text proposal with
respect to the interaction of subject clitics and object clitics; we
leave this question open.

TOBY PAFF
INDIANA UNIVERSITY

SENTENCE COMPLEMENTS ON NOUNS

This paper concerns noun phrases of the following sort, which I will call the "noun-complement" construction.

(1) Marie accepte *le fait que Paul est arrivé.*

(2) *La suggestion que nous fassions cela* a été rejetée par tout le monde.

For convenience, let us call the noun on which the complement depends, the "head noun", for example, *le fait.* Let us call the phrase introduced by *que,* for example, *que Paul est arrivé,* the complement. The contention of this paper is that the complement is an "appositive" on the "head noun", that is, the complement comes from an underlying non-restrictive relative clause of the form, *qui est que S,* which modifies the head noun. Let us first consider some of the restrictions on the noun complement construction.

In his "Remarks on Nominalization", Chomsky (1970:197) notes that while there are sentences like (3a), there are none like (3b).

(3) a. Le fait (que Marie accepte) est que Paul est arrivé.
     b. *le fait que Paul est arrivé est que Marie est riche

Chomsky suggests that deriving (3a) from (5) would account for the non-occurrence of (3b).

(5)

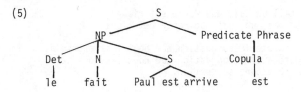

A transformation would move the complement, *Paul est arrivé,* after the copula, yielding (3a).

Consider, however, the following sentences.

(6) a. Le fait (que Marie accepte) est le fait que Paul est arrivé.
    b. Le fait que Paul est arrivé est le fait que Marie accepte.
    c. *le fait que Paul est arrivé est le fait que Marie est riche

(7) a. La suggestion que Marie accepte est la suggestion que nous fassions cela.
    b. La suggestion que nous fassions cela est la suggestion que Marie accepte.
    c. *la suggestion que nous fassions cela est la suggestion que Paul parte

Chomsky's suggestion, it seems clear, does not explain the non-occurrence of (6c) and (7c). Several other considerations also restrict the noun-complement construction.

A head noun with a complement sentence must refer to something which exists in the mind of the speaker. The noun must be "specific". To clarify the notion "specific", consider the following.

(8) a. Paul a acheté un livre.
    b. Paul a-t-il acheté un livre?
    c. Paul n'a pas acheté un livre.

In (8a), the speaker may have a particular book in mind; that is, *un livre* is "specific". In (8b) and (8c), the speaker does not have a particular book in mind. *Un livre* is "non-specific".

When a word like *suggestion* or *fait* takes a complement sentence, the word must refer to a particular suggestion or fact that the speaker has in mind; *suggestion* and *fait* must be "specific". When such words do not have a complement, they need not be "specific".

(9) a. Paul accepte le fait que Marie est riche.
    b. Paul accepte-t-il le fait que Marie est riche?
    c. Paul n'accepte pas le fait que Marie est riche,

(10) a. Paul accepte un fait que Pierre a fait observer que Marie est riche.
    b. *Paul accepte-t-il un fait que Marie est riche?
    c. *Paul n'accepte pas un fait que Marie est riche

(11) a. Paul n'a pas accepté la suggestion que nous fassions cela.
    b. *Paul n'a accepté aucune suggestion que nous fassions cela.
    c. Paul n'a accepté aucune suggestion.

Chomsky's proposal does not appear to explain these facts.

Restrictive relative clauses may, of course, modify nouns which take complement sentences. What is curious is that the restrictive relative clause must precede the complement.

(12) a. La suggestion que Paul a acceptée, que nous fassions cela, était étonnante.
b. *la suggestion, que nous fassions cela, que Paul a acceptée, était étonnante

(13) a. Le fait que Paul a fait observer, que Marie est riche, ne me surprend pas.
b. *le fait, que Marie est riche, que Paul a fait observer, ne me surprend pas.

Nothing in Chomsky's solution indicates the correct explanation of this, though obviously various restrictions on the relevant transformations might exclude the unacceptable phrases.

Nouns like *fait* and *suggestion* may also take non-restrictive relative clauses. These nouns may, in particular, take non-restrictive relative clauses of the form, *qui est que S.*

(14) Le fait que Marie a fait observer, qui était que Paul est riche, a été accepté par tout le monde.

(15) La suggestion que Paul a acceptée, qui était que nous fassions cela, a été rejetée par tous les autres.

Considerations quite independent of the noun-complement construction have caused several people to suggest a transformation to delete *qui est* in relative clauses. This transformation, applied to (16a), produces (16b), for example.

(16) a. Marie a acheté un livre qui est intéressant.
b. Marie a acheté un livre intéressant.

Applied to (14) and (15), the transformation which deletes "qui est" yields, in fact, the noun-complement construction.

(17) Le fait que Marie a fait observer, que Paul est riche, a été accepté par tout le monde.

(18) La suggestion que Paul a acceptée, que nous fassions cela, a été rejetée par tous les autres.

But if we derive the noun-complement construction as Chomsky proposed and do not restrict the application of the transformation which deletes *qui est* so as not to apply to (14) and (15), (17) and (18) will have two deep structures; one in which the complement sentence is a part of a non-restrictive relative clause, and another in which the deep structure is

analogous to (5). This would mean that (17) and (18) are structurally
ambiguous, which does not appear to be true. While creating more problems
for Chomsky's solution, the preceding points to its own solution and a
possible solution to the problems mentioned in the foregoing paragraphs.

Let us derive the complement sentence in the noun-complement construction from the non-restrictive relative clause. Thus, for example, application of the transformation to delete *qui est* to (19a) produces (19b),
the noun-complement construction.

(19) a. Marie accepte le fait, qui est que Paul est arrivé.
      b. Marie accepte le fait que Paul est arrivé.

Let us ignore the question of the intonation break which seems to be absent
in (19b). The deep structure of (19a) will be the same deep structure that
underlies all non-restrictive relative clauses. For reasons that cannot
be dealt with here, I suggest that the phrase structure contain the following rules (Chomsky 1965:106-7):

(20) a. S ----> NP Predicate Phrase
      b. Predicate Phrase ----> Aux VP (Place) (Time) (S^n)

The node, S, dominated by the node, Predicate Phrase, is the source of
subordinate clauses introduced by the so-called subordinate conjunctions,
for example, *quoique, avant que, etc.*, the "absolute" construction,
"participial" constructions, and non-restrictive relative clauses on noun
phrases, verb phrases, adjectives phrases and sentences.* The non-restrictive relative clauses are formed by the following transformations.

(21) NP-fronting
      X_1, (Det) N, X_2, X_3, (Det) N, X_4, X_5
      1   2   3   4   5   6   7
      => 1, 2, 3, 5 # 4 - 6, 7
      where: (i)   4-6 = S and either Predicate Phrase immediately
                    dominates 4-6, or NP dominates 4-6
          and (ii) 2 = 5

Accepting (22) as the deep structure of (19a), (21) produces (23).

(22)
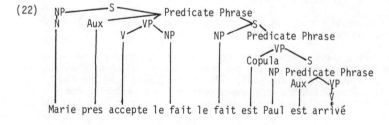

Marie pres accepte le fait le fait est Paul est arrivé

(23) (The embedded S only)

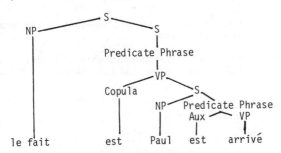

le fait   est Paul est arrivé

(24) Clause-movement
X_1, NP, X_2, NP, X_3, X_4
1 2 3 4 5 6
=> 1, 2 # 4, 5, 3, 6
where: (i) 4-5 = S and Predicate Phrase immediately
       dominates 4-5
   (ii) 2 = 4

(25) "Que" insertion
X, Y, (Det) N, W, Z => 1, 2, que + 3, 4, 5
1 2 3 4 5
where: (i) 3-4 = S immediately dominated by NP

These two rules, applied to (23), yield the following:

(26)

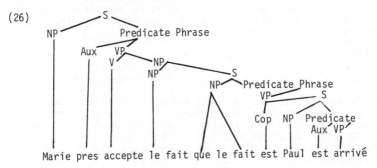

Marie pres accepte le fait que le fait est Paul est arrivé

At this point various transformations supply the proper relative pronouns.
Finally, a transformation may delete *qui est*.

(27) X_1, X_2, qui   Copula, X_3, X_4 => 1, 2, Ø, 4, 5
    1 2   3   4 5
    where: if 3-4 = S and NP that dominates 3-4 immediately dominates
           N, then 4 = Adjective Phrase

In particular, when 4 is a noun phrase, (27) produces what is ordinarily
called an "appositive". Applied to (26), after *qui* has replaced *le fait*,
(27) produces:

(28)

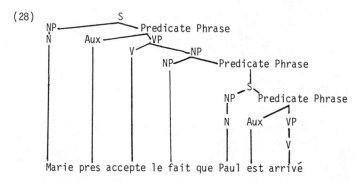

Marie près accepte le fait que Paul est arrivé

Clearly the above derivation results from transformations needed in the
grammar anyway to account for the non-restrictive relative clause. The
claim that the complement sentence is an appositive not only allows us to
make use of independently motivated rules, it removes several of the
problems we have mentioned in connection with Chomsky's proposals.

    Non-restrictive relative clauses, hence appositives, may modify only
nouns which refer to a particular item that the speaker has in mind,
that is, mouns which are "specific".

    (29) a. Paul a acheté un livre, grammaire française.
          b. *Paul a-t-il acheté un livre, grammaire française?
          c. *Paul n'a pas acheté un livre, grammaire française

The same considerations which exclude (29b) and (29c) will also prevent
nouns which are non-specific from taking complement sentences, if the
latter are derived in the same way as appositives. The semantic component
is, perhaps, the proper place for incorporating this restriction.

    Non-restrictive relative clauses and consequently appositives follow
restrictive relative clauses.

    (30) a. Paul a accepté le livre que je lui ai donné, grammaire
             française.
          b. *Paul a accepté le livre, grammaire française, que je lui
             ai donné.

(31) a. Marie a volé la fourchette que Paul m'a donnée, celle que
         vous vouliez acheter.
     b. *Marie a volé la fourchette, celle que vous vouliez acheter,
         que Paul m'a donnée.

The transformations presented, the reader will notice, do not allow the
reverse order of clauses (30b). The transformations are of this form
in order to handle appositives correctly. Treating complement sentences
as appositives means that we do not have to restate these restrictions in
some other rule.

Deriving complement sentences from non-restrictive relative clauses
of the form, *qui est que S*, of course, circumvents the problems raised by
(14)-(15) and (17)-(18). Since both sets of sentences have the same
deep structure, they mean the same. Since, furthermore, the only possible
deep structure for (17)-(18) is one analogous to (22), these sentences
cannot be structurally ambiguous. The hypothesis that the complement
sentence is an appositive explains several other phenomena which pose
problems for Chomsky's solution.

Consider, for example, the following sentences:

(32) a. Les faits, que Paul est riche, que Marie est pauvre, et que
         Pierre est voleur, sont évidents.
     b. *les faits que Paul est riche sont évidents.

(33) a. Les deux suggestions, que Paul parte, et que nous restions
         ici, ont été acceptées.
     b. *les deux suggestions, que Paul parte, que nous restions ici,
         et qu'on chante une chanson, ont été acceptées

(34) J'accepte le fait que Paul est riche, que Marie est pauvre, et
     que Pierre est voleur.

If the head noun is plural, there must be more than one complement sentence.
If a certain number precedes the head noun, that number of complement
sentences must follow the head noun. If the head houn is singular, several
complements, it appears, may follow the noun.

According to the hypothesis that the complement sentence is an appositive,
the deep structure for (32a) includes:

(35)

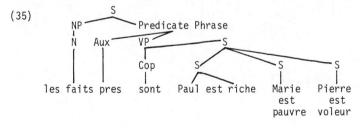

Clearly the non-occurrence of (36) precludes (32b).

(36) *les faits sont que Paul est riche.

Since, however, (37) is permissible, (34) is a sentence.

(37) Le fait est que Paul est riche, que Marie est pauvre, et que Pierre est voleur.

None of this requires a modification of the rules needed to produce appositives in any case.
    Let us now consider the problems created by the sentences in (3), (6) and (7) in light of the appositive hypothesis. I repeat the examples here.

(38) a. Le fait (que Marie accepte) est que Paul est arrivé.
     b. *le fait que Paul est arrivé est que Marie est riche

(39) a. Le fait (que Marie accepte) est le fait que Paul est arrivé.
     b. Le fait que Paul est arrivé est le fait que Marie accepte.
     c. *le fait que Paul est arrivé est le fait que Marie est riche

(40) a. La suggestion que Marie accepte est la suggestion que nous fassions cela.
     b. La suggestion que nous fassions cela est la suggestion que Marie accepte.
     c. *la suggestion que nous fassions cela est la suggestion que Paul parte

The deep structure of the sentences (38b) and (39c) would be the following:

(41)

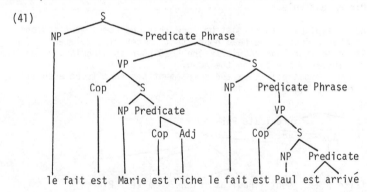

(42)

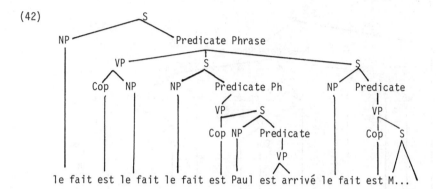

le fait est le fait le fait est Paul est arrivé le fait est M...

These deep structures say, in effect, the following:

(43) le fait = que Paul est arrivé = que Marie est riche

(44) le fait = que Paul est arrivé = le fait = que Marie est riche

Both (43) and (44) are equivalent to:

(45) que Paul est arrivé = que Marie est riche

The readings assigned to (38b) and (39c) by the semantic component will
contain (45). This reading, however, would seem anomalous, for when
one says *Paul est arrivé*, one does not mean *Marie est riche*, and so on.
The reading given (45), hence (38b) and (39c), is, nevertheless, precisely
that. If the semantic component marks (45) as anomalous, then (38b)
and (39c) will be marked semantically anomalous.
    A related problem is the following.

(46) a. Le fait que Paul est riche, (le) fait que Marie accepte,
          a été rejeté par tout le monde.
      b. Le fait que Marie accepte, le fait que Paul est riche,
          a été rejeté par tout le monde.
      c. *le fait que Paul est riche, le fait que Marie est arrivée,
          a été rejeté par tout le monde

The deep structure of (46c), according to the appositive hypothesis, is
the following.

(47)

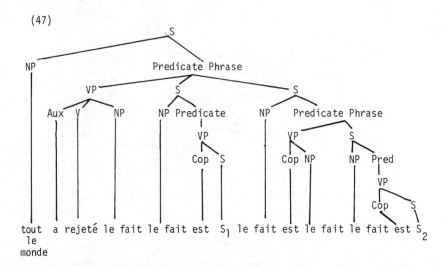

tout a rejeté le fait le fait est S_1 le fait est le fait le fait est S_2
le
monde

where S_1 is *Paul est riche*, and S_2 *Marie est arrivée*. This deep structure (47) contains an element similar to (45).

(48) que Paul est riche = que Marie est arrivée

The semantic component, if the explanation in the preceding paragraph is accepted, will mark (46c) as anomalous in the same way as it does (38b) and (39c). Even if some entirely different mechanism excludes (38b) and (39c), the appositive hypothesis allows us to use the same device to exclude (46c).
    The pronoun *ce* behaves like a noun such as *fait*. *Ce* is, of course, always "specific". When a restricitve relative clause modifies *ce*, the relative clause must precede the complement sentence.

(49) a. Ce que Paul a dit, que Marie est arrivée, ne m'étonne pas.
      b. *ce, que Marie est arrivée, que Paul a dit, ne m'étonne pas

A brief glance at the data also reveals that the other properties mentioned above in connection with *fait* are true of *ce*. For example, when *ce* takes a complement sentence, it may not be followed by ...*est que S*.

(50) Ce que Paul croit est que Marie est riche,

(51) *ce que Paul croit, que Marie est riche, est que Pierre est parti.

Another property of "ce" shows the appropriateness of the appositive hypothesis.

Consider the following:

(52) a. Ce que Paul croit, que Marie est riche, a étonné Pierre.
        b. *ce que Paul croit, voiture rouge, a étonné Pierre

(53) a. Ce que Paul a acheté, voiture rouge, a étonné Pierre.
        b. *ce que Paul a acheté, que Marie est riche, a étonné Pierre

The deep structure of (52b), according to the appositive analysis is:

(53)

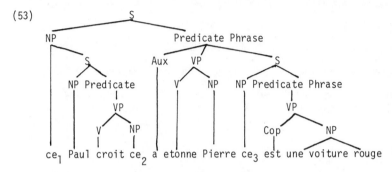

Since ce_1 must be indentical to ce_2 and ce_3 for relativeiztion to take place, and, in particular, ce_2 will be identical to ce_3, the phrase marker ((54)) will have a semantic interpretation which includes:

(55) Paul croit une voiture rouge.

This, of course, is anomalous. The deep structure of (53b) will be the same as (54) with *a achete* replacing *croit*, and *que Marie est riche* replacing *une voiture rouge*. Hence, the reading assigned to (53b) will contain:

(56) Paul a acheté que Marie est riche.

This, likewise, is anomalous. Without having to posit two underlying words, *ce*, we can explain the restrictions in (52) and (53) by means of rules needed to produce non-restrictive relative clauses.

    Sentences like the following appear to be counter-examples to the claim that complement sentences are appositives.

(57) a. Le général n'a pas accepté un ordre aux soldats de reculer.
        b. Le général a-t-il accepté un ordre aux soldats de reculer?

The problem arises if we derive the complement, *aux soldats de reculer* from an underlying sentence, *les soldats reculent*. *Ordre* takes a sentence complement, apparently, but is not "specific". This problem does not, however, refute the appositive hypothesis, for when the complement on *ordre* is a sentence introduced by *que*, not an infinitive, *ordre* must be specific.

(58) a. Le général a accepté l'ordre, que les soldats reculent.
b. *le général n'a pas accepté un ordre, que les soldats reculent
c. *le général a-t-il accepté un ordre, que les soldats reculent?

What the solution to this problem is is not obvious. Perhaps infinitival complements have some separate source. Sentences like those in (57) do not, at any rate, constitute clear-cut counter-examples to the claims made earlier.

The hypothesis that complement sentences on nouns are appositives explains several properties of the noun-complement construction, using rules which are independently motivated to account for non-restrictive relative clauses and ordinary appositives.

NOTE

*For further details, see Paff (1970).

DANIEL E. GULSTAD
UNIVERSITY OF MISSOURI

FUNCTIONS AND STATES IN THE DEEP STRUCTURE OF SPANISH

There are many alternative ways to look at grammar--many vantage points
from which to observe grammatical relations. Certainly every theoretical
approach has provided some new insights, and it is probable that all have
also by the very nature of their orientation left particular phenomena
obscured. For a few examples, we may consider the now notorious attention
to surface structure that limited structuralist analyses to what Chomsky
called taxonomies, Chomsky's own adoption of a phrase-structure basis that
permitted only constituent categories, or the case grammar advocated by
Fillmore which generates all constituent categories from function categories.
Despite the fact that looking back today we find few of Chomsky's premises
to have survived a decade and a half of critical testing by the best minds
in Linguistics, it is obvious that those premises initiated a renaissance in
linguistic inquiry, and that the manner of their formalization was a methodological breakthrough of immeasurable value to subsequent research.
Conversely, were it not for the careful attention to constituent structure
that occupied the generation on whose shoulders Chomsky rose, there would
not have existed the means or the challenge of applying formal notation
to the description of sentence relations. As for the current dissenters
who desire in one way or another to account for deep functional relations
that Transformational Generative Grammar excludes, while it is too early
to attempt an overall appraisal of their work (except to acknowledge its
importance), it is not unfair to emphasize the degree to which they are
indebted to the Transformational theory they have chosen to abandon; an
indebtedness so pervasive and obvious that it need not be pointed out in
detail.
    Some of the points I wish to make have been made in a previous paper
(Gulstad 1971), but since the focus here is on Spanish syntax rather than
on syntactic theory *per se*, I will limit theoretical discussion to that
which is relevant to the linguistic data chosen for this analysis. It
will be my practice also to explain theoretical matters as they come up,
rather than to present a separate introduction to the metatheory in
anticipation of its application. Among the characteristics of natural
language that have led me to doubt certain tenets of existing theories

of analysis there are two which hold particular prominence. First there
is the peculiar but to-date unexplained relationship between anaphora and
passiveness that shows up in Spanish in the so-called pleonastic pronouns
and in the variety of passive forms. Secondly, there is the predicative
nature of prepositional phrases and conjuctive clauses, known to traditional grammarians when they referred to the noun as the "object of a
preposition"; both Transformational Grammar and Case Grammar slight the
importance of these "function words" except as surface manifestations of
deep features. Let us begin by re-examining the notion "passive".

It is common for the passive to be treated in syntax as a transformation
of an active sentence. This viewpoint, as Chomsky has reminded us, was
the essence of what traditional grammar had to say on the subject. Chomsky
himself accepted that notion in his early work, (1957:42) with the relations formalized and represented as transformations. Later, after Katz
and Postal (1964:72-3) proposed a dummy passive morpheme in the deep
structure, Chomsky (1965:128) also accepted that version, generating the
agent constituent from a manner adverbial, as they had. Several new
proposals are gaining currency (e.g. Fillmore, 1968a; Chafe, 1970a, 1970b,
and 1971), but although they are the result of case-oriented or semantics-
oriented syntactic theories, they have not entirely eschewed the notion
that the passive is a paraphrase of the active, differing from it only in
regard to topicalization, which imposes a different ordering on its
constituents. There are several compelling reasons for rejecting these
approaches and seeking a new one.

First of all, there is not the same relationship of an underlying passive
morpheme to the constituents of the surface phrase marker of the passive
sentence as there is in, say, the case of WH and YES-NO Interrogatives.
Chomsky's earlier transformation rules were extremely unconvincing, and
the later association of the agent phrase (BY + Passive) with Manner
Adverbials borders on the ad hoc. Recent theories expressed by Fillmore,
Chafe, and.others carefully document the relation of Verb to NP, but
their disenchantment with Subject-Predicate categories militates against
an intuitively satisfying representation of native competence.

Secondly, although it is as much a part of native competence to relate
the *María* of (1) *Roberto dio flores a María* (that is, the indirect object)
with that of (2) *María recibió flores de Roberto* ("grammatical subject"
but "logical-object" of the verb in this case), there is nothing in the
above-mentioned approaches that sheds any light on this matter, nor--
furthermore--that offers a plausible explanation as to why the native
speaker senses an affinity between a passive sentence (3) *?María fue
dada un beso por Carlos* and (4) *María recibió un beso de Carlos*. That is,
recibió functions seemingly as a lexicalization of a passive *fue dada*,
with the Object of the "force" of the Verb functioning as the Subject,
and the Subject of the "force" of the verb as an Agent constituent to the
right.

Thirdly, there is a relationship between sentences with passives
utilizing the so-called "reflexive" particle, such as (5) *Este edificio
se construyó de mármol*, and those with passives that employ *ser* plus Past

Participle, such as (6) *Este edificio fue construido de mármol.* According
to the various methods of handling passives that we have been reviewing,
there is an extreme amount of irregularity in the surface structure of
Spanish, dividing passives as it does among several different types of
representation, particularly the types we have been examining, but including also some uses of the infinitive as well as some instances where the
sentence structure is active but the interpretation is passive.

Fourthly, there is the problem of the adjective. In recent work there
has been a progressive tendency to treat adjectives as verbs in the Deep
Structure, but the approaches employed have been varyingly unsuccessful
in establishing the proper relationship of the underlying verb to the
surface adjective. That is to say, although there has been quite general
agreement that the adjective has a stative function that parallels certain
non-stative functions in the verb, no-one to my knowledge has produced a
theory that places the adjective systematically within the underlying
verbality categories.

Fifthly, the seemingly unquestioned assumption that the agent constituent of passive sentences represents an underlying subject-of-the-verb
(or agent *qua* subject-of-the-verb), rather than an adjunct to the passive
sentence, severely handicaps any relationship between the sentences
(7) *El orador parecía acobardarse de Jorge* and (8) *El orador parecía ser
acobardado por Jorge,* since the "reflexive" element in (7) is commonly
assumed to represent the grammatical object of *acobardar,* creating an
underlying (9) *El orador acobardó (a) el orador,* pronominalized to (10)
El orador lo acobardó and reflexivized to (11) *El orador se acobardó,* to
which is appended the adjunctive agent *de Jorge.* It is questionable
whether whatever generality is achieved by considering (12) *Jorge parecía
acobardar al orador* as the active string representing the same underlying
constituents as (8) is sufficient to compensate for a generality of another
kind which is obscured, namely the fact that neither (7) nor (8) is either
incomplete or unintelligible without the adjoined *de Jorge* and *por Jorge,*
respectively. That is to say, in both sentences an agent is implied,
regardless of whether the optional specific agent is appended adjunctively
to compensate for the original occurrence of the agent in the deep structure which was subsequently deleted in the interest of topicalization.

In this paper I propose an alternative to theories which derive the
entire set of sentence classes for a given language from a single set of
ordered or unordered, optional and obligatory non-terminal category symbols, whether the transformational apparatus is called upon to reorder
syntactic constituents or to map a set of non-syntactic categories or
features (semantic or case) into syntactic constituents. This alternative
is by no means the answer to all syntactic problems, nor is it--at least
in its present stage--invulnerable to criticism from various points of
view. On the other hand, there are a number of characteristics of those
natural languages familiar to me which do not strike me as being satisfactorily described under any of the existing approaches to grammatical
analysis, a circumstance which prompts me to offer these suggestions.

Let us consider some of the typical relations of Spanish sentences that we might wish to elucidate.

The tree diagram of figure 1 is an abbreviated representation of the tree that results from the recurrent application of the rules:

(13) S ---> *Topic* + *Comment*,

      Comment ---> *Functive* (*Topic*),

      Topic ---> $\left\{ \begin{array}{l} S \\ (D)\ N\ (T) \end{array} \right\}$,

      Functive ---> $\left\{ \begin{array}{l} Verb + Tns\ (=Tense) \\ Predicative \\ Case\ Marker \\ \\ Nexus \end{array} \right\}$,where

any application of a non-terminal symbol has an absolute memory of the functional levels through which it has passed, and the capacity to predict exactly the series of levels through which it is yet to pass. That is, in addition to the formal category equivalent to Noun Phrase represented by the symbol T, and the functional category of Subject (versus Predicate, or *Comment*), there is a case-level constraint on the ordering of sentence types, and a sentence-topicalization constraint that applies whenever the *Comment* of the dominating *S* is rewritten as *Case Marker* or Nexus. To illustrate this, let us first trace the recurrent applications of the rewrite rules in figure 1. For the present we will withhold function classification from the node symbols, letting these functions reveal themselves only in a translative paraphrase (underlined) of the main verb, and global function labels (such as Caus*ative*, Pat*ient*, etc.); we will also expand the *Comment* as *Functive* (*Sentence*), eliminating the node labels of the dominating *Topic*. In order to conserve space and to facilitate reading, the *Sentence Topic* will be represented, without node labeling, by a surface noun or determiner + noun in standard orthography; the *Functive* will be represented by the surface form of the verb or connective that the deep structure implies.

In figure 1 the highest S has an Ag*entive Topic* and a Caus*ative Comment*. The verb form shown is the surface representation of the sentence (14) *Juan busca un lápiz*, but the subscript translative *causa* comes nearer the functional value of the underlying *Verb*, which may be verified by substituting one of the many pro-verbs, such as *hacer, cometer, ejecutar, arreglar*, or *causar* itself. When this is done the result is to deprive the sentence of the semantic content required in order to make the sentence intelligible, but if we glance down to the bottom of the tree diagram we find the answer to this dilemma--whenever the Caus*ative* verb is represented by a pro-verb, recourse must be taken to the Res*ulative* below, producing such sentences as (15) *Juan hace una busca* $\left\{ \begin{array}{l} de \\ a \end{array} \right\}$ *su lápiz*. This suggests

that a strict surface representation of the underlying structure here
would produce something on the order of (16) *Juan busca un lápiz una
busca, to which a set of rules is applied that says: (a) if the Caus*ative*
Verb is not pro-verbed, redundancy constraints delete the Resu*ltative;*
(b) if the Caus*ative Verb* is pronominalized, focus constraints delete
the Pat*ient*, then the entire sentence must be topicalized under a higher
Top*ic*, dominated by a higher S, to which a Com*ment* is appended, producing
(17) [[Top*ic*: *Juan hace una busca*] [Com*ment*: ${3 \atop de}$ *un lápiz*]], where the
Com*ment* simply recovers something from the deep structure of the original
Sent*ence* and places it in the proper functional relation to that Sent*ence*.

Let us now return to our examination of the tree in figure 1. If we
adopt the Caus*ative* explanation, we must accept the presence of at least
two sentences here, paraphrasable as (a) *Juan causa* and (b) *Un lápiz busca.*
This could be achieved by reducing the structure of the tree in figure 1 to

(18)

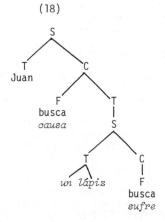

but to do so would obscure some functions in the syntax of Spanish as well
as that of the handful of other languages I have considered in this light,
so until some natural language data are shown definitely to contradict this
assumption, I shall continue to consider it an optional--if not obligatory--
universal of deep structure. One reason for taking this viewpoint is the
fact that, as we have seen, the Pat*ient* may be deleted, but only if the
Resu*latative* is present either in the Caus*ative Verb* or in the Top*ic* to
its right, which cogently argues that (18) is incorrect, since it permits
the equivalent of *Juan causa* _____ and *un lápiz sufre* _____ but does not
fill the blank with the necessary Resu*ltative*. Furthermore, although the
language could dispense with some sentences, such as (19) *?Un lápiz es
buscado (por Juan)*, any consideration of the syntax of the Spanish verb
must take this type of sentence (normally called the passive) into consideration. Since we have to account for the occurrence of the surface-

structure direct object of the transitive verb, on the one hand, and the "passive" sentence with the topicalized direct object on the other, and since they are properly sequenced to be considered as reciprocal matrices and embeddings, it is worthwhile considering whether *un lápiz*, occurring as the surface direct object of the transitive verb, is not a residual vestige of a "passive" sentence (20) *Un lápiz es* + *Topic*, where this *Topic* is in turn a residual vestige of an underlying active sentence (21) *Juan buscó* + *Topic*, etc. If we take this to be the case, we now have an explanation for several vexing problems of Spanish syntax. We are provided with the generative mechanism that produces the "unstressed" or clitic pronouns of the surface structure, as well as a means of generating the "stressed" or preposition-introduced pleonastic constituents as independent but related structures. Moreover, the fourth and fifth S nodes down from the initial Caus*ative* explain the existence of a second level of "passive", as well as to clarify the question of so-called reflexives as passives. They provide an explanation of "predicate adjectives" and "predicate nouns", and they relate the intransitive verb to the transitive verb. Suppose we now test these assertions against the empirical facts.

Some languages, such as English, employ the type of sentence generated in our diagram as S_2 for the majority of passive situations, although it is a well-known fact that some "passives" do not permit the optional agent constituent, which is evidence that (22) *The house was built of good material* is not derived from the same level as (23) *The house was built by skilled carpenters;* (22) must be derived from an S_4 level, farther away from the Caus*ative*, and just one level above the true Pass*ive*. English and Spanish differ considerably in the employment of the true Pass*ive*, a circumstance which is evident if we compare some sentences of English to their Spanish paraphrases. (24) *The dishes are washing* would be satisfactory only if the washing is being done automatically, as by a machine. If there are people washing the dishes, only (25) *The dishes are being washed* will do. Spanish, on the other hand, uses (26) *Se lavan los platos* in either case. If the function of the people is considered instrumental, then Spanish and English do not differ: (27) *La casa se llenaba de gente;* (28) *The house was filling with people* (not: *The house was being filled BY PEOPLE.*) So we see that what one is led to suspect about the several levels of passivity from the conditions in English becomes very clear and necessary to an understanding of Spanish sentence levels. Spanish has the S_2 type passives, such as (29) *El gato fue mordido (por el perro),* the S_4 type, such as (30) *El agua está agotada,* and the S_5 type, such as (31) *Se conoce que él es amigo suyo.*

There is more to be said about these passives, about the relationship between passives and intransitives, and about the similarity of the adjective to the passive, but these matters must wait to be elaborated when we come to appropriate examples. First we must examine some more trees, to see what other constituents or functions there might be. In figure 2 we find a tree with a human Caus*ative* Agent as in figure 1, but this time the Pat*ient* Topic is human rather than inanimate. Nevertheless,

the functions are similar: Causative, Patient, and Resultative, producing
such sentences as (32) El escritor (lo) asustó (al público), (33) El
público fue asustado (por el escritor), (34) El público está asustado, (35)
El público se asustó, (36) El escritor le causó un asusto al público, (37)
El público sufrió un asusto del escritor, (38) Un asusto fue sufridó del
público, (39) Un asusto se sufrio, (40) Se lo asusto al público. The tree
in figure 3 is almost identical to that of figure 2, except that the Agent
of figure 2 is replaced by an instrument, or so at least it appears at first.
Sentences (32)-(40) are all possible for figure 3, with periódico substituted
for escritor, but there is one sentence that can be generated only when
the Topic is an Agent: (41) El escritor asustó al público con el periódico.
This suggests that even though no Agent appears in figure 3 we must assume
the existence of a higher Causative sentence with an Agent, deleted in the
surface structure. If we move on now to figure 4 we encounter a tree similar
to that of figure 1, except that the global classes Causative and Patient
are separated by a new class, labelled Benefactive. This new class moti-
vates such sentences as (42) Juan le busca un lápiz $\left\{\begin{smallmatrix}a\\para\end{smallmatrix}\right\}$ Carlos, (43)
?Carlos es buscado un lápiz por Juan, (44) Se le busca un lápiz $\left\{\begin{smallmatrix}a\\para\end{smallmatrix}\right\}$
Carlos, etc.
     If we put these all together now as in figure 5, we note that the causa-
tivity of the highest S transfers through. Thus the Passive Sentence
(45) Enrique construyó is Passive only insofar as it reflects the benefi-
cence of the Causative. It also reflects the causativity of the Causative,
as do the Instrumental Passive and Patient Passive. This may seem an
excessively long series of function classes, and perhaps it is, but there
is considerable motivation for accepting it. There are also some classes
not present in this diagram which perhaps should be, such as Transfer,
but since the evidence for these is not as compelling as the evidence for
the classes of figure 5, it is better not to attempt to include them,
at least until we have had greater opportunity to study them.
     Another interesting phenomenon is clarified by sentences of the type
seen in figure 6. Many verbs of this sort spawn a new active verb from
their passives, which remain passive in their meanings. (46) ?Juan fue
dado un regalo has a meaning identical to (47) Juan recibió un regalo.
(48) Carlos fue perseguido por Enrique is the same as (49) Carlos huyó
de Enrique. This explains how the speaker is able to reconstruct the order
of events instantaneously and with ease: he merely converts recibió or
huyó into the underlying passive and then reads back to the Causative.
     In figure 7 we see how the sense verbs begin as Causatives of perception
whose Passives state the conditions that are perceived   Figure 8 illustrates the fact that even intransitive verbs of the surface structure
must be regarded as having Causatives dominating them in the deep
structure, and that they must be understood to dominate Resultatives.
This fact helps to clarify the evident kinship in Spanish of surface-
structure reflexives and intransitives, but it requires some further
elucidation, since there are reflexives in Spanish that are truly reflexive whose forms do not differ from those of the Passives masquerading
as reflexives. For example, (50) María le lava las manos al niñito,

a Causative sentence, has the same deep structure as (51) *María se lava
las manos (*a María)*, equally Causative, and we therefore do not wish
to confuse such legitimate cases of reflexivization with the pseudo cases.
If we examine such sentences as (52) *El navío se hunde* or (53) *El señor se
cae*, it is evident that they are not Causatives themselves, but are Passives dominated by Causatives. *Hundir* without the pronoun does indeed have
a Causative function, and although *caer* does not happen usually to be used
as a Causative, The underlying need for Causatives is filled by such
verbs as *derribar, derrocar, precipitar*. This is in fact an example of
the sort of lexical irregularity common to all languages, and it illustrates
the problem speakers often encounter when their intuitive grasp of deep
structure tells them that they need the Causative of a common Patient,
or *vice versa*, but are unsure which of several verbs of related meaning
to use in order to fill in the accidental gap of the defective verb. In
other words, while the native speaker always knows intuitively the functional level and the semantic content that a verb should have, he is not
always certain that he knows such a verb. We might add, in passing, that
since Spanish seems to have more verbs which are not defective than some
other languages, such as English, it is extremely common to encounter the
passivized Causatives, such as *derribarse, derrocarse, precipitarse,
encontrarse, matarse*, etc., in environments where their ambiguity with the
reflexive function--identical in surface form--is high.

Figure 9 illustrates the source of surface-structure adjectives. It
is in the nature of adjectives to be defective on the Causative level, although this defectiveness is often compensated by the creation of such
adjectivally derived Causatives as *ensuciar, aclarar, acomodar*, and so
on. Another evidence of the underlying Causative is the use of pro-verbs,
such as in (54) *Juan se pone nervioso*, where *se pone* is susceptible to
either of two interpretations, depending on whether we read the deep
structure of the pro-verb as Causative or Passive. We must, however, assume
that the deep structure contains a Causative Verb which for convenience
we render here as *nerviosar*, and this leads to a further question, which
is how this Verb differs from other Causative Verbs. The answer is that
the Resultative of the adjectival Causative is a state rather than a function, and that this is reflected in the Passive. Thus, in place of (55)
*Juan $\begin{Bmatrix} es \\ está \end{Bmatrix}$ *nerviosado*, we get (56) *Juan* $\begin{Bmatrix} es \\ está \end{Bmatrix}$ *nervioso*, by simply
marking the Passive as -Function. In those cases where a Causative form
of the adjective is present in the surface structure, such as *ensuciar*,
the +Function option will determine whether the form that emerges in the
Passive is *ensuciado* or *sucio*. Predicate nouns, such as *presidente* in
(57) *Mario es presidente*, are nominalizations of similar Causative adjectives. That is, (57) results from a nominalization or -Function option
applied to (58) **alguien presidentó Mario* at the Passive stage, getting
(57) in place of (59) **Mario es presidentado*.

Although this account has scarcely scratched the surface, the limita-
tions of space demand that we bring it to a close. Since the subject of
this paper has been the functions and states, and since these are so
intimately concerned with the Topic classes, there is a great deal about

the *Verb* that has not been discussed. These matters will have to remain
unattended to for the present, even in the list of tentative rules below.
Another extremely important matter has been barely mentioned in passing,
which is the predications involving -- *Verb Functives,* particularly those
that are traditionally considered conjoinings. All we can do for the
present is assert that a complete account of the deep structure of Spanish
must account for all adjunctive classes as well as all dominated classes,
and that a projected more complete study will give each of these matters
its share of consideration.

The following set of rules is tentative and merely intended to illustrate how the tree in figure 5 is generated. Many of the labels caused
me hours of deliberation and were ultimately chosen not as the perfect
representation but as the most appropriate term I could come up with, given
my limited understanding of some of the functions observed. It must be
added that no attempt was made here to include the category symbols for
such sentence types as Interrogatives, Emphatics, Negatives, and the
like, not because of any major difficulty imposed by such categories,
but simply in the interest of clarity and brevity.

THE RULES

S ---> *Topic* + *Comment*

$T ---> S_{caus\ act_1}$

$S_{caus\ act_1} ---> T_{ag_1} + C_{caus\ act_1}$

$C_{caus\ act_1} ---> F + T_{caus\ inact_1}$

$T_{caus\ inact_1} ---> S_{caus\ inact_1}$

$S_{caus\ inact_1} ---> T_{ben_1} + C_{caus\ inact_1}$

$C_{caus\ inact_1} ---> F + T_{caus\ act_2}$

$T_{caus\ act_2} ---> S_{caus\ act_2}$

$S_{caus\ act_2} --->T_{ag_2} + C_{caus\ act_2}$

$C_{caus\ act_2} ---> F + T_{caus\ inact_2}$

$T_{caus\ inact_2} \dashrightarrow S_{caus\ inact_2}$

$S_{caus\ inact_2} \dashrightarrow T_{ben_2} + C_{caus\ inact_2}$

$C_{caus\ inact_2} \dashrightarrow F + T_{ben\ pass\ (caus\ act)_1}$

$T_{ben\ pass\ (caus\ act)_1} \dashrightarrow S_{ben\ pass\ (caus\ act)_1}$

$S_{ben\ pass\ (caus\ act)_1} \dashrightarrow T_{ben\ ag} + C_{ben\ pass\ (caus\ act)_1}$

$C_{ben\ pass\ (caus\ act)_1} \dashrightarrow F + T_{inst\ inact_1}$

$T_{inst\ inact_1} \dashrightarrow S_{inst\ inact_1}$

$S_{inst\ inact_1} \dashrightarrow T_{inst_1} + C_{inst\ inact_1}$

$C_{inst\ inact_1} \dashrightarrow F + T_{ben\ pass\ (caus\ act)_2}$

$T_{ben\ pass\ (caus\ act)_2} \dashrightarrow S_{ben\ pass\ (caus\ act)_2}$

$S_{ben\ pass\ (caus\ act)_2} \dashrightarrow T_{ben\ ag_2} + C_{ben\ pass\ (caus\ act)_2}$

$C_{ben\ pass\ (caus\ act)_2} \dashrightarrow F + T_{inst\ inact_2}$

$T_{inst\ inact_2} \dashrightarrow S_{inst\ inac_2}$

$S_{inst\ inact_2} \dashrightarrow T_{inst_2} + C_{inst\ inact_2}$

$C_{inst\ inact_2} \dashrightarrow F + T_{inst\ pass\ (caus\ act)_1}$

$T_{inst\ pass\ (caus\ act)_1} \dashrightarrow S_{inst\ pass\ (caus\ act)_1}$

$S_{inst\ pass\ (caus\ act)_1}$ ---> $T_{inst\ ag_1}$ + $C_{inst\ pass\ (cause\ act)_1}$

$C_{inst\ pass\ (caus\ act)_1}$ ---> F + $T_{pat\ inact_1}$

$T_{pat\ inact_1}$ ---> $S_{pat\ inact_1}$

$S_{pat\ inact_1}$ ---> T_{pat_1} + $C_{pat\ inact_1}$

$C_{pat\ inact_1}$ ---> F + $T_{inst\ pass\ (caus\ act)_2}$

$T_{inst\ pass\ (caus\ act)_2}$ ---> $S_{inst\ pass\ (caus\ act)_2}$

$S_{inst\ pass\ (caus\ act)_2}$ ---> $T_{inst\ ag_2}$ + $C_{inst\ pass\ (caus\ act)_2}$

$C_{inst\ pass\ (caus\ act)_2}$ ---> F + $T_{pat\ inact_2}$

$T_{pat\ inact_2}$ ---> $S_{pat\ inact_2}$

$S_{pat\ inact_2}$ ---> T_{pat_2} + $C_{pat\ inact_2}$

$C_{pat\ inact_2}$ ---> F + $T_{pat\ pass\ (caus\ act)_1}$

$T_{pat\ pass\ (caus\ act)_1}$ ---> $S_{pat\ pass\ (caus\ act)_1}$

$S_{pat\ pass\ (caus\ act)_1}$ --->$T_{pat\ ag_1}$ + $C_{pat\ pass\ (caus\ act)_1}$

$C_{pat\ pass\ (caus\ act)_1}$ ---> F + $T_{res\ inact_1}$

$T_{res\ inact_1}$ ---> $S_{res\ inact_1}$

$S_{res\ inact_1}$ ---> T_{res_1} + $C_{res\ inact_1}$

$$C_{res\ inact_1} \dashrightarrow F + T_{pat\ pass\ (caus\ act)_2}$$

$$T_{pat\ pass\ (caus\ act)_2} \dashrightarrow S_{pat\ pass\ (caus\ act)_2}$$

$$S_{pat\ pass\ (caus\ act)_2} \dashrightarrow T_{pat\ ag_2} + C_{pat\ (caus\ act)_2}$$

$$C_{pat\ (caus\ act)_2} \dashrightarrow F + T_{res\ inact_2}$$

$$T_{res\ inact_2} \dashrightarrow S_{res\ inact_2}$$

$$S_{res\ inact_2} \dashrightarrow T_{res_2} + C_{res\ inact_2}$$

$$C_{res\ inact_2} \dashrightarrow F + T_{res\ pass}$$

$$T_{res\ pass} \dashrightarrow S_{res\ pass}$$

$$S_{res\ pass} \dashrightarrow T_{res} + C_{res\ pass}$$

$$C_{res\ pass} \dashrightarrow F$$

CONCLUSIONS

In this paper I have made the claim that all verbs in Spanish, including those that appear in the surface structure as adjectives, predicate nouns, or intransitives, must be considered to be dominated by a Causative level. I have offered some empirical evidence in an attempt to support this claim. It is further claimed that certain classes of *Verbs*, such as verbs of sense, have a mirror-image Pass*ive* form that is ordinarily thought of as an intransitive verb, such as *oler* in (60) *Este cuarto huele mal*. In regard to such classic problems as pleonastic pronouns, it is my claim, for which I have sought to offer some supporting evidence, that the answer lies in accepting the clitics as vestiges of the Pat*ient* and/ or the Ben*efactive Topics,* and the prepositionally introduced constituents as independent but related adjuncts (*Comments*) dominated by a higher S. A similar explanation is given for the traditional passive, the agent of which is optionally introduced by a preposition. Although space has not permitted coverage of complements, they too can be accounted for by accepting the above notion of the deep structure of Spanish.

Finally, it must be stated that although this is a sincere attempt to render more meaningful certain syntactic relationships, it is not motivated by any desire to innovate *per se*, and I will consider the effort worthwhile if it leads to nothing more fruitful than an enlightening refutation.

Figure 1.

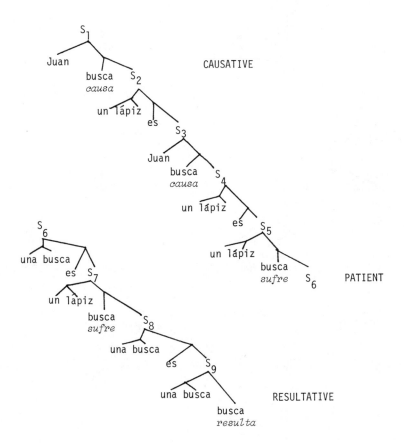

Figure 2.

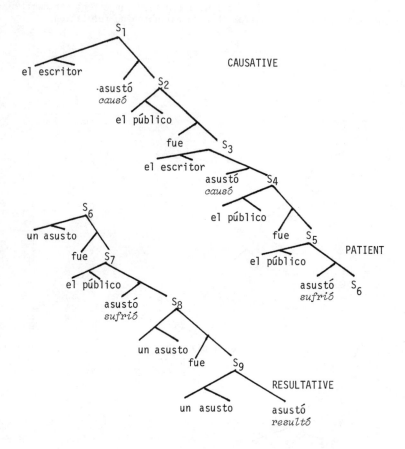

Figure 3.

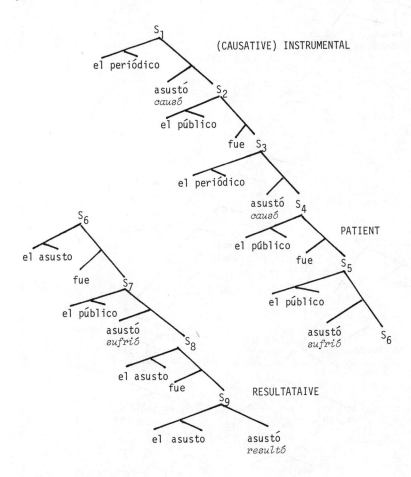

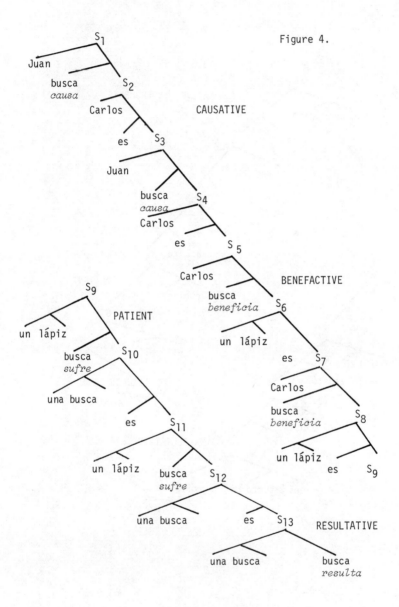

Figure 4.

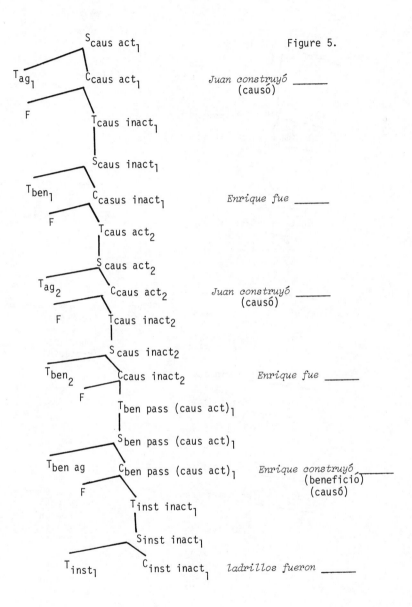

Figure 5.

$S_{caus\ act_1}$

T_{ag_1} $C_{caus\ act_1}$ *Juan construyó* _____
(causó)

F $T_{caus\ inact_1}$

$S_{caus\ inact_1}$

T_{ben_1} $C_{casus\ inact_1}$ *Enrique fue* _____

F $T_{caus\ act_2}$

$S_{caus\ act_2}$

T_{ag_2} $C_{caus\ act_2}$ *Juan construyó* _____
(causó)

F $T_{caus\ inact_2}$

$S_{caus\ inact_2}$

T_{ben_2} $C_{caus\ inact_2}$ *Enrique fue* _____

F $T_{ben\ pass\ (caus\ act)_1}$

$S_{ben\ pass\ (caus\ act)_1}$

$T_{ben\ ag}$ $C_{ben\ pass\ (caus\ act)_1}$ *Enrique construyó* _____
(beneficio)
(causó)

F $T_{inst\ inact_1}$

$S_{inst\ inact_1}$

T_{inst_1} $C_{inst\ inact_1}$ *ladrillos fueron* _____

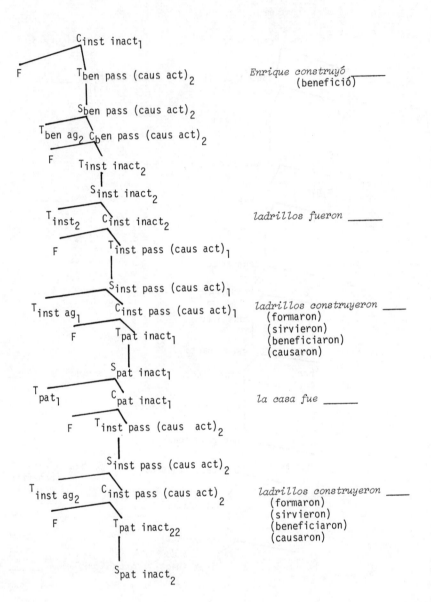

$C_{inst\ inact_1}$

F $T_{ben\ pass\ (caus\ act)_2}$

Enrique construyó ____
(benefició)

$S_{ben\ pass\ (caus\ act)_2}$

$T_{ben\ ag_2}$ $C_{ben\ pass\ (caus\ act)_2}$

F $T_{inst\ inact_2}$

$S_{inst\ inact_2}$

T_{inst_2} $C_{inst\ inact_2}$

ladrillos fueron ____

F $T_{inst\ pass\ (caus\ act)_1}$

$S_{inst\ pass\ (caus\ act)_1}$

$T_{inst\ ag_1}$ $C_{inst\ pass\ (caus\ act)_1}$

ladrillos construyeron ____
(formaron)
(sirvieron)
(beneficiaron)
(causaron)

F $T_{pat\ inact_1}$

$S_{pat\ inact_1}$

T_{pat_1} $C_{pat\ inact_1}$

la casa fue ____

F $T_{inst\ pass\ (caus\ act)_2}$

$S_{inst\ pass\ (caus\ act)_2}$

$T_{inst\ ag_2}$ $C_{inst\ pass\ (caus\ act)_2}$

ladrillos construyeron ____
(formaron)
(sirvieron)
(beneficiaron)
(causaron)

F $T_{pat\ inact_{22}}$

$S_{pat\ inact_2}$

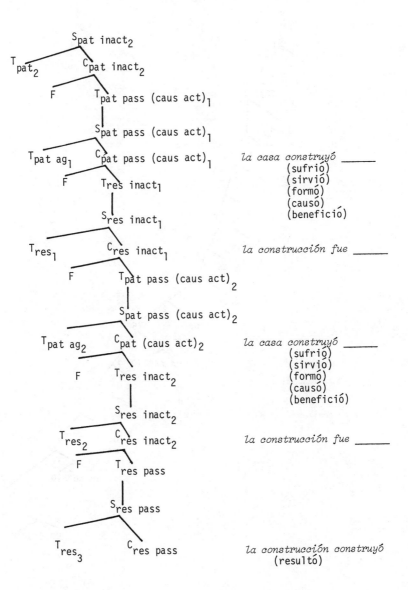

$S_{pat\ inact_2}$

T_{pat_2} $C_{pat\ inact_2}$

F $T_{pat\ pass\ (caus\ act)_1}$

$S_{pat\ pass\ (caus\ act)_1}$

$T_{pat\ ag_1}$ $C_{pat\ pass\ (caus\ act)_1}$ *la casa construyó* _____
                                        (sufrió)

F $T_{res\ inact_1}$ (sirvió)
                                          (formó)

$S_{res\ inact_1}$ (causó)
                       (beneficio)

T_{res_1} $C_{res\ inact_1}$ *la construcción fue* _____

F $T_{pat\ pass\ (caus\ act)_2}$

$S_{pat\ pass\ (caus\ act)_2}$

$T_{pat\ ag_2}$ $C_{pat\ (caus\ act)_2}$ *la casa construyó* _____
                                          (sufrio)

F $T_{res\ inact_2}$ (sirvio)
                                          (formó)

$S_{res\ inact_2}$ (causó)
                       (benefició)

T_{res_2} $C_{res\ inact_2}$ *la construcción fue* _____

F $T_{res\ pass}$

$S_{res\ pass}$

T_{res_3} $C_{res\ pass}$ *la construcción construyó*
                                            (resultó)

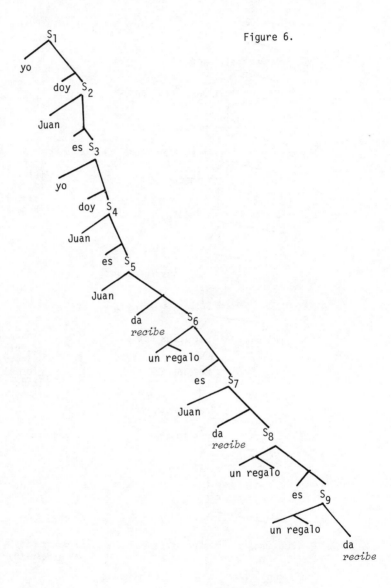

Figure 6.

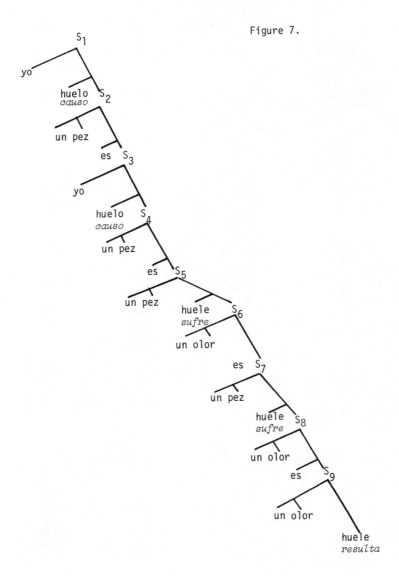

Figure 7.

Figure 8.

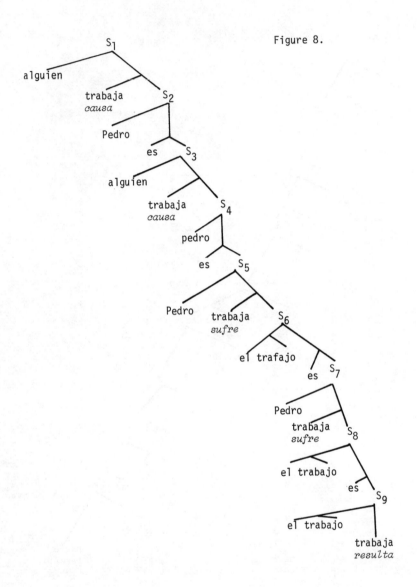

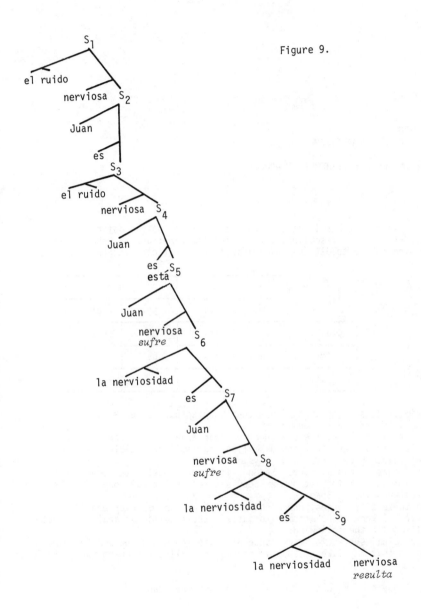

Figure 9.

MARTA LUJÁN
UNIVERSITY OF TEXAS AT AUSTIN

ON THE SO-CALLED NEUTER ARTICLE IN SPANISH

Spanish is traditionally said to have three forms of the definite article: *el/los*, the masculine; *la/las*, the feminine; and *lo*, the neuter.[1] The follwing is the traditional classification of articles in Spanish.

(1)

	Def.		Indef.	
	sg.	pl.	sg.	pl.
masc.	el	los	un	unos
fem.	la	las	una	unas
neut.	lo	---	---	----

The aim of this paper is to argue that Spanish has no neuter article, but that *lo* is instead a pronoun.

There is, in fact, little reason other than tradition to consider *lo* an article. It differs from the masculine and feminine articles, *el* and *la*, in at least three conspicuous ways.

First *lo* has no plural form. Second, it has no indefinite counterpart. Third, and most striking, it never occurs before a lexical noun, for there are no neuter nouns in Spanish.

Given these differences, one might well ask why *lo* was ever considered an article. I know of no attempt to justify the traditional analysis. But we might surmise the following.

The principal syntactic resemblance of *lo* to the masculine and feminine articles is that *lo*, like *el* and *la*, stands initially in noun-phrases like (2) - (4)

(2)   el bueno[2] (he who is good)   (the good one, masc.)

(3) la buena   (she who is good) (the good one, fem.)

(4) lo bueno   (that which is good)

These noun-phrases are said to contain "substantivized" adjectives; that is, their heads are adjectives which are functioning as nouns. Thus, *"bueno"* in (4) is considered an abstract noun of neuter gender, and, therefore, *lo* is its determiner, the neuter definite article.

If this reconstruction of the traditionalist's reasoning is correct, then his assertion that *lo* is an article rests heavily on the assumption that the so-called substantivized adjectives are, in fact, nouns. But if it could be shown that they are not, then there would be virtually no reason to consider *lo* an article. Moreover, one would be led to suspect that *el* and *la* in (2) and (3) are not articles, either.

There are, in fact, at least three arguments that substantivized adjectives, like *"bueno"*, are not nouns.

The first argument stems from a rule that changes singular feminine articles to their masculine counterparts before nouns that begin with stressed *a*.

(5) *la ala   (the wing)
     el ala

(6) *la ama   (the housekeeper)
     el ama

This rule applies only before nouns; when *la* precedes a modifier that begins with stressed *a*, as in (7) and (8), it does not change to *el*:

(7) la ágil ala   (the agile wing)
     *el ágil ala

(8) la alta ama   (the tall housekeeper)
     *el alta ama

Clearly, if substantivized adjectives are nouns, then this rule should change *la* to *el* before substantivized adjectives which begin with stressed *a* like *"alta"* (tall) and *"árida"* (arid), in (9) and (10).

(9) la alta   (the tall one, fem.)
     *el alta

(10) la árida (the arid one, fem.)
     *el árida

Evidently, the rule does not apply; and this fact, therefore, argues that substantivized adjectives are not nouns.

A second argument concerns question-words. Consider the following sentences:

(11) Compré *el material*. (I bought the material)

(12) Compré *el bueno*. (I bought the good one, (masc.))

"*Qué*" (what) is the appropriate word to ask for the italicized phrase of (11), but not that of (12), as can be seen in (13) and (14), respectively.

(13) Qué compraste? - Compré *el material*.
(*What* did you buy? - I bought *the material*.)

(14) *Qué compraste? - Compré *el bueno*.
(*What* did you buy? - I bought *the good one*, (masc.))

The italicized phrase "*el bueno*" of (12) requires, instead, the question-word "*cuál*". That is, it requires the same question-word as the modifier "*bueno*" in (15) does. Compare (15) and (16) below:

(15) *Cuál* material compraste? - Compré *el* material *bueno*.
(*Which* material did you buy? - I bought *the good* material.)

(16) *Cuál* compraste? - Compré *el bueno*.
(*Which one* did you buy? - I bought *the good one*, (masc.))

That phrases containing substantivized adjectives require a question-word related to modifiers and are incompatible with the question-word appropriate to phrases that contain nouns, strongly suggests that substantivized adjectives are not nouns.
A third argument is to be found in the fact that nouns are not readily modified by adverbs, as (17) below illustrates. But substantivized adjectives, like any ordinary adjective, admit a large variety of modifying adverbs, such as, "*muy*" (very) and "*extremadamente*" (extremely) in (18) and (19).

(17) *el extremadamente libro (the extremely book)

(18) el muy bueno (the very good one, masc.)

(19) lo extremadamente bueno (that which is extremely good)

It seems clear that if "*bueno*" above were a noun it could not, like the noun "*libro*", be modified by an adverb.
The facts presented in these three arguments constitute persuasive evidence that the so-called substantivized adjectives do not function as nouns. But if they are not nouns, then the only reason for supposing that "*lo*" is an article has been undermined, and we have no reason to consider it so. Moreover, there is compelling evidence that it is not.

In the first place, consider a class of verbs in Spanish like "proveer de", verbs that govern prepositions. A verb of this class provides a clear diagnostic frame for articles, because when its preposition is present, the object of the verb cannot be preceded by a determiner.[3] Thus, we have (20) but not (21):

(20) Me proveyó de libro. (He provided me with (a) book.)

(21) *Me proveyó de el libro   (He provided me with the book)
      *Me proveyó de un libro   (He provided me with a book)
      *Me proveyó de su libro   (He provided me with his book)
      *Me proveyó de ese libro (He provided me with that book)

On the other hand, when a determiner is present the preposition must be deleted, as in (22).

(22) Me proveyó el libro
      Me proveyó un libro
      Me proveyó su libro
      Me proveyó ese libro

Obviously, then, articles cannot co-occur with the associated preposition in the object of a verb like *"proveer."* But *"lo"* is perfectly grammatical when preceded by such a preposition, as (23) illustrates, a fact which indicates that *"lo"* cannot be an article.

(23) Me proveyó de lo necesario. (He provided me with what was necessary.)

A second construction in which articles cannot occur, but *"lo"* can, is that where the preposition *"con"* (with) and *"sin"* (without) introduce a prepositional phrase that functions as a manner adverbial, as in the sentences that follow.

(24) Peleó *con coraje.* (He fought with courage.)

(25) Vive *sin lujo.* (He lives without luxury.)

In such adverbial phrases, the noun cannot take a determiner,[4] so the various examples that follow are clearly ungrammatical.

(26) *Peleó *con* el *coraje.* (*He fought with the courage.)
      *Peleó *con* su *coraje.* (*He fought with his courage.)

(27) *Vive *sin* el *lujo.* (*He lives without the luxury.)
      *Vive *sin* su *lujo.* (*He lives without his luxury.)

But, *"lo"* is readily accepted in such adverbial phrases, as can be seen in the following examples, where its deletion would produce an ungrammatical sentence.

(28)   Vive *con lo necesario*.   (He lives with what is necessary)

(29)   *Vive *con necessario*.

But if *"lo"* can freely occur where articles cannot, then we are led to conclude that it is not an article.

Articles are, furthermore, barred from noun-phrases where a singular noun is constructed with *"todo"* (every). Thus we have (30) but not (31). *"Lo,"* however, can be preceded by *"todo"* as in (32).[5]

(30)   Todo hombre debe trabajar.   (Every man must work)

(31)   *Todo el hombre debe trabajar.

(32)   Todo lo necesario no siempre es bueno.   (Everything that is necessary is not always good)

There are, then, at least three instances in which the behavior of *"lo"* is exactly the opposite of that which we expect of an article.[6] In other words, the evidence strongly suggests that *lo* is not an article.

So far it can be seen (1) that there is no reason to believe that *lo* is an article, and (2) that there is good reason to believe that it is not. If these statements are correct, then a new analysis of *lo* must be found.

Such an analysis is suggested by a number of the observations advanced before, in which the substantivized adjectives like "bueno" of (2) - (4) behave like ordinary adjectives: they are modified by adverbs, they must be questioned as if they were modifiers and so forth. Such observations suggest that in phrases like (2) - (4), the so-called substantivized adjective is only an ordinary predicate adjective. But if this is so, then the adjective must be modifying something and the supposed articles *"el"*, *"la"*, and *"lo"* are conspicuous candidates, as the Spanish grammarian Andrés Bello noted more than a century ago with respect to (4). Regarding *"lo"* in construction with adjectives, he considers *"lo"* to be substantive in nature and thus the head of such phrases (Bello-Cuervo, 1958:101).

Following this lead, I propose that *"lo"* in *"lo bueno"* is a pronoun and that rather than the adjective being the head and *lo* a determiner, as traditionally analyzed, *"lo"* is the head and the adjective is its modifier. The source of the modifier is an underlying relative clause, so that *"lo bueno"* is directly related to the unreduced phrase *"lo que es bueno"*.

Since *"el bueno"* and *"la buena"* appear to have a similar structure (notice that they, too, are related to unreduced phrases, *"el que es bueno"*, *"la que es buena"*, respectively), we may extend our hypothesis to include them as well. That is, we hypothesize that *"el* and *"la"* are also pronouns and heads of these constructions and that the modifying adjective is no-thing more than the remnant of a reduced relative clause.

But *"el bueno"* and *"la buena"* are ambiguous (see glosses of (2) and (3) on p.   ) and must be derived from another deep structure source, different

from the one they share with *lo*-phrases, one in which *el* and *la* are determiners.[7] This deep structure will be discussed later in this paper.

As stated previously, *"lo bueno"*, *"el bueno"* and *"la buena"*, and their
corresponding unreduced paraphrases noted above, share an underlying structure roughly of the following form:

(33)
$$\left[_{NP} \begin{bmatrix} +N \\ +PRO \end{bmatrix} \left[_{S} \; que \frown Aux \frown Cop \frown Adj \; Phrase \; \right]_{S} \right]_{NP}$$

Phrases (2)-(4) are derived from (33) by way of Relative Clause Reduction, and are thus transformationally related to (34)-(36) below.

(34) el que es bueno (he who is good)

(35) la que es buena (she who is good)

(36) lo que es bueno (that which is good)

I will point out several relevant aspects pertinent to the justification
of this analysis.

First it can be argued that treating *"lo"* as a pronoun simplifies the
system of articles in Spanish without complicating the pronominal system
at all, for it can be shown that *"lo"* is merely the weakened form of the
well-known pronoun *"ello"* (it), which commonly stands for sentential
nominals.[8] Tradition already treats certain occurrences of *"lo"* as the
accusative form of *"ello"*. For instance, the nominative *"ello"* in (37)
is traditionally related to the accusative *"lo"* in (38).

(37) Les di*j*e *que Juan estaba loco* aunque sabia que *ello* no los
      preocuparia. (I told them *that John was crazy* though I knew
      it would not worry them.)

(38) Les dije *que Juan estaba loco*, pero no me *lo* creyeron.
      (I told them *that John was crazy* but they did not believe
      it.)

Moreover, that the *"lo"* that precedes adjectives is one and the same
"ello" (or *"lo"*) in the previous examples is further confirmed by the fact
that *"ello"*, unlike other third-person pronouns and *like* the so-called
neuter article, has no plural. Notice that in Spanish a pronoun that
refers to two or more coordinated singular noun phrases must be plural,
as shown in (39). However, if another nominal clause is added to sentence
(38), the pronoun *lo* remains singular, as in (40).

(39) *La mesa y la silla las* compré yo. (As for *the table and the*
      *La mesa y la silla la compré yo.   *chair*, I bought *them*.)

(40) Les dije *que Juan estaba loco y que se había escapado,* pero no me
      lo creyeron. (I told them *that John was crazy* and *that he had
      escaped* but they did not believe *it.*)

Still another piece of evidence of the basic identity of our *"lo"* and
"ello" is illustrated in (41) and (42) where the two forms are in complementary distribution: *"lo",* but not *"ello",* can co-occur with a modifier,
as in (41); while *"ello",* but not *"lo",* can stand alone, as in (42).

(41) Lo *que es bueno* no es obvio. (That which is good is not obvious.)
      *Ello *que es bueno* no es obvio.

(42) Ello no es obvio. (That is not obvious.)
      *Lo no es obvio.

But this alternation is not a special feature of this pronoun *"ello".*
It also obtains in the third-person pronouns *"él"* (he) and *"ella"* (she).
In (43) and (44) is illustrated the alternation of the pronoun *"ella"*
and its weakened form *"la".*

(43) Ella se casará por dinero. (She will marry for money.)
      *La se casará por dinero.

(44) La *que es ambiciosa* se casa por dinero.[9]
      *Ella *que es ambiciosa* se casa por dinero.
      (She who is ambitious marries for money.)

The fact that this alternation of strong and weak forms also takes place
in the personal pronouns lends support to the hypothesis that the wrongly
called neuter article *"lo"* is simply a weakened form of the pronoun *"ello"*
and that *"el"* and *"la"* of (2) and (3) are, in one reading, weakened forms
of the personal pronouns *"él"* and *"ella",* respectively.

The reduction of these pronouns is a consequence of the reduction of
their stress in the context immediately preceding a restrictive clause.[10]
The reduction rule deletes the first syllable of the bisyllabic forms when
unstressed.

(45) Pronoun reduction:

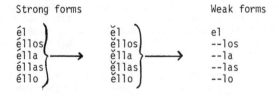

Strong forms		Weak forms
él	ĕl	el
éllos	ĕllos	--los
élla	ĕlla	--la
éllas	ĕllas	--las
éllo	ĕllo	--lo

An important consequence of our analysis of *"lo"* as a pronoun is that it eradicates the anomaly of having a three-way gender distinction in the forms of the definite article when there is only a two-way distinction in nouns. There is no neuter gender in Spanish. Nouns are either masculine or feminine and agreement is made observing this binary distinction. That the neuter gender is non-existent is obvious when one considers sentential nominals. They can take the definite article and they are neither masculine nor feminine. If *"lo"* were the neuter form of the definite article, then one ought to expect this to be the determiner for sentential nominals. But this is not the case. These nominals take the masculine definite article:

(46)   El *que Ana lo sepa* no me sorprende.
       *Lo *que Ana lo sepa* no me sorprende.
       (*That Ann knows* it does not surprise me.)

(47)   El *tener amigos* nunca daña.
       *Lo *tener amigos* nunca daña.
       (*Having friends* is never harmful.)

Precisely because there is no neuter gender, masculine functions as the unmarked member of the masculine-feminine opposition and thus is present when gender distinctions are neutralized.

Traditional grammarians, quite misleadingly, talk about a neuter gender in the pronominal system. These assertions are erroneous, too. The distinction which in fact obtains among the pronouns is [+HUMAN] versus [-HUMAN], or perhaps [+ANIMATE] versus [-ANIMATE]. Semitic languages, which have masculine and feminine gender, and languages that lack gender, such as Finnish or English, make use of a similar distinction in their pronouns. In Spanish *"ello"* is [-HUMAN] as opposed to *"él"* and *"ella"* which is [+HUMAN], masculine and feminine, respectively. This is why the latter cannot refer to the italicized phrases in (48) and (49) even when these phrases are masculine and feminine, respectively.

(48)   Compré *este libro* porque *él me interesaba.
       (I bought *this book* because he interested me.)

(49)   Modifiqué *esta mesa* porque *ella tenía tres patas.
       (I modified *this table* because she had three legs.)

Co-referentiality in these sentences may be indicated either by leaving the pronoun position vacant or by filling it with the phrase *"el mismo/ la misma"* (the same one). *"ello"* cannot be used here because this pronoun must refer to a class of (abstract or concrete) elements and not to individual ones.[11]   This is also true for the demonstrative pronouns *"eso"*, *"esto"* and *"aquello"* which, like *"ello"*, are also [-HUMAN].

The correctness of the deep structure assumed to underlie one reading of the so-called substantivized adjectives, shown in (33), is corroborated by independent syntactic motivation. Consider the rule in (50), a rule that replaces a sequence of personal pronoun plus complementizer by the pronoun *"quien"*.

(50) *Quien*-replacement rule:

$$\begin{bmatrix} +HUM \\ +PRO \end{bmatrix} \frown que \quad =======> \quad quien$$

This rule provides strong motivation for keeping the italicized phrases of (51) and (52) distinct, for it is clear that only the structure that underlies (51), where "el" is a pronoun, can undergo the rule, as can be seen by comparing (53) and (54) below.

(51) *El que es bueno* merce ser premiado.   12
      (He who is good deserves to be rewarded.)

(52) *El que es bueno* es mayor que el malo.
      (The good one is older than the bad one.)

(53) *Quien es bueno* merece ser premiado.
      (He who is good deserves to be rewarded.)

(54) **Quien es bueno* es mayor que el malo.

It follows, then, that by assuming the deep structure (33) to underlie the subject NP of (51) we satisfactorily account for the fact that only the italicized phrase in (51) is transformationally related to a *"quien"* phrase. The italicized phrase of (52) lacks that paraphrase because it does not have the same underlying structure, and in particular because *"el"* in this phrase is the definite article.

The second deep structure analysis of substantivized adjectives, alluded to earlier, is one in which *"el/ los/ la/las"* are the forms of the definite article, a structure roughly of the following form:

(55)
$$\begin{bmatrix} Det \begin{bmatrix} UNO \\ +PRO \end{bmatrix}_S \begin{bmatrix} que \frown Aux \frown Cop \frown Adj\ Phrase \end{bmatrix}_S \end{bmatrix}_{NP}$$

This is the structure that underlies the phrases that follow, in the readings shown.

(56) el bueno   (the good one, masc.)

(57) la buena   (the good one, fem.)

(58) el que es bueno   (the one that is good, masc.)

(59) la que es buena   (the one that is good, fem.)

The bare adjectives in (56) and (57) result from application of Relative Clause Reduction. The derivation of the four phrases, on the other hand, includes the application of an obligatory rule that deletes the pronoun *"uno"* when preceded by a determiner. There are two reasons to believe that there is such a rule. First, notice that although we can have phrases with *"uno"*, as in (60),

(60) Conozco a *uno que es bueno.*
      (I know one that is good.)

the same phrase cannot be preceded by the definite article:

(61) Conozco *al* *uno que es bueno.*[13]

But (62), where "uno" is not present, is perfectly grammatical.

(62) Conozco *al que es bueno.*
      (I know the one that is good.)

Second, although this pronoun is never realized in the phrases in question, it must be assumed to be in their deep structures since it shows up under conditions of emphasis in contrastive contexts, where apparently the deletion rule does not apply, as in (63).

(63) Tenía dos hijos, el *uno* bueno y el otro malo.
      (He had two sons, the *one* good and the other bad.)

There are at least three pieces of evidence that shows that *"el"* and *"la"* of (56)-(59) are determiners, as specified in (55).
First, other determiners may occur before substantivized adjectives, as shown in (64).

(64) Preferimos la nueva.   (We prefer the new one.)
      Preferimos esta nueva.   (We prefer this new one.)
      Preferimos tu nueva.   (We prefer your new one.)

Second, these phrases cannot occur in the object of *"proveer"* (to provide) when the preposition *"de"* is present. Recall the incompatibility of this preposition with immediately following determiners. Thus, the ungrammaticality in (65) is due to the fact that the preposition *"de"* is followed by the definite article.

(65) Compré la cartera marrón y Juan me proveyó *de la negra.
      Compré la cartera marrón y Juan me proveyó la negra.

(I bought the brown purse and John provided me the black one.)

Finally, recall that determiners are also incompatible with *"todo"*. Thus, these phrases should be ungrammatical when preceded by *"todo"*. Consider our earlier examples (51) and (52). The former but not the latter was known to contain the pronoun *"él"* because it was related to a sentence that had a *"quien"*-phrase, namely (53). Sentence (52), on the other hand, cannot contain a pronoun since it has no paraphrase with a *"quien"*-phrase. It is precisely (52) that becomes ungrammatical if *"todo"* is added to it, as shown below.

(51) *El que es bueno* merece ser premiado.
(He who is good deserves to be rewarded.)

(52) *El que es bueno* es mayor que el malo.
(The good one is older than the bad one.)

(66) Todo el que es bueno merece ser premiado.
(Everyone who is good deserves to be rewarded.)

(67) *Todo el que es bueno es mayor que el malo.

This second analysis of substantivized adjectives is to be preferred over one which assumes the occurrence of a lexical noun which is deleted when preceded by an identical noun (see for instance, Langacker 1968), if only because such an analysis cannot account for equivalent phrases that occur regardless of the presence of an identical noun in the immediate context. The facts, moreover, indicate that if there is such a deletion process it must deal with noun phrases rather than with nouns. Observe that in the following sentence *"el fácil"* (the easy one) includes not just *"libro"* (book), but at least *"libro técnico"* (technical book).

(68) Leí *el libro técnico difícil* y Pedro leyó *el fácil*.
(I read *the difficult technical book* and Peter read *the easy one*.)

This fact accords with our analysis since *"uno"* stands for noun phrases. If we assume a pronominalization rule for sentences such as (68), whereby *"uno"* replaces an identical noun phrase, then our analysis allows the noun phrases that result from pronominalization and the ones that do not, to be treated alike by later rules in the process of becoming surface structures.

The arguments and conclusions presented so far concerning the grammatical status of *"lo"* and the homophonous forms of the pronouns and the definite article are true not just when they are constructed with adjectives but in phrases such as the following:

(69) lo que sigue   (that which follows)

(70) lo de María   (that which is Mary's)

Such instances of *"lo"* are also wrongly analyzed in traditional grammar as the neuter article.
Likewise, no distinction is made between the two readings of the ambiguous sentence in (71), which our analysis accounts for.

(71) *El que te dice la verdad* te estima.
(He who tells you the truth loves you.)
(The one who is telling the truth loves you.)

In its first reading (71) is a paraphrase of (72) and *"el"* must be analyzed as a pronoun. In its second reading it is the definite article.

(72) Quien te dice la verdad te estima.

CONCLUSIONS

In summary, then, I have argued first, that there is no justification for the traditional classification of *"lo"* as an article. Second, that there is compelling evidence that *"lo"* is not an article. Finally, that there is substantial evidence to support the hypothesis that *"lo"* is instead a pronoun, and that phrases traditionally analyzed as neuter article plus substantivized adjective are instead pronoun plus relative clause. Thus, I conclude that the evidence shows that the neuter article in Spanish does not exist.

NOTES

1. This research was supported in part by NSF Grant GS 2468. I am indebted to P. Stanley Peters for invaluable discussion of the arguments made in the paper, to Emmon Bach for his encouragement and comments on an earlier version, and to Philip B. Gough for his helpful suggestions regarding its style. This paper challenges the current notion that Spanish has a neuter article. Evidence is presented that *lo* in *lo bueno* is substantive in nature, as first suggested by Bello (1820), and thus is the head of such noun-phrases. We claim that *lo* is related to the pronoun *ello* and that the source of *lo*+ADJ phrases is pronoun plus relative clause. An account is also provided of hitherto poorly understood nominalizations, such as *el bueno*. These are ambiguous, their two deep structures being distinguished in that *el* is a pronoun in one, and the definite article in the other.
2. The examples throughout this paper are given in the singular for the purpose of simplifying the presentation, but the arguments and conclusions are intended to apply to plural noun phrases as well.

3. Except, of course, when the object is modified by a relative clause as in:

Me proveyó del libro *que necesitaba.*
(He provided me with the book that I needed.)

The presence of the article in this instance must be due to relativization since an article is possible after the preposition *only* when there is a relative clause. It is easy to show that the article in these cases does not occur in deep structure and it is added to the antecedent of a relative clause as a result of relativization. For arguments to this effect, see Perlmutter (1968), for they are also applicable in Spanish.

4. Here again a determiner is possible only in the presence of a relative clause, as in:

Peleó con *el* coraje *que da la lucha.*

5. It might be objected that determiners *do* occur in certain phrases with *"todo"* on the basis of instances such as:

Todo el café se vendió. (All the coffee was sold.)
Todas las sillas se vendieron. (All the chairs were sold.)

These phrases, however, must be distinguished from those of (30) and (32), for they clearly have different syntactic properties. First, notice that while determiners are prohibited in (30) and (32), in these phrases a determiner must be present, otherwise the sentence becomes ungrammatical, as illustrated below.

*Todo café se vendió.
*Todas sillas se vendieron.

Secondly, *"todo"* can be postposed in these phrases, as in:

El cafe todo se vendió.
Las sillas todas se vendieron.

But *"todo"* in (30) and (32) cannot be postposed without rendering the sentences ungrammatical:

(30)'*Hombre todo debe trabajar.

(32)'*Lo necesario todo no siempre es bueno.

6. For more evidence bearing on this point see my "Adjectives in Spanish", doctoral dissertation, University of Texas (1972), in preparation.
7. This is the only thing in which traditional grammarians were correct. Unfortunately, it is also the very thing that led them to the error of

considering the adjective preceded by the definite article a noun, and to extend that analysis to *"lo"*+ Adj.

8. *"Ello"* does not only stand for sentential nominals. For an exhaustive study of old and modern usage of this pronoun, see an article by Pedro Henriquez Ureña in Revista de Filología Hispanica I, num. 3, 1939, 209-30. Among many other examples, he cites the following:

> "Et fué por *ello* et tráxogelo todo" (Juan Manuel, Conde Lucanor)
> (And he went for it and brought it all)
> "Una pareja..., el transeúnte ..., un coche..., éste que me saluda, aquél que me llama la atención, el otro que parece mirarme, a cada momento rostros nuevos ..., todo *ello* exige una serie de adaptaciones," (Unamuno. Ensayos III, p. 169)

9. That *"la"* in this sentence is a pronoun and not the definite article is corroborated by the fact that it can be constructed with *"toda"*, as in:

> Toda la que es ambiciosa se casa por dinero.
> (Everyone (woman) who is ambitious marries for money.)

10. For details of the interaction of stress rule and transformations, see my "Adjectives in Spanish", ibid.

11. In some dialects, however, it might refer to individual elements. For more detail, see Henriquez Ureña, P. ibid.

12. This sentence is ambiguous. It also means "The good one deserves to be rewarded."

13. The definite article here is contracted with the preposition "a", i.e., *"al"* is *"a"* plus *"el"*. But (53) is unambiguous.

DANIEL A. DINNSEN
UNIVERSITY OF TEXAS AT AUSTIN

ADDITIONAL CONSTRAINTS ON CLITIC ORDER IN SPANISH

0.   In his recent paper, "Surface Structure Constraints in Syntax,"
David Perlmutter (1970) argues for the necessity of surface structure
constraints on clitic pronoun sequences in Spanish.* In addition, he
claims that surface structure constraints are of two kinds, global and
nonglobal, and that Spanish provides evidence for the necessity of such
a distinction.
      This paper denies the necessity of any distinction bewteen global
and nonglobal constraints for Spanish. It can be shown that it is possible to formulate precise surface structure constraints all of one kind -
equally general, simple and consistent in notation - that will correctly
characterize the set of data in Spanish noted by Perlmutter. By broaden-
ing the scope of data beyond that considered by Perlmutter, the existence
of additional constraints becomes evident. These constraints may be
collapsed without loss of generality and stated as one constraint accounting for a much wider range of phenomena than could the constraints proposed by Perlmutter. Even if it could be shown that a global-nonglobal
distinction was necessary, I argue that the one constraint specifically
proposed by Perlmutter as a nonglobal constraint could not be nonglobal.
1.   Surface structure constraints are output conditions which the output
of the transformational component must satisfy. These constraints filter
out ungrammatical sentences that the transformational component for some
reason has failed to block. The necessity of surface structure constraints
is argued for convincingly by Perlmutter on the grounds that a number of
Spanish pronoun sequences in surface structure always result in ungrammatical sentences no matter which transformations applied to produce them.
He shows that the facts cannot be accounted for by restrictions on transformations or on deep structures. The following sentences should serve
as a partial list of evidence necessitating surface structure constraints:

    (21)   a.   Te escapaste.
                  'You escaped.'

    b. Te me escapaste.
       'You escaped from me.'

(22) a. Me escapé.
       'I escaped.'

    b. *Me te escapé.
       'I escaped from you.'

(31) a. Me le complicaron la vida a mi hija.
       'They complicated my daughter's life on me.'

    b. *Le me complicaron la vida a mi hija.
       'They complicated my daughter's life on me.'

(38) A Sarita se le permitió dormir toda la mañana, pero a mi no se
     me lo ha permitido.
     'Sarita was allowed to sleep all morning, but I wasn't allowed
     to.'

(39) a. *A mi se me permitió dormir toda la mañana,
       pero a Sarita no se le lo ha permitido.

    b. *A mi se me permitió dormir toda la mañana,
       pero a Sarita no se se lo ha permitido.

       'I was allowed to sleep all morning, but Sarita wasn't
       allowed to.'

    The proposed surface structure constraint for Spanish is expressed
in the following notation:[1]

(86) Output condition on clitic pronouns

        se   II   I   III

(86) is a constraint on the relative order of the morpheme *se* and the
object pronouns in terms of person. The notation of (86) is interpreted
in a positive sense in that it is a statement of the grammatical (as
opposed to the ungrammatical) pronoun sequences. Also, by virtue of the
positive interpretation, it follows automatically that a sequence of two
or more consecutive clitics from the same slot in the chart notation is ungrammatical. The clitics are strictly ordered; that is, the order is
transitive, irreflexive, and antisymmetric.
    Perlmutter demonstrates the insufficiency of (86) for some dialects
of Spanish by providing evidence from those dialects of ungrammatical
pronoun sequences not filtered out by (86). He correctly notes that the
inadequacy of (86) does not necessarily compromise the validity of the

constraint or the notation developed to express the constraint. However, if it could be shown that (86) incorrectly filtered out grammatical sequences of clitics (thus characterizing them as ungrammatical), then one could conclude that either the constraint or the notation is incorrect. It would be possible to argue against the notation specifically if, for example, it could be shown that the constraint must be interpreted negatively. It is not the intent of this paper in any sense to argue against the necessity of (86) or its notation. The scope of this paper will, however, focus on Perlmutter's solution to the inadequacy of (86) and the subsequent introduction of nonglobal constraints.

It is a more interesting question to ask whether, in the absence of any constraints on clitics other than (86) and (121), the grammars of Spanish and French will generate any ungrammatical sentences with clitic sequences which (86) and (121) do not filter out. If there is evidence that the ungrammaticality of these sentences is due to the clitic sequences they contain, and if the same clitic sequences are grammatical in other constructions, one can tentatively conclude that their ungrammaticality is due to construction-particular or *nonglobal constraints* on clitics. Such nonglobal constraints would be additional constraints, super-imposed on the *global constraints* (86) and (121), which set an upper limit on grammatical sequences of clitics in Spanish and French. [2]

The above excerpt roughly characterizes Perlmutter's intended dis-tinction between global and nonglobal constraints. That is, output condition (86) and presumably its notation and interpretation are consis-tent with global constraints. The peculiar nature of nonglobal constraints is emphasized by being 'construction-particular' and by being limited to filtering out ungrammatical sentences (1) not blocked by (86) and (2) whose ungrammaticality is due to the clitics they contain and (3) whose clitic sequence is grammatical in other constructions. Demonstrating the insufficiency of (86) simply involves providing a sentence with a clitic sequence that conforms to (86) but that is still ungrammatical. The ungrammaticality of the sentence being due to the clitics is evidenced if a sentence with the same meaning is grammatical in the corresponding strong form, i.e. if one of the clitics is expressed as a prepositional phrase. The construction-particular nature of nonglobal constraints would seem, at first glance, to be especially motivated if there were certain ungrammatical clitic sequences which are grammatical in other constructions. However, it should be noted that all that Perlmutter could possibly mean by 'construction-particular' is that certain sequences of clitics are ambiguous with regard to case specification. The fact that only these sequences of clitics are identical phonologically and syntacti-cally with regard to person seems, at best, accidental.
2. Perlmutter claims to have provided two examples of nonglobal con-straints necessitated by evidence from Spanish. For the sake of exposition,

I will consider the two examples in the reverse order. It is noted that for some dialects of Spanish, in addition to (86), there is a constraint which requires that the reflexive pronoun precede the nonreflexive dative of interest (Perlmutter 1970:231-2). Consider the following sentences:

(143) *Te me escapé.
      'I escaped from you.'

      *Te me acerque.
      'I approached (to) you.'

The order of clitics in these sentences corresponds to the order prescribed by output condition (86); however, the consequence of conforming to (86) is that the nonreflexive *te* incorrectly precedes the reflexive *me*. For this dialect, then, (86) is insufficient. The ungrammaticality being due to the clitics is clear since use of a corresponding strong form is grammatical, e.g. *'Me escapé de tí.'* The same sequence of clitics ('same' in Perlmutter's sense) is grammatical in other constructions:

(142) Te me escapaste.
      'You escaped from me.'

The conclusion that the ungrammaticality of (143) is due to a non-global constraint is, however, unnecessary. It is possible to formulate a constraint with the notation and interpretation of global constraint (86). A somewhat broader investigation of those dialects exhibiting the constraint noted above will show that there are additional constraints on clitics which, when considered together, will allow a more cohesive and general statement of the facts - facts which Perlmutter apparently did not consider. As the following sentences will illustrate, dative cannot follow accusative, benefactive cannot follow dative, and reflexive cannot follow any clitic pronoun:

DATIVE BEFORE ACCUSATIVE

(1)   Te me presentó.
       'He presented me to you

(2)   a. *Te me presentó.
       b. *Me te presentó.
           'He presented you to me.'

Since the order of the clitics in (1) conforms to (86) and since dative precedes accusative, the sentence is grammatical. Either order of clitics is ungrammatical in (2) when the second person *te* is specified as accusative. That is, even though the order of clitics in (2) a. does not violate (86), it is ungrammatical since accusative precedes dative; in (2) b. dative precedes accusative, but the order of pronouns characterized according to person violates the order specified by (86).

BENEFACTIVE BEFORE DATIVE

(3)   Te me escribió la carta.
          'He wrote the letter to me for you.'

(4)   Me le escribió la carta.
          'He wrote the letter to him for me.'

(5)   Te le escribió la carta.
          'He wrote the letter to him for you.'

(6) a. *Me le escribió la carta.
     b. *Le me escribió la carta.
        'He wrote the letter to me for him.'

(7) a. *Te me escribió la carta.
     b. *Me te escribió la carta.
        'He wrote the letter to you for me.'

(8) a. *Te le escribió la carta.
     b. *Le te escribió la carta.
        'He wrote the letter to you for him.'

In (3)-(5), benefactive precedes dative, and the clitic order does not violate (86). However, (6)-(8) are ungrammatical since either dative precedes benefactive or (86) is violated.

REFLEXIVE BEFORE BENEFACTIVE

(9)   Te me escribiste la carta.
          'You wrote the letter to yourself for me.'

(10) a. *Te me escribí la carta.
      b. *Me te escribí la carta.
         'I wrote the letter to myself for you.'

Since the order of the clitics in (9) does not violate (86) and since reflexive does not follow benefactive, the sentence is grammatical. Even though the order of clitics in (10) a. does not violate (86), the reflexive pronoun incorrectly follows another clitic. (10)b. is ungrammatical because it violates (86).

Since the grammatical order of clitics is transitive, irreflexive, and antisymmetric, it is possible to express the order as a surface structure constraint in the notation of (86). That is, the constraint responsible for filtering out ungrammatical sequences of clitics not filtered out by (86) would be characterized as follows:

(OO) Output condition on clitic pronouns

REFLEXIVE   BENEFACTIVE   DATIVE   ACCUSATIVE

The interpretation of (OO) is consistent with the notation of (86):
(OO) is a constraint on the relative order of clitics in terms of case
specifications and is a positive statement of the grammatical order of
clitics. Sentences with more than one clitic from a given column of the
chart will be ungrammatical. In terms of complexity, (OO) may even be
more general than (86). That is, (OO) is expressed entirely by case;
whereas, (86) requires a person specification for three clitics and a
phonological spelling for the morpheme *se*. If there is a distinction
between global and nonglobal constraints, the example noted by Perlmutter
does not motivate it.
3.   Perlmutter's second example of a nonglobal constraint also fails to
establish a distinction between global and nonglobal constraints. Furthermore, even if such a distinction were motivated, the constraint sketched
by Perlmutter could not be a nonglobal constraint. First, the existence
of a nonglobal constraint is argued for on the basis of the following
evidence:

(135) a.   *Me le recomendaron.
            'They recommended me to him.'

      b.   *Te le recomendaron.
            'They recommended you to him.'

(86) alone would not filter out the above sentences since the order
of clitics does not violate (86). Perlmutter demonstrates that the
ungrammaticality of (135) is due to the clitics since sentences in the
corresponding strong form are grammatical, and he points out that the
same sequence of clitics is grammatical in other constructions. Perlmutter
(1970:231) then states:

It is necessary to conclude that some nonglobal constraint
involving clitics is responsible for the ungrammaticality
of *(135).

The alleged nonglobal constraint is as follows:[3]

(140) If the direct object ... is first or second person, use of the
      clitic form of the indirect object results in an ungrammatical
      sentence.

Another fact of this dialect noted by Perlmutter is that speakers
do not accept sentences like:

(141) Te me recomendaron.
      'They recommended me to you.'
      'They recommended you to me.'

Excluding (141) from consideration temporarily, one could conclude
that the ungrammaticality of (135) is due to output condition (OO).
That is, since accusative precedes dative in (135) and since (OO) filters
out any sequence of clitics which violates the order 'dative before accusative' and since there is no evidence in this dialect that the additional constraints incorporated in (OO) do not hold, it is possible that (OO)
is the correct constraint. However, since neither reading of (141) is
possible in this dialect, it becomes evident that (86) and (OO) are not
sufficient as presently formulated. Only one of the readings of (141)
is filtered out by (86) and (OO), i.e. 'They recommended you to me.'
This reading succeeds in being filtered out by (OO) because the clitic
order is 'accusative before dative.' The other reading fails to be
blocked since second person precedes first person and dative precedes
accusative as prescribed by the two constraints. Given the fact that
speakers of this dialect do not accept the clitic order *te me*, it is
possible to make the generalization that first and second person clitic
pronouns simply may not co-occur. The notation of (86) provides a means
of capturing the generalization that two clitics are mutually exclusive
(Perlmutter 1970:216). (86) may be appropriately revised as follows:

(86)'   Output condition on clitic pronouns

                se   II   III
                         I

The revised constraint incorporates the single generalization that
first and second person clitics are mutually exclusive as a natural and
predictable consequence of a more comprehensive constraint on clitics.
(OO) conjoined with (86)' adequately characterize the data without
necessitating the distinction at least implied by the introduction of
nonglobal constraints.
The negative statement of (140) might at first appear to establish a
possible distinction between global and nonglobal constraints. That is,
Perlmutter shows that global constraints cannot be stated negatively;
they must be stated positively. Therefore, if it could be shown that one
distinguishing characteristic of nonglobal constraints was their obligatory
negative statement, a formal distinction might be imposed. It could be
claimed that global constraints filter out ungrammatical sequences by
specifying what is grammatical while nonglobal constraints would do the
same by specifying what is ungrammatical. This attempt to establish a
distinction also fails, however, since the positive formulation of both
(OO) and (86)' has shown that it is unnecessary to state these constraints
negatively.

Even if there were a motivated distinction between global and non-global constraints, the constraint responsible for ruling out the ungrammatical sentences of this second dialect could not be a nonglobal constraint. It should be recalled that one of the conditions for a nonglobal constraint is that it filter out ungrammatical sequences of clitics which are grammatical in other constructions. If it is the case that speakers do not accept sentences like (141) because first and second person clitics are mutually exclusive, then it will never be the case that the sequence 'II I' will be grammatical in any other construction. The facts obviously do not accomodate the conditions required of nonglobal constraints.

4.   In summation, this paper has attempted to show that Perlmutter intended a necessary distinction between global and nonglobal constraints. In arguing that the distinction was unnecessary and empirically inconsequential, the existence of additional constraints became evident. The nature of these constriants permitted their being collapsed into one general constraint accounting for a wide range of facts not previously accounted for.

Even though no arguments were presented for the necessity of stating the additional constraints as surface structure constraints, in general the formulation developed here is to be preferred since it does not require the costly metatheoretical introduction of a distinction between global and nonglobal constraints. It seems fairly clear that within a framework where surface structure constraints have already been shown to be necessary, there could be no added cost in stating the above constraints as surface structure constraints. Even if the constraints could be stated as restrictions on transformations, it is doubtful that the restrictions could be stated more generally.

NOTES

*I am grateful to Gerald Sanders for his comments and the interest he inspires.

1.   In Perlmutter 1970:213 the phonological spelling of the clitics is as follows:

II - *te*, sg. dative, accusative, and reflexive.
I - *me*, sg. dative, accusative, and reflexive.
     nos, pl. dative, accusative, and reflexive.
III - *le*, sg. dative
      los, pl. dative and accusative
      lo, *la*, sg. accusative

2.   (121), Perlmutter (1970:230), is the surface structure constraint for French and does not immediately concern this topic.

3.   It should be noted that, of the two examples of nonglobal constraints, Perlmutter actually only proposes the one constraint (140) and does not formulate the constraint for the other dialect.

PAULA L. MEYER
UNIVERSITY OF CALIFORNIA, SAN DIEGO

SOME OBSERVATIONS ON CONSTITUENT-ORDER IN SPANISH

The following is an informal discussion of the various orders of the
constituents in sentences spoken by a native Spanish speaker.[1] It is an
attempt to show that the constraints governing these orders can be accounted
for rather interestingly and with some facility by considering such notions
as topic and focus.[2] To attempt a definition, I would call the focus of
a sentence that part[3] which is new to the discourse, i.e. the non-presup-
posed part. A good example of focus is the NP in the answer to a question
which questions that NP, e.g., *WHO has the lunch? ROSS has the lunch.*
A topic is somewhat harder to define, but it is generally thought of as
the thing which the sentence "is about" or "concerns", e.g., *About the
concert, it's been cancelled*, which is equivalent to *The concert's been
cancelled*. I would go further and suggest that the topic is already
somehow present in the context of the discourse, as, for example, we
cannot have, **About a concert, it's been cancelled*.[4] With this contextual
constraint in mind (that the topic be already there), I think it safe to
assume that any NP cannot be both the focus and the topic of the same
sentence; that is, it cannot both have and not have a referent in the discourse. Now, if we partition sentences into topic-comment and into focus-
presupposition, then the topic is an element of the presupposition and the
focus is an element of the comment; but these two relationships cannot be
collapsed into one, with the topic equalling the presupposition and the
comment equalling the focus, because they are not necessarily equivalent.[5]

The Spanish data which I will examine here consist of sentences that
contain a subject, an object and a verb, with possible and impossible
permutations and arrangements of these constituents. I want to suggest
that, with basic word order verb-subject-object and with topic and focus
marked in deep structure, we can derive all possible surface orders involving these constituents with the following kinds of rules: a focus-
subject rule which moves the subject to the right only if it is the focus;
subject-permutation to the left for topics and contrastive subjects; WH-
fronting; dislocation, which copies the topic outside the S; and object-
pronoun clitic movement to the front of the verb. There are two apparently
separate constraints on the surface order of constituents[6] which, rather

than having to be stated explicitly, will be seen to follow from these rules. Declarative sentences will behave differently from the others; this last probably has to do with the performative verb 'to say'.

First, looking only at simple sentences, we see that there appears to be a surface-structure constraint on the relative order of the verb and the direct object, requiring that non-pronominalized objects not precede the verb (within a single S). Thus we never find such sentences as:

a. *José/un coche/se ha comprado   SOV ('José has bought a car')
b. *Un coche/José/se ha comprado   OSV
c. *Un coche/se ha comprado/José   OVS.

These orders never occur in any of the sentences that I have examined, but we do find the other three permutations.[7]

Now, the relative order of the direct object and the verb remaining constant,[8] we are left with subject-verb-object, verb-subject-object and verb-object-subject, in which the thing that varies appears to be the position of the subject. These arrangements, however, do not vary freely, but are governed by certain restrictions which we will now examine.

Looking first at simple declarative sentences, it is evident that SVO is by far the most normal order:

(1)   Paco se ha comido la manzana   SVO
              has eaten   the apple

(2)   El niño se ha comido la manzana
       the child

(3)   Un niño se ha comido la manzana.
       a child

SVO may be replaced by VSO, but only if the subject is not definite:

(4)   *Se ha comido Paco la manzana

(5)   *Se ha comido el niño la manzana

(6)   Se ha comido un niño la manzana.

And VOS can replace SVO only if the subject is the focus of the sentence, e.g., if it is an answer to a question on the subject, such as 'Who did x?':[9]

(7)   Se ha comido la manzana Paco
       (if answer to
       ¿Quién se ha comido la manzana?).[10]
           who

So, we can posit a focus-subject rule which backs the subject when it is the focus. The alternating positions for indefinite subject (non-focus) and the invariant position for definite subject seems at the moment to be unexplainable, at least in any regular or general fashion.

Still with declarative sentences, I shall now introduce another phenomenon which I think relevant to the problem at hand, and this is dislocation of NP's. Dislocation is a copying rule which moves an NP outside the original S (usually to the front[11]) and leaves a pronoun copy where it was moved from.[12] Dislocation occurs in declaratives as follows:

Subjects can dislocate out of the SVO order given for simple declaratives, but not from (focus-subject) VOS order:

(8)   Paco, *él* se ha comido la manzana
            he

(9)   *Paco, se ha comido la manzana *él*.

Nor can the subject dislocate from VSO:

(10)   *Paco, se ha comido *él* la manzana.

Objects can be dislocated from the above simple S's when the subject follows the verb, but not otherwise:

(11)   La manzana, se la ha comido *Paco*
                            it

(12)   *La manzana, *Paco* se la ha comido.

Finally, only definite NP's may be dislocated:

(13)   *Un niño,* él se ha comido la manzana

(14)   *Un niño,* se ha comido él la manzana

(15)   *Una manzana,* se la ha comido Paco.
            an apple

A constraint which seems to be present on dislocation is that the copied NP tends to have a referent already in the context. Note again, in relation to this, that this copied NP cannot be indefinite. This explains why subjects cannot dislocate from VSO (example 10), as only indefinite subjects may fall into this configuration VSO, as in example 6.

If we say that only the topic can be dislocated, then we will be consistent both with these data and with the definition given earlier of topic. Also, this will explain the non-occurrence of subjects dislocated from VOS (example 9), because the topic and the focus are, by definition, mutually

exclusive. Now, what about the fact that definite subjects must be at
the beginning while indefinite ones may either precede or follow the verb?
Judging from the dislocation data (examples 8, 9 and 10), the topic of a
declarative sentence seems to always be at the beginning of the sentence.
To say that the definite subject of a declarative is its topic and thus
comes first (by use of an obligatory permutation rule (or, if you want to
start with SVO underlying word order, of the converse of that rule) would
be consistent with the definition of topic and would explain non-sentences
such as example 10. Now we still have to explain the optionality of positions of indefinite subjects, which occur in both VSO and SVO order. What
seems to be at work here is a sort of tendency toward there always being a
topic (which is marked by fronting) in declarative, and only declarative,
sentences,[13] or, more simply, toward a "declarative" form.

We have not yet dealt with the ungrammaticality of sentences in which
the direct object is dislocated and the subject precedes the verb. (This
is shown in example 12.) It would be nice to avoid any separate rule
for this and to have the constraint fall out as the result of already-
needed considerations. Looking at large numbers of sentences from the data
with topics marked by dislocation, I discovered that there are never any
with more than one topic. For example:

d.   *José, el coche, él se lo ha comprado
            the car he   it has bought

e.   *José y el coche, él se lo ha comprado.
          and

Therefore, if an initial-position subject is the topic, and a dislocated
NP is also the topic, the fact that we can have only one topic would rule
out any sentence in which both an initial-position NP and a dislocated NP
occur, but are not identical; in particular, example 12.[14]

Of the rules to be used in this paper, the following have now been
introduced: focus-subject backing, right- and left-dislocation of the
topic (either subject or object), and topic-subject permutation. (Let us
for the moment accept the last rule, topic-subject permutation, with the
underlying subject following the verb, as opposed to its converse, non-
topic-subject permutation from SVO.)

Now let us go ahead and look at some sentences other than declaratives.
In yes-no questions, VSO is the preferred normal order, with definite as
well as indefinite subjects:

(16)   ¿Se ha comido Eva la manzana?   VSO

(17)   ¿Se ha comido una niña la manzana?.

SVO is perfectly acceptable, however; but here there is some emphasis on
the subject, generally showing disbelief that this NP is the subject,

or contrasting it with some other subject NP. These questions were often paraphrased by my informant as cleft questions with anaphoric pronoun subjects or as negative cleft questions with a different subject:

(18) *¿Eva* se comió la manzana?
      ate
  ¿Fue ella quien se comió la manzana?
  was she who
  ¿No fue María quien se comió la manzana?
  ('was it not María....')

With VOS in yes-no questions, the subject was also emphasized (or questioned), but, put impressionistically, it did not seem to be so much a matter of disbelief of an already-stated NP or of contrast:

(19) ¿Se comió la manzana *Eva?*
  ¿Fue Eva quien se comió la manzana?.

In dislocation from these questions, the pronoun trace of a dislocated subject most normally follows the verb:

(20) Eva, ¿se comió *ella* la manzana?.

If it precedes, the sentence is quite marginal, and there is a strong emphasis on the subject, this again indicating disbelief:

(21) Eva, ¿*ella* se comió la manzana?
       she

Subject dislocation with VOS is once again impossible:

(22) *Eva, ¿se comió la manzana *ella*?,

and so is dislocation of any indefinites:

(23) **Una niña,* ¿se comió ella la manzana?

(24) **Una manzana,* ¿se la comió Eva?.

Besides having this constraint on definiteness, object dislocation is still the same as in declaratives, the subject having to be after the verb:

(25) La manzana, ¿se la comió *Eva?*

(26) *La manzana, *Eva* se la comió?.

Besides yes-no questions, I looked at indirect yes-no questions, NP-complements, and *if*-clauses, and they seem to conform to the same pattern just given, with dislocated NP's going to the beginning of the entire sentence. Some examples of these various clauses are given in examples 27-34:

(27) Si tuviera *María* el libro, me lo daria
      if   had   the book· me it would give

(28) Si *María* tuviera el libro, me lo daria
      Si fuera María la que tuviera el libro,....
          it were   the one who

(29) Es verdad que tiene *María* el libro
      it's true that has

(30) Es verdad que *María* tiene el libro

(31) María, espero que tenga *ella* el libro
                I hope   has

(32) ?María, espero que *ella* tenga el libro
                          she

(33) El libro, espero que lo tenga *María*

(34) *El libro, espero que *María* lo tenga.

Imperatives are always VSO:

(35) Cierre usted la puerta.
      close you the door

VOS, with the su ject 'you' being the focus, is ungrammatical:

(36) *Cierre la puerta *usted*.

SVO may be said to occur as an imperative, but it always occurs in a conjoined sentence with contrasted subjects. And, moreover, this last type sentence alternates with one containing the indicative instead of the imperative form of the verb:

(37) *Usted* cierre la puerta

(38) *Usted* |cierre| la puerta, y *yo* abriré la ventana.[15]
              |cierra| I will open the window

   The facts given here seem to be consistent with the earlier choice of verb-initial basic order, reasonably suggesting that declarative sentences,

in having obligatory topic-subject permutation, are in some way set apart
from the other types of sentences. But then, what is the rule that gives
us SVO in other kinds of clauses besides simple declaratives? I think it
is very similar (and I would expect, upon closer examination of this problem,
to come up with one general principle), but the constant feeling of contrast in non-declarative initial subjects leads me to posit another permutation
rule for contrastive subjects in non-declaratives.

However, there is one exception that I found to VSO order in complements
and to the contrastive feeling on initial subjects. This is complements of
the verb *decir* 'to say'. Here, VSO is questionable, although not out altogether, and SVO is definitely preferred:

(39)   Dice que *María* tiene el libro
       he says

(40)   ?Dice que tiene *María* el libro.

This fact would lead me to consider a performative analysis for declaratives,
decir being the performative verb which somehow triggers the declarative
topic-subject permutation.

We now have focus-subject backing, dislocation, and subject-permutation
for declarative topics and non-declarative contrastive subjects.

The only group of sentences left to examine is WH-questions (and indirect
WH-questions, which are just the same). The first thing we notice in WH-
questions is that there is a general WH-word fronting rule, fronting WH-
subjects, objects, and things such as adverbs:

(41)   ¿*Quién* se ha tomado la sopa?
        who   has eaten   the soup

(42)   ¿*Qué* se ha tomado la niña?
        what

(43)   ¿*Cuándo* se compró Luis la bicicleta?.
        when   bought   the bicycle

Non-sentences such as

(44)   *¿Qué *la niña* se ha tomado?
and
(45)   *¿Cuándo *Luis* se compró la bicicleta?

show us that the subject, not being allowed in front of the verb when
another constituent is questioned, either has to be moved back (as a
non-contrastive) or has to start out after the verb. In such sentences as:

(46)   ¿Cuándo se compró la bicicleta *Luis*?,

the subject can be moved to the right, giving VOS, but the subject here receives extra emphasis.[16]

Dislocation occurs in WH-questions in the following way. When the object is questioned, the subject can be dislocated (if it is definite), and, just as a full NP subject must follow the verb, as shown in examples 42 and 44, the pronoun trace must be after the verb:

(47)   La niña, ¿qué se ha tomado *ella*?

(48)   *La niña, ¿qué *ella* se ha tomado?

(49)   *Una niña, ¿qué se ha tomado ella?.

The same thing (the subject following the verb) is seen to be true when the subject is dislocated from a WH-adverb question, although even the only good one (i.e. VSO) is for some reason still quite strange:

(50)   *Luis, ¿cuándo se compró la bicicleta *él*?

(51)   *Luis, ¿cuándo *él* se compró la bicicleta?

(52)   ?Luis, ¿cuándo se compró *él* la bicicleta?.

The object can be dislocated from WH-subject questions:

(53)   La sopa, ¿quién se la ha tomado?

and WH-adverb questions:

(54)   La bicicleta, ¿cuándo se la compró Luis?,

but only if the subject again follows the verb:

(55)   *La bicicleta, ¿cuándo *Luis* se la compró?.

If we want to start from SVO to derive these WH-questions, then we have to always back their subjects on the basis of their not being contrastive. This would be true also of other non-declaratives, for instance, example 20. The backing rule would be paired with the rule for backing non-topic subject NP's in declaratives. Now, it seems not at all necessary and even somehow backwards to have rules based on such conditions as *non*-topics and *non*-contrastive. That is, to point something out as a topic or a contrast, we move it to a special position, not vice-versa, as in 'Cornflakes I hate.' So it seems, finally, that SVO, while not being ruled out, certainly appears no better qualified as deep-structure order than VSO, and, moreover, it involves the use of negative conditions on rules, something which I feel makes for rather awkward, non-intuitive explanations.

Using example 47 as a sample, a derivation from SVO would be:

```
[ [la niña] [ [se ha tomado]  [qué] ] ]
S NP +T   NP V P V          V  NP NP VP S

[ [qué] [la niña] [ [se ha tomado] ] ]        WH-fronting
S NP NP NP +T   NP VP V          V VP S

[la niña] [ [qué] [ella] [ [se ha tomado] ] ]   dislocation
NP +T   NP S NP NP NP +T NP VP V          V VP S

[la niña] [ [qué] [ [se ha tomado] ] [ella] ]
NP  +T NP S NP NP VP V          V VP NP+T NP S   non-contrastive subject
                                                 permutation
```

Starting with VSO, the derivation looks like:

```
[ [se ha tomado] [la niña] [qué] ]
S V            V NP  +T  NP NP NP S

[ [qué] [se ha tomado] [la niña] ]            WH-fronting
S NP NP V            V NP +T   NP S

[la niña] [ [qué] [se ha tomado] [ella] ]  dislocation
NP  +T NP S NP NP V            V NP +T NP S
```

In summary then, if in deep-structure the constituents are in the order
verb-subject-object and are marked according to their relation to the
context of the discourse, then we can account for all possible permutations
of these constituents with rules that reflect the native intuitions associated with them. These rules are, once more:

I.   focus-subject backing

II.   subject-permutation for declarative topics and non-declarative
       contrastive NP's

III.   (WH-fronting)

IV.   dislocation of topics

V.   (clitic placement of object pronouns).

Evidently then, intuitions about single sentences are inseparably tied up
with the surrounding context.
    Finally, I should like the trends presented in this paper to suggest a
perspective from which to view this problem on a more general level. That
is, I think we should look at the different dialectal and ideolectal

variants of these constraints on word-order and NP-movement (and there are quite a few) in order to discover the tendency of the language in general and to try to get some idea what it is that governs the variation.

NOTES

1.   This paper owes its life to a lot of people, but mostly to R. W. Langacker, Don Forman, and the informant Eva Fusi. Eva happens to be from Madrid, and is thus naturally influenced by the language spoken there. However, many of the phoenomena discussed herein seem to be determined not geographically, but by some other means of dialect differentiation which is as yet unexplored but which is certainly not unique to Spanish. Although there is considerable disagreement about the data among various speakers of Spanish, the general trends introduced here appear to be present in all ideolects. In not purporting to describe more than one dialect, this paper is intended principally to give a perspective from which to go on and examine the language as a whole. Since my informant's intuitions on the more subtle aspects of word order seem at this point to be somewhat rare, and since she had to go back to Spain before I finished the paper, there are a few gaps in the data which will doubtlessly become apparent to the reader. However, I do not think that these affect the general conclusions presented.
2.   In particular, the tendency for the topic to precede the comment and for the focus to come after the presupposed part of the sentence.
3.   The focus, but not the topic, can probably be other than a NP, for example, in the answer to, *What did Ann do?*.
4.   Sentences with what seem to be indefinite topics are in some way I think related to existentials.
5.   For example, in the answer to *What did Don eat?*, *Don ate the pie.* *(Don, he ate the pie.)*, I think the topic is *Don* (and *he*), the comment thus being *ate the pie*. However, the focus in only *the pie*, not the entire *ate the pie*.
6.   These are: first, that more than one full (i.e. non-pronominalized) NP may not precede the verb in any sentence, and second, that a non-pronominalized direct object may not precede the verb in a single S.
7.   SVO, VSO, and VOS.
8.   Within the S, and if the object is not pronominalized.
9.   A focus need not be backed if it receives heavy stress. Stress on a constituent, however, generally shows distortion in the position of that constituent. I have eliminated consideration of stress from the present paper, although it is relevant to the problem and should certainly be included in a broader study.
10.   A subject can also be backed if it is "heavy", i.e. if it is complex. For example,

Se ha comido la manzana *el niño que vi ayer*
                                  that I saw yesterday
need not follow a question on the subject.
    11.   It can equivalently be to the right, although this is not so common.
Actually, I suspect that there is some semantic difference between left-
and right- dislocation, but it was impossible to discerne from the informant. As examples of right-dislocation, we find:
    (corresponding to example 8) *El* se ha comido la manzana, *Paco*
    (corresponding to example 11) Se *la* ha comido Paco, *la manzana*.
The constraints on right-dislocation are the same as those for dislocation
to the left.
    12.   Except that there is a general rule in Spanish that object clitic
pronouns are placed to the front of their (finite) verbs.
    13.   This topic is generally the subject of the sentence, the close
relationship between topic and subject being already rather well known.
For an interesting discussion of this as it relates to Japanese, see
Kuroda (1969). Also, 'Sentences in Discourse: An analysis of an Essay
by Bertrand Russell' by Carlota Smith (1971) has a very nice discussion of
underlying and surface subjects and the notions topic and comment. Also
extremely interesting are two dissertations from UCLA, those of Soemarmo
(1970) and Terry Moore (1967). The affinity between topic and subject
can be seen in Spanish in the behavior of object-topics, which, instead of
merely being at the beginning of the sentence, have to be dislocated
outside, a less natural situation. Also, in dialects which use the
passive, topic-objects become the subject of the corresponding passive.
Note that these passive sentences must state the agent (the underlying
subject), consistent with the notion that, if not the focus, it is at
least part of the comment. Keep in mind the above-stated tendency for
the topic to precede the comment. As for passives, for some reason they
seem to be fading out. This is especially evident in such languages as
Spanish and Russian, where they are totally unacceptable for many speakers,
but it is also true for English, where they are generally felt to be formal
and a little archaic. But a whole other paper is needed to discuss the
demise of the passive. I somehow think that the tendency for declaratives
to have their subjects act as topics may have developed from some sort of
trend toward one form for declaratives; this would go along with the
development of a more constrained word order from Latin to present
Spanish.
    14.   It at first appears that these could be ruled out by the surface
structure constraint given above that more than one full NP cannot occur
before the verb. However, we can see that this is not the case from the
following example involving right-dislocation:
    *La manzana, *Paco* se la ha comido (example 12)
    *_Paco_ se la ha comido, la manzana
    Se la ha comido *Paco*, la manzana
    La manzana, se la ha comido *Paco* (example 11).
Note that the ungrammaticality depends on the fronting of the subject, *Paco*.

15. The incompatability of topic with subjects of imperatives can be seen perhaps more clearly in the English *About you, eat your eggplant.*
16. Is this the focus?

MARÍA-LUISA RIVERO
UNIVERSITY OF OTTAWA

ON CONDITIONALS IN SPANISH

INTRODUCTION

This paper studies the structure of conditional sentences in Spanish, and motivates two different assumptions about those types of structures. In the first part of the study we will present evidence which argues in favor of the hypothesis that the particle *si* 'if' is the matrix verb of the protasis in a conditional configuration and that as a verbal element it belongs to the set which G. Lakoff (1968) has termed 'world-creating' verbs. In the second part of the paper we will argue that the protasis and the apodosis function as coordinated sentences.

We will call conditional sentence the combination of the protasis (the if-clause) and the apodosis (the consequent).

I. SI 'IF' AS A WORLD-CREATING VERB.

1. The first argument in favor of the assumption that *si* is a verbal form is provided by the behavior of conditionals in connection with clefting. Consider the following examples:

(1) a. Si Juan viene, nos iremos 'If John comes, we'll leave'.
     b. Si es que Juan viene, nos iremos 'If it is that John comes, we'll leave'.

All conditionals, including counterfactual ones, admit the kind of clefting represented by 1b:

(2) a. Si Juan hubiera venido, nos habríamos ido 'If John had come, we would have left'.
     b. Si fuera que Juan hubiera venido, nos habríamos ido 'If it were that John had come, we would have left'.

As 1b and 2b indicate, those strings which follow a conditional particle function as NP's, and the particle *si* may be left out of that NP structure.

If the protasis in a conditional sentence is assigned an underlying structure of the type of (PM1), we can easily explain this phenomenon:

(PM1)

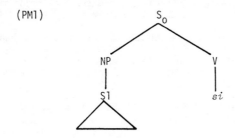

Notice that this argument applies only to *si* and not to temporal or causal
clauses:

(3) a. Cuando venga Juan, nos iremos 'When John comes we'll leave'.
     b. *Cuando sea que Juan venga nos iremos.

(4) a. Porque Juan viene nos iremos 'Because John is coming we'll
         leave'.
     b. *Porque es que Juan viene, nos iremos.

3b has a grammatical reading with the English gloss 'Whenever it is that
John comes, we'll leave', which is unrelated to 3a.
    Equative sentences indicate as well that what follows a *si* element is
an NP:

(5) a. Si María se enfada, nos creará un problema 'If Mary gets mad,
         it'll be a problem'.
     b. Si es esto: que María se enfada, nos creará un problema
         'If it is this: that Mary gets mad, it'll be a problem'.

Furthermore, in this type of cleft sentence not only the string which
follows a *si* functions as an NP, but the conditional particle itself functions
as a verb plus its complementizer:

(6) a. Imagina que Juan nos encuentra ... 'Imagine that John finds
         us ...'.
     b. Imagina que es que Juan nos encuentra ... 'Imagine that it is
         that John finds us ...'.

(7) a. Si Juan nos encuentra ... 'If John finds us ...'.
     b. Si es que Juan nos encuentra ... 'If it is that John finds
         us ...'.

In 7b *si* has the same role as *imagina que* in 6b.

The verb which follows *imagina que* in sentences of the type of 8b must mirror the mood of the verb in the NP-clause, and the same holds true for the verb *ser* 'to be' which follows the *si* particle in sentences like 9b:

(8) a. Imagina que Juan hubiera cantado ... 'Imagine that John had sung ...'.
     b. *Imagina que es que Juan hubiera cantado, ...
     c. Imagina que fuera que Juan hubiera cantado ... 'Imagine that it were that John had sung ...'.

(9) a. Si Juan hubiera cantado, ... 'If John had sung, ...'
     b. *Si es que Juan hubiera cantado, ...
     c. Si fuera que Juan hubiera cantado, ... 'If it were that John had sung, ...'.

All this receives a simple explanation if *si* is analyzed as a verb.

In summary, the behavior of the protasis when involved in clefted constructions indicates a) that what follows *si* is an NP, and b) that *si* is a verb. In other words, the conditional particle is a verbal form with transitive complementation.

2.   The second argument deals with S-pronominalization. Consider the following example:

(10) Si Juan hubiera venido, lo comprenderia 'If John had come. I would understand it'.

In the above string the pronoun *lo* refers back to *Juan hubiera venido,* that is, to an antecedent without conditionality, without the semantic content which *si* adds to the string.

Under the assumption which treats *si* as a verb this is easy to explain: there is a constituent sentence, S1 in (PM1), with no conditional particle or no conditional meaning attached to it, and *lo* is pronominalizing such a structure. If *si* were a constituent of the sentence which serves as an antecedent, there would be no explanation for the disappearance of the conditional meaning in the reference of the pronoun.

There is no pronominalization process which replaces the whole protasis, that is to say that the conditional particle can never be included in the reference of a pronoun.

It could be argued at this point that the reason why *si* is never part of the pronominalization is because it is a complementizer introduced in deep structure within a configuration of the type of (PM2):

(PM2)

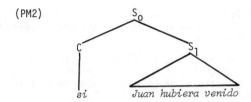

The pronominalization process applies to Sl and does not affect the complementizer. This is the proposal made by J. Bresnan (1970) in a recent
article in *Foundations of Language* for English complementizers in general,
although conditionals are not mentioned there. At the end of the first
part of this study we will briefly argue against the proposal to treat
the conditional *si* as a deep structure complementizer, but we would like
to point out at this moment that the fact that *si* is not part of any
pronominalization is not an isolated phenomenon under the hypothesis which
treats *si* as a verb. *Si* functions in 10 in the same way as the set of
world-creating verbs. To see this consider the following sentences:

(11) a. Imagina que viene, pues lo comprenderé 'Imagine that he comes,
          well, I'll understand it'.
      b. Supón que se cansa, eso sería lo más lógico 'Suppose he
          gets tired, that would be the most logical thing'.

In 11a *lo* refers back to *que viene* and it can never refer back to *imagina
que viene*. In 11b we find a similar situation, *eso* refers back to *que se
cansa* but never to *supón que se cansa*. In other words, there are constraints
on sentences whose main predicate is a world-creating verb (i.e. *imaginar,
suponer*) to the effect that the pronominalization can only refer to the
newly created universe of discourse.

In connection with argument number 1 and in view of the parallelisms
between world-creating verbs and protases in conditional configurations,
which we will discuss in the following sections, we conclude that the
non-pronominalization of *si* correlates with the non-pronominalization of
world-creating verbs, and not with the non-pronominalization of complementizers. That is to say that together with the rest of the evidence, we
take this argument to favor the hypothesis that *si* is a verb and one of
the group of world-creating verbs.

3. The third argument favoring the assumption that *si* is a verb which
can be classified as world-creating deals with factive verbs. Factive
verbs are those which take complements which are presupposed to be true,
i.e. *darse cuenta* 'to realize', *evidente* 'evident'.

(12) a. Me doy cuenta que mintieron 'I realize that they lied'.
      b. Es evidente que copiaron 'It is evident that they copied'.

When a factive verb is embedded in a so-called world-creating verb, it loses its factivity, that is to say that its complement ceases to be considered as obligatorily true:

(13) a. Imagina que me doy cuenta que mintieron 'Imagine that I realize that they lied'.
      b. Supón que es evidente que copiaron 'Suppose that it is evident that they copied'.

Compare sentences 12a and 13a and sentences 12b and 13b respectively. In 12a and 12b it is presupposed that it is true that somebody lied and that somebody copied, but this is no longer true in the sentences in 13; in this last example it could very well be that nobody lied or nobody copied. The hearer is simply asked to envision the possibility, to create a new world of reference.

When factive verbs appear in the protasis of a conditional structure, they also lose their factivity:

(14) a. Si me doy cuenta que mintieron, les recriminaremos su conducta
          'If I realize that they lied, we will recriminate them for their behavior'.
      b. Si es evidente que copiaron, no les aceptaremos el examen
          'If it is evident that they copied, we will not accept their exam'.

Si has the same effect on factive verbs as world-creating verbs. If we treat *si* as a verb of this group, the meaning of the sentences in 14 and the meaning of the sentences in 13 correspond to a unique phenomenon: when embedded in a world-creating verb, the factive interpretation of a factive verb is neutralized.

4. The fourth argument which favors the assumption that *si* is a world-creating verb deals with counterfactual readings.

The combination of a matrix world-creating verb and a pluperfect subjunctive in the embedded clause create a counterfactual reading, that is, a meaning in which it is presupposed that what is being asserted did not happen or is not true. The combination of a conditional *si* with a pluperfect subjunctive produces the same type of counterfactual reading:

(15) a. Imagina que hubiera contado la verdad ...
          'Imagine that he had told the truth ...'.
      b. Supón que hubieran descubierto la verdad ...
          'Suppose that they had discovered the truth ..'.
      c. Si hubieran descubierto la verdad ...
          'If they had discovered the truth ...'.

The readings which we obtain in 15a-b-c presuppose that somebody didn't tell the truth in a, that the truth was not discovered in b and c.

This kind of counterfactual reading is connected with the set of world-creating verbs and not with just any kind of verb. Consider the following examples in which the combination of a verb of command with a pluperfect subjunctive in a. and the co-occurrence of a verb of emotion with the same tense in b do not have a counterfactual reading:

(16) a. Ordenó que hubiera terminado la función a las tres
       'He ordered that the performance be finished at three o'clock'.
     b. Le sorprende que la función hubiera terminado a las tres
       'It surprises him that the performance had (already) finished
        at three o'clock'.

If *si* is analyzed as a world-creating verb, the readings obtained in 15 can be treated in the same way, otherwise we would be dealing with two unrelated phenomena: the first one concerning world-creating verbs, the second one specifically concerning the conditional particle.

5. The fifth argument which correlates the conditional *si* with world-creating verbs deals with Neg-transportation.
Although I have no explanation of why this is so, Neg-transportation cannot apply within the protasis of a conditional sentence, and it cannot apply if the highest verb of a P-Marker is a world-creating verb and the two clauses embedded in the highest one meet the structural description of the rule. Consider the sentences below:

(17) a. Si Juan quiere que no hables palabra de francés, no vayas a
       Francia 'If John wants you not to speak a word of French,
       don't go to France'.
     b. *Si Juan no quiere que hables palabra de francés, no vayas a
       Francia.

(18) a. Imagina que Juan quiere que no hables palabra de francés, ...
       'Imagine that John wants you not to speak a word of French, ...'.
     b. *Imagina que Juan no quiere que hables palabra de francés, ...

Palabra de ... is a constituent whose grammaticality depends on its appearing in the negated clause in underlying structure. Its deviance in 17b and 18b indicates that the negative there could not have been transported from the lowest embedded clause, that is to say that there is no structure derived through Neg-transportation from the one which underlies 17a and 18a.
If we treat *si* as one of the world-creating verbs, this phenomenon can receive but one explanation, whatever that may turn out to be.

6. It has been noticed by B. Fraser (1969) that if a conditional particle *if* is preceded by an *even*, the hypothetical force of the conditional is neutralized. I would like to point out that this is not an isolated event which relates uniquely to conditionals. It is a general phenomenon

which is connected with world-creating verbs. It indicates that *if*, or
its Spanish counterpart *si*, behave exactly in the same manner as verbs of
this group and that they should be treated as one of them. *Even* neutralizes
the property of referring only to new universes of discourse which world-
creating verbs share. In other words, the semantic effect of *even* is
'in all possible worlds'.

(19) a. Incluso suponiendo que no viene, nos marcharemos
       'Even supposing that he is not coming, we'll leave'.
     b. Incluso imaginando que no viene, nos marcharemos
       'Even imagining that he is not coming, we'll leave'.
     c. Incluso si no viene, nos marcharemos 'Even if he doesn't
       come, we'll leave'.

The sentences in 19 are all affected by *incluso* 'even' in a similar way.
They all imply that a condition will be met in the world created by *imaginar*
'to imagine', by *suponer* 'to suppose', and by *si* 'is', and in all other
worlds as well.

In summary, the semantic effect of *even* on *if* and the parallel effect
of *incluso* on *si* provide further evidence for the assumption that the
conditional particle is a world-creating verb.

7.   J. L. Morgan has pointed out (1969) that the comparison involved
between a sentence with a world-creating verb and a second sentence is a
comparison between two worlds. Comparisons within the protasis of a conditional are comparisons between two worlds as well. To support the
assumption that *si* is a world-creating verb, we find the same behavior
in comparisons within a protasis as in comparisons involving overt world-
creating verbs:

(20) a. Si soy más inteligente de lo que creo, aprobaré
       'If I am more intelligent than I think, I will pass'.
     b. *Si soy más inteligente de lo que soy, aprobaré
       *'If I am more intelligent than I am, I will pass'.

(21) a. Supón que soy más inteligente de lo que creo, entonce aprobaré
       'Suppose that I am more intelligent than I think, then I will
       pass'.
     b. *Supón que soy más inteligente de lo que soy, entonces aprobaré
       *'Suppose I am more intelligent than I am, then I will pass'.

In 20a and 21a *si* and *supón* define the real world while *creer* defines a
different world. In 20b and 21b we are comparing within the same world
which makes both sentences anomalous. The above examples demonstrate
that the conditional *si* and world-creating verbs behave alike.

Furthermore, it is the case that the conditional particle and world-
creating verbs define universes in parallel fashion. We have already
mentioned that in 20a and 21a the conditional particle and the verb,

respectively, define the real world. However, this is not always the case. In combination with other tenses and moods we find that *si* and the verbs we are discussing do not define the real world:

(22) a. Si fuera más inteligente de lo que soy, aprobaría
          'If I were more intelligent than I am, I would pass'.
      b. Supón que fuera más inteligente de lo que soy, entonces aprobaría
          'Suppose that I were more intelligent than I am, then I would pass'.

In 22a and 22b *si* and *supón* define a possible world but not the real one. What is important to our discussion is that the conditional particle functions exactly like the verb *suponer*.

Still a third possibility of defining universes of discourse is presented by the following examples in which the conditional *si* and the world-creating verb behave in parallel fashion again:

(23) a. Si fuera más inteligente de lo que creo, aprobaría
          'If I were more intelligent than I think, I would pass'.
      b. Supón que fuera más inteligente de lo que creo, entonces aprobaría 'Suppose I were more intelligent than I think, then I would pass'.

The difference between 20a and 23a, and 21a and 23b is that in the examples in 23 *si* and *supón* do not define the real world but a possible world and that world is different from the one determined by *creer*.

It is outside the scope of this paper to study the ways in which tenses combine with world-creating verbs to define worlds, my objective is simply to show that *si* and the set of world-creating verbs relate to the creation of universes of discourse exactly in the same way. I feel that I have clearly demonstrated with three different sets of sentences (20-21; 22; 23) that the parallelism is not accidental.

8. The conditional particle *si* may be deleted in the same manner as verbs are deleted:

(24) a. Si muriese el burro, lo enterraríamos 'If the donkey died, we would bury it'.
      b. Muriese el burro, lo enterraríamos.

(25) a. Te mando que vengas 'I command you to come!'.
      b. ¡Que vengas! Lit.: 'That you come!'.

24a-b are paraphrases. Notice that in Spanish complementizers are not deletable, so that the existence of 24b argues against the hypothesis of *si* as a complementizer.

9. Consider the following examples:

(26) a. María sabe que el niño llorará si su padre no viene
'Mary knows that the child will cry if his father doesn't come'.
b. Si su padre no viene, María sabe que el niño llorará 'If his father doesn't come, Mary knows that the child will cry'.

The *si* clause in 26b is clearly part of the complement, it is never the protasis of the matrix sentence. We can find examples in which the preposed protasis of a conditional can only relate to the most deeply embedded complement clause:

(27) a. María dice que piensa que Luis cree que el niño llorará si su padre no viene 'Mary says that she thinks that Louis believes that the child will cry if his father doesn't come'.
b. Si su padre no viene, María dice que piensa que Luis cree que el niño llorará 'If his father doesn't come, Mary says that she thinks that Louis believes that the child will cry'.

This is due to restrictions requiring that the time reference of the apodosis be ulterior to that of the protasis, and in 27 and 26 the most deeply embedded clause is the only one which does not violate this restriction.

If the tense of one of the higher clauses has a future reference with respect to the protasis, it can be considered as the apodosis of the conditional sentence:

(28) Si su padre no viene, María dirá que la niña llorará 'If her father doesn't come, Mary will say that the child will cry'.

In 28 the apodosis is *María dirá que la niña llorará.*

What is interesting to our discussion is that the same restrictions apply when there is a world-creating verb involved in a similar situation to that of the conditional particle. Consider:

(29) Imagina que la madre se enfada, María dice que piensa que Luis cree que el niño llorará 'Imagine that the mother gets angry, Mary says that she thinks that Louis believes that the child will cry'.

In 29 the possibility of the child crying exists within the world created by *imaginar*, but all the other actions specified by the clauses which dominate the most deeply embedded one are not within the sphere of the world-creating verb. *Imaginar* in 29 behaves exactly like *si* in 27b.

If the tense of *decir* in 29 takes a future reference, or if any other does, it falls immediately within the sphere of the world-creating verb:

(30) Imagina que la madre se enfada, María dirá que piensa que Luis cree que el niño llorará 'Imagine that the mother gets angry, Mary will say that she thinks that Louis believes that the child will cry'.

María dirá ... is within the universe of discourse defined by *imaginar*. In this last example the semantic effect of *imaginar* is parallel to the effect of *si* in 28.
   Within a theory which treats *si* as a world-creating verb, the above sentences constitute examples of the same phenomenon.

   10. Finally, it should be obvious at this point that meanings which can be expressed by the conditional particle *si* can be expressed by an overt world-creating verb:

(31) a. Suponiendo que María hubiera venido, no estaríamos aquí 'Supposing that Mary had come, we would not be here'.
      b. Si María hubiera venido, no estaríamos aquí 'If Mary had come, we would not be here'.

I find that 31a and 31b are paraphrases.
   It could be argued at this point that the semantic similarity between 31a and 31b is due to the presence in the underlying structure of the former of a configuration of the type of *Si supusiéramos* ... 'If we supposed ...', which is a protasis; the conditional particle is then deleted by trans- formation. That this cannot be so is demonstrated by the fact that 32 is not a paraphrase of 31a-b:

(32) Si supusiéramos que María hubiera venido, no estaríamos aquí 'If we supposed that Mary would had come, we would not be here'.

Si and *suponiendo* have the same semantic effect on the sentences in 31, and 32 paraphrases a string of the form *Suponiendo que supusiéramos* ...

   11. I have limited myself to the study of Spanish examples to motivate the analysis of the conditional *si* as a world-creating verb, but I would like to point out that I feel that the phenomena I have discussed are not simply features of the syntactic behavior of *si* in Spanish but reflections of the semantic nature of the expression of conditionality. Our conclusions do not try to explain Spanish conditionals in particular, but the notion of conditional sentence in general.
   To show how the general semantic characteristics of the expression of conditionality can explain other phenomena in different languages I would like to discuss an interesting case in Classical Greek.
   There are two types of negation in Classical Greek: μή and οὐ(κ) . οὐ(κ) is used within the universe of discourse considered as the real world, μή to negate other worlds. Or, in the words of Meillet and Vendryes (1948:604):

"La négation οὖ s'applique à un fait réel ou présenté comme tel; la négation μῆ à tout ce qui implique une volonté ou une supposition de l'esprit"

Within the conditional sentence the protasis is negated with μη while the apodosis is negated with an ουκ

(33) Ταῦτα οὐκ ἂν ἐδύναντο ποιεῖν, εἰ μὴ διαίτη μετρίᾳ ἐχρῶντο

'They would not be able to do this if they did not lead an abstemious life' X.C., 1, 2, 16.

The negative μῆ , naturally, is found in other structures besides the protasis of a conditional sentence. We will not study these constructions in detail since it would be well beyond the scope of this paper, but we would like to point out that verbs which require a μῆ as the negation of their complement include expressions denoting possibility, verbs of wishing, hoping, promising, and expecting, that is, world-creating verbs. Within our theory it is completely predictable that the protasis of a conditional sentence and the complement of a world-creating verb should have the same kind of negation. Εἰ , the Greek conditional particle is but one of the world-creating verbs and its complement is the protasis. If the complements of world-creating verbs are negated with a μῆ , then the protasis should be negated with a μῆ as well.

12. To conclude the first part of this paper, I would like to indicate why I do not take *si* to be a complementizer which is introduced in deep structure, in the event such a hypothesis is accepted for other complementizers.
One of Bresnan's arguments (1970) to introduce complementizers in deep structure is that they subcategorize verbs. This argument could never apply to the conditional particle in that all verbs can take a complement with a conditional particle (under the assumption that the protasis is a subordinate clause) while not all verbs admit all complementizers.
The second argument provided by J. Bresnan to prove that complementizers should be in deep structure deals with Conjunction Reduction. Bresnan first shows that in any P-Marker containing conjoined S nodes at a deeper level of embedding than the governing VP, Conjunction Reduction should precede Complementizer Insertion, should there be such a rule:

(PM2)

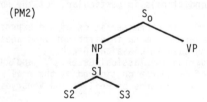

This is because the structural description of Conjunction Reduction is met in the Sl cycle while that of Complementizer Insertion is only met in the S_0 cycle. Should there be a rule of Complementizer Insertion applying after Conjunction Reduction, sentences with symmetric predicates would be undistinguishable at this point from those which are derived from Conjunction Reduction. The grammar would then derive the ungrammatical 34:

(34) *I prefer that a man and that his wife $\begin{cases} \text{be similar} \\ \text{resemble} \\ \text{each other.} \end{cases}$

Spanish evidence would lead us to the opposite conclusion, though. The translation of 34 is a perfectly grammatical sentence in Spanish:

(35) Prefiero que un hombre y que su mujer $\begin{cases} \text{sean iguales.} \\ \text{se parezcan.} \end{cases}$

Therefore this does not constitute an argument for the inclusion in deep structure of Spanish complementizers and we will not discuss it in connection with *si*.

As we have seen throughout this paper, the semantic properties of *si* correlate with the semantic properties of world-creating verbs.

We saw in section 8 that the conditional particle *si* is deletable while complementizers are not.

Therefore we conclude that there are arguments against the hypothesis that *si* is a deep structure complementizer and none in favor of it.

There is still another possibility which I have not discussed: *si* is the transformationally inserted complementizer of a world-creating verb which is abstract. The verb is then obligatorily deleted while the complementizer remains. To consider the conditional particle a complementizer of this type or the verb itself is merely a terminological question at this point. One advantage of this proposal would be the possibility of explaining the *si* of conditionals and the *si* of indirect questions as one and the same complementizer, but we will leave this question open for the moment.

We have discussed ten different phenomena which motivate the assumption that *si* is a verb and that it should be classified among world-creating verbs of the type of *imaginar* 'to imagine', *suponer* 'to suppose'. We have generalized our conclusions indicating that the characteristics of *si* in Spanish reflect the semantic properties of conditionality in general and that these semantic properties are common to all conditionals in all languages. Our Classical Greek case shows how a unique phenomenon can be explained in terms of those general characteristics. Finally, we have concluded the section by rejecting the possibility that the conditional particle should be treated as a complementizer introduced in deep structure.

II. PROTASIS AND APODOSIS AS COORDINATED

The second part of this paper deals with the relationship between the protasis and the apodosis in a conditional.

In traditional grammars there have been two different proposals concerning the relationship between the protasis and the apodosis:

(1) The most common assumption is that the apodosis is the main clause or the matrix and that the protasis is a subordinate clause embedded into it. In her structural study of Spanish conditionals Lidia Contreras (1963) takes this position although she gives no arguments for her choice.

(2) A less common assumption is that the apodosis and the protasis are interdependent. This is the position taken by Ernout and Thomas (and the one accepted for Portuguese by Vaz Leão 1961):

> "Les propositions conditionnelles introduites par *si,*
> *nisi, sive,* etc. sont étroitement unies à la proposition
> que paraît leur servir de principale, mais qui indique
> en fait la conséquence de la condition supposée... L'en-
> semble ainsi formée s'appelle PHRASE CONDITIONNELLE, où,
> à proprement parler, il n'y a ni principale ni subordon-
> née, mais interdépendence de deux propositions solidaires,
> qui ne peuvent exister l'une sans l'autre et n'ont de sens
> que l'une par l'autre"
> (Ernout and Thomas, 1953:374).

We feel that this second position is the correct one and we will proceed to motivate a coordinate structure for the two clauses of the conditional configuration.

1. It has often been noticed that the protasis and the apodosis do not stand in the relationship of a subordinate and a matrix respectively, but that they are interdependent. A few facts which support this observation are given below but there are, no doubt, many others.

The mood of the apodosis and that of the protasis are independent of each other:

(35') a. Si hubieras venido, te asombras   'If you had come (*Subj.*), you would have been amazed (*Ind.*)'.
     b. Si hubieras venido, te hubieras asombrado   'If you had come (*Subj.*), you would have been amazed (*Subj.*)'

We find examples of conditionals in which there is an overt correlation rather than dependency between protasis and apodosis. For instance, consider the following sentence from the *Chanson de Roland* where the *sis* place the two clauses within the same rank:

(36) Si l'orrat Charles, si retornera l'oz 'So Charles will hear it,
     so the army will turn back'.

or the correlation established by *si... entonces* in Spanish (*se... então*
in Portuguese, *si... alors* in French, to remain within the Romance group):

(37) Si comprendes, entonces perdonarás 'If you understand, then you
     you will forgive'.

We find surface strings which are semantically conditionals but in
which the two clauses are juxtaposed or coordinated:

(38) a. Se enfada él, me enfado yo 'He gets angry, I get angry'
     b. Háblase de esta manera, y nadie le escucharía 'Should he
        talk in such a manner and nobody would listen to him'.

Furthermore, a *que* complementizer may appear either in front of the
apodosis or in front of the protasis when no conditional particle is
present:

(39) a. Que respete las leyes y no le condenarán 'Let him obey the
        laws and he will not be condemned'.
     b. Respete las leyes que no le condenarán 'Let him obey the laws,
        (that) he will not be condemned'.

39a-b are paraphrases and indicate that neither clause can be considered
as subordinate to the other.
    There are no movement transformations between protasis and apodosis.
    We find that the protasis can be an interrogative sentence, an imperative,
or a declarative. This would go against the hypothesis that it is embedded
in the apodosis:

(40) a. ¿Has compredido el problema? Pues soluciónalo.
        'Did you understand the problem? Then solve it'.
     b. Soluciónalo y te darán una buena nota 'Solve it and they'll
        give you a good mark'.
     c. Me ayudas y te ayudo, no me ayudas y no te ayudo 'You help me
        and I'll help you, you don't help me and I won't help you'.

All these facts can be easily captured if we accept the hypothesis that the
apodosis and the protasis of a conditional sentence are coordinated.
    Before I consider some additional evidence which brings support to this
hypothesis, I would like to discuss it in connection with the results presented in the first section of the paper.
    If the conditional particle *si* is a world-creating verb whose complement
is the protasis as proposed in the first part of this study, and the protasis

and the apodosis are coordinated, we have two possible underlying structures for a conditional sentence: (PM3) and (PM4).

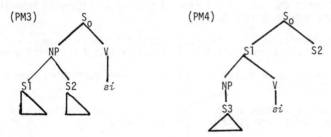

(PM3)   (PM4)

In (PM3) the protasis and the apodosis are coordinated but they are both
embedded in the sentence whose verb is the conditional *si*. In (PM4) the
protasis and the apodosis are also coordinated, but only the protasis is
embedded in the sentence whose predicate is *si*. It is easy to show that
(PM4) is the correct structure. Consider the following examples:

(41) a. *Dudo que los otros, si lo supieran, actuarían (*Ind.*) de manera
            tan honrada.
       b. Dudo que los otros, si lo supieran, acturan (*Subj.*) de manera
            tan honrada 'I doubt that the others, if they knew it, would
            act in such an honest way'.

When a conditional structure is embedded in a sentence with a verb which
requires a subjunctive complement, such as *dudar* 'to doubt' in 41, the
apodosis can only be in the subjunctive. If it is in the indicative, as
in 41a, the string is deviant. The mood of the protasis is not affected
by the highest verb in the tree. In other words, the apodosis functions
as any other sentence when embedded, while the protasis remains independent.
(PM4) can easily explain these facts: if S_0 is embedded, the verb of S2
will be directly affected by the verb of the matrix, but the verb of S3
will remain unaffected because there is an intervening predicate *si*.
Notice that the hypothesis which considers the protasis as a subordinate
clause could explain as well the sentences in 41, but not the rest of the
evidence we have discussed and the arguments which follow.

2. The first set of facts in favor of a coordinate protasis and apodosis
dealt with the independence of the two clauses in a conditional sentence.
   The second set of facts which support our assumption deal with tenses
in conditionals and in sentences with world-creating verbs. The relationship between a protasis and an apodosis is precisely the same as the one
found between two conjuncts of which the first one has a world-creating
verb as its predicate.

When a first conjunct of a structure has as its predicate a world-creating verb, the second conjunct must have a future time reference with respect to the first:

(42) a. Imagina que te escribió y te alegrarás 'Imagine that he wrote to you and you'll feel happy'.
b. *Imagina que viene, y te alegraste '*Imagine that he comes, and then you were happy'.

We find the same situation in conditional sentences. The apodosis must have a future reference with respect to the protasis:

(43) a. Si te escribió, te alegrarás 'If he wrote to you, you'll feel happy'.
b. *Si viene, te alegraste 'If he comes, you were happy'.

There is a consecutive reading in 43b which is grammatical, but not a conditional one. An argument to show that it is the consecutive meaning which is grammatical is that consecutive clauses can be paraphrased by causal structures of the type of 44b and 44c while true conditionals cannot. 45a is a true conditional.

(44) a. Si lo entiende, se lo explicaste 'If he understands it, you explained it to him'.
b. Si lo entiende es porque se lo explicaste 'If he understands it it is because you explained it to him'.
c. Lo entiende porque se lo explicaste 'He understands it because you explained it to him'.

(45) a. Si no lo entiende, se lo explicarás 'If he doesn't understand it, you will explain it to him'.
b. *Si no lo entiende es porque se lo explicarás '*If he doesn't understand it it is because you will explain it to him'.
c. *No lo entiende porque se lo explicarás '*He doesn't understand it because you will explain it to him'.

45b and 45c are starred because they do not paraphrase 45a. The sentences in 43 show that *si* should be treated as a world-creating verb as we have already concluded, but they also show that the relationship between the protasis and the apodosis is that of two coordinated sentences where the protasis functions as a left conjunct. World-creating verbs control the time reference across conjuncts and the conditional particle *si* controls the time reference across conjuncts.

Correlation of tenses across coordinated sentences when the first clause has a world-creating verb parallel the correlation of tenses found between the protasis and the apodosis:

(46) a. Imagina que hubiera venido, pues nos habríamos asustado 'Imagine that he had come, then we would have been frightened'.

b. Si hubiera venido, pues nos habríamos asustado   'If he had
come, then we would have been frightened'.

If we assume that the protasis and the apodosis are coordinated we can
easily account for these correlations.

3. Consider again concessive conditionals in which the conditionality
is neutralized.

(47) a. No lo comprenderé incluso si me lo explicas 'I will not
understand it, even if you explain it to me'.
b. Ni siquiera si me lo explicas, lo comprenderé 'Not even
if you explain it to me, will I understand it'.
c. *No incluso si me lo explicas, lo comprenderé.

47a and 47b are paraphrases. There is an easy explanation for this common
meaning: Neg-transportation has applied to incorporate the negation which
precedes *lo comprenderé* in 47a to the element *incluso* 'even' to give 47b.
This is confirmed by the ungrammaticality of 47c.

Under the proposal which considers the protasis as an embedded clause
the structural description of Neg-transportation is not met by the structure which underlies 47:

(PM5)

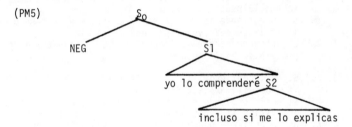

Sketchy as (PM5) might be it nevertheless reflects the basic point that
the element NEG is higher than *incluso,* and under those conditions Neg-
transportation cannot apply.

Semantically *incluso* does not only belong to the protasis but to the
apodosis as well:

(48)   a. { Ni siquiera }
b. { Incluso no } lo comprenderé si me lo explicas.
'Not even will I understand it, if you explain it to me'.

48 and the sentences in 47 are all paraphrases. If we assume that the
apodosis and the protasis are coordinated, and that *incluso* is a predicate

which dominates both of them, we explain this phenomenon and assign a configuration to these sentences where the structural description of Neg-transportation is met:

(PM6)

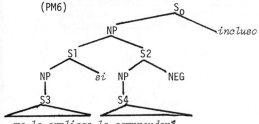

me lo explicas lo comprenderé

The NEG in S2 can now move up to *incluso*, producing *ni siquiera* as in 48a or 47b. If Neg-transportation does not apply we obtain 48b or 47a.

That the negation belongs over S4 is demonstrated by the grammaticality of the following sentences where *palabra de...* needs a negation within its underlying clause to be non-deviant:

(49) a. No comprenderé palabra del problema incluso si me lo explicas.
      b. Ni siquiera si me lo explicas comprenderé palabra del problema.
      c. $\left\{\begin{array}{l}\text{Ni siquiera}\\\text{Incluso no}\end{array}\right\}$ comprenderé palabra del problema
         si me lo explicas.
      (Gloss for all three) 'I will not understand a word of the problem even if you explain it to me'.

The set of sentences which we have discussed in this section indicate that the apodosis and the protasis are coordinated, that the protasis cannot be embedded in the apodosis.

CONCLUSIONS

In the second part of this paper we have presented three different types of evidence which argue in favor of the proposal that the protasis and the apodosis of a conditional sentence are coordinated. Together with the arguments presented in the first section in favor of the hypothesis that the conditional particle is a world-creating verb, we have motivated a structure for conditionals of the type of (PM4). This structure has the advantage of capturing two facts which have led grammarians to the postulation of conditional sentences as either formed by a matrix and an embedded clause, or as coordinated structures. First, the protasis and the apodosis are coordinated, which means that they are independent from each other to a certain degree. Contrary to what a matrix-subordinate hypothesis would lead us to believe, it is the protasis which determines the time reference of the apodosis. This coordination explains the interdependence noticed by Ernout and Thomas. Second, the protasis is the complement of the predicate *si*, which means that it is an embedded clause. These two aspects taken together explain both the independence emphasized by certain authors, and the subordinate nature of the protasis, emphasized by others.

PHONOLOGY

BOHDAN SACIUK
UNIVERSITY OF FLORIDA

PHONOLOGICAL STUDIES IN ROMANCE

1. Pre-1965

In the early stages of the evolution of generative phonology the study
and analysis of the Romance languages within this new theory were virtually
nonexistent.

Probably the first attempt to make use of this, then very young and quite
sketchy, theoretical framework took place one year after the publication of
Chosmky's *Syntactic Structures*. In his 1958 Indiana University dissertation
Sholes presented a series of "transformations" for French intended to
"relate morphemes to phonemes." Sholes (1958) included rules that inserted
word-boundaries into strings of morphemes, transformed morphophonemes into
phonemes at phrase level, and accounted for linking in French by eliminating
word-boundaries in certain consonant clusters.

In this period five other works appeared which can be considered as early
applications of the newly emerged school of phonology to the description
of Romance languages. All of these studies dealt with Spanish and two
(Alarcos 1961; Allen 1964) just employed the distinctive features developed
by Roman Jakobson, Gunnar Fant, and Morris Halle in *Preliminaries to Speech
Analysis*.[1] Alarcos (1961:50-82) after an exposition of Jakobson's acousti-
cally defined distinctive features, gave an analysis of Spanish phonemes
in terms of these features (1961:159-73). Allen (1964) arrived at some
interesting conclusions about the Old Castilian system of phonemes by
positing a tense/lax distinctive feature opposition for /p/, /t/, /k/, /f/,
/s/, /n/, /l/, and /r/. This tense/lax distinction survives in Modern
Castilian only in the trill/flap (/r̄/:/r/) opposition, while in some Spanish
dialects it is disappearing even here.

Leuschel (1960) and Anderson (1961) were only marginally related to
phonology. Leuschel's Indiana University dissertation, directed by Sol
Saporta, presented a transformational grammar of Spanish verb forms and
proposed a method for evaluating alternative grammars within each of the
three generative models discussed in the literature at the time (i.e.,
finite-state, phrase structure, and transformational grammars).

Anderson's article, which was a revised version of an M.A. thesis submitted at the University of Washington and directed by Sol Saporta, offered in an appendix entitled "Generative Grammar" several Phrase Structure Rules that would generate various types of Spanish nouns, including diminutives, augmentatives, and feminine forms with the "derivational morphemes" -*in*, -*es*, and -*is*- (*gallina*, *condesa*, *poetisa*, etc.). Due to the state of generative studies of Spanish at the time, Anderson is forced to include the zero allomorph for both the masculine and feminine gender morphemes. Foley (1965) and other investigators showed that the last formative in the underlying representations of words like *papel* (masc.), *mujer* (fem.), etc. is an /e/ which is deleted in the singular by an independently motivated rule of Spanish phonology, but which appears in the plural of these nouns (cf. *papeles*, *mujeres*).

Adopting the view proposed in Chomsky (1957) that a grammar of a given language should generate all the grammatical sequences of this language, but none of the ungrammatical ones, Saporta and Contreras (1962) presented "a phonological grammar of Spanish consisting of a set of rules that ideally are necessary and sufficient for generating all and only the phonologically grammatical sequences. (1962:30)" Their grammar included rules of expansion, lists, and obligatory and optional transformations. It was intended to generate all possible strings of phonemes that can occur in a phonological word of Spanish, without any reference to meaning or to the words or formatives that do in fact occur in this language. A very short section of Saporta and Contreras (1962:38-9) was labeled "Distinctive Features" and was in essence just the presentation of a chart of Spanish phonemes in terms of the features *vocalic, consonantal, nasal, compact, grave, tense, continuant,* and *strident,* which was not accompanied by any discussion. The final section in this brief book was devoted to the validation of a phonological grammar. It summarized an earlier article by the same two linguists (Contreras and Saporta 1960) in which, based on experiments they ran with native speakers of Spanish, they attempted "to develop an operational test of an informant's behavior which a) will distinguish grammatical from ungrammatical sequences, and b) will indicate whether two grammatical sequences are or are not in contrast."

2. 1965

After the isolated and fragmentary attempts of the preceding period to apply the theory of generative phonology to the description of the Romance languages, we come to a turning point -- the year 1965. It was this year that the ranks of American linguists increased by twelve (precisely twelve) "disciples" of the M.I.T. school. These were students of Chomsky and Halle who received their doctoral degrees that year and scattered throughout the North American continent to spread the teachings of transformational-generative grammar. This was a record year for M.I.T. linguistics not only in terms of numbers, but also in terms of quality and valuable contributions to linguistic science. Among the twelve linguists who were awarded the Ph.D. degree in 1965 we find such well-known names as James Foley, Bruce Fraser, Barbara Hall, Paul Kiparsky, Sige-Yuki Kuroda, Theodore Lightner,

James McCawley, Peter Rosenbaum, Sanford Schane, and Arnold Zwicky. Two of these linguists, James Foley and Sanford Schane, whose works appear in this volume, used the methods and principles of generative phonology in the description of Romance languages.

Foley's (1965b) dissertation on Spanish morphology presented the rules needed to account for phonological alternations in this language. This was the first generative study of Spanish phonology of some scope, and many of its proposals were adopted by later generative phonologists of Spanish, e.g. Harris, Saciuk, Willis, Wolfe, and others. One of Foley's most important contribution to Spanish phonology was the positing of an underlying final /e/ in nouns and adjectives which do not exhibit phonetically any final vowel in the singular, and the formulation of the Apocope Rule that deletes this final /e/ which is realized phonetically in the plural forms (cf. *voz, voces* < /bōke(s)/, *red, redes* < /rēte(s)/, etc.). This not only simplifies the process of plural formation in Spanish, but it makes the Main Stress Rule in this language much simpler and more general. Foley's description of Spanish phonology hinges on the division of the lexicon into two classes, *erudite* and *vulgar*, to which different sets of rules apply, although some rules may apply to forms of both classes.

Schane's dissertation, published in a revised version three years later (Schane 1968a), was the first description of French phonology and morphology within the generative framework. The rules presented in this work account for a great number of phonological alternations appearing in morphologically related forms. Schane's is the first generative analysis of *elision* and *liaison* in French. He showed that both of these are in reality a single phonological phenomenon, Truncation, which operates on special morphological and syntactic constraints. Schane also found it necessary to divide the French lexicon into two major categories -- learned and non-learned -- and claimed that "the applicability or nonapplicability of numerous rules [of French] is contingent on this morphological distinction. (Schane 1968a: 143)" Just as Foley (1965b) had established the need for underlying tense and lax vowels in Spanish, of which only the latter undergo some phonological rules (e.g. Diphthongization), so did Schane's description of French contain seven tense and seven lax underlying vowels.[2] A major portion of Schane's dissertation and monograph deals with the morphology of the French verb system and the phonological rules that account for the different paradigms.[3]

1965 was a crucial year because it marked the beginning of a new period in the development of Romance linguistics. In addition to the two pioneering works just mentioned, other phonological studies of Romance languages appeared that year making use of the generative theory. At the 11th International Congress of Romance Linguistics held in Madrid, R. J. Di Pietro's paper presented an outline of a generative phonology of Italian. Foley (1965a) claimed that all forms of the Latin verb *sum* could be generated from the underlying root *s* by the application of 5 phonological rules for which he found independent motivation. Saporta (1965) used several facts from Spanish dialects with the aim to give support to some claims made by Halle (1962) that the descriptions of two related dialects very often differ by the deletion, addition, or reordering of a small number of rules.

A student of Saporta at the University of Washington applied the ideas of this article in her M.A. thesis (Sableski 1965), in which she presented a generative phonology of a rural dialect of Spanish spoken in Panama.

On the other side of the world, in the Soviet Union, Igor Mel'čuk was also very active in 1965. Three of his papers (Mel'čuk 1965a, 1965b, 1965c) dealing with Spanish phonology appeared in print. Although his main interest was machine translation and computational linguistics, he did discuss some theoretical aspects of generative phonology, made use of distinctive features in describing phonological processes of Spanish, and offered an algorithm to generate the simple forms of the Spanish verb system (1965c).

3. 1966-1969

The last four years of the sixties saw a proliferation of studies and descriptions of the Romance languages within the framework of generative phonology. The two most important works of this period were, undoubtedly, Mario Saltarelli's 1966 University of Illinois dissertation on Italian, and James Harris' 1967 M.I.T. dissertation on Spanish.

Saltarelli's dissertation, published in monograph form in 1970, was "the first extensive application of generative techniques to the study of Italian phonology."[4] The most important claim of this description of the sound system of a variety of modern Italian was that the feature of vowel length rather than stress is of primary importance in Italian. Saltarelli's rules assigning stress in Italian operate on the basis of syntactic and lexical strata[5] information. Harris' dissertation on Spanish phonology, published as a monograph two years after its defense (Harris 1969b), was not only the most detailed and thorough description of the phonology of a Romance language, but it was an important contribution to the theory of generative phonology since it was the first in depth study of a language other than English from the point of view of the universal phonological theory proposed by Chomsky and Halle in *The Sound Pattern of English*. Harris' study of Spanish phonology led him to postulate some revisions in the theory of markedness, namely an amended universal interpretive convention for stridency, the need for upgrading the role of the feature [distributed] in linguistic theory, etc. One of the areas of Spanish phonology not covered in Harris (1969b), that of the irregular verbs, is discussed in the studies of Foley, Cressey, and Harris that appear in this volume.

Within the same period a large number of doctoral dissertations and M.A. theses in which Romance languages were analyzed from the point of view of generative phonology were completed in American and Canadian universities. Campbell (1966), after reviewing and evaluating the most important analyses of Spanish phonology done in pre-generative terms, offered a set of rules to account for phonological processes found in this language. Wolfe (1966) proposed an analysis of Spanish verb forms. His stress rules seem simple, but he achieved this apparent simplicity by setting up three different types of underlying vowels (plain vowels, double vowels, and weak vowels), which seems totally counterintuitive. Zull (1966) proposed a selfconsistent set of rules for a sub-system of the French verb system stated in terms of

distinctive features. She concluded that phonological rules written in
distinctive features could be tested by computer. Willis (1969) gave in
his dissertation a set of rules to account for four degrees of stress in
Spanish. In the second part of my own dissertation (Saciuk 1969a) I offered
a generalized Main Stress Rule for Spanish, and made the claim that penultimate syllable stress is the normal case for [+Native] words of Spanish,
giving supporting evidence for this from nativized borrowings, from the process
of lexical simplification, and from dialectal data.[6] Augerot (1968) developed
a set of distinctive features to describe morphophonemic alternations in
Romanian. To be able to account for the phonological phenomena of this
language, he found it necessary to divide the lexicon into at least two parts
(Latin-derived vocabulary and fully assimilated borrowings vs. unassimilated
borrowings and neologisms) on the basis of application or non-application of
rules.

Diachronic and dialectal studies of the Romance languages viewed through
the prism of generative theory also appeared during this productive period.
Loy's (1966) dissertation presented a set of phonological rules reflecting
the development of Modern French from Latin. Delisle (1968) proposed the
rules needed to derive the Modern French first person plural verb forms
from the Latin underlying forms.[7] In his dissertation Burstynsky (1967)
applied the distinctive feature framework to historical Spanish phonology
and compared the diachronic rules with the rules of a morphophonemic description of Modern Spanish. Willis' 1967 M.A. thesis was a generative diachronic
study of Spanish vowels.

Among the linguists who made a contribution to the generative approach
to Romance dialectology in the late sixties, we find the names of Vasiliu,
Calvano, Burstynsky, and Saltarelli. Vasiliu (1966 and 1967) used the
generative framework to offer a classification and comparison of Daco-
Romaniam dialects and showed how a dialectological study done in terms of
a system of ordered rules, and its subsets, was more powerful and more revealing than a purely historical or a purely distributional synchronic analysis.
Calvano in his M.A. thesis (1966) compared the phonemic systems (analyzed in
distinctive features) and the phonological rules of four Ibero-Romance
dialects (Castilian, Aragonese, Catalan, Portuguese). Calvano (1969) based
his dissertation on five Italian dialects (Catanese, Palermitano, Caposelese,
Roccagorghese, Galtellese). He suggested "that a language consist[s] of a dictionary or lexicon of cognates plus those rules and only those rules needed
to convert these items to the correct form of the individual dialect dictionary
(Calvano 1969:162-3)," and used these criteria in his comparison of the five
dialects. Burstynsky (1968) was a generative treatment of some phonological
phenomena of Canadian French. Another dialectological study of French was
Patterson's M.A. thesis (1969), which compared the vowel system of Standard
French and that of the dialect spoken at Falher. Saltarelli (1968) formulated
the rules needed to account for vocalic processes in three areas of the
Marsian dialect of Italian with the rules of Standard Italian and proposed
a hypothesis for dialect "intelligibility." Another study to be mentioned in
this group is Fontanella (1967), in which, using Saporta's (1965) proposals

for dialect description, the author offered four rules to be found in the Spanish dialects that exhibit word-final and syllable-final s-deletion and s-aspiration (s>h).[8]

A number of other synchronic descriptions and studies of individual Romance languages carried out within the generative theory appeared in print in 1966-1969. Although Romanian had been completely neglected by generative phonologists until this period, in the late sixties there was a flourish of generative publications on the phonology of this language (Belchiţa 1967-1968, 1968, 1969; Golopenţia-Eretescu 1967a; Hamp 1968; Ionescu 1969). French and Spanish were also well represented. In addition to the works already mentioned, we find articles by Gross (1967), Milner (1967), Schane (1967a, 1967b, 1968b) on French phonology, and Contreras (1969b), Foley (1967), Hoffman (1969),[9] Mel'čuk (1967) on Spanish. To the generative analyses of topics of Italian phonology that appeared in these years we must add Saltarelli (1966a) and Di Pietro (1967). Foley (1966) dealt with Latin.

The major Romance language least studied from within the framework of generative phonology in the sixties was Portuguese. Probably, the first generative analysis of its sound system was my paper entitled "Some Basic Rules of Portuguese Phonology," read at the 1967 Winter meeting of the Linguistic Society of America. The first published work on Portuguese phonology was Hensey (1968). No other generative study of Portuguese phonology was made public before 1970. The minor Romance language (e.g., Catalan, Provençal, Gallego, etc.) were completely neglected.

Several of the phonological studies of the Romance languages of this period, mentioned so far, touched upon theoretical issues.[10] But there was also a small number of works that dealt primarily with the theory of phonology espoused by the generative-transformational school of linguistics. In all of them, the theoretical considerations and proposals were based on data from the Romance languages. Thus, contreras (1969a) used Spanish, primarily, in his article on "Simplicity, Descriptive Adequacy, and Binary Features." Harris (1969a)[11] used evidence from the diachronic development of Spanish sibilants to argue for some needed revisions in the theory of markedness and in the universal interpretive conventions proposed in *The Sound Pattern of English*. Saciuk (1969a)[12] proposed a language-independent generative approach to account for the different lexical strata that form part of the phonology of a given language,[13] and then applied the proposed method to the analysis of Spanish stress and of several phonological phenomena from Spanish and Portuguese. On the basis of phonological data from Ibero-Romance and Italian dialects, Saltarelli (1966b) outlined a strategy for comparing generative-transformational grammars of related dialects and languages with the goal of developing a theory of dialectology. He attempted to provide grammatical definitions of various dialectologically important concepts (e.g. relatedness, variation, distance, intelligibility, dialect).

4. RECENT WORK

The seventies stated very promisingly. The impetus of the last decade acquired even greater momentum. Over 40 works[14] appeared in the first two years of the new decade, in which the theory of generative phonology was applied to the description and analysis of Romance languages or that presented new proposals for the revision or improvement of the current generative-trans-formational theory, namely that formulated in Chomsky and Halle (1968).

It is safe to assume that master's theses and doctoral dissertations continue to be written, analyzing topics in the phonologies of the Romance languages from the generative point of view. But because it takes sometimes a year or more for a thesis or dissertation to be mentioned in the literature or to be entered in *Dissertation Abstracts*, at this time we can list only a few of these works. In his M.I.T. dissertation, Dell (1970) treats some of the most important late phonological processes of French. He also restates the phenomenon of *liaison* and consonant truncation, and, on the basis of French data, attempts to establish the foundations of a theory of derivational morphology. Lleó's University of Washington M.A. thesis is a generative analysis of the basic rules of the phonology of Catalan. Catalan is also described in Vogt's 1970 bachelor's thesis at Harvard. Walker (1971) is a Ph.D. dissertation on Old French phonology and morphology directed by Schane at the University of California-San Diego. Wilson (1970) is a University of Michigan dissertation on the phonology of Costa Rican Spanish.

The seventies bring with them generative works on two Romance languages heretofore not studied from within this theory of phonology — Catalan and Portuguese.[15] In addition to Lleó (1970) and Vogt (1970), Catalan is analyzed in Phelps (1972) and Vogt (1971). Descriptions of topics from Portuguese phonology are found in Brasington (1971), Hensey (1971), Naro (1970a, 1971a, 1971b, 1971c, 1971d), and Saciuk (1970).[16] Spanish is represented by Berschin (1971), Cressey (1970b), Harris (1970a, 1970c, 1970d), Mayerthaler (1971), Naro (1970b), Saltarelli (1970b), and Willis (1970). Works that deal with Romanian phonology are Augerot (1971), Belchiţa (1970), and Ionescu (1971). Descriptions of questions of Italian phonology appear in the works of Clivio (1970,1971), Saltarelli (1970c), and Wanner (1970). The only work solely devoted to French phonology is Morin (1972).

Theoretical investigations and proposals based on data drawn from the Romance languages are becoming more frequent. In the first two years of this decade works devoted to many areas of the generative theory of phonology itself are: Cressey (1970b), Harris (1970d), Ionescu (1971), Naro (1970a, 1971a, 1971b, 1971c, 1971d), Phelps (1972), Schane (1970, 1971a, 1971b), Vogt (1971), and Wanner (1970).

5. THE FUTURE

In addition to providing descriptions of the major Romance languages as well as of heretofore untouched minor languages and dialects, generative studies of these languages will help to re-examine, validate or reject some of the existing theoretical claims.

In our future work we should look for data that validate or annihilate some of the recent theoretical proposals. One of these is the notion of *GLOBAL RULES*, "where the structural description of a phonological rule may refer not only to properties of the structure which is [the] input to the rule, but also to properties of that structure at an 'earlier' point in the derivation." That is to say, if phonological rules must have access to 'derivational history', as has been suggested by Charles Kisseberth. If this notion is correct, our theory of phonology will have to be re-examined in order to allow rules to refer to the derivational history of the forms to which they apply.

The nature of linguistic change as seen from the generative perspective should be investigated on the basis of Romance languages. These studies may support or call for a revision of our theory, as delineated by Chomsky and Halle, which claims that "a rule that is added to the grammar may continue to function for many generations without causing changes in the lexical representations (1968:251)." Diachronic studies of the Romance languages within the generative framework may reveal good arguments for the retention, rejection, or modification of the current view that lexical restructuring is a slow process and that rule addition takes place at the end of a set of rules. It may also shed some light on the types of rules that can be added to a grammar and if indeed "the constraints on [these] rules...[are] more severe than those on rules that can figure in a grammar," as has been proposed in Chomsky and Halle (1968:259).

The relationship between diachronic changes and synchronic descriptions is still not clear. Do historical explanations "point the way towards a more natural synchronic analysis," as was suggested by Cressey in his 1970 LSA paper. The Romance languages are in a very good position to confirm or disprove this suggestion, because of the abundance of available information on historical developments. If an affirmative conclusion is reached on this topic, then the theoretical knowledge gained from the examination of the Romance languages can be applied to American Indian, Siberian, and other languages which lack written sources and historical information.

The careful analysis of the Romance languages will also provide our theory of language with a better understanding of lexical strata.[17]

Answers to many theoretical and language-specific descriptive questions will emerge in the years to come as the result of the interaction between generative-transformational grammar and the Romance languages.

NOTES

1. Cambridge, Mass.: The MIT Press. First published in 1951. The second edition of 1952 was corrected and revised and went through several printings. In 1963 the article "Tenseness and Laxness" by Jakobson and Halle was added as a supplement and it has appeared in all subsequent printings of *Preliminaries*.

2. Foley established ten underlying vowels for Spanish, five tense and five lax.

3.   Smith (1969) is an excellent and very informative review of Schane (1968a), where the author updates Schane's analysis in light of the theoretical innovations proposed in *The Sound Pattern of English* (Chomsky and Halle 1968).   Smith formalizes, in terms of the new distinctive features and with the theory of markedness in mind, some of the rules of French phonology presented verbally by Schane, and offers some changes in the theory of phonology on the basis of the French data described by Schane and reanalyzed by Smith. Schane (1966) was a shortened version of the analysis of the French verb presented in detailed form in Schane (1968a).   It was intended to exemplify the principles of generative phonology.

4.   Di Pietro (1971b:718). This is a very detailed review of Saltarelli (1970a).

5.   I.e., he assigns to words the features [+Native], [-Native], [+Greek x], etc., and some rules (e.g., Primary Stress Rule P11, and the phonological rules of FEM, MASC, and PLUR inflection) apply to words belonging to one lexical subset differently than to those which are members of another lexical category.   Saciuk (1969a and 1969b) claimed that a word in a language may be made up of morphemes belonging to different lexical strata and that features like [±Native], etc. should be assigned to individual formatives and not to whole words.

6.   The analysis of Spanish stress given in Saciuk (1969a) accounts correctly for forms like *Venezuela, abuelo, tropiezo,* etc. which were a problem for Foley (1965b) and Harris (1969b).

7.   He postulated that the underlying form of the root of the Latin verb *sum* is /sm/ and made some slight modifications of the rules presented in Foley (1965a).

8.   Although the analysis is based on the Spanish dialect spoken in Buenos Aires, identical or similar rules would be needed for certain levels of speech in a number of American-Spanish dialects, e.g. Cuban or Caribbean Spanish in general.

9.   This is the first generative study of Spanish hypocoristics (i.e., nicknames).   The rules needed to account for hypocoristics reflect many processes of child language. To the best of my knowledge, this is the first generative work on hypocoristics in any language to appear in print.

10.   Agard (1967), for example, in his analysis of stress in Spanish, Portuguese, Italian, and Romanian, tried to show, among other things, the necessity of revising generative theory so that the underlying systematic morphophonemes are first converted into phonemes before the application of phonological rules.

11.   This is a section of Harris (1969b).

12.   Saciuk (1969b) is just the first part of this work.

13.   The theoretical discussion was based on data from a variety of languages, especially Spanish.

14.   Since these works are so recent, most of them readily available, and very often mentioned or brought up in the literature, I will not discuss them individually.

15. As was mentioned above, only one publication on Portuguese phonology appeared prior to 1970.

16. This is a revised and enlarged version of the 1967 paper.

17. The matter of [±Native] and other classes that form the lexicon of a language was treated in Augerot (1968), Foley (1965b), Harris (1969b), Saciuk (1969a), Saltarelli (1970a), Schane (1968a), Willis (1969).

JAMES FOLEY
SIMON FRASER UNIVERSITY

ASSIBILATION IN SPANISH FIRST SINGULAR VERB FORMS:
INTERRUPTED RULE SCHEMATA

In earlier analyses of Spanish morphology I claimed that certain verbs generally considered irregular in the first person singular could be considered regular by application of certain rules in the proper order. Thus for *hacer/hago* the derivation was

(1)   haker   hako

(2)   haser   "   (assibilation)

(3)   "   hago   (lenition)

The *s/g* alternation results from assibilation applying to *k* when followed by a front vowel but not when followed by a back vowel, in which case lenition occurs.

Harris (1969b:97) objects to this analysis, though he offers no other:

Let us dispose once and for all of the fiction that the present indicative of *hacer* and *decir* is regular.
It has been shown in some detail in Section 3.3 why the irregularities of *hacer* and *decir* cannot be "explained" away as in the above simple but impossible derivation. If *hacer* and *decir* are regular (contrary to all grammarians), then *mecer* (*me[s]o, me[s]es*), *cocer* (*cue[s]o, cue[s]es*), *vencer* (*ven[s]o, ven[s]es*), *torcer* (*tuer[s]o, tuer[s]es*), to mention only a few of the huge number of relevant examples, cannot be.

Several comments are worth making:

(1)   Section 3.3 deals with the present subjunctive. There is no
      discussion in detail of the stem alternations in *hacer* and
      Nor does Harris explain why the derivation is impossible.

(2)   That all grammarians consider *hacer* and *decir* irregular means
       nothing. Grammarians consider all verbs exhibiting alternations
       irregular.

(3)   The claim that both *hacer/hago* and *vencer/venzo* cannot be regular
       is simply false, as will be shown in this paper.

The problem of assibilation in Spanish first person verb forms resolves
itself into the following categories:

(1)   failure of assibilation in *hacer/hago*.

(2)   assibilation in *vencer/venzo, torcer/tuerzo, mecer/mezo, cocer/cuezo*.

(3)   failure of assibilation in *conocer/conozco, nacer/nazco, lucir/luzco,
       crecer/crezco*.

(4)   assibilation in *regir/rijo, proteger/protejo, dirigir/dirijo*.

The derivation of *hacer/hago* is not quite as simple as given above.
The underlying forms are

(1)   hak-e-r   hak-e-o

with thematic vowel *e* before both infinitive ending *r* and first person
ending *o*. If assibilation applied first, incorrect **hazo* would result.
But before assibilation can apply, thematic *e* is deleted by rule

         A vowel elision

$$e \longrightarrow \emptyset \ / \ \underline{\quad} + V$$

giving

(2)   hak-e-r   hak-o

to which applies first assibilation

(3)   hatser   "

and then lenition

(4)   haser   hago

If the same rules applied in the same order to *vencer/venzo* the incorrect
*venko would result:

(1)   venk-e-r   venk-e-o

(2)	"	venk-o	(vowel elision)
(3)	venser	"	(assibilation)
(4)	"	"	(lenition)

The solution lies in an analysis of the rule A vowel elision. We can make at least three statements concerning vowel elision:

(1)   for reasons unclear, it occurs in the environment ___ + V but not in ___ V or ___ + C. This particular characteristic plays no role in differentiating the first person reflexes (where all occur in the environment ___ + V) and no further reference will be made to it.

(2)   weak vowels are elided before strong vowels are elided. Thus in Romance languages e is dropped before o is, o before a is, note

Latin	Spanish	French
mare	mar	mer
amicus	amigo	ami
amica	amiga	amie

First e drops (Spanish) then e and o (medieval French) then e and o and a (modern French). The rule is

B V_n ---> $\emptyset$ / ___ #

where $\emptyset \leq n \leq m$

    for Latin m = $\emptyset$
    for Spanish m = 1
    for medieval French m = 2
    for modern French m = 3

based on the Romance vowel strength scale

$$\begin{array}{ccc} e & o & a \\ \hline 1 & 2 & 3 \end{array} \rightarrow$$

which gives the relative phonological strength of Romance vowels.

Stated differently, if o drops then so must e, if a drops then so must o and e. Or given the three vowels e,o,a we predict that e will be the first to drop.

This characteristic of vowel elision has no relevance to the problem at hand except to illustrate the role that phonological strength plays in the statement of rule schemata. The rule schema B is an abbreviation for a series of rules

B_1 e ---> $\emptyset$ / ___ # (m = 1)

B_2 e,o ---> $\emptyset$ / ___ # (m = 2)

B_3 e,o,a ---> $\emptyset$ / ___ # (m = 3)

(3)   Our third and relevant comment on vowel elision refers to the role of the number of preceding consonants.

$$C \quad V ---> \emptyset \ / \ C^n \ \underline{\quad} \ \#$$
where n refers to the number of consonants
where $1 \leq n \leq m$
for Spanish m = 1
for French m = 2

Thus in Spanish final *e* is deleted after one consonant, but not after two consonants, whereas in French final *e* is deleted also after two consonants:

Latin	*Spanish*	*French*
mare	mar	mer
*habitante	habitante	habitant

Important is the realization that rule C is a rule schema for

C_1 V ---> $\emptyset$ / C^1 ___ #

C_2 V ---> $\emptyset$ / C^1___# and / C^2 ___#

and that C_1 applies before C_2.

From the foregoing we see that the elision of thematic *e* in *hak-e-o* occurs earlier than the elision of *e* in *venk-e-o*.

$$D \quad e ---> \emptyset \ / \ C^n \ \underline{\quad} \ + V$$
where $1 \leq n \leq m$

which is an abbreviation for

D_1 e ---> $\emptyset$ / C^1 ___ + V

D_2 e ---> $\emptyset$ / C^2 ___ + V

Thus

(1)   hak-e-o   venk-e-o

(2)   hak-o   "   (rule D_1)

(3)   "   venk-o   (rule D_2)

When the subrules of a rule schema apply contiguously there is no visible reflection of their sequential application. But the sequential application becomes apparent when their application is not contiguous, but rather interrupted by insertion of another rule. Thus in the derivation of *hago* and *venzo* the order of rules is:

(1) vowel elision D_1

(2) assibilation

(3) vowel elision D_2

giving the derivations

(1) hak-e-o   venk-e-o

(2) hak-o   "   (vowel elision after one consonant)

(3) "   venz-e-o   (assibilation)

(4) "   venzo   (vowel elision after two consonants)

The assibilation in *venzo* but not *hago* results from the two consonants preceding the thematic vowel in *venzo*. This consonant group delays vowel elision until assibilation has applied. Both *hago* and *venzo* are regular under the concept of interrupted rule schemata. Like *vencer/venzo* are *torcer/tuerzo*, *mecer/mezo*, *cocer/cuezo* through each requires separate discussion.

As concerns Spanish, *torcer/tuerzo* is exactly like *vencer/venzo* but from a historical view *torcer* is anomalous, since assibilation does not normally apply to a labial-velar (Latin *torquere*, though *vincere*). *Torquere* differs from e.g. *quem > quien*, *aquila > aguila* in the preceding back-rounded vowel which attracts the labial element of k^w, thus *tork^{w}ere > to^{w}rkere* from which development as in *vincere > vencer*. The rule is

$$E \quad \varepsilon_1 \, \varepsilon_2{}^x \quad \text{----} \rightarrow \quad \varepsilon_1{}^x \, \varepsilon_2$$

where ε_1 and x are sufficiently more similar than ε_2 and x.

In Bulgarian $sk^s > s^sk > sk$ and in Greek $uk^w > u^wk$. Examples are:

(1)   Greek . IE *wlk^wos gives in Greek *luk^{w}os > lu^{w}kos > lukos* with *u* absorbing the *w* of k^w (the usual reflex of k^w is *t* before *i* or *e*: Latin *quis*, Greek *tis*, or *p* before *a* or *o*: Latin *sequor*, Greek *hepomai*).

(2)   Bulgarian (after Koutsoudas 1966) has singular *ezik*, plural *ezici*, but *vipusk*, pl. *vipusk'i*, where *k* assibilated to *ts* before *i* unless preceded by *s*. The development is

(1)   ezik-i   vipusk-i

(2)   ezik^{s}i   vipusk^{s}i   (k ---> k^s / __ i)

(3)   "   vipus^{s}ki   (sk^s ---> s^{s}k)

whence *ezitsi* but *vipusk'i*.

   Superficially anomalous in Spanish is *mecer/mezo* where we expect **mego*
as reflex of simple intervocalic *k*. But the reflex *z* as in *venzo* suggests
a preceding consonant K such that K prevents vowel elision long enough to
allow assibilation and is then deleted

(1)   meKk-e-o

(2)   "   (vowel elision D1 fails)

(3)   meKs-e-o   (assibilation)

(4)   meKso   (vowel elision D_2 applies)

(5)   messo   (assimilation)

(6)   meso   (simplification)

The chief constraint on *K* is that it must assimilate to the following *s*.
Thus it cannot be *n* (as in *venzo*) and certain other consonants, but of the
possible consonants, the most likely to assimilate to *s* is *s* itself.
Assuming that K = s (as historically *miscere* > *mecer*) the development is

(1)   mesk-e-o

(2)   "   (vowel elision D_1 fails)

(3)   messeo   (assibilation)

(4)   messo   (vowel elision D_2 applies)

(5)   meso   (simplification)

   Mecer/mezo does not follow *hacer/hago* but rather *vencer/venzo* differing
from the latter in having a penultimate thematic consonant which has no
phonetic reflex.

   We note a group of verbs which might be expected to behave like *mecer/
mezo* but which retain unassibilated *k* in the first singular:

       conocer/conozco
       nacer/nazco

lucir/luzco
crecer/crezco

In the infinitive *$conosker$ > $conosser$ > $conoser$ like *$mesker$ > $messer$ > $meser$, but in the first singular *$conosk$-e-o > $conosko$ without the expected assibilation.

We notice that these verbs differ from type $mecer/mezo$ in possessing the inchoative suffix sk. The failure of assibilation in $conozco$ is apparently related to the catalytic influence of the morpheme boundary (+sk) though a detailed discussion is beyond the scope of this paper.

Problematic is the appearance of zc in verbs having no sk of whatever origin in Latin: $placer/plazco$ (Latin $placere$), $yacer/yazco$ but also $yago$ (Latin $jacere$), $deducir/deduzco$ (Latin $deducere$).

The verb $cocer/cuezo$ presents two problems

(1)   as in $mecer/mezo$ there appears to be only one stem-final consonant in $cuezo$, yet the reflex is that of a stem-final cluster.

(2)   historically $cocer$ is anomalous, for from Latin $coquere$ we expect *$coguer$ or *$coguir$ as $sequere$ > $seguir$. The thematic labial-velar should not undergo assibilation.

Fortunately the difficulty of solution does not increase as the anomalies increase, but rather decreases. Were there only one anomalous development the solution would be more difficult, for we would know less. As it is, we know that $cuezo$ suggests two underlying consonants, one of which must be k, and from Latin $coquere/coquo$ we know the other to be w. As in $tork^w ere$ > $to^w rker$ > $torcer$ the development is

(1) $kok^w er$ kok^w-e-o

(2)   kowker   kowkeo   (rule E)

(3)   "   "   (vowel elision D_1 fails)

(4)   kowser   kowseo   (assibilation)

(5)   "   kowso   (vowel elision D_2 applies)

The essential step is the transference of w from k to o, since w is more similar to o than to k. Once this occurs, k is relieved of w and can undergo assibilation, and the cluster wk prevents vowel elision long enough to allow assibilation.

Where the radical vowel is not o, rule E cannot apply and assibilation cannot occur: $sequere$ > $seguir$, $sequo$ > $sigo$.

To summarize this section, the thematic cluster of $venzo$ retards vowel elision long enough to allow assibilation, while the simple consonant of *hago* allows immediate elision, thus preventing assibilation. Like *venzo* are *tuerzo, mezo* and *cuezo*.

Differing both from roots with k (*hacer/hago*) and from roots with Ck (*vencer/venzo*) are roots with g

 regir, rijo
 proteger, protejo

with assibilation in first singular like *venzo*, though with the single consonant characteristic of *hago*.

It is perhaps not immediately clear why k and g should give different reflexes. Presumably either

(1) dik-i-o   rig-i-o

(2) dik-o   *rig-o   (vowel elision)

(3) "   "   (assibilation fails)

or

(1) dik-i-o   rig-i-o

(2) disio   rižio   (assibilation)

(3) *diso   rižo   (vowel elision)

Either order of application of the rules gives an incorrect reflex. The problem is the assibilation of g (*rijo*) but not of k (*hago*). (The assibilated reflex of g is not z (as s the assibilated reflex of k) but rather $ž$ for reasons not discussed here. $ž$ devoices to $š$ with subsequent development to X.)

It is not meet to go into a detailed discussion of assibilation here, but we notice certain characteristics of assibilation:

(1) It depends on the quality of the following vowel, being more likely to occur before i than before e, more likely to occur before e than before a.

(2) It is more likely to occur to velars than to labials.

(3) It is more likely to occur to voiced consonants than to voiceless consonants.

 1. In Spanish assibilation occurs before i or e, whereas in French it occurs before i, e or a

Latin	Spanish	French
circus	circo	cirque
centum	centavo	cent
carus	caro	cher

and presumably in some language assibilation occurs before i but not before e or a. The rule is

F $k \longrightarrow s / \underline{\quad} V_n$

where n refers to phonological strength of vowel
where $\emptyset \leq n \leq m$
where m $= \emptyset$ for Latin (no assibilation)
m = 1 for some language
m = 2 for Spanish
m = 3 for French

Rule F is a rule schema for

F_1 $k \longrightarrow s / \underline{\quad} i$

F_2 $k \longrightarrow s / \underline{\quad} i,e$

F_3 $k \longrightarrow s / \underline{\quad} i,e,a$

2.   We note also that assibilation is more likely to occur to velars than to labials. Compare Spanish and French

Latin	Spanish	French
centum	centavo	cent
gens, gentis	gente	gens
sapiam	sepa	sache
rabiēs	rabia	rage

Referring to the relative phonological strength of velars and labials

$$\frac{k \quad p}{1 \quad 2} >$$

we have the rule for assibilation.

G $C_n \longrightarrow s / \underline{\quad} V$

where n refers to the strength of the consonant
where $\emptyset \leq n \leq m$
where m $= \emptyset$ for Latin (no assibilation)
m = 1 for Spanish
m = 2 for French

We note that G is a rule schema standing for

G_1 k,g --->s,$\check{z}$ / ___ V

G_2 k,g,p,b --->s,$\check{z}$ / ___ V

In short, from the above two observations, we notice that assibilation applies preferentially to weak consonants in weak vocalic environments.

3. We come finally to the pertinent observation, that assibilation is more likely to occur to voiced velars than to voiceless velars. This follows from the principle that assibilation is more likely to occur to phonologically weak consonants than to phonologically strong ones.

H C_n ---> s / ___ V

  where n refers to strength of consonant
  where $\emptyset \leq n \leq m$
  where m = $\emptyset$ for Latin
  m = 1 for some language
  m = 2 for Spanish

with reference to the relative phonological strength of velars

$$\frac{g \quad k}{1 \quad 2} \longrightarrow$$

We note again that H is a rule schema for

H_1 g ---> z / ___ e

H_2 g,k ---> z,s / ___ e

Finally we realize that the assibilation of *g* in *protejo* but not of *k* in *hago* results from the interruption of rule schema H by vowel elision.

(1)   hak-e-o   proteg-e-o

(2)   "   proteǧ-e-o   (H_1 assibilation of g)

(3)   hako   proteǧo   (D vowel elision)

(4)   "   "   (H_2 assibilation of k fails)

Recalling from the previous discussion that vowel elision itself is interrupted by assibilation, we combine our results.

(1)   hak-e-o   venk-e-o   proteg-e-o

(2)	"	"	protežeo	(H_1 assibilation of g)
(3)	hako	"	protežo	(D_1 vowel elision after C)
(4)	"	venseo	"	(H_2 assibilation of k)
(5)	"	venso	"	(D_2 vowel elision after CC)

The different reflexes *hacer/hago*, *vencer/venzo*, and *proteger/protejo* are easily explicable, resulting from the mutual interruption of the rule schemata for assibilation and vowel elision.

WILLIAM W. CRESSEY
GEORGETOWN UNIVERSITY

IRREGULAR VERBS IN SPANISH

In a generative phonology, a verb is considered irregular, not simply because its paradigm differs from that of other verbs, but only if the differences cannot be explained in terms of general principles of pronunciation of the language under analysis. For example, those verbs usually designated as "radical changing verbs" have been analyzed without recourse to special lexical markings both by Foley (1965b) and by Harris (1969b). Once these verbs, and certain others, have been disposed of, we are still left with a substantial number of verbs having irregular conjugations which must be accounted for in terms of exception features associated with their lexical entries.[1]

Naturally, whether or not a given verb requires a special marking in the lexicon is a function of the set of rules which are formulated for the analysis of the language in question. Furthermore, whenever it is asserted that the forms of some class of verbs can be accounted for in terms of a particular set of rules, it must be the case that either (a) the set of rules can apply to the regular forms of the language without yielding incorrect results, or (b) some special lexical feature must be used in order to assure that only the appropriate forms will undergo the proposed rules. For this reason, I have used the rules and derivations proposed in Harris (1969) as a starting point. This will make it possible to determine when and in what ways the rules used in the derivation of the irregular verbs which I propose to discuss differ from the set of rules required for the analysis of regular verbs.

In particular, I will make the claim that, among those verbs which require special marking, given Harris' rules, there is a large subset whose phonetic shapes can be explained, or at least partially explained, in terms of the informal concept of athematicity, that is, the absence of the theme vowel at a point in the derivation when it would normally be present.

For a number of reasons, one of which will be discussed somewhat below, Harris (1969b:67ff.) assumes that the theme vowel must be present in the underlying forms of present subjunctive and first person singular present indicative verbs. He therefore has formulated a rule which deletes the theme vowel from these forms:

(1)   Theme Vowel Deletion (13):[2]

$$V \rightarrow \emptyset \ / \ + \underline{\hspace{1em}} + \begin{bmatrix} V \\ +\text{tense} \end{bmatrix}$$

As illustrated in the following derivations, this rule deletes the theme vowel from forms such as *amo* and *ame* when it is followed by a tense vowel, but not from forms such as *amas* when what follows the theme vowel is a consonant.[3]

(2)   am+a+o   am+a+s   am+a+e+Ø
         Ø   -   Ø   Theme Vowel Del.
       [amo]   [amas]   [ame]

"Athematicity", as used in this paper, will mean that there is something irregular about the way that this rule, theme vowel deletion, applies to a particular verb form: Either the verb form is subject to the rule, although it does not meet the structural requirement of the rule, or the rule applies at an earlier point in the derivation of the verb than it would normally.

For the purpose of establishing the claim that athematicity is a bona fide phenomenon in Spanish, I will begin by briefly summarizing two cases of athematicity which have been discussed in previous work, and I will then suggest analyses of two other classes of irregular verbs in terms of this same concept. In addition, I will attempt to show that the analyses proposed here have certain implications for the overall theory of generative phonology.

One case of athematicity, discussed in Foley (1965b) is the set of irregular past participles. If the past participle ending is assumed to be -*to* rather than -*do*, the irregular forms listed below can be explained by assuming that the theme vowel has been deleted from these forms before voicing of intervocalic stops occurs.

(3)

Infinitive	Underlying Form	Past Participle
abrir	aper+i+to	abierto
cubrir	cuper+i+to	cubierto
morir	mor+i+to	muerto
volver	volv+e+to	vuelto
soltar	solt+a+to	suelto
escribir	scrip+i+to	escrito
ver	vid+e+to	visto
poner	pos+e+to	puesto
decir	dik+i+to	dicho
hacer	ak+e+to	hecho
romper	rup+e+to	roto

In order to fully explain the phonetic shapes of many of these past participles, additional rules are required and in some cases the underlying form given above is not the most obvious one. For a full discussion of these rules and these underlying forms see Harris (1969b) and Foley (1965b). As an illustration, derivations, for the regular form *amado* and for the irregular forms *muerto* and *dicho* are given below:

(4) am+a+to   mor+i+to   dik+i+to
      -           Ø   Ø   Theme V. Del.(13)
                              y   č   Palatalization(12)
      d   Voicing(19)
                              Ø   y-deletion(23)
                  we   Diphthongization(26)
      [amado]   [mwerto]   [dičo]

Although Harris lists palatalization (rule 12) before theme vowel deletion (rule 13), I am not aware of any case which depends crucially upon this ordering. Therefore we can assume tentatively that the order of these two rules can be reversed as shown in (4), above, without affecting the rest of the grammar. The analysis of irregular past participles, then, is carried out in terms of a lexical feature which stipulates that these forms undergo theme vowel deletion in spite of the fact that they do not meet the normal structural requirement of the rule. Thus we should add to theme vowel deletion a second case which will be designated as a minor rule (that is, it applies only to those lexical items which are specially marked to undergo it):

(5) Theme vowel deletion(13), revised:

$$V \rightarrow \emptyset \ / \ + \underline{\quad} + \begin{Bmatrix} \begin{bmatrix} V \\ +tense \end{bmatrix} & (a) \\ \dots \quad MINOR & (b) \end{Bmatrix}$$

The second previously discussed case of athematicity is the set of irregular future tense forms as analyzed by Harris (1969b:96ff.). The first four forms in (6), below, can be accounted for solely in terms of theme vowel deletion. The middle group requires, in addition, a *d*-insertion rule which serves to break up the alveolar sonorant clusters *n+r* and *l+r*, and *decir* and *hacer* require a special rule to delete the stem final consonant.

(6) *Infinitive*   *Athematic Future Stem*
      haber   habr-
      querer   querr-
      poder   podr
      saber   sabr-

poner	pondr-
tener	tendr-
venir	vendr-
salir	saldr-
valer	valdr-
decir	dir-
hacer	har-

Thus these verbs must be marked to undergo theme vowel deletion in the future tense. Inspection of the lists given in (3) and (6) reveals that there is some overlap between the set of verbs which must be marked [+Theme Vowel Deletion in Past Participle] and the set which must be marked [+Theme Vowel Deletion in Future Tense]. Clearly, then, some system of redundancy rules is required to assign these exception features in the most efficient manner possible.

Having established abnormal theme vowel deletion as an existing process in Spanish phonology, I turn now to the analysis of irregular preterites, and of the present indicative and subjunctive of *hacer* and *decir*.

In (7), below, the first and third persons singular of the irregular preterites are given along with the infinitives of the verbs in question:

(7) *Infinitive*	*1st. sg.*	*3rd. sg.*
venir	vine	vino
poder	pude	pudo
poner	puse	puso
saber	supe	supo
caber	cupe	cupo
estar	estuve	estuvo
andar	anduve	anduvo
tener	tuve	tuvo
haber	hube	hubo
traer	traje	trajo
decir	dije	dijo
hacer	hice	hizo
(pro)ducir	(pro)duje	(pro)dujo

At first glance, the penultimate stress of these forms would appear to be more regular and natural for Spanish than the final stress of regular preterite forms, for example *amé, amó*. Indeed the final stress of these regular forms has been one of the most puzzling aspects of the Spanish verb system. Harris has proposed an analysis of these regular preterites in terms of special person number endings for preterite and a set of rules which, although quite complex, is well motivated in his discussion (Harris 1969b:79ff.). Harris' analysis of regular preterites is further supported, it seems to me, by the fact that it is quite possible to account for irregular preterites in terms of his rules with very little lexical marking (in fact, by changing one single feature specification). Harris' derivations for the regular first and third person singular forms *amé*, *amó*, *comí*, and *comió* are as follows:

(8)

am+a+ĭ	am+a+ŭ	com+e+ĭ	com+e+ŭ	
		i	i	Past Raising(1)
		-	-	Theme V. Del.(13)
á	á	í	í	Stress(16)
é	ó			a-assimilation(18)
∅	∅	∅	i ṷ	High Deletion(22)
			ó	Stress shift(27)
				Lowering(28)
			y	Glide Formation(37)
[amé]	[amó]	[comí]	[comyó]	

In these derivations, normal theme vowel deletion fails to apply to the first and third person singular forms because their endings are lax *i* and *u* and theme vowel deletion applies only before a tense vowel. Returning to the irregular forms such as *vine* and *vino*, it would seem that the most natural way to explain why the stress patterns of these forms differs from that of the regular verbs, would be to assume that these two persons (but not *viniste*, *vinimos*, etc.) are athematic. It would also seem that the simplest assumption that could be made as to why these two forms, but not the other persons, are athematic is that the endings for the irregular preterites are tense rather than lax (as for regular preterites). Furthermore, Harris' analysis of regular verbs includes a rule which converts lax vowels to tense vowels:

(9) Raising(1):

$$\begin{bmatrix} V \\ -low \end{bmatrix} \rightarrow \begin{bmatrix} +high \\ +tense \end{bmatrix} \Bigg/ \left\{ \begin{matrix} \underline{\quad} \ [+past] & (a) \\[2ex] \left[\overline{3conj}\right] C_0 \ [V]_v & (b) \end{matrix} \right.$$

Since this rule mentions the feature [+past] it is an intriguing thought that the special marking required for the analysis of irregular preterites might be accomplished most economically in terms of a minor case of this rule which would apply only to irregular preterites, tensing the first and third person singular endings:[4]

(10)

$$\Bigg/ \ \left[\overline{+past}\right] \ \# \ MINOR \quad (c)$$

Derivations for the forms of *venir* are as follows:

(11) ven+i+í̆   ven+i+ste   ven+i+ŭ̆   ven+i+mos   ven+i+ron
        i   i   i   i   i   (1b)
              ī̃   ū̄   (1c)
           ∅   ∅   (13)
        ↑   ↑   ↑   ↑   ↑   (16)
                                                          ↑̃   (25)
                                                          yé̃   (26)
           e   o   (28)
      [víne]   [viníste]   [víno]   [viní̃mos]   [vinyéron]

Rule (1b) raises the vowel of third conjugation verb stems, (1c) tenses the preterite endings for first and third person singular, thus allowing theme vowel deletion (13) to apply to these forms. Rule (16) then correctly assigns stress to the stems of these two forms and to the theme vowel of all the others. Rules (25) and (26) account for the diphthong in the third person plural form in the same manner as for regular verbs, and finally rule (28) lowers the final vowels of *vine* and *vino* producing the correct phonetic outputs.

In these derivations, the key difference between regular and irregular preterites is seen to be the athematicity of first and third person singular forms. If the tensing of these preterite endings by a minor case of rule (1), as suggested here, seems ad hoc, it is clear that there are other ways to trigger the required theme vowel deletion. For example, these verbs could be lexically marked to undergo the minor case of rule (13) for first and third person singular forms. However, it would seem that my formulation explains in a more straightforward way why the irregular preterites should be athematic only in these two forms, rather than throughout the entire paradigm.

As in the case of the forms discussed earlier, the shapes of the stems of a number of these forms requires explanation as well. Foley (1965b: Sec. 1.7, 4.4) has proposed analyses of *decir* and *saber* in terms of *s* and *w* increment rules respectively, and the latter could be applied to *saber*, *tener*, *caber*, *haber*, and *andar* as well. The high stem vowels of *pude* and *puse* offer one additional reason to examine the possible relationship between Harris' rule (1) and this class of irregular preterites. The stem *o*'s of *poder* and *poner* cannot be raised to *u* by either case of Harris' rule (see (9), above)--case (a) fails because these stem vowels are not in the correct position immediately before the preterite ending, and case (b) fails because the verbs in question are not third conjugation verbs. Nor could this vowel raising be accomplished by my proposed case (c) of this rule. However, it could be accomplished by a strange combination of (a), (b), and (c), which I have formulated as case (d). (The entire rule is repeated below):

(12)

$$\begin{bmatrix} V \\ -low \end{bmatrix} \rightarrow \begin{bmatrix} +high \\ +tense \end{bmatrix} / \left\{ \begin{array}{ll} \underline{\qquad} \text{ [+past]} & \text{(a)} \\ \overline{[3conj]} \ C_0 \ V]_V & \text{(b)} \\ \\ \overline{[+past]} \ \# \qquad\qquad \text{MINOR} & \text{(c)} \\ \underline{\qquad} \ C_0 \ V \ \text{[+past]} \ \text{MINOR} & \text{(d)} \end{array} \right\}$$

Although, given our present notational system, it seems unlikely that it is possible to combine cases (a) through (d) of this rule in a way that eliminates repetition of the feature [+past] and the configuration C_0 V, the generalization expressed by the rule as a whole is relatively easy to state -- non-low vowels in irregular preterite forms are raised and tensed wherever they happen to be in the verb form.

I turn now to a consideration of the present indicative and subjunctive forms of the verbs *hacer* and *decir*. With the exception of some vowel alternations, these two verbs can be explained identically. Thus only forms of *decir* will be cited here. Foley (1965b:Sec. 1.7) proposed an analysis of these forms in terms of velar softening and voicing of intervocalic stops. His derivations of *digo, dice,* and *diga* are given below:

(13) dik+o   dik+a   dik+e
      -        -   s   Velar Softening (9)
      g   g   Voicing (19)
      [digo]   [diga]   [dise]

At first glance, it would appear that the forms are regular and that these forms require no special lexical marking to account for them. However, as I stated earlier, Harris has provided strong evidence for assuming that the theme vowel of forms like *digo* and *diga* must be present in the underlying forms. Furthermore, in order to derive forms such as *togue* and *cueza*[5] correctly, the theme vowel deletion rule must follow velar softening, as illustrated below:

(14) tok+a+e   kŏk+e+a
      -          s   Velar Softening(9)
      ∅   ∅   Theme Vowel Deletion (13)
                 we   Diphthongization (26)
      [toke][6] [kwesa]

Moreover, this sequence of rules cannot produce the correct results in the case of *hacer* and *decir*. In spite of these facts, the phonological processes cited by Foley in his derivations of *digo*, *dice*, and *diga* appear to be correct--the application of velar softening to some instances of stem-final /k/ and not to others seems to be conditioned by the vowel which follows the stem in phonetic representations in spite of the fact that this vowel does not follow the stem final /k/ at the point in the derivation when velar softening usually applies. One rather straightforward way of explaining why this should be so would be to assume that the theme vowel is missing in these verb forms at the point in the derivation when velar softening normally applies. This approach would have the added advantage of explaining the forms of these two verbs in a way which is related to the explanations of other irregular verb forms (i.e., in terms of athematicity).

Now, in the present forms of *hacer* and *decir*, the theme vowel is not deleted from any forms from which it would not be deleted from a regular verb -- it is deleted in exactly the environment specified by rule (13a). Therefore, it would seem that the only way to accomplish the deletion at the necessary point in the derivation is to stipulate that these two verbs are marked with a special feature which reverses the order of application of theme vowel deletion and velar softening, as illustrated below:[7]

(15) dik+e+o   dik+e+a   dik+e+s
        Ø   Ø   -   Theme V. Del.(13)
        -            -   s   Velar Soft.(9)
        g   g   Voicing(19)
      [digo]   [diga]   [dises]

Thus it seems that in addition to exception features which stipulate that a given lexical item undergoes a rule which it should not, and vice versa, we need exception features which stipulate that in the case of lexical items to which they apply. The "normal" order of certain rules is reversed.

Everything I have said thus far has been in the context of a system of ordered rules such as that described in Chomsky and Halle (1968) and currently in use in most phonological research. However, the mechanism of reversing the order of two rules would appear to be a much more natural one within the context of a somewhat different ordering system proposed by Stephen Anderson (1970:394ff). The aspect of Anderson's Local Ordering Theory relevant to the present discussion is the suggestion that some phonological rules are not ordered explicitly by being listed in a particular order, but rather implicitly in the following manner: two rules will apply to a given lexical item in the order which will allow maximum application of both rules to that lexical item (What Kiparsky (1968b:197ff) calls a feeding order). feeding order and bleeding order of theme vowel deletion and velar softening to the lexical item *cuezo* is illustrated below:

(16)   feeding   bleeding
                 order   order

	kŏk+e+o	kŏk+e+o	
Vel. Sof.	s	∅	T.V.D.
T.V.D.	∅	-	Vel. Sof. fails
	[kweso]	*[kweko]	

If these two rules apply in the feeding order, both rules apply and the correct result is obtained. However, if they apply in the bleeding order, velar softening fails and the incorrect result *[kweko] is obtained.

In Anderson's ordering theory, rules designated as locally ordered will apply automatically in the feeding order (which he calls the unmarked order) unless otherwise stated for a particular lexical item. As demonstrated earlier, in the case of *hacer* and *decir*, these two rules must apply in the opposite order, which for these verbs is a bleeding order, and must be marked explicitly:

(17)   feeding   bleeding
                 order   order

	dik+e+o	dik+e+o	
Vel. Sof.	s	∅	T.V.D.
T.V.D.	∅	-	Vel. Sof. fails
Voicing[8]	-	g	Voicing
	*[diso]	[digo]	

Thus in terms of Anderson's Local Ordering Theory, *decir* and *hacer* must undergo these two rules in the marked order, and the irregular property of the forms in question is expressed in terms of a mechanism which is intrinsic to his overall ordering theory.

It should be noted that the verbs *hacer* and *decir* must be marked as irregular given either ordering theory. The difference is simply that the irregularity is expressed more naturally in the local ordering theory than in the standard ordering theory.

Now, all this looks pretty good, and works fine for the analysis of these two verbs with respect to these two rules. However, as has been the case so many times in recent work in phonological theory, when we broaden our scope and consider other verbs and other rules a simple straightforward mechanism such as the Local Ordering Theory runs into difficulties and requires fixing up in terms of not-so-straightforward, not-so-simple provisos. One difficulty was mentioned by Harris (1970b). When we consider verbs like *tocar*, which are perfectly regular by any account, the correct order of the rules is the bleeding order:

(18)   feeding   bleeding
                         order   order

                        tok+a+e   tok+a+e
T.V.D.   Ø   -   Vel. Sof. fails
Vel. Sof.   s   Ø   T.V.D.
                        *[tose]   [toke]

Thus in terms of the Local Ordering Theory as stated here, *tocar* must be just as heavily marked as *decir*, which is obviously not correct.

However, the notion that local ordering, as defined by Anderson, plays some part in phonological systems does seem quite well motivated, and it is possible that some proviso, perhaps along the "paradgmatic regularity" lines suggested by Harris, might be formulated to remedy this difficulty.

In conclusion, it appears that athematicity is a property shared by many Spanish irregular verb forms, and that the particular manifestation of athematicity exhibited by the present forms of *hacer* and *decir* lends some support to a fairly significant revision of the theoretical framework of generative phonology.

NOTES

1. That is, in terms of the phonological system outlined in Chomsky and Halle (1968). Foley, in his paper in this volume, proposes an analysis of many of these verbs as regular, but only at a cost of considerable increase in the total power of the theory. (See also footnote 7).

2. The numbers in parentheses next to names of rules throughout this paper refer to the cumulative list of ordered rules in Harris (1969b: 183ff.).

3. The present subjunctive forms and the first person singular, present indicative are the only forms to which this rule will apply in the case of a regular verb, since all the other person-number and tense morphemes which follow the theme vowel begin either with a consonant or a lax vowel (in the case of first and third person singular preterite endings, see discussion below).

4. I leave aside for the moment the question of whether there is any way to combine cases (a) and (c) of this rule, and thus take advantage of the fact that [+past] is mentioned in both.

5. The stem of *cocer* must be derived from /kok/ because of the word *cocción*.

6. The verb *tocar* does not undergo voicing. This is due to a subdivision of the lexicon discussed both in Foley (1965b) and in Harris (1969b). The subdivision in question is almost equivalent to the historical distinction between vulgar and learned words. Learned words are not subject to the voicing rule (nor to a great many others).

7. As in the case of irregular preterites, alternative analyses suggest themseleves. *Hacer* and *decir* could simply be marked as exceptions to velar softening in the first person (and consequently throughout the present subjunctive). However, this simply restates the facts without making any effort to explain them. We could improve upon this somewhat by eliminating reference to a particular person and mark these verbs [-velar softening if stem+V+ V (+back)]. However this still does not explain why *decir* and *hacer* should undergo velar softening except in cases where the second vowel following the stem would prevent the rule from applying were this vowel in contact with the stem. It seems that the rule reversing feature is the most straightforward assumption we can make concerning the forms of *hacer* and *decir*. Furthermore, this exception feature is more economical in a mechanical sense as well, since it can be applied to the verb stem as a lexical entry without any restrictions, which is not true of the alternate proposals sketched here. For an interesting attempt to explain the forms of *hacer* and *decir* without assuming any exceptional lexical marking what- soever, see Foley's paper in the current volume. As stated earlier, Foley's proposals can only be carried out at considerable cost in the total power of the system.

8. Voicing is not a locally ordered rule, and thus applies after the two rules under discussion here. As mentioned earlier, local ordering applies only to some of the rules in a grammar, others are ordered explicitly as in the standard theory.

JAMES W. HARRIS
MASSACHUSETTS INSTITUTE OF TECHNOLOGY

FIVE CLASSES OF IRREGULAR VERBS IN SPANISH

0. INTRODUCTION

By traditional criteria, most Spanish verbs are "regular." With a few
exceptions, the relatively small number of verbs called "irregular" can be
grouped into several classes with common peculiarities. We shall be concerned here with verbs that have irregular forms in the present indicative
and present subjunctive. No other paradigms will be considered, although
some of the verbs studied here have other irregular forms. The verbs we
will examine can be grouped as follows:[1]

(a) Verbs like *conocer, crecer, producir*, etc., with a "*k*-extension,"
     e.g. *produŝe*[2] but *produŝko, produŝka*, etc.
(b) Verbs like *salir, tener, poner*, etc., with a "*g*-extension," e.g.
     pone but *pongo, ponga*, etc.
(c) Verbs like *traer* and *caer*, with an "*ig*-extension," e.g. *trae* but
     traigo, traiga, etc.
(d) Verbs like *destruir, incluir, atribuir*, etc., with a "*y*-extension,"
     e.g. *destruimos* but *destruyo, destruye, destruya*, etc.
(e) *Oír*, unique, with an "*ig*-extension" like *traigo* plus a "*y*-extension"
     like *destruye: oímos* but *oigo, oiga* and *oye*, etc.

Among the questions we want to ask about these verbs are the following:
To what extent are they idiosyncratic? That is, must their peculiarities
simply be noted individually or group-by-group, or are there non-obvious
regularities to be discovered? How do these verbs differ from "regular"
verbs? To what can the irregularity be attributed, in each case, and how
is the grammar affected by the existence of these irregularities? What
light, if any, can study of these particular verbs shed on the nature of
complex inflectional systems in general?

From the outset, I would like to stress two points about this paper as
a whole: One, it must be taken as a report on work in progress rather
than as a finished product; two, it ends with a number of questions whose
weight is considerably greater than that of the factual observations, rules,

etc., which lead to these questions. I am quite sure that more study of
the same and additional data will suggest ways of correcting many details,
for example, in the rules given and their ordering, and of deepening the
analysis. I am almost equally sure, however, that such modifications of
detail will leave essentially unaltered the bearing this material has on
certain fundamental questions that I attempt to bring into focus at the
close of the paper.

In order to provide some perspective for the discussion of irregular
verbs, a few observations must be made about regular verbs. Traditionally,
a verb is considered to be "regular" if all its inflected forms are deduc-
ible from the infinitive. Take for example, the present indicative and
subjunctive of the regular first conjugation verb *buscar*, "to look for."
The following are broad phonetic representations of the forms spoken in
isolation (a hyphen separates stem and ending):

(1)   *Infinitive*
                              busk-ár

   Indicative   *Subjunctive*
  búsk-o   busk-ámos   búsk-e   busk-émos
  búsk-as busk-áys   búsk-es busk-éys
  búsk-a   búsk-an   búsk-e   búsk-en

One simply attaches the appropriate inflectional endings to the stem; stress
follows a simple fixed pattern. To be slightly more precise, the traditional
primary defining characteristics of "regularity" in verb forms are (a) that
the same sets of inflectional endings are used for all verbs of a given con-
jugational class, and (b) that the segmental composition of stems is invariable in phonetic representations of all inflected forms of a given verb.

This looks like a good definition, so good and simple that it could
hardly seem to involve problems. In fact, however, some serious questions
are raised by the fact that stems of regular verbs are invariable, except
for stress, in phonetic representations. It is well known that Spanish
has morphophonemic alternations between k and s (*opako/opasidad*, "opaque/
opacity") and between g and the voiceless velar fricative x (*antropólogo/
antropoloxía*, "anthropologist/anthropology").[3] These alternations are
controlled by the following rule:[4]

(2) *Velar Softening*

$$\begin{bmatrix} k \\ g \end{bmatrix} \rightarrow \begin{bmatrix} \acute{s} \\ x \end{bmatrix} / \underline{\hspace{1cm}} \begin{bmatrix} V \\ -back \end{bmatrix}$$

Why then does Velar Softening not apply in the present subjunctive of regular first conjugation verbs like *buscar* to give forms like *bússe, *bussémos*
instead of the correct forms shown in (1)? The problem is seen in its full complexity when one considers a regular second conjugation verb like *proteger*,
"to protect":

(3) (*x* is phonetic, not orthographic)

Infinitive
protex-ér

Indicative		*Subjunctive*	
protéx-o	protex-émos	protéx-a	protex-ámos
protéx-es	protex-éys	protéx-as	protex-áys
protéx-e	protéx-en	protéx-a	protéx-an

It is fairly straightforward to show that the underlying stem is /proteg-/.[5]
Stem-final /g/ appears unchanged except for voicing in *proteksión, protektor,*
and *protektivo,* for example. What is striking about the verb forms of (3)
is that they defy Velar Softening, like the forms of *buscar,* but in the
opposite direction. In the subjunctive of *buscar,* Velar Softening FAILS
to apply where the environment seems to be met; in the forms of *proteger,*
on the other hand, Velar Softening applies not only as expected before the
front vowel *e,* as in the infinitive and five of the indicative forms, but
also where it SHOULDN'T, in indicative *protexo* and throughout the subjunctive.
How can this be accounted for? It is useless to simply state that in
all regular verbs of all conjugations the infinitive provides the model for
all finite forms. This only restates the problem. The question remains:
WHY does the same stem-final segment appear in all forms, infinitive and
finite forms alike, regardless of the frontness or backness of the following
desinential vowel? This question can be answered in terms of derivations
like the following:

(4)

First conjugation

/a/ = theme vowel	/o/ = 1st pers sing
/e/ = pres subjunct	Ø = 3rd pers sing

	Indic		Subjunct	
1 sing	3 sing		3 sing	
/busk+a+o/	/busk+a+Ø/		/busk+a+e+Ø/	
-	-		-	Velar Softening (fails)
Ø			Ø	Truncation: V→Ø/+—+V
bus*ko*	bus*ka*		bus*ke*	

Second conjugation

/e/ = theme vowel	/o/ = 1st pers sing
/a/ = pres subjunct	Ø = 3rd pers sing

/proteg+e+o/	/proteg+e+Ø/	/proteg+e+a+Ø/	
x	x	x	Velar Softening
Ø		Ø	Truncation
prote*xo*	prote*xe*	prote*xamos*	

In underlying representations, unlike phonetic representations, all
INDICATIVE forms consist of *stem + theme vowel + person-number ending;*
all SUBJUNCTIVE forms consist of *stem + theme vowel + subjunctive marker +
person-number ending.* The configuration of vowels in the UNDERLYING

representation, not the PHONETIC representation, determines the applicability of Velar Softening. And since the UNDERLYING vowel immediately
following the stem, namely the theme vowel, is the same in all forms of a
given verb, the result is that the same stem-final consonant appears
phonetically in all forms, regardless of the following PHONETIC vowel.
Now we have more than a mere restatement of easily observable facts: The
rule of Truncation accounts for the non-appearance of the theme vowel in
phonetic representations of first person singular indicative forms as well
as all subjunctive forms; the ordering of the rule of Velar Softening
BEFORE Truncation provides an explanation of the apparently mysterious
distribution of "softened" and "unsoftened" stem-final velars in all
conjugations.
    We have dwelt at some length on certain properties of regular verbs
and on the rules of Velar Softening and Truncation because they are important for an understanding of irregular verbs, to which we now turn.

1. VERBS LIKE *PRODUCIR,* "TO PRODUCE," *CONOCER,* "TO KNOW," AND *CRECER,*
    "TO GROW"

    This group contains most, but not all, second and third conjugation
verbs whose infinitives end in orthographic -*cer* and -*cir*. Some such verbs
that do NOT belong in this group are irregular *hacer,* "to make, do," and
decir, "to say, tell," and regular *cocer,* "to cook," *mecer,* "to rock, sway,"
and *vencer,* "to conquer." In order to show clearly how irregular *producir,*
etc., differ from regular verbs, I give the forms of (regular) *mecer:*

(5)   *Indicative*   *Subjunctive*
    meśo   meśemos   meśa   meśamos
    meśes   meśéis   meśas   meśáis
    meśe   meśen   meśa   meśan

Thus, if *producir, crecer,* etc., were regular, we would expect first person
singular indicative **produśo, *creśo,* and subjunctive **produśa, creśa;*
*produśas, *creśas, etc. But the actually occurring forms are the following
(hereafter I use *producir* as the representative of the class):

(6)   produśko   produśimos   produśka   produśkamos
        produśes   produśís   produśkas   produśkáis
        produśe   produśen   produśka   produśkan

To the question "Is the '*k*-extension' part of the underlying representation
of the stem?" two answers are logically possible, "Yes" and No." Not
surprisingly, BOTH have been given in fairly recent work.
    Foley (1965b) says "Yes." He proposes that the underlying stem is
/produsk-/ (NOT /produśk-/; Foley does not consider Castilian), and that
the phonetic forms are derived essentially as follows:[6]

(7) /produsk+i+o/   /produsk+i/   /produsk+i+a/
    produsk   o   produsk   a   Truncation
                   produss i   Velar Softening[7]
                   produss e   Lowering
                   produ s e   Degemination
       produsko   *produse*   *produska*

Saporta (1965) takes the opposite position, namely that the "*k*-extension" is inserted in the appropriate forms, rather than being part of the underlying representation of the stem. His view is that the underlying stem is /produθ-/ in both Castilian and non-Castilian dialects, and that *k* is inserted after θ before a back vowel, as in (8):

(8) /produθ+o/   /produθ+e/   /produθ+a/
    produθko   -   produθka   Insertion

The non-Castilian forms are produced by a later rule, absent from the grammar of Castilian, that changes θ to *s* in all environments.

Both Foley and Saporta fail to take into account at least one well-motivated rule of Spanish, as well as non-verb forms like *produkśión*, "production," *produkto*, "product," and *produktivo*, "productive," which surely must have the same stem as the verb *producir*.

The rule they overlook is Cluster Simplification, whose effect is roughly that of deleting the middle of three consecutive consonants. For example, *esculpir*, "to sculpt," but (/(e)sculp+tura/→) *escultura*, "sculpture"; *absorber*, "to absorb," but (/absorb+to/→) *absorto*, "absorbed"; *distinguir*, "to distinguish," but (/disting+cion/→) *distinción*, "distinction," and so on.

Now if the nouns *producción*, *producto* and the adjective *productivo* have the same stem as the verb *producir*, then Foley's proposal would apparently entail the following incorrect results:

(9) /produsk+cion/   /produsk+to/   /produsk+tivo/
          Ø   Ø   Ø   Cluster Simpli-
    produsción   *produsto*   *produstivo*   fication

And on Saporta's analysis, the corresponding forms would presumably be the following, although one can only guess here because of the limited scope of his general analysis of Spanish phonology:

(10) /produθ+θión/   /produθ+to/   /produθ+tivo/
    produθión   *produθto*   *produθtivo*   Castilian
    produsión   *produsto*   *produstivo*   non-Castilian (θ→s)

When we cease to consider verb forms *in vacuo*, and bring forms like *producción*, *producto*, and *productivo* into the picture, then it becomes reasonably clear that the stem in question is /produk-/. This stem appears unchanged except for matters of phonetic detail in non-verb forms. The

"k-extension," not being part of the underlying representation, must be inserted, as Saporta has claimed. As a first approximation, the insertion rule may be stated as follows:

(11) *K-insertion*

$$\emptyset \rightarrow k \; / \; [+\text{Stem}_k] \text{———} [^{V}_{-\text{back}}]V$$

We thus have derivations like the following:

(12)

/produk+to/	/produk+i+mos/	/produk+i+o/	/produk+i+a/	
–	š	š	š	Velar Softening
		k	k	K-insertion
		∅	∅	Truncation
produkto	*produšimos*	*produško*	*produška*	

Note particularly that the $š$ derived from stem-final /k/ in all verb forms is the normal result of the normal order of Velar Softening and Truncation, as shown in the derivations of (4). This result is achieved by ordering K-insertion AFTER Velar Softening, as shown in (12). We will return to the rule of K-insertion below, where it will be revised somewhat.

Lest any confusion should arise, let me emphasize that I claim no virtue for the suggested analysis on the basis of the fact that it RELATES Castilian and non-Castilian dialects in a certain way. There is no a priori reason why SYNCHRONIC grammars of the two sets of dialects should be related in this particular way, or any other way. In fact it is quite conceivable that the two sets of dialects could have diverged so much that by now there IS no very close relation between the underlying forms and rules necessary to account for the facts in the two sets of dialects. What the present account attempts to do, for each set of dialects INDEPENDENTLY, is elucidate the relation of verb forms with intrusive k to verb forms without this k and to nouns with the same stem (also without intrusive k). It does so in the least ad hoc way possible: k is inserted in just those forms in which it appears phonetically, and the grammar is otherwise unmodified.

A word about the last point. It could be said that the rule of K-insertion simply restates observable facts without explaining them. This is correct, but cannot be taken as a serious criticism. We could achieve an illusion of greater generality in any number of ways. For example, we could posit a "k-augment" that appears in the underlying representation of ALL verb forms (but not in nouns, adjectives, etc.), thus eliminating the less general rule of K-insertion, which inserts k only before a sequence of two vowels in underlying representations. But then we must propose not only some mechanism to generate the "k-augment" in the appropriate (morphological) environment in the first place, but also phonological rules in addition to those already in the grammar, that would give the correct phonetic results. This would not tax anyone's ingenuity. However, until some independent motivation were found for the extra machinery, it would remain exactly as ad hoc as the rule of K-insertion, and more complicated. Therefore any "explanation" said to be provided by the supposedly more general "k-augment" would be spurious. There is no virtue in abstractness for the sake of abstractness.

We will return to the rule of K-insertion below. First let us return to the fact that some verbs in -*cer* and -*cir* insert k while others don't (like irregular *hacer* and regular *mecer*). Which of the two sets is "irregular" with respect to the total grammar? As stated, K-insertion is a "minor" rule, in the sense that it applies only to a specified class of forms, tentatively labeled "Stem$_k$." The implication is clearly that this is the special, irregular class. Yet at first glance, it seems that "Stem$_k$" verbs vastly outnumber non-k-inserting verbs like *hacer*, *mecer*, etc. It would be somewhat surprising for the IRREGULAR Class to constitute a majority. When we look more closely, however, this may not be the case. The "Stem$_k$" class is highly interrelated. For example, many members seem to have the single stem /duk/ with a variety of prefixed elements: *pro+ducir*, *in+ducir*, *re+ducir*, *tra+ducir*, *de+ducir*, *se+ducir*, ... Also an extremely large number of "Stem$_k$" verbs are formed with the single suffix written -*ecer*: *en+nobl+ecer* (cf. *noble*), *en+lo[k]+ecer* (cf. *loco*), *a+tard+ecer* (cf. *tarde*), *a+par+ecer* (cf. *aparente*), ... Clearly ALL the verbs with the stem /duk/ count as only ONE ITEM in a tally of "stem$_k$" forms, as do ALL the verbs with the suffix -*ecer*, and so on. Non-k-inserting verbs, on the other hand, are largely "independent" and unrelated to one another. Thus each counts as ONE ITEM in a tally. It is not at all obvious on this kind of count that k-inserting stems outnumber non-k-inserting stems. In any event, one or the other class must be marked as exceptional with respect to K-insertion, and it would seem idle to argue at this point about which class is "really irregular."

2. VERBS LIKE *SALIR*, "TO LEAVE, GO OUT," *TENER*, "TO HAVE," AND *PONER*, "TO PUT"

This group contains the verbs just mentioned plus *valer*, "to be worth," *venir*, "to come," *asir*, "to grasp," and apparently no others (but see Sections 3 and 5 below). Using *salir* as the representative of this group, the forms of the present indicative and subjunctive are as follows:

(13)

Indicative		Subjunctive	
salgo	salimos	salga	salgamos
sales	salís	salgas	salgáis
sale	salen	salga	salgan

Since all the stems in this group end in the dentals *l*, *n*, and *s* and belong to the second or third conjugation, it might be imagined that there is a basis for predicting membership in this group, hereafter "Stem$_g$." But this is unfortunately not the case; there are other second and third conjugation verbs with the same stem-final consonants that do not belong to the "Stem$_g$" class:

(14) *Indicative* *Subjunctive*
    moler, "to grind" muelo, mueles, muele, ... muela, muelas, ...
    unir, "to unite" uno, unes, une, ... una, unas, ...
    coser, "to sew" coso, coses, cose, ... cosa, cosas, ...

Thus membership in the class "Stem$_g$" is apparently unpredictable.

We must now ask a question analogous to the one asked in the previous section: "Is the 'g-extension' part of the underlying representation, or is it inserted by rule?" Unfortunately there are very few related forms that provide any evidence one way or the other. For example, in the noun *ad+vento* (cf. *ad+venir*, verb) the *g* of a hypothetical /ad+veng+to/ would be deleted in any event by the Cluster Simplification rule (which, as will be recalled, deletes the second of three consecutive consonants). But decisive forms do exist. Consider the noun *valor*, "value, worth." This must consist of the same stem as the verb *valer*, "to be worth," plus the common noun-forming suffix *-or*. Now compare *valor* with first person singular *valgo*. The NON-appearance of *g* in the noun *valor*, in precisely the same immediate phonetic environment as the appearance of *g* in the verb form *valgo*, is quite strong evidence that the *g* is inserted, in verb forms only. We may thus propose the following as a first approximation to the rule that inserts *g*:

(15) *G-insertion*
$$\emptyset \rightarrow g \;/\; [\text{+Stem}_g] \;\underline{\hspace{1.5cm}}\; [_{-back}^{V}]V$$

We thus have derivations like the following:

(16) /val+or/ /val+e+mos/ /val+e+o/ /val+e+a/
                            g   g   G-insertion
                            ∅   ∅   Truncation

    valor   *valemos*   *valgo*   *valga*

We may now note that the order of G-insertion is the same as that of K-insertion (G-insertion must also be ordered after Velar Softening, to prevent the inserted *g* from being changed, ultimately, to *x*), and that the two rules are extremely similar. So similar in fact as to suggest the following generalizations: There is only one class of velar-inserting verbs, call it "Stem$_v$"; and the distribution of *g* and *k* is predictable since *k* appears always and only after *š*, within the class "Stem$_v$." We may thus collapse G-insertion and K-insertion into the single rule of Velar Insertion:

(17) *Velar Insertion*
$$\emptyset \rightarrow \begin{bmatrix} \text{+obstruent} \\ \text{+back} \\ \text{-continuant} \\ \alpha\text{tense} \end{bmatrix} \;/\; \begin{bmatrix} \text{+Stem}_v \\ \alpha\text{F} \end{bmatrix} \;\underline{\hspace{1.2cm}}\; [_{-back}^{V}]V$$

The ad hoc notation [αF] is shorthand for whatever feature(s) distinguish š from [l, n, s] at this very early stage of derivation.[8] This notation cannot be clarified completely until some investigation of general phonological processes in Castilian Spanish is available. In other words, the exact form of the generalization we seek to express in the rule of Velar Insertion is not known; but it is reasonably clear that such a generalization exists, and we know exactly how to go about finding out what [αF] is now a substitute for.

Let us now clarify a few other points about the rules of K-insertion and G-insertion which have been collapsed as (17). Since the velars inserted by (17) are always before back vowels in phonetic representations, it might appear attractive at first glance to state the right-hand environment more simply as —— [V, +back]. This, however, is inadequate to distinguish, say, the verb form *val(g)o* from the noun *valor*, where *g* is not inserted to give **valgor*. Also, the first vowel of the right-hand environment of (17) is, perhaps redundantly, specified as [-back] to express the fact that there are in the class "Stem$_V$" no FIRST CONJUGATION stems, which are always followed by the back vowel *a* in the underlying representations of verb forms. There are other facts which remain unexpressed by (17), for example, that all of the stems to which this rule applies end in a SINGLE [+consonantal] segment, as opposed to verbs like *vencer, torcer, zurcir, fruncir*, etc. At the moment we do not have enough facts available to know whether this is accidental or not.

There are a few other residual problems with verbs like *salir, tener, poner*, etc., for example, the vowel alternations in the stem of *tener* and *venir*. About these, I have no proposals interesting enough to warrant discussion here.

3. *TRAER*, "TO BRING," AND *CAER*, "TO FALL"

Traer and *caer* have a "g-extension" like the verbs in the previous group, but this *g* is preceded by *i*:

(18)   *Indicative*   *Subjunctive*

   traigo   traemos   traiga   traigamos
   traes   traéis   traigas   traigáis
   trae   traen   traiga   traigan

   caigo   caemos   caiga   caigamos
   caes   caéis   caigas   caigáis
   cae   caen   caiga   caigan

One other verb, *roer*, "to gnaw, eat away," has, among three alternate sets of forms, one that belongs in this group: indicative *roigo, roes, roe*, etc., subjunctive *roiga, roigas*, etc.

There are no derivatives of these simple stems that would indicate directly what the underlying forms are. The same stems, apparently, do

occur with prefixed elements in nouns and adjectives as well as verbs.
For example:

(19)   *Verb*   *Noun/Adjective*
a+traer, "to attract"   *atracción*, "attraction," *atractivo*, "attractive"
de+caer, "to decay"   *decadente*, "decaying," *decadencia*, "decay"
cor+roer, "to corrode"   *corrosión*, "corrosion," *corrosivo*, "corrosive"

It is argued in Harris (1969b), Chapter 5, that forms like those in (19)
point to the underlying representations /trag-/, /cad-/, and /rod-/,
respectively, for the stems in question. If this is correct, as seems likely,
then all the verb forms WITHOUT the "*ig*-extension" are no problem: the *g* of
/trag-/ is deleted by the rule of G-deletion in *traes, trae, traemos*, etc.,
and the *d* of /cad-/ and /rod-/ is deleted by the rule of D-deletion in *caes,
cae*, etc., and *roes, roe*, etc.[9]
This is no help, however, for the forms WITH the "*ig*-extension." As a
start, we may observe that the distribution of this extension is exactly the
same as that of the *k* and *g* extensions in verbs of the "Stem$_v$" class. Also
since the surface *g* of *traer, caer, roer* is NOT preceded by *s̆*, this *g* could
be inserted by Velar Insertion. In short, these three verbs belong to the
class "Stem$_v$."
But what is the source of the *i*, phonetically [y], of the "*ig*-extension"?
Note that the forms with -*ig*- are just those with a sequence of two adjacent
vowels in underlying representations (if the surface *g* is inserted by Velar
Insertion); for example, first person singular indicative /trag+e+o/ →
traigo, /cad+e+o/ → *caigo*, /rod+e+o/ → *roigo* and subjunctive /trag+e+a/ →
traiga, /cad+e+a/ → *caiga*, /rod+e+a/ → *roiga*. Such forms are opposed to,
say, third person singular indicative, with no *VV* sequence: /trag+e/ →
trae, /cad+e/ → *cae*, /rod+e/ → *roe*. This suggests a rule with the following
effect:

(20)   *Lax→glide*

$$[g, d] \rightarrow y / \text{\textemdash} VV$$

Incorporating the Lax→glide rule into the grammar developed so far, we have
derivations roughly like the following (actually, these derivations contain
an inaccuracy that will be corrected directly below):

(21)

/trag+e+o/	/trag+e/	/trag+e+a/	/cad+e+o/	/cad+e/	
y		y	y		Lax→glide
g		g	g		Velar Insertion
∅		∅	∅		Truncation
	∅				G-deletion
				∅	D-deletion
traygo	*trae*	*trayga*	*cayga*	*cae*	

We will now marshall other data that support the Lax→glide rule and lead to a better formulation of it than (20).

It was mentioned above that *roer* has three alternate sets of forms, one of which is like *traer* and *caer* (with indicative *roigo, roes,* etc., and subjunctive *roiga, roigas,* etc.). One of the other sets is the following:

(22)   *Indicative*   *Subjunctive*
    royo   roemos   roya   royamos
    roes   roéis   royas   royáis
    roe   roen   roya   royan

It is immediately obvious that this set of forms differs from the set like *traer* and *caer* precisely in that Velar Insertion does not apply. In other words, the stem /rod-/ may or may not belong to the class "Stem$_V$." *Roer* undergoes Lax→glide, however, whether or not it undergoes Velar Insertion.[10]

Consider now the present subjunctive of *haber*, the perfect auxiliary:[11]

(23)   haya   hayamos
                      hayas   hayáis
                      haya   hayan

The underlying forms, if they were perfectly regular, would be /hab+e+a/, /hab+e+a+s/, /hab+e+a+mos/, etc. Underlying /b/, followed by two adjacent vowels, appears on the surface as *y*. This striking coincidence with the corresponding forms of *traer, caer,* and *roer* suggests that the Lax→glide rule should apply to *b* as well as to *d* and *g*. This of course results in a much more natural rule: the features [αcoronal, αanterior] necessary to characterize *d* and *g* to the exclusion of *b* may be dropped, allowing the rule to apply to all lax obstruents:

(24)   *Lax→glide*

$$\begin{bmatrix} \text{+obstruent} \\ \text{-tense} \end{bmatrix} \rightarrow y\ /\ \text{—— VV}$$

But there is more to the subjunctive of *haber*. Interestingly enough, there exists a substandard variant *haiga, haigas, haigamos,* etc. *Haber* is thus quite similar to *roer*: *haber* ALWAYS undergoes Lax→glide, but only the substandard variant is subject also to Velar Insertion. The existence of these particular sets of variants of these two verbs is a surprising kind of evidence for the existence, the independence, and the optional character of the rules of Lax→glide and Velar Insertion.

We have left out of the account so far the rules of Velar Softening, A-assimilation, G-deletion, and High Deletion. (A-assimilation changes *a* to *e* before high front *i* and *y* (and, symmetrically, to *o* before high back *u* and *w*); High Deletion deletes *i* and *y* after *e* and *i* (and, symmetrically, *u* and *w* after *o* and *u*).) For reasons we cannot go into here, these rules must apply in the order (Velar Softening, A-assimilation, G-deletion, High Deletion). Lax→glide, in turn, must be ordered AFTER A-assimilation;

otherwise it would provide the environment for A-assimilation in forms
like *traigo*, which would then become **treigo*, and ultimately **trego*.
Lax→glide then must follow Velar Softening. We thus have the order (Velar
Softening, A-assimilation, Lax→glide, G-deletion, High Deletion). But
what effect does this order have on the formulation of Lax→glide and G-
deletion, which have to operate on the output of Velar Softening? There is
no effect at all. The first step of Velar Softening changes g to $\check{J}$.
Lax→glide affects all lax obstruents, and G-deletion affects high lax
obstruents; $\check{J}$ is no less a (high) lax obstruent than g, so the formulation
of these two rules is entirely unaffected. For clarity, I repeat as (25)
the derivations originally given as (21), now with all the crucial steps
shown, including the rules that cannot (must not) apply:

(25) /trag+e+o/ /trag+e/ /trag+e+a/ /cad+e+o/ /cad+e/
       J̌   J̌   J̌   Velar Softening
                                                      A-assimilation (fails)
       y   y   y   Lax→glide
         g   g   g   Velar Insertion
         ∅   ∅   ∅   Truncation
                   ∅   G-deletion
                                                      High Deletion (fails)
                                       ∅   D-deletion
       traygo   trae   traygo   caygo   cae

I will close this section with a historical footnote: At an earlier
stage of the language, the forms of *traer* were indicative *trayo*, *traes*,
trae, etc., and subjunctive *traya*, *trayas*, etc. Those of *ca(d)er* were
indicative *cayo*, *cades*, *cade*, etc., and *caya*, *cayas*, etc. This suggests
derivations like the following (details omitted):

(26) /trag+e+o/ /trag+e/ /trag+e+a/ /cad+e+o/ /cad+e/
       y   y   y   Lax→glide
                 ∅   G-deletion
         ∅   ∅   ∅   Truncation
       trayo   trae   traya   cayo   cade

In other words, in the synchronic grammar at this stage, neither *traer* nor
ca(d)er had joined the class "Stem$_y$" (although this class existed at the
time). The ancestors the rules Lax→glide and G-deletion had already become
a part of the grammar, but the rule of D-deletion had not yet appeared in
anything like its modern form.

4. VERBS LIKE *DESTRUIR*, "TO DESTROY," *INCLUIR*, "TO INCLUDE," AND *ATRIBUIR*,
   "TO ATTRIBUTE"

The present indicative and subjunctive of verbs of this group are illustrated with *destruir:*

(27)　　　*Indicative*　　　　　　　　*Subjunctive*
　　　destru*y*o　　destruimos　　　destru*y*a　　destru*y*amos
　　　destru*y*es　　destruís　　　　destru*y*as　　destru*y*áis
　　　destru*y*e　　destru*y*en　　　destru*y*a　　destru*y*an

Virtually all verbs whose infinitives end in *-uir* belong to this group.
The only exceptions known to me are *luir*, "to wear away by friction,"
which many speakers don't know and others are not sure how to conjugate;
and the extremely marginal *inmiscuir*, "to intermeddle." According to
authorities *luir* is regular (*lúo*, *lúes*, etc.); and *inmiscuir* has two sets
of forms, one of which is regular (*inmiscúo*, *inmiscúes*, etc.) and the other
is like *destruir* (*inmiscuyo*, *inmiscuyes*, etc.).
　　The most obvious thing shown in (27) is that the distribution of the
intrusive *y* is not the same as that of *k* and *g* in "Stem$_V$" verbs. *Y* appears
in ALL forms except first and second person plural indicative. The DISTRI-
BUTION, as opposed to the ORIGIN, of this *y* is transparently due to the
operation of the rule of Y-deletion:[12]

(28)　destruyo　　destruyes　　destruyimos　　destruýs
　　　-　　　　　-　　　　　∅　　　　　　∅　　　Y-deletion
　　destruyo　*destruyes*　*destruimos*　*destruís*

　　But the question remains where the intrusive *y* comes from. Is it
really "intrusive"? We must again attempt to determine what the underlying
stems are, by considering all the forms, non-verbs as well as verbs, in
which the same stem presumably occurs. Fortunately there is an abundance.
Consider, for example, for *destruir*, "to destroy," the noun *destru[k]ción*,
"destruction," and the adjective *destru[k]tivo*, "destructive"; and for *incluir*,
"to include," the noun *inclu[s]ión*, "inclusion," and *inclu[s]o*, "inclusive, including." Thus the stems must be /destrug-/ and /includ-/, as is argued in
Harris (1969b:140-5.) We might imagine then that the surface *y* in these verbs
is somehow derived from underlying stem-final /g/ and /d/.
　　This prospect will be short-lived however. One difficulty, which could
be overcome, would be to distinguish stems like /destrug-/ and /includ-/
from /trag-/ of *traer* and /cad-/ of *caer*, also with stem-final /g/ and /d/
but with an entirely different distribution of *y* in surface forms.
　　A more serious difficulty is found in consideration of verbs like *atribuir*,
"to attribute," of which there are a good many. Here, non-verb forms with
the same stem give no indication of a stem-final consonant in underlying
representations: *atribuŝión* (NOT *atribu[kŝ]ión* like *destru[kŝ]ión* or
atribu[s]ión like *inclu[s]ión*), "attribution," *atributo* (NOT *atribukto* or
atribuso), "átribùte," and *atributívo* (NOT *atribuktīvo* or *atribusīvo*),
"attribùtive."
　　We can conclude only that (a) the stem is /atribu-/, with no final consonant, and (b) the surface *y*, having no underlying source, must be inserted.
There must be, then, derivations ROUGHLY like the following:

(29) /atribu+to/ /atribu+i+o/ /atribu+i/ /atribu+i+mos/
                       ∅   Truncation
                       y   y   y   Y-insertion
                                      e   Lowering
                                                  ∅   Y-deletion
    atributo   *atribuyo*   *atribuye*   *atribuimos*

Now, since surface *y* must be inserted in forms of *atribuir*, it is natural to insert it also in *destruir* and *incluir*, which are conjugated exactly like *atribuir*, even though some way could in principle be invented to derive surface *y* from underlying stem-final *g* and *d* in the latter cases. Thus we can apparently formulate the rule of Y-insertion as follows:

(30) *Y-insertion*

$$\emptyset \rightarrow y \ / \ [_{+\text{Stem}_y}^{\text{u}}] \underline{\quad\quad} V$$

As noted above, membership in the class of *y*-inserting verbs is almost, but not quite, predictable. Thus we could almost, but not quite, dispense with the restriction "Stem$_y$" in (30). The motivation for ordering Y-insertion as shown in (29) is, at the moment, hardly overwhelming, and a number of alternatives could be considered. We will return to this rule in the next section.

It remains to be seen exactly how forms of *destruir*, with stem-final /g/, and *incluir*, with stem-final /d/, are derived with the set of rules developed so far. Sample derivations that illustrate the application of all the rules are given in (31):

(31)
/destrug+i+o destrug+i destrug+i+mos/ /includ+i+o includ+i/
    ĵ   ĵ   ĵ   Velar Softening
    y   y   Lax glide
      ∅   ∅   Truncation
            ∅   ∅   G-deletion
                            ∅   D-deletion
          y   y   y   Y-insertion
          e   e   Lowering
               ∅   Y-deletion
 destruyo   *destruye*   *destruimos*   *incluyo*   *incluye*

At first glance these derivations may seem rather complex, but in fact the underlying representations are well motivated and perfectly regular, and the longest derivations contain only four steps.

A final historical note: The present situation seems to have arisen roughly as follows: At an early date, the ancestor of the rule Lax→glide produced forms like *destruyo*, in which surface *y* derives from underlying *g*. Then this surface *y* was propagated analogically not only to other forms of

verbs like *destruir* (e.g. *destruyes, destruye, destruyen*), but also to verbs
like *atribuir*, which have no underlying stem-final lax obstruent. The result
is an increase in the surface regularity of the paradigms in question, but a
more complex, less natural grammar.[13]

5. *OÍR*, "TO HEAR"

Oír is unique. Its present indicative and subjunctive forms are the
following:

(32)   *Indicative*   *Subjunctive*
     oigo   oímos   oiga   oigamos
     oyes   oís   oigas   oigáis
     oye   oyen   oiga   oigan

It may help the reader to regain his bearings to see what the forms of
oír would be if they were perfectly regular:

(33)   *oo   oímos   *oa   *oamos
     *oes   oís   *oas   *oáis
     *oe   *oen   *oa   *oan

Actually, it is none too clear that the forms of (32) would be the expected
ones if *oír* were perfectly regular. The rule of Raising normally applies to
third conjugation verb stems, changing all vowels except *a* to high vowels.
Then some verbs undergo the "minor" case of the rule of Lowering, which
dissimilates high vowels to mid in the environment ——C_0 í. Since the
infinitive in question now is *oír* rather than *uir*, it seems that this verb
undergoes the case of Lowering just mentioned. Thus *oímos* and *oís* would be
expected, but it is not clear why the remaining forms would not be as shown
in (34):

(34)   *úo   oímos   *úa   *uamos
     *úes   oís   *úas   *uáis
     *úe   *úen   *úa   *úan

Aside from these peculiarities, we can see in (32) that *oír* seems to have a
"*y*-extension" like *destruir*, etc., but UNLIKE *traer, caer*; and that it has
a "*g*-extension" like *traer, caer* but UNLIKE *destruir*, etc.
    Of these last two oddities, perhaps the more surprising is that *oír* has a
"*y*-extension." This is surprising because all other verbs in the "Stem*y*"
class have *u* as the last vowel in the stem IN UNDERLYING REPRESENTATIONS,
while the last (and only) vowel of the stem of *oír* seems to be *o*, although,
as was just remarked, it could be *u*, lowered to *o* by Lowering in certain
forms. Even so, there seems to be no explanation for the *o* in ALL forms
of (32), since the environment of Lowering is met only in *oímos* and *oís*.
    But both the surprising membership of *oír* in the class "Stem*y*" and the
strange behavior with respect to Raising and Lowering would be explained if

we took the stem to be not /o-/ but rather /aud-/ or /awd-/. This is suggested by non-verb forms such as the noun *audición*, "hearing," and the
adjective *auditivo*, "auditory." If the stem were /aud-/ or /awd-/, the
membership of *oír* in the class "Stem$_y$" would be expected. And the strange-
ness with Raising and Lowering would disappear: Raising never applies to
low *a*, and it would apply vacuously to *u*, at best. Now recall that the
rule of A-assimilation changes *a* to *o* before high back *u* and *w*, under
certain conditions, and that High Deletion deletes *u* and *w* after *u* and *o*.
Thus /aud-/ or /awd-/ become *oud-* or *owd-* by A-assimilation, and the latter
become *od-* by High Deletion. Thus the lowering rule plays no role whatso-
ever, and the *o* is accounted for in all forms.

Everything else falls into place if the forms of *oír* are subject to BOTH
Velar Insertion and Y-insertion. Full derivations of illustrative forms
are given in (35):

(35)

/awd+i+o	awd+i	awd+i+mos	awd+i+a	awd+i+a+mos/	
-	-	-	-	-	Raising (fails)
owd i o	owd i	owd i mos	owd i a	owd i a mos	A-assimilation
owy i o			owy i a	owy i a mos	Lax→glide
owygi o			owygi a	owygi a mos	Velar Insertion
owyg o			owyg a	owyg a mos	Truncation
ówyg o	ówd i	owd í mos	ówyg a	owyg á mos	Stress
	ów i	ow í mos			D-deletion
	ów yi	ow yí mos			Y-insertion
ó yg o	ó yi	o yí mos	ó yg a	o yg á mos	High Deletion
	ó ye				Lowering
		o í mos			Y-deletion
óygo	óye	oímos	óyga	oygámos	

We are now in a position to give at least a tentative answer to the
question of whether the underlying stem of *oír* is /aud-/ or /awd-/. It
apparently must be /awd-/, as anticipated in the first line of (35). This
is because stress is always assigned to the PENULTIMATE VOWEL in present
indicative and subjunctive verb forms. Thus stress would be assigned
INCORRECTLY to *oúygo, *oúdi, etc., but is assigned CORRECTLY to *ówygo,
ówdi, owdímos, etc.[14]

In order not to stretch an already difficult exposition past the breaking point, I have so far refrained from giving second person plural forms
in sample derivations. Now the time has come. The second person plural
present indicative of *oír* is *oís*, and the subjunctive is *oigáis*. The
underlying shape of the second person plural person-number ending is -*dĕs*,
where *ĕ* = lax *e*.[15] Thus the derivations of *oís* and *oigáis* are as follows:

(36)

	Indicative	*Subjunctive*	
	/awd+i+dĕs	awd+i+a+dĕs/	
	-	-	Raising (fails)
	owd i dĕs	owd i a dĕs	A-assimilation

			owy i a děs	Lax→glide
			owygi a děs	Velar Insertion
			owyg a děs	Truncation
owd í děs			owyg á děs	Stress
ow í ěs			owyg á ěs	D-deletion
ow yí ěs				Y-insertion
o yí ěs			o yg á ěs	High Deletion
o yí ys			o yg á ys	New Glide (roughly ě→y/V——)[16]
o í s				Y-deletion[17]
oís			oygáys	

The derivations in (36) are somewhat awesome. I know of no others in the language, except those of (35), that even approach them in complexity and what I will call "abstractness," for want of a better word. These derivations will be discussed further in the concluding section.

I will close the present section with a historical footnote. At an earlier stage of the language, *o(d)ir* was conjugated as follows: indicative *oyo, odes, ode,* etc., and subjunctive *oya, oyas,* etc. This suggests derivations entirely analogous to those of *ca(d)er* given in (26). That is, *o(d)ir* had not yet joined the class "Stem$_V$," as is seen in the fact that it does not yet have the forms *oigo, oiga,* etc. Also, the ancestor of Lax→glide was in the language (/awd+i+o/→... → *oyo*), but that of D-deletion was not (/awd+i/ → ... → *ode*). In time, of course, *o(d)ir* joined both the "Stem$_V$" and "Stem$_y$" classes. (*Ca(d)er,* on the other hand, has joined "Stem$_V$", but it did not, COULD not, join "Stem$_y$.") Interestingly enough, *destru/g/ir* and the ancestors of other modern *-uir* verbs have been conjugated as follows: indicative *destruigo, destruyes, destruye,* etc., subjunctive *destruiga, destruigas,* etc. That is, *destru/g/ir* was once a member of the "Stem$_V$" class, but no longer is. Thus the histories of *caer, oír,* and *destruir* show that in the course of time verbs are free to move in and out of the "Stem$_V$" class independently.

6. FURTHER DETAILS

The point of departure of this study has been the grammar of Harris (1969b) as modified in Harris (forthcoming *a*).[18] To that grammar we have added three rules: Velar Insertion (17), Lax→glide (24), and Y-insertion (30). With the addition of these three rules, we have been able to account for quite a variety of apparently disparate facts, for example the extremely odd and puzzling collection of phonetic shapes of the forms of *oír*. Before proceeding to the concluding section, I would like to comment further on a few of the many details of the analysis given so far that could profit from more intensive study.

Let us turn first to the rule Lax→glide. What precisely is the domain of this rule? So far we have said only that it applies to a specifically designated set of forms.[19] We must now ask whether membership in this set is totally arbitrary, or whether some generalization can be found. It would

seem worthwhile to explore the possibility that the domain of Lax→glide is
precisely the set of second and third conjugation verbs that are [+S].[20]
I am suggesting, for example, that perhaps the "regular" set of forms of
roer (*roo, roes,* etc.), which do NOT undergo Lax→glide are [-S], while both
"irregular" sets (*royo, roes,* etc. and *roigo, roes,* etc.), which DO undergo
Lax→glide are [+S]. I give in (37) below all the verbs I have been able to
find that at first glance seem to invalidate the suggestion that the domain
of Lax→glide.is just the set of [+S] non-first conjugation verbs. All the verbs
in (37) satisfy each of the following conditions: (a) they are second or third
conjugation, (b) the stem apparently ends in one of the lax obstruents /b/
(sometimes orthographic *v*), /d/, /g/, (c) they are demostrably [+S], say,
because of diphthongization of *e* to *ie* or *o* to *ue*, and (d) they do NOT undergo
Lax→glide:

(37) Group I: defender; morder; perder; hender; ascender, descender,
                condescender, encender; atender, contender, entender,
                desentender, extender, tender; hervir
     Group II: heder, poder
     Group III: leer (= le/g/er, *cf.* le[x]ible, lector, lectura)
     Group IV: conmover, mover

Group I of (37) contains stems that end in a consonant cluster. Thus
it would be possible to maintain the generalization that Lax→glide is
applicable to all [+S] non-first conjugation stems, by simply restricting
the environment as shown in (38)

(38) *Lax→glide* (revised)
$$\begin{bmatrix} +\text{obstruent} \\ -\text{tense} \\ +\text{S} \end{bmatrix} \rightarrow y \ / \ V \text{——} VV$$

Group II contains stems that end in a single consonant; thus the restriction just proposed does not seem to be strong enough. It is entirely conceivable, however, that our generalization can still be maintained. The
UNDERLYING stem-final consonants of Group II may not be LAX, as the rule
requires: *hed+er,* "to stink, reek," may have the same stem as *fét+ido,*
"foul-smelling, reeking"; and *pod+er,* "to be able, have power," may have
the same stem as *pot+ente,* "potent, powerful." The rule of Lenition, which
would change underlying /t/ to *d* in these cases, is independently motivated,
applies only to [+S] forms, and must necessarily be ordered considerably
later than Lax→glide. Thus the generalization could stand. However, in
my opinion at least, the synchronic relatedness of *poder* to *potente,* and
especially, of *heder* to *fétido* is hardly self-evident.
The single member of Group III, *leer,* is no problem. Lax→glide may very
well apply, but its effect would be wiped out in any event by High Deletion:

(39)　/leg+e+o/　　/leg+e/　　/leg+e+a/
　　　　ǰ　　　　　　ǰ　　　　　ǰ　　　　　Velar Softening
　　　　y　　　　　　　　　　　y　　　　　Lax glide
　　　　ø　　　　　　　　　　　ø　　　　　Truncation
　　　　　　　　　　　ø　　　　　　　　　G-deletion
　　　　ø　　　　　　　　　　　ø　　　　　High Deletion
　　　leo　　　　　*lee*　　　　*lea*

This leaves *(con)mover* as the only case in which Lax→glide does not
apply to a [+S] non-first conjugation stem ending in a single lax obstruent.
It could conceivably be argued that the underlying representation of this
stem is not /mob-/ but rather /mov-/, /mow-/, /mou-/, or even /mop-/; but
in fact I know of no such argument that I find at all convincing.

Given all these facts I think it fair to say that the following is a
good generalization, though not an absolutely unexceptionable one:　the
domain of Lax→glide (with the environment ammended as in (38)) is just the
class of [+S] stems.

The change of the environment of Lax→glide to the one shown in (38)
suggests an intriguing possibility, which I shall pursue briefly but leave
as an open question.　Rule (38) still requires an additional MORPHOLOGICAL
restriction to non-first conjugation stems.　We could trivially convert
this restriction into a PHONOLOGICAL one by changing the environment to the
one shown in (40):

(40)　　　　　　　　　/V ── [$_{-back}^{V}$]V

Now recall that it was observed at the close of section 2 that the rule of
Velar Insertion affects only stems that end in a SINGLE [+consonantal] segment.
We thus have the striking coincidence that Lax→glide and Velar Insertion,
the two rules that play the major roles in the derivation of irregular
present tense verb forms, both affect strings of segments of the form:

(41)　　　　　　　V[+consonantal][$_{-back}^{V}$]V

This "coincidence" suggests that something is missing in the analysis; in
other words, that the sequence (41) should not have to appear twice in the
grammar, once in the rule of Lax→glide and again in the rule of Velar
Insertion, but rather only once somewhere else in the grammar in such a
way that a generalization is captured on which Lax→glide and Velar Insertion
can depend.　A number of things suggest themselves, but I have so far found
no one thing that is significantly more attractive than others, so I leave
the question at this point.

7. CONCLUDING REMARKS

In conclusion, let us return to the derivations of *oír* (35) and, especially, (36).　As noted near the end of section 5, these derivations are
extraordinarily complex and "abstract."　By this I mean that in (36), for

example, the underlying representations /awd+i+dĕs/ and /awd+i+a+dĕs/
differ only in the present subjunctive marker -*a*- of the latter; yet the
respective phonetic outputs share only initial *o* and final *s*. Also, the
only underlying segments that survive intact in the phonetic representations
are final *s* and the (eventually) stressed vowels *i* and *a*. It is a striking
fact, however, that, taken one by one, each of the rules that figure in
These derivations is relatively easy to justify, at least as far as its
existence and gross effect are concerned, although not down to the last
feature. That is, forms can be found in which the effect of each of
these rules is visible to the naked eye; forms whose phonetic representations have derivations of two, three, or at the outside, four steps —including stress assignment, which figures in the derivation of all "major
lexical class" forms. Such derivations would presumably stretch the
credulity of no one who is not repelled by the idea of ordered rules altogether. In other words, it is quite plain that the derivations of (35)
and (36) are latent in the grammar of Spanish, in the sense that they are
"valid deductions" given the rules of the language, and would still be so
even if there happened to be no verb with exactly the forms of *oír* (like
other theoretically possible but actually non-occurring derivations).

There is another side to the same coin. Not only do the derivations
in question grind out the correct phonetic forms when we need them, but
also they DON'T PRODUCE the incorrect, but EXPECTED, forms. I do not
think this is a tautology. Consider the fact that *oír* is absolutely unique
in the following way: no other non-defective third conjugation verb, not
a single one, has a mid vowel in the first and second person plural of the
present subjunctive. Compare:[21]

(42) *oír: oigamos, oigáis* versus *morir: muramos, muráis*
dormir: durmamos, durmáis
pedir: pidamos, pidáis
sentir: sintamos, sintáis
reír: riamos, riáis

.
.
.

If the underlying representation of the stem of *oír* were /o-/ or /od-/
rather than /awd-/, then we would have no explanation for either (a) the
NON-OCCURRENCE of a high vowel in certain forms,[22] or (b) the membership of
oír in the class "Stemy." Instead, we would simply have to note these facts
in some ad hoc way. In short, the somewhat dubious (when made a priori)
assumption that *oír* has the same stem as *audición* and *auditivo* finds
empirical confirmation in a quite subtle way.

In spite of all of the above, one can still seriously question the
"psychological reality" of the derivations shown in (35) and (36). I think
it is a fair guess that every Spanish-speaking child memorizes as individual
items a good many of the forms of *oír*—surely *oye* and *oiga*—long before he
has had a chance to digest enough data to permit him to internalize a

grammar containing all the rules of (35) and (36) in their proper order. Yet, as we have already observed, the derivations of (35) and (36) are presumably AVAILABLE to any mature speaker of Spanish, even though he has probably long ago memorized the phonetic outputs without the benefit of the rules.

For the sake of argument, let us grant that Spanish speakers do memorize the forms of *oír* before they have acquired a grammar that will generate the derivations of (35) and (36). What then is the status of these derivations and of the grammar that generates them? Are they simply fictions, the products of the linguist's overactive fantasy? Should phonological theory be so constrained that such derivations and grammars are ruled out? It is not at all clear that this could be done, if it were deemed desirable, without throwing the baby out with the bathwater; that is, without producing a phonological theory that would also rule out obviously desirable grammars. To give just one small bit of support for this view, as far as I can see —although the matter is not entirely straightforward—the derivations in question seem to pass through, or can easily be reformulated so that they do, the types of constraints suggested in Kiparsky's "How abstract is phonology?" (which many people believe are too severe, although a perhaps equally large number of people think are not severe enough). One could easily run through a list of other types of constraints that everyone would consider inappropriate, and still others about which agreement could not easily be reached.

Derivations as long and complicated as (35) and (36) are not terribly unusual in treatments of suprasegmental phenomena like stress (usually English), but for (non-cyclical) derivations almost exclusively of segmental features, (35) and (36) are extreme cases. Thus they serve to bring into sharp focus timely questions, such as that of the degree of abstractness or concreteness of phonology, already alluded to. Other questions that are less familiar and that can hardly even be formulated coherently at present are "What is the psychological, as opposed to the descriptive, status of phonological rules?" and "Given that human beings have the competence to formulate phonological rules with such-and-such properties, what good are these rules to human beings as language USERS?" It is easy to be dogmatic about such questions, but less easy to give good answers, or even to think of promising directions for research. In my opinion, however, the interrelated problems of the relative abstractness of phonology and of the psychological status of phonological rules are among the most pressing issues confronting generative phonological theory today. I have no serious suggestions to offer; in this paper I have merely tried to call attention to the problem, and I will close by voicing the opinion that careful working out of dilemmas of the sort posed by the forms or *oír* will provide valuable grist for the mills of future study.

NOTES

1. These will NOT be taken into account: (a) The very large group whose only "irregularity" consists of a vowel-diphthong alternation in the stem, e.g. *pensar: pensamos, pienso,* and *contar: contamos, cuento.* This alternation is discussed in my *Spanish Phonology.* (b) Third conjugation verbs whose only "irregularity" is an alternation in the stem between a high and a mid vowel, e.g. *pedir: pedimos, pido* or a three-way alternation, e.g. *sentir: sintamos, sentimos, siento* and *morir: muramos, morimos, muero.* These too are discussed in my book. (c) *Hacer* and *decir* which are treated at length in my paper "On the order of certain phonological rules of Spanish." (d) High idiosyncratic verbs like *ser, ir, saber,* and a few others.

2. The symbol *š* is to be read as [θ] for Castilian and as [s] for other dialects.

3. See, for example, Saporta (1959), especially section 1.18, pages 43-5.

4. What is stated here for illustrative purposes is actually a summary of the effects of several rules. Fuller discussion can be found in Harris (1969b), pages 163-177. An ordered list of all the rules discussed in the present paper is given in the Appendix. Suggestive names are supplied here as a convenience.

5. For discussion see Harris (1969b), Chapter 5.

6. The names of the rules are my own, but the derivations themselves do not depart in any relevant way from Foley's proposals.

7. Notice that Truncation applies before Velar Softening here, although these rules apply in the opposite order in the derivation of regular verbs, as shown in (4). If the stem is /produsk-/, then the "regular" order is clearly incorrect; e.g. *produsk+i+o* → (Velar Softening) *produssio* → (Truncation) *produsso* → (Degemination) **produso.* These facts about rule ordering, however, are only a minor problem; a more serious objection to Foley's account is given below (8).

8. Recall from notes 2 and 4 that *š* itself is shorthand for the "softened" reflex of *k,* and that the relevant stage of derivation is after the first step in the series of rules we have referred to collectively as Velar Softening.

9. In Harris (1969b) G-deletion and D-deletion are formulated as the single rule of G/d-deletion. It is argued at some length in Harris (forthcoming *a*), however, that there must be two rules, an early rule of G-deletion and a late rule of D-deletion, that cannot be collapsed.

10. The third and, mercifully, only other alternative set of forms of *roer* is completely regular: indicative *roo, roes, roe,* etc., subjunctive *roa, roas,* etc. It follows from this set of forms, and from those of other regular verbs with stem-final *d* and *g,* that Lax glide applies only to a specifically designated set of stems. We return to this below.

11. The present indicative is unique--*he, has, ha, hemos, habéis, han*--and will be ignored.

12. This rule, which deletes *y* on either side of any high non-back segment, was originally proposed in Harris (1969b); it is discussed further and refined somewhat in Harris (forthcoming *a*).

13. This is the topic of Harris (1970b); more detailed remarks can be found in Harris (forthcoming *b*).

14. A change, in fact a simplification, is required in the rule of Y-insertion: the *u* of the environment is generalized to [-consonantal, +high, +back], as shown in the Appendix.

15. This is argued in Harris (forthcoming *a*). Actually, the motivation for the *d* of -*dĕs* is not overwhelming, so that -*es* might be the correct shape. The choice does not affect the following derivations in any crucial way, and the -*dĕs* alternative is given for the sake of illustration.

16. This rule is not mentioned in Harris (1969b), but is discussed at some length in Harris (forthcoming *a*). A slightly more precise formulation is given in the Appendix to the present paper.

17. Recall that Y-deletion is a mirror image rule (see note 12). Notice that in converting *oyĭys* to *oĭs*, both "reflections" of Y-deletion are used, with the single segment *ĭ* as environment, to delete the two flanking *y*'s.

18. Recall (see notes 9, 12, and 15) that the modifications directly affecting the present study are (a) separation of G/d-deletion into the two rules of G-deletion and D-deletion, (d) official recognition of the mirror image property of Y-deletion, and (c) incorporation of the rule New Glide.

19. See note 10

20. See Harris (1969b) for discussion of this diacritic. (Consult index for a large number of references.)

21. The analogous observation holds for other forms, not included in this study: present participle *oyendo* versus *muriendo, durmiendo, pidiendo, sintiendo, riendo,...;* Third person singular preterit *oyó* versus *murió, durmió, pidió, sintió, rió,...;* third person plural preterit *oyeron* versus *murieron, durmieron, pidieron, sintieron, rieron,...*

22. Expected but non-occuring **uamos, *uáis,* or, with Y-insertion, **uyamos, *uyáis,* are not impermissible forms on any count. The latter are in fact the correct first and second person plural present subjunctive forms of *huir*.

APPENDIX

Numbers in parentheses on the right refer to Harris (1969b), pages 183-8.

1. *Raising:* $\begin{bmatrix} V \\ -low \end{bmatrix} \rightarrow [+high] \: / \: [\overline{3conj}]C_0V]_{Verb}$ (1)

2. *Cluster Simplification:* $\begin{bmatrix} +obstr \\ -contin \end{bmatrix} \rightarrow \emptyset \: / \: [+cons] \underline{\hspace{1em}} [+obstr]$ (4)

3. *Velar Softening*
   Summary: $\begin{bmatrix} k \\ g \end{bmatrix} \rightarrow \begin{bmatrix} ś \\ x \end{bmatrix} \: / \: \underline{\hspace{1em}} \begin{bmatrix} -cons \\ -back \end{bmatrix}$ (9)

   First step: $\begin{bmatrix} k \\ g \end{bmatrix} \rightarrow \begin{bmatrix} č \\ ǰ \end{bmatrix} \: / \: \underline{\hspace{1em}} \begin{bmatrix} -cons \\ -back \end{bmatrix}$ i.e. [+obstr]→[-back]/...

4. *A-assimilation:* $\begin{bmatrix} V \\ +low \\ +S \end{bmatrix} \rightarrow \begin{bmatrix} -low \\ \alpha back \end{bmatrix} \: / \: \underline{\hspace{1em}} \begin{bmatrix} -cons \\ +high \\ \alpha back \end{bmatrix}$ (18)

5. *Lax→glide:* $\begin{bmatrix} +obstr \\ -tense \\ +S \end{bmatrix} \rightarrow y \: / \: V \underline{\hspace{1em}} VV$

6. *Velar Insertion:* $\emptyset \rightarrow \begin{bmatrix} +obstr \\ +back \\ -contin \\ \alpha tense \end{bmatrix} \: / \: \begin{bmatrix} +Stem_V \\ \alpha F \end{bmatrix} \underline{\hspace{1em}} \begin{bmatrix} V \\ -back \end{bmatrix} V$

7. *Truncation:* $V \rightarrow \emptyset \: / \: + \underline{\hspace{1em}} +V$

8. *Stress:* $V \rightarrow [1stress] \: / \: \underline{\hspace{1em}} ((]_{Stem} C_0V)C_0V)C_0\#]_{Verb}$ (16)

9. *G-deletion:* $\begin{bmatrix} +obstr \\ -tense \\ +high \\ +S \end{bmatrix} \rightarrow \emptyset \: / \: \underline{\hspace{1em}} \begin{bmatrix} V \\ -back \end{bmatrix}$ (8)

10. *D-deletion:* $d \rightarrow \emptyset \: / \: V \underline{\hspace{1em}} V$ (and additional restrictions)

11. *Lenition:* $\begin{bmatrix} +obstr \\ +S \end{bmatrix} \rightarrow [-tense] \: / \: V \underline{\hspace{1em}} [-obstr]$ (19)

12. *Y-insertion:*

$$\emptyset \rightarrow y \ / \ \begin{bmatrix} -cons \\ +high \\ +back \\ +Stem_y \end{bmatrix} \text{---}V$$

13. *High Deletion:*

$$\begin{bmatrix} +high \\ -cons \\ -stress \\ \alpha back \end{bmatrix} \rightarrow \emptyset \ / \ \begin{bmatrix} V \\ -low \\ \alpha back \end{bmatrix} \text{---} \tag{22}$$

14. *Lowering:*

$$V \rightarrow [-high] \ / \ \begin{cases} [-stress]C_0 \# & \text{(a)} \\ \text{---}C_0 \acute{1} & \text{(b) MINOR} \end{cases} \tag{28}$$

15. *Degemination:*

$$C_i C_j \Rightarrow C_k \quad \text{where } C_i = C_j = C_k \tag{31}$$

16. *New Glide:*

$$\begin{bmatrix} -tense \\ -stress \\ -back \\ +S \end{bmatrix} \rightarrow [-syllabic] \ / \ V\text{---} $$

17. *Y-deletion:*

$$y \rightarrow \emptyset \ // \ \begin{bmatrix} +high \\ -back \end{bmatrix} \quad \text{(mirror image)} \tag{23}$$

ROBERT L. RANKIN
UNIVERSITY OF KANSAS

A MINOR RULE WITH HISTORICAL IMPLICATIONS IN RUMANIAN

It is generally accepted (Bourciez 1956; Elcock 1960; Grandgent 1962; Iordan 1965) that Classical Latin stressed vowels have the following context free reflexes in Rumanian:[1]

This schema yields an assymetrical historical system, and the question has often been raised whether stressed ŏ might not have diphthongized to *[u̯ó] at an early date. This would parallel nicely developments in several of the western Romance languages as well as development of ĕ in Rumanian,[2] e.g.

	Short ŏ	Short ĕ
Latin	fŏcus 'fire'	*fĕlem (literary fĕl) 'bile'
French	feu	fiel
Italian	fuoco	fiele
Portuguese	fogo	fel
Spanish	fuego	hiel
Rumanian	foc	fiel

The comparative evidence, coming as it does from over a broad geographical area, coupled with considerations of phonetic and phonological symmetry has led some linguists to actually posit such a development in the early stages of Rumanian.

Luigi Romeo,[3] in his Martinet based treatment of Romance diphthongization, claims such a development on grounds of structural pressures operating in a four height vocalic system. Other linguists (Romeo 1968:96)[4] have generally favored arguments based on more or less ill defined considerations of symmetry. These include Adolph Zauner, Friedrich Schürr, and the Rumanians Sextil Puşcariu and Alexandru Philippide.

What sort of internal evidence might one look for in Rumanian which would confirm or disconfirm the diphthongization hypothesis? Naturally, the first place a well trained Romanist will look is the earliest written records of the language. The earliest purely Rumanian documents,[5] however, date from the 16th century; the first is a personal letter relating military moves of the Turks, dated 1521. A series of religious texts, translations from Slavic, follows in 1544, but all of these early sources show forms quite similar to the modern spoken language. In any event, no light is shed on the problem at hand.

A second possible source is the body of Latin inscriptions, numbering some 3000 in the ancient province of Dacia, which date from the early centuries of Roman conquest and colonization. Unfortunately, most of these appear to be the work either of transients, soldiers and the like, or of persons who knew the literary norms of Latin and/or Greek reasonably well. There is no *Appendix Probi* for the eastern edges of the Empire. There are two instances of Classical Latin *uo* as *o: quattuor* as *quattor,* found in Macedonia but also in Rome, and *suorum* as *sorum* in Pannonia (Mihăescu 1960:271). There are also two instances of classical ŏ turning up as *uo* in inscriptions (Mihăescu 1960:67-8): *soror* as *suora* (Dalmatia) and *posuit* as *puosuit* (Lower Moesia c. 157 A.D.). Of the two, the Dalmatian example is too far removed geographically to be relevant. The other inscriptions show orthographic *o* or *u* as a reflex of the classical ŏ.

It is unfortunate but true that we have almost no direct evidence from the period of formation of the Rumanian language. The Latin inscriptions are too early and show almost none of the well known peculiarities of Rumanian, while the earliest native documents come too late. We must turn to the third source; phonological evidence from the modern spoken and literary dialects.

In the literary language and in most dialects the diphthong [ᵘo] occurs infrequently. The most common source for it is utterence initial, under-lying /o/, regardless of whether it is etymologically long or short or even Latin, e.g.,

(1a) /omu/ ⟶ [ᵘóm] < L. *hŏmo* 'man'

(1b) /óu/ ⟶ [ᵘóᵤ] < L. *ōvum* 'egg'

(1c) /oraš/ ⟶ [ᵘoráš] < Hungarian *város* 'city'

(1d) /obrazu/ ⟶ [ᵘobráz] < OCS *obrazŭ* 'face'

This phonetic [ᵘo] alternates with [o] when not in absolute initial position. It never contrasts with [o] in any environment.

The dialects of Moldavia and the Banat, in extreme eastern and western Rumania respectively, provide another source of phonetic [ᵘo] from under-lying /o/. In these two areas all stressed /o/, again regardless of etymology, appear as dipthongs, e.g.,

(2a) /foku/ ⟶ [fu̯ók] < L. fŏcus 'fire'

(2b) /dosu/ ⟶ [du̯ós] < L. dorsum 'back'

(2c) /košu/ ⟶ [ku̯ós] < OCS košĭ 'basket'

This dialect phenomenon is recent. Its spread in the areas in question can be seen comparing the earliest and most recent Rumanian linguistic atlases. As in the case of utterance initial [u̯o], there is no contrast with [o].

A third, more interesting source for a possible [u̯o] exists. There are a few cases of underlying /u/ and /o/ juxtaposed at a morpheme boundary.[6] These cases are historically old and in the literary dialect can be seen most clearly in the paradigm of the present participle of the verb with its suffixed object pronouns:

Underlying forms	*Surface forms*	*Gloss*
(3a) /vedendu-me/	[vəzɨndumə]	seeing me
(3b) /vedendu-te/	[vəzɨndute]	seeing you
(3c) /vedendu-lu/	[vəzɨndul]	seeing him
(3d) /vedendu-o/	[vəzɨndo]	seeing her

In the Rumanian dialect of the Yugoslav Banat the past participle also takes a reduplicated object pronoun as a suffix. The resultant paradigm (Flora 1962:112) shows the same reduction of /u-o/ to [o]: [vədzútul]. 'saw him' but [vədzúto] 'saw her', never *[vədzútu̯o].

Some dialects, notably those of Transylvania, preserve underlying word final /u/ which is normally deleted in the literary dialect, e.g. [un ómu] compared with literary [un óm] 'a man'. Here the prerequisite combination of segments may occur with an intervening word boundary. Even so, the reduction of the underlying dipthong occurs. The same generally holds true for the very small number of such cases in literary Rumanian[7] (but see rule 4, below).

Of the above sets of examples groups one and two are the result of low level phonetic rules, yet they account for practically all observable sequences of [u̯o] in Rumanian. Juxtaposition of underlying /u/ and /o/ as in the third set of examples, however, never produces the expected [u̯o] diphthong.

There must be a higher level phonological rule which reduces all instances of underlying /uo/ to [o] wherever they occur. There is no reason to believe that this rule is context sensitive. The reason that all of the above examples occur at a morpheme boundary is that only in that environment can one find overt evidence for underlying /u/ plus /o/ in modern Rumanian.

Internal evidence presented above from the spoken language, then, suggests the following ordering for rules relating to the diphthong [u̯o]:[8]

(1) /uo/ ——→ [o] in all contexts.[9]

(2) /o/ ——→ [u̯o] following a pause.[10]

(3) /ó/ ——→ [u̯ó] in all environments (dialectal, Moldava and Banat only).

(4) /-l/ of the postposed masculine definite article is deleted, often yielding the following surface representations:
(a)   /un bou o vede/ ——→ [umbŏovéde] 'An ox sees her'.
but (b) /boul o vede/ ——→ [bŏu̯ovéde] 'The ox sees her'.

Thus, there are at least four possible sources for the [u̯o] diphthong in Rumanian. The one that is most interesting, however, is the one which never actually produces [u̯o] as a surface output: Underlying /uo/, which undergoes rule 1 above.

It is now evident why no evidence for dipthongization of Latin ŏ has been uncovered by linguists in the past. Once the active synchronic nature of the /uo/ ——→ [o] rule is apparent, it becomes clear that there can be no such evidence. Assuming that the present sequential constraint operated across the board and was added to the grammar of Common Rumanian at an early date, all possible evidence for the putative diphthongization would have been wiped out. And since Rumanian was not written until the 16th century, at least 500 years after the disintegration of Common Rumanian, it is futile to search for evidence in early texts. Restructuring would have taken place long before in morpheme internal position where no alternation was present to preserve an underlying */uó/.

This small insight into the history of Rumanian is obscured in a descriptive treatment which does not separate underlying from superficial *uo* and which does not treat the relationship /vedendu-o/ ——→ [vəzɨndo] in terms of actively operating synchronic rules.

NOTES

1. This is only a slight oversimplification. There is some contextual variation from this schema, but for the purposes of this paper it is sufficient.
2. In addition to the languages listed there is also diphthongization in one or another environment in Rheto-Romance, Sicilian, Provençal, Dalmatian, and even reputedly, in the Portuguese dialect of Baixo-Minho (Iordan and Manoliu 1965:88).

3. Romeo's (1968:95-102) discussion of Rumanian is interesting and very involved. Unfortunately, an apparent lack of familiarity with the language led him to treat the diphthong [oá] as the reflex of Latin /ŏ/. [oá], however, is the reflex of *both long and short* Latin /o/ when it precedes /e/ or /a/ (including phonetic [ə] from /a/). This synchronic rule applies invariably throughout the native Romance vocabulary and simply never distinguishes etymologically short from long /o/.

4. The author gives a convenient resumé of these views in a footnote.

5. Isolated occurrences of personal and place names appear in Slavic and Hungarian texts of somewhat earlier date, but the forms cited are not markedly different from 16th century native sources.

6. Here I refer to all classes of juncture lower than /word boundary/. Underlying /u/ and /o/, may also be juxtaposed across a word boundary, of course, but the outcome is not as predictable, i.e. external sandhi rules tend often to apply optionally. The internal rules for /u+o/ are always obligatory, and I confine this discussion to them.

7. E.g. rapid speech: /domnul ionésku o vede/⟶ [dòmnu̯ionéskovêde] 'Mr. Ionescu sees her'.

8. Any number of rules unrelated to the [u̯o] diphthong may intervene between any two of these rules, especially between 1 and 2.

9. If added to Common Rumanian before the 10th century the same rule would occur in the dialects south of the Danube; Arumanian, Megleno-Rumanian and Istro-Rumanian. In Arumanian, the best attested of the three with over 200,000 speakers in Greece, Yugoslavia and Albania, all cases of post tonic /o/ have become [u] obscuring possible evidence. In addition, the present participle takes a form different from that of Daco-Rumanian in all three dialects.

10. Rules 2 and 3 are not ordered with respect to one another in dialects having both. They must, however, follow 1 and precede 4.

MARY CLAYTON WANG
UNIVERSITY OF TEXAS AT AUSTIN AND INDIANA UNIVERSITY

WHAT STOPS A SOUND CHANGE?

The notion "living" or "productive" sound change is an old and obvious one which has been largely ignored in generative phonology, aside from the observation that sound changes don't really "die" as was once thought, but often live on as synchronic phonological rules. Let us take as examples two changes in the history of Spanish: e-epenthesis, and palatalization of /ks/ and /kt/ clusters. The traditional historical linguist would say that e-epenthesis is a living sound change, or phonological process, since new words entering the language still undergo it. In contrast, he would say that palatalization is totally dead, since new /ks/ and /kt/ clusters are not affected by it. Generative phonologists, on the other hand, have ignored the distinction between productive and non-productive sound changes, thus claiming that it is not relevant whether a phonological process is still active in the traditional sense, but only whether a rule corresponding to it is required to derive surface forms from underlying representations.

Is the productive or non-productive status of a phonological process represented in the synchronic generative phonology? I hope to show that it is, and to explore the possible implications for generative phonology of the distinction between living and non-living phonological processes.

As a definition of "living sound change", we may refer to a straightforward statement in Meyer-Lübke (1901:73) that "A sound change lives as long as all words newly admitted by the language participate in it." In terms of a synchronic generative grammar, this seems to be equivalent to a requirement that nothing in the output of the grammar--whether native word, newly coined, or borrowed--may violate the rule which corresponds to the sound change in question. Thus, there are a number of words in Spanish that do not conform to the above mentioned palatalization rule, but there are no exceptions to the rule of e-epenthesis. The usual words of caution should be mentioned here concerning possible confusion between the terms "sound change" and "phonological rule". Since the relationship between rules and sound changes is often direct and obvious, we must be especially careful to avoid the assumption that it *must* be so. In speaking

of a correspondence between a sound change and a certain phonological
rule, I mean only that the alternations introduced by the sound change
are at least in part accounted for by the phonological rule in question--
certainly not there must be a synchronic rule which has all and only
the effects of the sound change. Also, it should be noted that I am
using the term "sound change" in the traditional sense, to mean change in
output as well as change in system, rather than in the more restricted
sense of generative phonology, to mean only change in the underlying
grammar.

Given our current model of language, in which language change is seen
as grammatical change, we may expect that the cessation of a sound change
will be reflected in some change in the synchronic grammar. My claim is
that only those sound changes which correspond to last rules in the synchronic grammar can be productive, and that just these *must* be productive.
That is to say, when a phonological process ceases to be active in the
language, the corresponding rule has lost its last-rule status in the
grammar.

1. LAST RULES

The "last rules" referred to above are those rules which need not
precede any other rule in the grammar. That is, their output does not
undergo any further modification, except for the possible action of
certain late rules which I will say more about below. Notice that I am
speaking of more than one last rule. Since there are many pairs of
phonological rules which are not ordered with respect to each other, the
rule order is only partial. Thus, one might picture a phonological
component as being composed of layers of rules, the rules in each layer
being unordered. I will assume that rules are ordered as close to the
end of the grammar as is allowed by the presence of rules crucially
ordered after them.[1] Thus, the bottom layer consists of last rules, the
next layer up of rules crucially ordered before at least one of these last
rules but not ordered before any others, and so on. It is the last or non-
last status of a rule which will concern us in this paper.

Before discussing an example of this notion of rule ordering, let us
return for a moment to the late rules mentioned above. I am treating
rules involving stylistic (that is, tempo) restrictions as belonging to
a separate sub-component of the phonology, to be ordered after all of the
rules required to derive systematic phonetic representations. For convenience, I will arbitrarily call the former "phonetic rules" and the
latter "phonological rules". The suggestion is certainly not a new one.
Stylistic rules, and some others, are generally felt to be somehow separate
from the rest of the phonology. By treating these phonetic rules as
separate from phonological rules, whose ordering is my main concern, I am
claiming that none of them may be ordered before any of the "last rules"
mentioned above, which are last phonological rules.

For examples of last and non-last rules, let us take a brief and
superficial look at a familiar series of sound changes in the history of

Spanish, assuming that these changes are indeed reflected in the synchronic phonology.[2] These changes involve Latin intervocalic stops, of which I will use the dentals for illustration. The environments for the changes and for the corresponding rules in Spanish vary somewhat, but this variation does not affect the ordering.

(Latin)   d   t   tt
           ↓   ↓   ↓
           ∅   d   t
                    ↓
                    δ

If these changes correspond to rules in the synchronic grammar of Spanish, these rules must be ordered as follows:

(1)   d --> ∅ / ...

(2)   t --> d / ...

(3)   tt --> t / ...   (4)   d --> δ / ...

```
           (1)
            |
           (2)
          /   \
        (3)   (4)
```

Both (3) and (4) are last rules.[3] No rules apply to their output, and their input is not allowed to surface in Spanish. That is, any new word appearing in the language must conform to these rules. Geminate or long obstruents are not permitted, and voiced stops must be continuant in the proper environments. Rules (1) and (2), on the other hand, are non-last rules, as they must be ordered before (3) and (4), and (1) must be ordered before (2). They correspond to non-productive phonological processes, which new /t/ and /d/ in Spanish do not undergo.

2.   [-LAST] AND [+SPECIAL]

Notice that the two non-last rules correspond to Harris' [+Special] rules. Rules that require the feature [+Special], or [+S], belong to a small group of rules which only the native vocabulary is marked to undergo. These rules must be set apart because a large part of the Spanish vocabulary was borrowed from Latin too late to undergo the sound changes to which they correspond. Thus, when native and non-native words show alternations that the phonologist wants to ascribe to the same underlying form, the non-native words must somehow be barred from the rules for the native vocabulary.

Does this mean, then, that all rules which do not correspond to active processes must be marked with [+S] or some equivalent? No, it does not, because it happens that some rules, by their very nature, will not apply to new vocabulary, and obviously, a rule need not be blocked unless it applies wrongly to some part of the vocabulary.

A rule may have as its input a sequence that arises from a previous [+S] rule, and that is unlikely to be found aside from this intermediate stage in the derivation. Thus, to draw an example from Harris' rules, rule (23) deletes /y/ before /č/ and /š/. These segments are the output of rule (12), which converts the clusters /kt/ and /ks/ into /yč/ and /yš/ respectively, and which must include [+S], since a number of words must be protected from the rule. But (23) need not mention [+S], because it applies to nothing but the output of (12), and it doesn't seem likely that /yč/ and /yš/ will occur in any new words. The only function of (23) is to finish up the process that (12) began.

> *nokte*

(12) [+S]   noyče

(23)   noče

If /yč/ and /yš/ should appear in new words, my claim that only last rules apply to new words predicts that, in the case of /ey/ or /iy/ before /č/, /š/, rule (22), which deletes glides after non-low vowels which agree in roundness, would apply, as this rule is apparently a last rule. However, since there are no last rules which would affect other vowels + y before /č/, /š/, the prediction is that they would remain.

             eyč iyč ayč oyč uyč

(22) [last] eč   ič   --- --- ---

The example discussed above illustrates one type of rule that need not be marked for application only to the native vocabulary, even though it does not correspond to any active phonological process. There is at least one other case in which a rule representing a non-productive process does not have to be singled out as applicable only to native words. It is sometimes possible to build into a rule a restriction on the environment that excludes productive morphological classes. For instance, Harris uses the features [-1conj] and [+3conj] to insure that the respective rules will not apply to new verbs, which join the first conjugation. Likewise, the feature [+past], in combination with the feature [-low] for vowels, blocks rule (1) in the only productive conjugation, which has /a/.

So, we see that some non-last rules require a special feature to block their application to new vocabulary, while others do not. But I hope I have shown that it would be wrong to draw from this fact the conclusion that rules requiring the special marker are somehow in a special class by themselves. Rather, all non-last rules have in common the fact that they correspond to non-productive processes; and thus it might be said that a sound change is stopped by the addition of a rule ordered after the rule which corresponds to the sound change in question.

3. WHAT ELSE STOPS A SOUND CHANGE?

Are there any other possible changes in a grammar which would correspond to the cessation of a sound change? An obvious possibility is restructuring of underlying forms as a result of a sound change which does not bring about new alternations. In such cases, since there would be no rule corresponding to the change for new words entering the language to undergo, one would not expect the change to remain as a productive phonological process.

The change of initial /š/ to /x/ in Spanish is an example of such a change. Restructuring seems to provide the most plausible generative account of the change of /š/ to /x/ in initial position, since there are no alternations, and thus, no reason to derive initial /x/ from any other segment. As one would expect, /š/ can occur initially in borrowings, a fact which shows that there is no active phonological process involved. It would be possible, of course, to derive initial /x/ from /š/ (or whatever segment underlies /š/) in an analysis which recognizes alternations medially between /ks/ and /x/, and between /kt/ and /č/, since š--> x might well be needed to relate /ks/ and /x/. It is interesting to note that a rule š-->x to derive initial /x/ would be a counter-example to my claim that last rules are productive. I know of no rules that must be ordered after this putative rule, and yet, it does not correspond to a productive process. This may indicate that my claim is wrong. But, of course, there is also a possibility that the use of the rule is wrong. And given the unusual nature of the rule, which does not set up any new alternations, but rather, changes every instance of a segment, this latter possibility is not unreasonable.

4. SPECULATIONS

I would like to speculate that last phonological rules represent a significant level in generative phonology, and to suggest that this level is distinguished by other properties in addition to being the location of productive phonological processes. In general, and very impressionistically, one might say that this is the level at which speakers are able to play around with their grammars.

I suspect it is at this level that hypercorrection takes place. One type of hypercorrection might be thought of as an informal rule that says, essentially, "Hey, you know that rule that changes X into Y? Well, you shouldn't use it, so change Y's back into X's." It seems, though, that

speakers don't have access to derivational information in such cases,
because instead of just undoing the rule, they change *all* Y's into X's,
regardless of whether they were derived from X's. These two rules are
represented schematically below, where (a) represents the rule being
rejected, and (*) represents the hypercorrection.

(a)   X --> Y / Z

(*)   Y --> X / Z

Now, I know of no cases in which a phonological rule must apply to the
output of such a hypercorrection, a fact which suggests that a hypercorrection can only "reverse" a last rule. As evidence for this, I
would like to mention a couple of examples of hypercorrection from the
tenth and eleventh century.[4] The segments in question are italicized,
and the Latin and Spanish words are given beneath.

"inte*c*ritate", "inte*c*ridade"   "iu*c*o"

(integritatem integridad)   *(iugum yugo)*

It can readily be seen that the rule being reversed incorrectly is rule
(2) mentioned above, which voices obstruents intervocalically and also
before /r/. Notice the second hypercorrect form, which incorrectly
devoices an original /g/ before /r/, but at the same time voices an
intervocalic /t/. What makes these forms interesting is the fact that
they are no longer possible hypercorrections. It is hard to imagine
that even the most pompous speaker of Spanish could say "intecridad".
Why are these once-possible hypercorrections no longer possible?
Simply, I think, because the rule which the hypercorrection was intended
to reverse is no longer a last rule. This rule, (2), must now be ordered
before rule (3), which replaces the segment removed by (2), and also
before rule (4), which further changes the output of (2). Thus, rule
(2) has moved higher into the grammar, and is, so to say, out of reach of
the whims of the speaker. Below is a comparison of the "normal" and
hypercorrect derivations with the modern derivation.

	lacrima	*integritate*
(2)	g	g
(*)	c	*c
-----	---------	-------------
(2)	g	g
(4)	ɣ	ɣ

I also suspect that rule simplification takes place while rules are at the level of last rules; however, I know of no crucial examples. A counter-example would be a rule (X) ordered before some rule (Y), and having a more restricted structural description than (Y). Then, if (X) should lose a feature and become more general, the result would be that additional outputs of (X) would be in feeding order with (Y), and the output forms involved in the change would undergo two changes: one from application of the simplified (X), the other from application of (Y) to this new segment.

5. QUESTIONS

The claim that I am making is clearly falsifiable, since either a last rule which is not productive, or a productive rule which is not last would be a counter-example. The possible existence of such counter-examples provides the most obvious questions that should be asked of the claim.

In addition, I would like to mention a couple of other questions which might be asked of the claim that productive phonological processes correspond to all and only last rules. What if only one expansion of a rule schema is ordered before some other rule in the phonology? Of course, it cannot be the case that a rule is crucially ordered between two parts of the same rule, but it should be possible for, say, part (a) of a rule (X) to be ordered before rule (Y), while part (b) of (X) is unordered with respect to (Y). Now, if rules (Y) and (Xb) should happen to be last rules, is it the case that (Xb) is productive, but (Xa) is not? And if (X) should indeed have a productive and a non-productive expansion, are we making specious use of our formalism by collapsing these into one rule? One might also want to ask whether a last rule can be reordered or lost.[5] Such a possibility makes the unlikely prediction that some formerly dead rule will be resurrected, and will once again become productive.

NOTES

1. Wallace Chafe (1968) discusses this version of partial ordering.
2. Whether one agrees or disagrees with the analysis implied by the claim that a certain rule is indeed in the synchronic phonology of Spanish is irrelevant to the claim I am making about the relation between rule order and productivity. Later in the paper, I will mention several rules from Harris (1969b) for illustration, as they should be generally known to generative phonologists working in Romance; but the exact formulation of the rules is not relevant to the present discussion on ordering, so it is not necessary to state the rules in full, or even to accept all of them as they are given.

3. One may object that (4) is not a last phonological rule, but rather a phonetic rule, since Harris (1969b) provides separate environments for Andante and Allegretto (rule (36). Rules quoted from Harris are numbered according to his Cumulative List of Rules pp. 183-8.) But there are other possibilities. As the Andante form of the rule must be in any description of any style of Spanish, and as the entire environment of the Andante rule must be repeated for Allegretto, with only the addition of optional word boundary, one might want to claim that the two are spearate rules, the Andante rule appearing as a last phonological rule, the Allegretto rule belonging to the phonetic rules. Simplicity is not a factor in the decision, since the two environments must be separate anyway. Indeed, taking this suggestion, one might be able to make another generalization namely, in Allegretto, certain assimilation rules present in the phonological rules (e.g. 34, 35, 36, in Harris) also apply across word boundaries. This generalization would be one rule in the phonetic rules, involving some general characterization of the phonological rules in question--something like "rules having only α-variables in the structural change apply across word boundary in Allegretto." I don't see how this would be possible in the current formalism, but it is certainly no accident that all three of the rules just mentioned must have two separate environments which differ only in the presence or absence of optional word boundary.

4. R. Menendez Pidal (1964:248). It seems likely that these particular examples do not really represent the type of hypercorrection that I mentioned above, but simply involve a spelling rule "/gr/ is usually spelled *cr* in Latin." There may well be earlier examples that are more convincing as cases of true hypercorrection. But these examples may at least be treated as hypothetical cases of what is involved in hypercorrection.

5. This suggestion was made by Emmon Bach, with whom I have had several useful discussions on earlier versions of this paper. I would also like to thank Robert Harms, Robert King, and Mike Brame for reading and commenting on the paper.

FRITZ G. HENSEY
UNIVERSITY OF TEXAS AT AUSTIN

PORTUGUESE VOWEL ALTERNATION

In Portuguese, vowel alternations of one type or another occur as regular and seemingly productive morphological processes. These alternations
are analogous to processes found in other Romance languages and, like
them, are consequences of the restructuring of the Vulgar Latin vowel
system.[1] On the other hand, the Portuguese alternations are of special
interest because of their great regularity. As a result of their having
become generalized in the grammar, Portuguese vowel alternations lend
themselves to a much simpler description than do the analogous ones of
Spanish, Italian, etc.[2]
The major areas in which systematic vowel alternation occurs are:

Verbs:
Present system (e.g., *botár/bóta;*[3] *escrêvo/escrévem*)
Strong or rizotonic preterites (e.g., *quiséram,* cf. *coméram;*
puséste, cf. *corrêste*)
Certain preterites (e.g., *fiz-fêz-fizemos; pus-pôs-puseram*)
Certain imperfects (e.g., *ponha/punha; venha/vinha*)
Deverbal nouns (e.g., *chorar:chôro; apelar:apêlo*)

Demonstratives and Personal Pronouns:
Demonstratives (e.g., *isso-êsse-éssa*)
Personal Pronouns (e.g., êle(s), éla(s))

Nouns and Adjectives:
Nouns (e.g., *ôvo/óvos; jôgo/jógos* (a deverbal also)
Adjectives (e.g., *nôvo/nóvos/nóva(s)) famôso/famósos/famósa(s)*)

The various areas of vowel alternation were listed here in order of
decreasing interest and importance to the analyst attempting to write a
synchronic description. The nouns and adjectives which undergo alternation
of open and close /o/ belong to a limited group; there are numerous exceptions (e.g., *espôso(s), tôdo/tôda,* etc.). The demonstratives and 3d

sg. nominative personal pronouns form a closed set with few members, to
wit: ((*êle(s) êla(s)*) (*êste êsse aquêle* and variants)). The area of most
interest is that of the verb, and the five topics given under this heading
are also listed in order of decreasing importance.

Portuguese is traditionally analyzed as having a seven-vowel system; on
the surface, it shows more phonetically distinct vowel segments than does
Spanish and less than French or (some variants of) Italian. Nevertheless,
recent work in some languages which share a great many rules with Portuguese shows that, historical considerations aside, phonological rules for
Romance languages operate on a basic seven-vowel system:[4]

(i)

	i	e	ε	u	o	ɔ	a
High	+	-		+	-		
Low		-	+		-	+	+
Front	+	+	+	-	-	-	-
Round					+	-	

In Portuguese, most vowel alternations involve the feature Low (alternations of *e/ε* and *o/ɔ*, although a few may refer to the feature High.

In Spanish and Italian (and to a lesser extent in French) the corresponding alternations involve a simple vowel and a dipthong (*e/ie, o/uo,*
and the like); in Portuguese, two simple vowels are involved: a mid and
a laxer, lower variant of the mid vowel.

To the extent that this alternation is predictable, an underlying form
need not specify the feature Low (nor, in some cases, the feature High)
for the vowel which undergoes such regular alternation. In Spanish, however, surface forms like *sienta* (vs. *presenta*) and *cuenta* (vs. *monta*)
clearly point to the need for differences in the underlying forms: e.g.,
/sεnta/ vs. /presenta/, /kɔnta/ vs. /monta/; or /s e nta/ vs. /pres e nta/,
/k o nta/ vs. /m o nta/.   [+D]   [-D]
[+D]   [-D]
We shall show here that in Portuguese, underlying forms (especially
those of verbs) need not specify the feature Low for vowels other than
/i u a/ nor make use of some special feature, like *D*(iphthongizing),
tense, long, etc. What we have in effect is a language in which vowel
alternation has become much more general than is the case in other major
Romance languages.

Suppose that verbstems are given a canonical form something like /XCVC/,
where V is defined as the stem vowel. Lexical features will include the
specification of the theme vowel as

(ii)

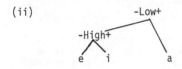

Other lexical features will include mode, person, number, tense or aspect, and special traits of the particular verb such as "minus rule such-and-such". Deverbal nouns will be identified as dominated by *Verb* but specified "+Noun". Rules for specifying the feature *Low* (and occasionally *High* as well) will occur at a rather low level, certainly after the theme vowel and the affixes have been put in place and stress has been assigned.

Let us first consider the most interesting case of vowel alternation in verbs, that of the present system. In general, what happens is that a-theme verbs lower the stressed stem vowel: *lévo, móras, péga, córtam;* since the 1st sg. pres. indicative stem is normally the basis for the present subjunctive, forms like *léve, móres, péguem,* and *córte* result.[5] The rule, so far, is quite simple:

(iii)
$$
\begin{bmatrix}
V \\
\alpha \text{front} \\
-\alpha \text{ ound} \\
-\text{high} \\
+\text{stress}
\end{bmatrix}
\text{----> +low / } \underline{\qquad}]_{\text{stem}}
\;\;[\text{+low theme}]
$$

Rule (iii) is applicable to e-theme verbs except in 1st. sg. and, consequently, in the present subjunctive. Here, the stressed stem vowel is specified -Low:

(iv)
$$
\begin{bmatrix}
V \\
\alpha \text{front} \\
-\alpha \text{round} \\
-\text{high} \\
+\text{stress}
\end{bmatrix}
\text{-----> -low / } \underline{\qquad}]_{\text{stem}}
\begin{bmatrix} -\text{high} \\ -\text{low} \end{bmatrix}_{\text{theme}}
\;\;[\text{+I}]
$$

The case of *i*-theme verbs is rather complex. First, there are some *i*-theme verbs which do not undergo alternations of the type *e/ɛ, o/ɔ,* but rather *e/i* (*agredir:agride*); others do undergo a similar form of alternation but show a high vowel in their stems (*destrUir, sUbir*); and others conform to the general requirement that the stem vowel be (-High) (*sentir, dormir*). Further, these verbs show three levels of alternation (*i:e:ɛ, u:o:ɔ*) under stress. Thus; there is a rule similar to (iv) for *i*-stem verbs in 1st person sg. while for the other persons (iii), without specification of theme vowel, will apply.

(v)
$$
\begin{bmatrix}
V \\
\alpha \text{front} \\
-\alpha \text{round} \\
+\text{stress}
\end{bmatrix}
\text{----> +high / } \underline{\qquad}]\text{ stem } [\text{+I}]
\;\;[\text{+high theme}]
$$

These three rules may be collapsed into one, since what happens is that in all three conjugations the stressed stem vowel is lowered to /ɛ/, /ɔ/, in all persons but first singular; in first singular, the stressed stem

vowel assimilates to the theme vowel for the two features *High* and *Low*.
Consequently, in *a*-themes (+low) the stem vowel is specified as (+low);
in *e*-themes, as mid (-high -low); and in *i*-themes as (+high).

Many i-stems show /u/ rather than /o/ as their unstressed stem vowel,
yet they undergo the same sort of alternation as do others which show the
expected stem vowel /o/: *subir, construir* vs. *dormir*. To capture the
historical observation that this alternation in 3d conjugation verbs spread
by analogy, we may have underlying forms in /sob/, /konstro/, and /dorm/.
This would make them subject to a vowel alternation rule whose output would
include forms like *subo, sóbe, constróem*, and *durma*. The phonetic [u] which
appears as the pretonic stem vowel of these verbs (including *dormir*, despite
its current spelling), may be accounted for by a low level rule to the effect
that atonic /e/ and /o/ may (and often must) be specified (+high). Such
a rule gives not only *sUbia, construUimos*, and the like, but also the common
pronounciation of forms like *melhor, política* and the like as *milhor, pulítica*.
This is to argue that setting up /sob/, /konstro/ etc., is not merely ad hoc.

The following general rule applies to stressed stem vowels /E/ and /O/:

(vi) a.
$$\begin{bmatrix} V \\ \alpha front \\ -\alpha round \\ -high \\ +stress \end{bmatrix} \quad \text{----->} \quad +low \ / \ \underline{\hspace{2cm}}]_{stem} \ [-I]$$

b.
$$\begin{bmatrix} V \\ \alpha front \\ -\alpha round \\ -high \\ +stress \end{bmatrix} \quad \text{----->} \quad \begin{bmatrix} \beta low \\ \gamma high \end{bmatrix} \ / \ \underline{\hspace{2cm}}]_{stem} \ [+I] \\ \begin{bmatrix} \beta low \\ \gamma high \end{bmatrix}_{theme}$$

We may illustrate the effects of this rule for six verb forms: levas,
moro, escrevem, corro, sirvo, dormes

(vii)

		lEvas	mOro	skrEven	kOrro	sErvo	dOrmes
	THEME	a	a	e	e	i	i
	PERSON	II	I	III	I	I	II
vi	a.	lévas	-	skréven	-	-	dŏrmes
	b.	-	mɔ́ro	-	kɔ́rro	sírvo	-
		lévas	mŏro	escrévem	côrro	sírvo	dŏrmes

The present subjunctive stem is that of the 1st sg. present indicative,
with a small set of exceptions (*haver, saber*, etc.). This is true of some
other Romance languages as well. In Portuguese, an obvious consequence is
that in *a*-themes, the stem vowel in the present subjunctive will be (+low),
in *e*-themes (-low -high), and in *i*-themes (+high): *môres, côrra, sírvam*,

etc. We need a rule to the effect that the stem of certain verbs is replaced in 1st. sg. present indicative; e.g., that /mid/ is replaced by
/mɛs/, /pod/ by /pɔs/, and the like: *medir:méɡo, poder:pôsso*. After this,
a more general rule will state that for all verbs not marked as exceptional...
haver, saber, and some others...the stem of the present subjunctive is
identical to that of the 1st sg present indicative.

The remaining cases of vowel alternation in verbs are dealt with much
more quickly because of their simplicity. One of them involves some twenty
verbs with rizotonic preterites: *querer, fazer, por* (underlying /pone/),
etc. They are called rizotonic in that in the 1st. and 3d. singular of the
preterit, stress falls on the stem vowel rather than elsewhere (*quís, fíz,
pôs, trôuxe, dísse*, and others, as compared with so-called arrizotonics like
levar (levôu), comer (comî), etc.).

The alternation which applies to all rizotonic verbs except *ir, ser*, and
ver is as follows: the person/number markers -*ste*, -*mos*, -*steis*, and *ran* of
2d sg, 1st pl, 2d pl, and 3d pl respectively, are normally preceded by the
stressed theme vowel: *falâste, comêmos, escrevêram, saîsteis*. The cited
rizotonic verbs resemble *e*-stems except that the stressed theme vowel is
/ɛ/ rather than /e/. There should be a rule, then, which lowers the theme-
vowel in such cases.

Furthermore, the stem of several other tenses is predictable (as happens
also in Spanish) from the 3d. pl. preterite form; removing the person-
number marker -*ran*, we have the stem for the imperfect subjunctive (*fi-
zésse*), the future subjunctive (*quiser*), and the pluperfect indicative
(*pudéra*). The rule which replaces the present stem with that of the 3d.
pl. preterite minus -*ran*, must follow the one which lowers the stressed
theme vowel of rizotonic verbs. For most verbs, of course, the stem-
changing rule would apply vacuously because the present stem is the one
normally used for all finite verb forms.

Five verbs show a special type of alternation in the preterit: *fazer,
estar, ter, poder, pôr*. Their basic stems are replaced in the preterit
with /fIze/, /stIve/, /tIve/, /pUde/, and /pUze/; the spellings I and U
refer to non-low vowels unspecified for High. The stem vowel is (-high)
in 3d. sg. of the preterit, and (+high) elsewhere: 3d. sg. *fêz, têve,
estêve, pôde, pôs*; other forms: *fiz, tiveste, estivemos, pudemos, pus*.
The corresponding rule applies only to these five verbs, but since it gives
the vowel quality for the 3d. pl. preterite, it accounts for a good many
other forms based on the 3d. pl. pret.

The verbs *ter, vir*, and *pôr* (probable underlying stems: *tene, veni,
pone*) share a number of idiosyncracies, among them the formation of an
imperfect stem whose stem vowel is stressed throughout and related systematically to the stem vowel of the 1st sg pres ind: *tenho: tính-,
venho: vính-, ponho:púnh-*, being the 1st sg. pres. ind. and the imperfect
stem respectively, illustrate the process. The corresponding rule, of
very limited scope, proves to be of some use pedagogically; these three
verbs may be taught as a group, since they share a good many special
rules; e.g., loss of -*n*- in the present stem, assuming that forms like

ven(s), ten(s), and *põe(s)* are based on forms like /véne(s)/, /téne(s)/, and /póne(s)/, respectively.[6]

There is a limited set of deverbal nouns, already illustrated by *chorar: chôro, apelar:apêlo*. All that is involved, in terms of rules, is to specify (-low) for the stem /E/ or /O/ of verbs which make use of this particular process of nominalization. This is a small segment of the derivational morphology.

Before leaving verbs, it is important to discuss counterexamples, real or apparent, to the scheme of vowel alternation outlined above. In Brazilian dialects, for instance, nasalized vowels are (-low); *come*, for instance, is /kóme/, while in Portugal it may be /kɔ́me/. The latter follows from (vi a) above; the former appears to be a counterexample. A simple treatment of this problem would be to allow (vi) to lower the stressed /E/ or /O/ of all verbs (and not only those, say, specified (-nas). Later, there would be a rule to the effect that a nasalized vowel is non-low. This would permit the nasal-/E/-stems like *sentir* to undergo (vi), which would give correctly the 1st sg. /sínto/, as well as */sɛ́nte /, */sɛ́nten/, etc. The later rule would restore the proper mid level for those dialects which do not admit open nasalized vowels.

A second problem area is that of *a*-themes which on the surface have /o/ or /e/ as their stressed stem vowels, without a following consonant: *corôa, vôam, passêia, odêias* rather than **corôa, *vôam, *passéiam, *odéias*. The *-oar* group involves loss of *-n-* or *-l-*, at least from a diachronic viewpoint (assuming underlying /korona/, /vola/, for "crown" and "fly", respectively. The glide in *-ear* verbs appears to be a hiatus-breaker. For such verbs, one might restrict the environment in which (vi) may apply to those stems where there is at least one consonant after the stem vowel. Such a restriction is too strong, however, for it would eliminate verbs like *destruir* and *moer* (probable base, /mole/), to which (vi) does apply.

Related to the *-ear* group is that in *-ejar* (/-eẑar/) like *desejar, almejar*, which do not undergo (vi): *desêjo, almêjas* rather than **deséjo, *almêjas*.

A solution which may be worth considering would be to mark all such verbs as idiosyncratic (in this case, "minus rule (vi)"; to do so, however, would ignore the phonetic similarities among these apparently exceptional verbs. One might, for instance, set up stems in /ei/ and /ou/ for these verbs: /korona/ --> /koroua/; /vola/ --> /voua/; /pasesa/ --> /paseia/ /dezea/ --> /deseia/. In this way, the stems would be comparable to other dipthong stems, like *roubar*, which does not undergo alternation is Std. Portuguese.[7]

If this proceedure were followed, applying it only to *a*-stems, the environment of (vi) could be restated so as to eliminate diphthong stems; i.e., the stressed stem vowel must not be followed by another, non-syllabic vowel. Forms like /dezei-/, /vou-/, etc., would not undergo alternation. It may be noted that in Portuguese falling dipthongs whose nucleus is /E/ or /O/, those with an open nucleus are quite uncommon (*céu, idéia*, and the like). A third possible solution to this problem would be to let all verbs undergo (vi), and then to specify that unless otherwise indicated, stressed /E/ or /O/ followed by a second vowel or a glide are specified (-low).

A last, minor ser of counterexamples includes the commonly cited *chegar* and *fechar*, verbs which do not undergo (vi) in standard Portuguese. It may be noted, however, that *fechar* quite often undergoes alternation in familiar speech (*fécha a porta*). Some other verbs appear to be restructured, at least in familiar or reginal speech, to suit them for porcessing by (vi). *Roubar* is heard to be treated as though it were **robar....róbo....róbam....* and *viver* gets recast as **viver....vivo, *véve(m)*. It may or may not be an exaggeration to present such common substandard forms as evidence that (vi) is not only general in modern Portuguese, but productive as well.

In 3d. person personal pronouns, base /El/, the rule is simple:

$$(iii) \begin{bmatrix} V \\ -high \\ +stress \end{bmatrix} \longrightarrow \alpha low \; / \underline{\hspace{2cm}} \begin{bmatrix} -\alpha masc. \end{bmatrix} \; stem \\ \begin{bmatrix} +Pron. \end{bmatrix} \\ \begin{bmatrix} +III \end{bmatrix} \\ \begin{bmatrix} -nominative \end{bmatrix}$$

Thus, masculine is (-low): *êle(s)*; feminine is (+low): *éla(s)*. The same rule may be extended to the three demonstratives with bases /Est/, Es/, and /akEl/...*êste(s), éssa(s)*... except that there is in addition a neuter form for each, whose vowel is specified (+high): *isto, isso, aquilo*.

It would be economical enough to let (viii) apply both to personal pronouns and to these three demonstratives. The neuter formation would not represent the rule which matches vowel height with gender, but rather it would be part of another rule which would deal with the three demonstratives and the form *tudo*, which is the neuter corresponding to *todo*, "all".

The last alternation to be discussed here will be that represented in *ôvo/óvos* (for nouns) and *nôvo-nôvos/nóva(s)* (for adjectives). Both are minor subsets of their respective form classes. From a pedagogical viewpoint, it is interesting to group them, e.g., in a beginners text. It may be noted that the o/ɔ alternation persists in a certain very common substandard syntactic process, namely, the one whereby the last inflected member of a noun phrase loses its plural marker: **essas coisa* for *essas coisas, *dois pastel* for *dois pastéis, *os limão* for *os limões;* cf. **meus ôlho* (rather than **meus ólho*) for *meus ólhos*.[8]

Vowel alternations, as part of various processes of allomorphic variation, are interesting and important features of all the Romance languages. It is noteworthy that in Portuguese these processes have become especially regular in synchronic grammar.[9]

NOTES

1. For a recent summary, see Mendeloff (1969).
2. Said Ali (1964:129-82) discusses the chronology of this process of generalization along with other relevant aspects of the Portuguese verb.
3. In Portuguese orthography, the circumflex accent is used to indicate a stressed close /e/ or /o/, while the acute serves to indicate an open /ɛ/ or /ɔ/. In this article, I make use of this spelling device even where the standard spelling does not require any diacritic: *bóta* = /bɔta/ is actually written *bota*; *escrêvo* = /iskrévo/ is written *escrevo*.
4. Two well-known and recent treatments are Schane (1968a) and Harris (1969b).
5. A more complete treatment of Portuguese verb morphology will appear in several as yet unpublished articles, e.g., Hensey (1971 and forthcoming).
6. This approach is implicit in the grouping of "irregular" verbs in Barrutia et al (1970).
7. "Standard Portuguese", outside some academic texts, is of course a useful fiction pending extensive research in Portugal and Brazil. As regards the latter, see Thomas (1969). For a wide range of Brazilian viewpoints, see Anais (1958).
8. It is worth noting that this construction has long since invaded the written language; e.g., some official documents urge the user to *evitar o uso dos grampo* 'avoid using staples', advertisements refer to *os melhores café*, etc. Likewise, some folksongs alternate *os teus oio* with *os óios teu* 'your eyes'.
9. For a treatment of Portuguese stem replacement, vowel alternations, etc., in terms of allomorphic variation, see Mattoso Câmara (1970:59-105).

DIETER WANNER
UNIVERSITY OF ILLINOIS

THE DERIVATION OF INFLECTIONAL PARADIGMS IN ITALIAN

The question whether the paradigm is a meaningful linguistic unit is neither new nor has it ever been answered conclusively. The reluctance to introduce theoretical machinery which, unless appropriately constrained, might be too powerful leads to the rejection of paradigmatic and analogical forces in general as explanatory devices. Yet a number of studies have presented cases where it seems that the only reasonable explanation for the observed phenomena is the recognition of the paradigm as an active force. In the field of Romance linguistics Malkiel (1968) and Kuryłowicz (1968) reached such a conclusion for two related historical problems of Spanish and Italian verbal inflection respectively. At the 1970 LSA Winter Meeting, J. Harris (1970b) presented the difficulties involved in stating the applicability conditions of the Spanish Velar Softening rule in verbal forms. The most natural solution would require to give them as a function of a paradigmatic surface constraint.

This paper will investigate the same problem in nominal and verbal inflection in Italian where only a minor portion of stem final consonants undergo palatalization and related rules. Although the derivational description of the forms is complex, the surface results correspond to relatively simple patterns of alternation. Besides proposing a revised classification of Italian verbs based on rule applicability conditions, I will argue for a reconsideration of the paradigmatic dimension interpreted as a special case of functional, as opposed to formal, restrictions on rules.

I. PALATALIZATION IN NOMINAL FORMS

Most Italian nouns show distinct forms for singular and plural. The usual endings are:[1]

(1)							
I	(fem)	sg -a	pl -e		pianta - piante	'plant'
II	(masc)	-o	-i		punto - punti	'point'
III	(m or f)	-e	-i		ponte - ponti	'bridge'
IV	(masc)	-a	-i		artista - artisti	'artist'

Given the fact that Italian also possesses a palatalization (or velar softening) rule

(2)
$$\begin{bmatrix} C \\ +back \\ +high \end{bmatrix} \longrightarrow \begin{bmatrix} +del\ rel \\ -back \end{bmatrix} \bigg/ \ - \begin{bmatrix} V \\ -back \end{bmatrix}$$

whose effect can be seen in forms like

(3) [k] conduco 'I lead'   [č] conduci 'you lead'
          elettrico 'electric'   elettricità 'electricity'
     [g] dialogo 'dialog'   [ǧ] dialogizzare 'to have a
                                               dialog'

it seems reasonable to ask what happens with eventual velar consonants in stem final position when they occur with one of the ending pairs in (1): In all cases the plural ending is [-back] whereas all the singular endings (with the exception of III) are [+back]. The expected result should be a regular alternation between velar and palatal stem final consonants in I, II and IV; on the other hand III should only provide us with examples for invariable palatal. Consider the data in (4):

(4) I   [k] amica 'friend (f.)'   [k] amiche
                   pratica 'practice'   pratiche
              [g] strega 'witch'   [g] streghe
     II (a) [k] amico   [č] amici   'friend (m.)'
                   porco   porci   'pig'
              [g] filologo   [ǧ] filologi   'philologist'
         (b) [k] banco   [k] banchi   'bank, bench'
                   baco   bachi   'berry'
              [g] lago   [g] laghi   'lake'
                   astrologo   astrologhi   'astrologer'
         (c) [č] gancio   [č] ganci   'hook'
                   cacio   caci   'cheese'
              [ǧ] regio   [ǧ] regi   'royal'
                   collegio   collegi   'college'
     III   [č] voce   [č] voci   'voice'
                   codice   codici   'codex'
              [ǧ] strage   [ǧ] stragi   'bloodshed'
     IV   [k] duca   [k] duchi   'duke'
                   patriarca   patriarchi   'patriarch'

Only in the case of III is the prediction borne out fully; in addition, IIa shows regular palatalization. But IIc shows a palatal even before a back vowel. In I, IIb and IV on the other hand the palatalization rule fails for some reason to apply and to produce the expected variation.

Notice however that it is far from clear that all palatals in Italian should be derived from underlying velars by the palatalization rule. It

would make more sense to claim that the forms in IIc have an underlying
palatal consonant in stem final position so that the palatalization rule
will not have to apply to them; on the same grounds III can be reduced to
a straightforward representation. Since palatalization does not apply in
those cases it can be claimed consequently that it does not apply in
nominal paradigms at all. The non-alternating forms of I, IIb, IIc, III
and IV find their natural explanation. Nothing happens to them because
nothing should happen to them. The crux is the group IIa (fairly important
in number) which makes it necessary to include among the rules of Italian
phonology the palatalization process (2) which then has to be blocked on
non-phonological grounds from applying to a number of strings.

Not to recognize palatalization as a rule would make it unexplainable
why a stem final [k] or [g] alternates with a palatal, if it alternates at
all. Therefore a hopefully principled way of distinguishing between IIa
and the other classes will be found.

It has been argued that the Italian plural morpheme for nouns and adjectives is $+i\#$ and that there are two rules responsible for deriving the
surface endings resulting from the underlying hiatus of thematic vowel
(thV) and plural ending (Schane and Wanner 1969):

(5)   coalescence $a + i \longrightarrow e$

   elision $\begin{bmatrix} V \\ -stress \end{bmatrix} \longrightarrow \emptyset \ / \ - + V$

   therefore: $o + i$ and $e + i$ become i

As a consequence it would be sufficient to order palatalization crucially
after coalescence and elision to obtain the desired results. The [+back]
thV will protect the stem final consonant from meeting the structural description of (2):

(6)   / streg + a + i /   / bak + o + i /
   -------   ------   palatalization
              e   ------   coalescence
   ------- $\emptyset$ elision
   [strége]   [báki]   surface

But by the same token palatalization would have to fail for *amici* which has
the same structure as *bachi*: / amik + o + i /. The result of an ordering
solution would be inconsistent ordering given the same type of underlying
representation. Both forms are masculine nouns in the plural and have
the ending $k + o + i$. Given this situation, not even the theory of local
ordering (Anderson 1969) can do anything here. There are two classes of
otherwise identical forms, one blocking, the other one allowing palatalization
to apply.

Several means of producing such a difference come to mind utilizing the
full capacity of phonological theory; but none seems to appeal even at first

glance. We could claim that palatalization is ordered after coalescence
and elision; in addition the nouns IIa take exclusively a front unrounded
high vowel as plural morpheme whereas all other classes would have a back
unrounded high vowel which later on gets neutralized with the front vowel
plural morpheme. Or the stem final consonant of classes IIb and IV could
be a rounded velar k^w as opposed to the plain one of IIa; after palatalization had applied the rounding would be eliminated to produce the correct
output, etc. These are all tricks which work mechanically but do not have
any other value to them. The first solution has to give up the uniqueness
of the plural morpheme; the second one creates new problems because either
it gives up the natural relationship between *amico* and *amica* in underlying
representation or it has to accept inconsistent ordering of the rule which
eliminates the artificial rounding of the stem final consonant.[2]
  Blaming the difference on either the stem final consonant or the plural
morpheme cannot do more than just stating that there are two classes with
distinctive behavior regarding palatalization. Unless some other difference
between the two classes can be found which could only be explained in terms
of the proposed distinction, such a solution does not offer any insights
other than the ones provided by the equally adequate exception features
governing the application of palatalization.
  Even in derivational morphology, palatalization offers some surprises.

(7) (a) IIa: k - $\check{c}$ in sg. - pl.

amico:	amicare 'to become friends', amica 'friend (f.)'	k/a,o,u
'friend(m)'	amicizia 'friendship'	č/e,i
	amichetto 'little friend', amichevole 'friendly'	k/e,i
porco:	porcaccio 'ugly pig', porcone 'big swine'	k/a,o,u
'pig'	porcile 'pigsty', porcellino 'little pig'	č/e,i
	porchetta 'roasted pork', porcheria 'filthiness'	k/e,i
medico:	medicare 'to cure', medicabile 'curable'	k/a,o,u
'doctor'	medicina 'medicine'	č/e,i
	medichino 'little doctor', medichessa 'female doctor'	k/e,i
monaco:	monaca 'nun', monacale 'monastic'	k/a,o,u
'monk'	monacella 'little nun'	č/e,i
	monachella 'little nun', monachesimo 'monasticism'	
	monachetto/a 'little monk/nun'	k/e,i
pubblico:	pubblicare 'to publish'	k/a,o,u
'public'	pubblicità 'publicity'	č/e,i

IIb: k - k in sg. - pl.

fuoco:	focoso 'fiery'	k/a,o,u
'fire'	fuochetto 'little fire'	k/e,i
bianco:	biancume 'white things'	k/a,o,u
'white'	imbianchire 'to make white', biancheria 'linen'	k/e,i
cieco:	ciecaggine 'blindness'	k/a,o,u
'blind'	cecità 'blindness'	č/e,i
pudico:	pudicizia 'chastity'	č/e,i
'chaste'		

IIc: č - č in sg. - pl.

gancio: 'hook'	agganciare 'to hook up' gancietto 'little hook'	č/a,o,u č/e,i
calcio: 'kick'	calciatore 'soccer player'	č/a,o,u

(b) IIa: g - ǧ in sg. - pl.

teologo: 'theologian'	teologare 'to theologice' teologia 'theology' teologhessa 'female theologian'	g/a,o,u ǧ/e,i g/e,i
asparago: 'asparagus'	asparageto 'asparagus field'	ǧ/e,i
esofagos: 'esophagus'	esofageo 'of the esophagus'	ǧ/e,i

g - ǧ / g in sg. - pl.

antropologo: 'anthropologist'	antropologia 'anthropology'	ǧ/e,i
chirurgo: 'surgeon'	chirurgico 'surgical'	ǧ/e,i

IIb: g - g in sg. - pl.

dialogo: 'dialog'	dialogare 'to make/participate in a dialog' dialogico 'of a dialog' dialoghetto 'short dialog'	g/a,o,u ǧ/e,i g/e,i
fungo: 'mushroom'	fungaia 'mushroom field' fungiforme 'in the form of a mushroom' fungheto 'mushroom field'	g/a,o,u ǧ/e,i g/e,i
lago: 'lake'	lagone 'big lake' laghetto 'little lake'	g/a,o,u g/e,i
catalogo: 'catalog'	catalogare 'to make a list' cataloghino 'small catalog'	g/a,o,u g/e,i

IIc: ǧ - ǧ in sg. -pl.

grigio: 'grey'	grigiastro 'greyish'	ǧ/a,o,u

Although no principle of application is discernible at first glance, it is clear that palatalization cannot be anything else than a productive process of Italian phonology. Either it applies to a form (*amico: amicizia*) or it fails to do so (*amico:amichevole*); but never can we find an instance of unmotivated application before a back vowel.[3] There is no form corresponding to a type *ami[k]o:*ami[č]a-*. All cases where the rule applies conform to the natural environment before a front vowel.

The only hopeful solution will be in the direction of a subclassification of the various suffixes. Regularities which can be easily recognized include the following:

(a) Feminine and masculine nouns in *-a* do not palatalize in the plural.
(b) Native, productive derivations do not palatalize; e.g. the diminutive suffixes (which characteristically begin with a front vowel

like in *-ino, -etto, -ellino*) show very few exceptions: *mona[č]ella* (but also *mona[k]ella*), *por[č]ellino*. Notice the difference between *medi[k]ino* and *medi[č]ina*. Only in the function of a diminutive does the suffix /+*in*+/ block palatalization.

(c) Non-native (productive or unproductive) derivations usually palatalize regardless of whether palatalization applies in the plural or not: *cecità, pudicizia, dialogico, fungiforme.* The meaning of these words (especially with respect to the meaning of the basic form) tempts one to place them in a different lexical stratum, i.e. to classify them as [-native].

The point of the discussion is that palatalization does not apply across the board in Italian phonology; it is highly sensitive to morphosyntactic information and to lexical markings classifying single items as belonging to the [+native] or [-native] part of the lexicon. There is a high correlation between [+native] and [-palatalization rule] on the one hand, on the other between [-native] and [+palatalization rule].[4]

In the light of work done by Harris (1969b) and Saciuk (1969a and b) this correlation of [αnative] with [-αrule X] is rather strange. The native (or special) part of the vocabulary is usually characterized by undergoing rules which the non-native (non-special) forms do not undergo. The characteristic feature of such rules is that they are known to have existed at one time as a historical process. For the Italian case under discussion the situation is rather the opposite. The well known historical process of palatalization seems to be typical of non-native items.

None of the briefly discussed solutions seems to be really a desirable one. The only one which works, but which in turn is as uninsightful as may be, is the marking of each individual lexical item for its ability to serve as an environment for, or undergo, palatalization, with the possible benefit of some suffixes behaving in a consistent way. The situation expressed by the data is disorderly; perhaps this is the only motivated statement regarding palatalization in nominal forms.[5]

II. STEM FINAL CONSONANT ALTERNATIONS IN VERBAL FORMS

In the light of the problems encountered in the preceding paragraphs which revealed a considerable amount of fluctuation in the applicability of palatalization, it comes as no surprise that the situation in the verbal inflectional forms is not any better. The set of different forms is much larger (six amalgamated tenses with six forms each plus a number of nominal forms) and therefore the chances for finding exceptional paradigms are much higher.

In the conventional account of the different verbal forms a preliminary classification is established based on the thematic vowel and the paradigmatic dimension of regularity:

(8) I thV $\bar{a}$ IIa thV $\bar{e}$ IIIa thV $\bar{\imath}$
          (parláre)   (temére)   (dormíre)

$$\text{IIb} \quad \text{thV} \quad \breve{e} \qquad \text{IIIb} \quad \text{th}\underline{V} \quad \bar{\imath}/\check{\imath}\text{sk}$$
$$\text{(préndĕre)} \qquad\qquad \text{(finīre)}$$

Irregular verbs on the other hand escape this classification often: *dire*, *fare*, *porre* (all partially in IIb), *essere* (not in IIb) etc.[6]

What we are interested in here is again, as in the case of nominal paradigms, the behavior of the stem final consonant with respect to rules having the potential of alternating its surface manifestations. Therefore our main concern will be the forms where an ending is directly attached to the stem or to the thV (which in turn is directly attached to the stem), but not the endings which are attached to some intervening tense or other morpheme:

(9) parlano: / parl + *a* + *n*(o) / (stem + thV + person/number ending)
                               3 pl pres. indic. of *parlare* ' to speak'
    parlavano: / parl + *a* + *v*a + n(o) / (stem + thV + tense + ending)
                               3 pl imperf. indic. of *parlare* 'to speak'

This restriction will limit the discussion essentially to forms of the present indicative and subjunctive and to the stem + thV + tense morpheme configurations of the other tenses (to which then will be added the individual morphemes for number and/or person). Given a morphological structure of such a verb form as

(10) (prefix) + stem + (thematic vowel) + (tense/mood) + (person/number)

we will be talking about the following morphemes:

(11) (a) Thematic vowel: cf. (8)
      (b) Tense/mood: -*ya*/*a* (after a palatal) in all conjugation classes
                        for 1 pl pres. indic. and 1, 2 pl pres. subj.
                        -*i* pres. subj. in I, *a* pres. subj. in II - III
                        -*isk*/*išš* (before a front vowel) in IIIb for 1 - 3
                        sg, 3 pl in pres. indic. and subj.
      (c) Person/number: 1 sg *o*   1 pl *mo*
                         2 sg *i*   2 pl *te*
                         3 sg *a* or ∅ in I   3 pl *n* in I indic.[7]
                               e or ∅ in II   I - III subj.
                               e in III   *on* in II - III ind.

The resulting surface endings with schematic marking of the position of main stress in the form are the following:

(12) (a) indicative forms

1sg	I	´-o	IIa & b	´-o	IIIa	´-o	IIIb	-ísko
2sg		´-i		´-i		´-i		-íšši
3sg		´-a		´-e		´-e		-íšše

1 pl	-yámo	-yámo	-yámo	-yámo
2 pl	-áte	-éte	-íte	-íte
3 pl	´-ano	´-ono	´-ono	-ískono

(b) subjunctive forms

1 sg	´-i	´-a	´-a	-íska
2 sg	´-i	´-a	´-a	-íska
3 sg	´-i	´-a	´-a	-íṣka
1 pl	-yámo	-yámo	-yámo	-yámo
2 pl	-yáte	-yáte	-yáte	-yáte
3 pl	´-ino	´-ano	´-ano	-ískano

These endings follow the stem directly; eventual surface manifestations of
the thematic vowel are already included in the endings above. Additional
endings belong to the following tenses (quoted in 2 sg):

(13)

		I		II		III	
Imperfect indicative:		-avi		-evi		-ivi	
	subjunctive	-ássi		-éssi		-íssi	
Future		-erái		-(e)rái		-irái	
Conditional		-erésti		-(e)résti		-irésti	
Passato remoto[8]		-ásti		-ésti		-ísti	

By looking at these surface forms it is clear that a stem final velar
consonant will be alternatively before a front and before a back vowel. On
the basis of present linguistic theory we would expect such a consonant to
undergo the independently motivated palatalization rule (as was expected
for the nominal forms). This actually happens in at least some of the
classes. IIb and IIIb are subject to this variation.

(14) IIb: vínko, vínči, vínče, vinčámo, vinčéte, vínkono
      IIIb: -ísko, -íšši, -íšše; -- , -- , -ískono

Notice however that for IIIb it is not the stem which is shown to be subject
to palatalization but only a special ending morpheme. Whenever a verb
belongs to IIIb (i.e. has this stem or thV augment in forms which would
otherwise receive stress on the stem) it will undergo palatalization for
what concerns the augment, but not with respect to the stem. The constant
and predictable nature of the augment allows us to collapse IIIb with IIIa
for the present purposes.

Remain the verbs of IIb. Since their thV is *e* (a vowel which can usually
trigger palatalization) and since only the forms with an overt front ending
vowel palatalize, it appears that there are only two choices for a viable
underlying representation. Either the thV is present in all forms, in which
case, in order to prevent palatalization from applying to all forms without
discrimination, elision has to precede it;

(15)

	/ vink + e + o /	/ vink + e + i /
elision	Ø	Ø
palatalization	----	č̌

other rules   [vîŋko]   [vínči]

or else the thV is not included in the underlying representation and is inserted transformationally whenever the stem is directly followed by the word boundary or a consonant.

(16)   / vink + o /   /vink + i /   / vink # /   / vink + te /
     insertion   ---   ----   e   e
     palatalization   ---   č   č   č
     other rules   [vîŋko]   [vínči]   [vínče]   [vinčéte]

The second solution (16) has the advantage that it characterizes the surface form of the stem final consonant directly as a consequence of the attached ending whereas the former solution requires a crucial ordering of the bleeding type which conceals the obvious relation between ending and consonant shape.[9]

But the same situation does not obtain in I; here there is no palatalization in any form. The phonetic shape of the stem final consonant does not change between underlying representation and surface manifestation. Therefore we can find velars in all positions, or palatals in all positions, but certainly no alternations. Consider *mancare* 'to (be) miss(ing)' and *mangiare* 'to eat':

(17) (a) indicative: mango, mangi, manga, mangamo, mangate, mangano
                       manko, manki, manka, mankyamo, mankate, mankano
     (b) subjunctive: mangi, mangi, mangi, mangamo, mangate, mangino
                       manki, manki, manki, mankyamo, mankyate, mankino

One solution would be that thV is present in all forms and that elision follows palatalization. Therefore:

(18)   / mank + a + o /   / mank + a + i /
     palatalization   -----   -----
     elision   ∅   ∅
     other rules   [maŋko]   [maŋki][10]

Two problems arise. The order of elision and palatalization is exactly the reverse of what it would have to be in a comparative solution for IIb. However, the point is that in both cases the ordering is determined as a bleeding relation (due to the particular structure of the strings operated upon); in this case the theory of local ordering (Anderson 1969) is sufficient to explain the data provided that it can be stated in the grammar that elision has to be in a marked order with respect to palatalization given a string to which both rules can apply.

Even if this sounds convincing, it cannot solve at the same time the other problem connected with the *ya* morpheme. It replaces in all conjugations the thematic vowel in 1 pl indic. and 1, 2 pl subj. of the present.

Therefore it should be transformationally inserted. This has to happen
after palatalization has already failed on the form due to the [+back] thV
in I. But for the forms of IIb another ordering inconsistency appears.
Here *ya* induces palatalization in indicative and subjunctive. In the
indicative the previously present thV is [-back] so that no ordering argument can be based on it. Palatalization can take place anyway. But
in the subjunctive the original thV (or subjunctive morpheme) is *a*. In
order for the stem final consonant to be able to palatalize the insertion
has to precede palatalization. But this required ordering between insertion
and palatalization is feeding whereas it had to be bleeding for class I;
this cannot be accounted for even in the framework of local ordering.
There is an open inconsistency to be recognized.

   If the data are expanded to include III it will finally become clear
that ordering is an inadequate device for explaining the varying shapes of
stem final consonants in verbal paradigms. As was the case with class III
of the nouns (*voče* - *voči*) the front vowel can again be expected to have
an influence on the consonant. But neither of the two logical possibilities
(palatals throughout or velar/palatal alternation as in IIb) is the correct
guess. Palatalization is inapplicable to III in any form. In opposition
to the situation in class I the thV cannot take over the function of
stem protection due to its [-back] specification. Consider (19):

(19) arri[*kk*]ire   : arri[kk]isco, arri[kk]ite, arri[kk]iva etc.
                            'to make rich' from ri[kk]o- ri[kk]i 'rich'
      imbian[*k*]ire 'to make white' from bian[k]o- bian[k]i 'white'
      inva[*g*]ire   'to induce'
      addomesti[*k*]ire 'to train to live in a house' from domest + i[k]o-
                            domest +i[č]i 'domestic'
      inselvati[*k*]ire 'to run wild' from selvat + i[k]o- selvat + i[č]i
                            'wild'
      intisi[*k*]ire   'to get tuberculosis' from tis + i[k]o - tis + i[č]i
                            'having tuberculosis'

   It is significant that not even verbs with /*selvatik*/, /*tisik*/, /*domestik*/
as stem can undergo palatalization. The nominal plural forms of the
corresponding adjectives characteristically undergo the variation as does
any other nominal form in /*+iko*/. Consequently it cannot be the stem which
determines the applicability of palatalization here.

   The only solution for III is dictated by the absence of any ordering
hypothesis. The palatalization rule is not applicable to III. The blocking
of this rule has to be **part** of the content conveyed by the conjugation class
marking *III*. This means that we are to reinterpret a naive feature like
[+III] as (in one aspect) a rule feature [αrule R] such that by convention
the blocking is only effective with respect to the stem final consonant.
Notice that in *imbianchisce:* / in + byank + isk + e / only the first /k/
is exempt from palatalization.

   Since a reinterpretation of conjugation class features is needed in any
case to account for III, the question of how to treat class I in this respect

is open again. In other words, is there any evidence that the thV appears in underlying representation (or even by morphological insertion) in all forms other than the rather shaky rule order argument for the sake of the non-palatalizing character of I? In II and III the thV does not help to explain the palatal distribution. In these two classes then the thV is more of a burden than beneficial.

There is a big number of forms which exhibit the thV clearly: all the forms of imperfect indicative and subjunctive, future and conditional and some forms of the *passato remoto*. In all these cases there is a regular distribution of thV *a*, *e* or *i* according to the lexical marking of the conjugation class. In addition the 2 pl present indicative presents the same distribution. Interestingly enough, all of the endings following an overt thematic vowel are consonant initial. In addition, in one other form, the infinitive, the thV may be absent in surface form for some verbs; in 1 pl pres. indic. and 1, 2 pl pres. subj. the thematic differences between the conjugation classes are neutralized by the thV substitute *ya*. In the present framework of phonology the special morpheme *ya* is best introduced by an insertion rule given its invariability. As long as we decide that the most reasonable solution is to have the thV present in all forms we can claim it to be part of the underlying string for each verbal derivation. But notice that the morpheme *ya* points to another solution: insertion guided by lexical feature information. In order for this process to find at least some motivation (there is no apparent justification neither for its appearance nor for its particular phonological shape)[12] it would be preferable to have the thV inserted by rule rather than to assume it to be an integral part of the underlying representation.[13] In this way the morpheme *ya* is just exceptional in its phonological manifestation but not with respect to the position where it appears in the verbal forms. But as soon as the thV is not a part of the underlying representation and acts as a correction of the syllable structure (surfacing just in case the stem final consonant is directly followed by a consonant initial ending) there is no longer a justification for inserting it everywhere. This would require deleting it again in all cases where it does not have this corrective function. In terms of overall simplicity and meaningfulness of the grammar, it seems to me that the insertion solution is preferable.[14]

Remember now that up to this point nothing has been said about the difference in the thV between the classes IIa and IIb: the former is traditionally characterized by a long, the latter by a short vowel. This distribution is based on the infinitives.

(20) IIa temḗre 'to fear'   vs. IIb redímĕre 'to redeem'
         tacḗre 'to keep quiet'   nuócĕre 'to harm'

However, there is no motivation to distinguish between the two subclasses as soon as other forms which exhibit an overt thV are considered. In all of them the thV is long if stressed (exceptionally short in both classes in the imperfect subjunctive) and short if unstressed; but they are always parallel. It appears then that the exceptional form of the thV is in the infinitive of IIb. This can be handled by another ad hoc provision in the thV insertion rule that for some verbs of the comprehensive class II (thV *e*) a short vowel is required for the infinitive; otherwise the inserted vowel is unmarked, tense and long (cf. footnote (17) below). Looking at the question from the other side, if a basic length distinction is assumed, it is necessary to adjust the very length feature in all cases where the thV appears except for the infinitive. The collapsing of IIa and IIb is inevitable since there are no differences either where the thV appears or where it does not.[15] Consider for this point the relevant data in (21).

(21)	overt thV	teméte	rediméte	2 pl pres. ind.
		temévo	redimévo	1 sg imperf. ind.
		teméssi[16]	rediméssi	1 sg imperf. subj.
		teméro	rediméro	1 sg future
		temérei	redimérei	1 sg conditional
		temésti	redimésti	2 sg passato remoto
	no thV	témo	redímo	1 sg pres. ind.
		témi	redími	2 sg pres. ind.
		téme	redíme	3 sg pres. ind.
		temyámo	redimyámo	1 pl pres. ind. & subj.
		témono	redímono	3 pl pres. ind.
		téma	redíma	1-3 sg pres. subj.
		temyáte	redimyáte	2 pl pres. subj.
		témano	redímano	3 pl pres. subj.

To summarize up to this point, the thV is inserted just in those cases where it is phonologically functional; a conjugation class marker has as part of its content the information about the applicability of palatalization to the stem final consonant. The following classes have been established:

(22)   I: thV *a* ; palatalization is inapplicable
        II: thV *e* ; palatalization can apply
       III: thV *i* ; palatalization is inapplicable

Consequently there are two types of verbs: alternating and non-alternating ones. The presence vs. absence of alternation is not dependent on the phonological character of the thematic vowel but has to be expressed on the morphological/lexical level, so far as the traditionally 'fully regular' verbs go. But there are numerous irregular ones exhibiting various surface patterns of alternations.

Again as for the regular verbal paradigms the 'irregular' ones are centered around palatalization and related supplementary processes. The list in (23) gives the patterns in the two crucial forms (1 sg pres. ind. and 2 sg pres. ind.) on the basis of which all other forms can be extrapolated. The defining characteristic for the two forms is again, as in the regular class II, the position of the stem final consonant before a front vs. back vowel. The relevant verbs for this discussion belong mostly to class II with a small number coming from III.

(23) (a) [ŋg] spíŋgo   [lg] vǫ́llg   [rg] pǫ́rgo
           [ňǧ] spíňǧi   [lǧ] vǫ́lǧi   [rǧ] pǫ́rǧi
           II   'to push'   II   'to turn'   II   'to hand
      (b) [ŋg] spę́ŋgo   [lg] šélgo   over'
           [ňň] spę́ňňi   [ľľ] séľľi
           II   'to put out' II   'to choose'
      (c) [ŋg] tę́ŋgo   [lg] válgo
           [ň]   tyę́ňi   [l]   váli
           II, III 'to hold' II   'to be worth'
      (d)   [ľľ] sǫ́ľľo
                               [l]   swǫ́li
                               II   'to be used to'
      (e) [čč] táččo   [gg] léggo
           [č]   táči   [ǧǧ] léǧǧi
           II   'to be quiet' II,III 'to read'
      (f)   ∅   mwǫ́yo
                 [r]   mwǫ́ri
                 II, III 'to die'

The strange pair is (23f) *morire* because there are traces neither of a
velar nor of a palatal consonant; in the other patterns one or both are
present in varying shape.

Notice that there is a triple ambiguity in a stem form ending in [ŋg]
or [lg] before a back vowel. It may alternate with either of three different
forms before a front vowel. The first pair in (23a) is a straightforward
consequence of the alternating character of the regular class II verbs.
Assuming an underlying representation *sonorant + voiced velar* the application of the palatalizing process will yield the desired forms. The source
of the [g] in (23b and c) on the other hand is rather obscure. It should
be connected with some phonetic trait in which the r-patterns cannot participate, hence the characteristic absence of attested examples in the
third column. Another ambiguity exists for [l] before a front vowel ending
(23c and d, middle column) since for some verbs the back vowel alternant
is velar, for others it is palatal.

The pattern of *leggere* (23e, right column) is not surprising; it can
be understood as a direct consequence of the application of palatalization
to an originally long [g] producing a regular alternation velar - palatal.
The same pattern is not found for the voiceless [k]. Either the verb is
regular such as [víŋko] - [víňči] or it exhibits the all palatal pattern
of (23e) with a distinctive difference between a tense stem final palatal
before a back vowel and a lax one before a front vowel. The surface forms
do not reveal a natural way to characterize this difference. What is needed
is a condition X such that it will cause the stem vowel to be laxed just in
case the ending vowel is back.[17] There is already a rule in the language
which has to lax a vowel:

(24)
Laxing   V ----> $\begin{bmatrix} \text{-tense} \\ \text{-long} \end{bmatrix}$ / - C C (heavy cluster)

Instead of - C C we need here the environment - X, but the effect of the rule is exactly the one required by the data under consideration.

A comparision of the following historical (and perhaps also synchronic) doublets can clarify the content of condition X:

(25) dŭplice   'twofold'
     duplo̯   'double'   dőppyo   'double'
     plateǎle   'of a square'   pyássa   'square'
     dubitāre   'to doubt'   dŭbbyo   'doubt'
     labiale   'labial'   lăbbro   'lip'
                                fèbbre   'fever'
                                ákkwa   'water'
               pŭbblico 'public'

The transition from Latin to Italian is, among may other changes, character-ized by a rule which lengthened a consonant immediately followed by a non-syllabic non-obstruent (in the particular case l, r, y, w). After the elimination of post-consonantal l (cf. *dŭplu* > *dőppyo*, *planu* > *pyano* etc.) and due to the fact that r and w acted only as optional environments, the historical rule became reduced to the environment before a front glide. Finally the introduction of a great number of non-native items (cf. (25), left column) which did not obey the anyway reduced rule brought about the present state of affairs where this glide-laxing rule has essentially no basis for existing other than to state a few typical gaps in the phonological structure of the Italian native vocabulary.[18]

However weak the evidence for this glide-laxing rule in present day Italian (it would rather be envisaged as a minor, unproductive rule) it is exactly the rule which is conditioned by X:

(26) glide-laxing[19] $V \longrightarrow \begin{bmatrix} -\text{tense} \\ -\text{long} \end{bmatrix} / - C\ y$

There is one other phenomenon of Italian phonology which requires this rule and can therefore give it some additional motivation. All segments [ĺ], [ñ] and [ś] (voiceless dental affricate) are long except in absolute initial position. [ĺ] and [ñ] cannot occur in any cluster whereas [ś] can be found as a second member in a cluster (where it will be short due to general conditions on length in Italian). While the alternations in (27a) are simply due to different tenseness value in the governing vowels, the pattern in (27b) shows the operation of an additional rule, amalgamation (affrication for the dental), which has to apply obligatorily as soon as the governing vowel is lax (i.e. the consonant is tense).

(27) (a) kőpya   'copy'   kőppya   'couple'
          dŭbito   'I doubt'   dŭbbyo   'doubt'
          sóčo   'member   ríččo   'curl'
     (b) médyo   'middle'   mézžo   'half'
          *méddyo   *mézo

```
*-ítya                  pu̧dičíśśya  'chastity'
*-íṭtya                 *-íśya
zmánya      'frenzy'    són̆n̆o       'dream'
*zmánnya                *són̆o
fǫ́lyo      'folio'     fǫ́ľľa       'leaf'
*fǫ́llyo                 *fǫ́la
```

(28) amalgamation l, n ---- ľ, n̆ / $\begin{bmatrix} V \\ -\text{tense} \end{bmatrix}$ -- y

The rule (28) correctly expresses the fact that the palatal laterals and
nasals only occur long and exclusively in intervocalic position; the mentioning of [-tense] in the environment makes it necessary for rule (26) to
have applied to the string beforehand (or else the vowel has to be lax
already in underlying representation). The crucial point then is that
neither a non-palatalized long consonant nor a short palatalized one can
occur. In other words, instead of attaching an ad hoc statement to [n̆n̆],
[ľľ] and [śś] to the effect that they can only occur long we can derive
them by rules (26) and (28) from underlying /ly/, /ny/ and /ty/ so that
they will only show up as long consonants. This approach makes it also
possible to express naturally that in initial position the tenseness value
of these consonants is dependent on the preceding word final segment (tense
if a vowel precedes, otherwise lax).[20]

The purpose of this lengthy digression was to identify and motivate the
condition X which is needed to explain the distinct behavior of a stem final
palatal before a back vs. a front vowel as in [taččo - tači]. The problem
now is the source of the required glide such that it will be derived only
before a back vowel but not before a front vowel; this would enable the
glide-laxing rule to apply to the back vowel but not to the front vowel
form. There is some evidence that a glide may exceptionally appear in the
desired position: cf. [mwǫ́yo] vs. [mwǫ́ri] where the dropping of the r is
dependent on an immediately following glide. Similarly the pattern [sǫ́ľľo]
vs. [swǫ́li] needs a glide before the back vowel for the derivation of [ľľ].
The only possible source is the exceptional presence in underlying structure
of a thV which becomes a front glide before a back vowel but which will be
elided before a front vowel ending. For deriving the forms of (23e) and
(23f) the following rules are needed:

(29)
thV shortening $\begin{bmatrix} V \\ -\text{low} \end{bmatrix}$ ---> $\begin{bmatrix} -\text{long} \\ +\text{high} \end{bmatrix}$ / - + $\begin{bmatrix} V \\ +\text{back} \end{bmatrix}$

The independently motivated rule (30), glide formation, will then turn [ɪ̆]
to [y].

(30)
glide formation $\begin{bmatrix} V \\ +\text{high} \\ -\text{long} \end{bmatrix}$ ---> [-syll] / - V

(31) r-drop   r ----> ∅ / - y

(32)
      y-drop   y ----> ∅ / ⎡ C   ⎤
                              ⎢ +high ⎥
                              ⎣ -back ⎦

Consider now the derivations which they enable us to carry out:

(33)   / m ǭ r + ī + ō /   / m ǭ r + ī + ī /
        thV shortening   ĭ   ---
        glide formation   y   ---
        elision   ---   ∅
        r-drop   ∅́   ---́
        other rules   [mwǫ́yo]   [mwǫ́ri]

(34)   / s ǭ l + ē + ō /   / s ǭ l + ē + ī /
        thV shortening   ĭ   ---
        glide formation   y   ---
        elision   ǫ̆ ----   ∅
        glide-laxing   ǫ̆   ---
        amalgamation   ĭ   ---
        y-drop   ∅   ---
        other rules   [sǫ́ĭlo]   [swǫ́li]

(35)   / t āk + ē + ō /[21] / t āk + ē + ī /
        thV shortening   ĭ   ---
        glide formation   y   ---
        elision   ---   ∅
        glide-laxing   Ă̆   ---
        palatalization   č̆   č̆
        y-drop   ∅   ---
        other rules   [táččo]   [táči]

For what concerns the ordering of the rules in the derivation it has to
be stated that thV shortening and elision, r-dropping and glide-laxing are
characterized for a bleeding relationship. The other rules can apply in
normal unmarked order if any order is specifiable at all.
    What is still missing is a set of rules which would be capable of deri-
ving the alternations in (23b) and (23c). The front vowel stem form of
(23b) will be derived in the same way as the back vowel stem form of (24d)
from /ly/. What is needed in addition is a rule producing a [g] out of
the thematic vowel. Although this sounds like another piece of abstract
virtuosity, notice however that this rule (36) is to a certain degree the
inverse of the palatalization process. Instead of leaving an underlying
velar untouched before a back vowel as is the case for palatalization, the
velarization rule creates a velar before a back vowel from a non-velar.

(36)

$$\text{velarization} \quad \begin{bmatrix} -\text{syll} \\ -\text{obstr} \\ -\text{back} \end{bmatrix} \quad \text{---> } \quad \begin{bmatrix} +\text{obstr} \\ +\text{back} \end{bmatrix} \quad / -+ \begin{bmatrix} V \\ +\text{back} \end{bmatrix}$$

Again this rule is in a bleeding relationship to amalgamation as were the two other ad hoc rules thV shortening and r-dropping. At least it makes it possible to derive the remaining patterns of (23).

(37)
	/ v ā l + ḛ + ō /	/ v ā l + ḛ + ī /
thV shortening	ĭ	---
glide formation	y	---
elision	---	Ø
glide-laxing	Ă	---
velarization	g	---
other rules	[válgo]	[váli]

The derivation of [rimáŋgo] vs. [rimáni] runs paralles to (37). The difference in the derivation of the forms of *solere* to the one of *valere* is that in the latter velarization is applicable but not in the former; interestingly enough, the type *valere* with one additional ad hoc process in the derivation is by far the more common one. In the subclass of *solere* there are exactly two verbs, *solere* 'to be used to' and *volere* 'to want'.

The last pattern to be discussed here, (23b), requires in all forms either amalgamation (before a front vowel ending) or velarization (before a back vowel). If the glide /y/ is assumed as a constant part of the stem the correct derivation does not even have to contain a thV in all forms.

(38)
	/ s k ḛ l y + ō /	/ s k ḛ l y + ī /
glide-laxing	Ḛ	Ḛ
velarization	g	-ǐ-
amalgamation	---	ī
y-drop	---	Ø
other rules	[sélgo]	[sélli]

The derivations of / spḛny + ō / and / spḛny + ī / is completely parallel to the one shown in (38).

The net result of the preceding discussion is that all the patterns listed in (23) can be derived phonologically without having recourse to highly unnatural rules. But the price is the acceptance of three essentially unmotivated rules: *thV shortening, glide-laxing* and *velarization*. There is no real outside motivation for these rules. Two of them are category specific (thV shortening and velarization); they serve no other purpose than to describe the variations found in the mentioned verb paradigms. But on the other hand any analysis will have to accomodate these special forms in one way or another, and it seems to be that any analysis will be forced to recognize a number of ad hoc processes. Therefore, justification for an analysis dealing with the described phenomena can only be given in terms of what the complex of statements and processes expresses about the language and its conjugation system, i.e. on the basis of the functionality of the solution.

Let me summarize the foregoing considerations by making a proposal for a more accurate classification of Italian verbs. The concept of conjugation class is vital for predicting the correct verbal forms. The information to be contained in a conjugation class marker [αconj. X] is of several types. First it has to state which rules with the potential of alternating the stem final consonant are applicable and in which order. Secondly, the type of thematic vowel insertion has to be specified, i.e. if the thV occurs just before a consonant initial ending or throughout the conjugation. Minor information for the thV would include specification of the conditions under which ya has to be inserted, eventual irregularities in the phonetic shape of the thV etc. Thirdly, the thematic vowel would have to be determined in its phonological content: low, high, or mid. Any other irregularities of the surface paradigms will have to be stated either in terms of the verb stem if it is a lexical idiosyncrasy or on the particular tense/mood morpheme (e.g. the laxing of the thV in imperfect subjunctive).

On these bases it is possible to replace the traditional conjugation class markers by three more informative features: [+/-Alternation], [+/-Insertion] and [+/-Height]. The first of them expresses the dichotomy of alternating vs. non-alternating paradigms. Its interpretation has to be the bundle of the rule applicability features for the relevant processses: velarization, r-dropping, palatalization; thV shortening, coalescence, elision; glide-laxing; and any other rules of importance to the derivations which have not been considered here.

For the regular, productive, non-alternating verbs the feature has to be specified as [-Alt]. This shall mean:

$$(39) \quad [-\text{Alt}] = \begin{bmatrix} -\text{velar} \\ -\text{r-drop} \\ -\text{palat} \end{bmatrix} + \begin{bmatrix} -\text{thV short} \\ -\text{coalesc} \\ +\text{elision} \end{bmatrix} + [-\text{glide lax}]$$

Ordering specifications: elision precedes stress assignment
unless otherwise stated (cf. (42) below)

In addition, [-Alt] will imply invariably that the thV appears only where it has a phonological function and that the thV is either a or i ([+low] or [+high]), i.e. [-Alt] implies the condition thV: [αhigh, -αlow].

On the other hand, [+Alt] has to characterize the alternative verbs and will therefore receive the following interpretation:

$$(40) \quad [+\text{Alt}] = \begin{bmatrix} +\text{velar} \\ +\text{r-drop} \\ +\text{palat} \end{bmatrix} + \begin{bmatrix} +\text{short} \\ +\text{elision} \\ -\text{coalescence} \end{bmatrix} + [+\text{glide lax}]$$

Ordering specifications: velarization precedes palatalization
and amalgamation

r-dropping precedes glide laxing
thV shortening precedes elision
Other orderings are given by universal
conditions on rule applicability.

There is no particular implication as to whether an alternating verb only
shows critically conditioned thV insertion or constant thV.[22] On the
other hand, it is predictalbe that the thV will have the phonological
content [αhigh, -low].

The interpretation of the insertion feature is straightforward: [-Ins]
means that the thV is inserted only where it has a phonological function,
i.e. before a consonant initial ending as in the non-alternating verbs
regularly. [+Ins] equals thV insertion in all verb forms regardless of
their structure.

The height feature narrows down the possible phonological content of
the thV given in the thV conditions of the (non-)alternating verbs to one
specific thV: [+H] stands for [+high], [-H] for [-high].

This framework allows us to describe all the discussed verb stem alternation patterns in the following way:

(41) [-Alt, -Ins, +/-H]: traditionally I ([-H]) and III ([+H])
                            e.g. *parlare, finire*
      [+Alt, -Ins, +/-H]: traditionally the regular verbs of II ([-H])
                            and the simple palatalizing ones on III ([+H])
                            e.g. *temére, redímere, víncere; fúggire*
      [+Alt, +Ins, +/-H]: traditionally the irregular verbs of II and
                            III; e.g. *valére, tenére, venire, morire*

The description of *solere* will require one additional marking: [-velariza-
tion] to prevent the incorrect derivation of [*sǫlgo] instead of [sǫ́llo].
Given the minimal number of verbs corresponding to this pattern (only two),
it seems to be correct to require it to carry for its characterization a
bigger number of features than the more widespread pattern of *valere* etc.[23]

Notice that no independent or even universally valid status is claimed
for the complex new conjugation class markers; their purpose is only to
allow us to factor out the content which is predictable for the particular
case of Italian verb classes. The grammar of Italian will still have to
state what these ad hoc features mean; thus the relative simplicity of the
complex markers [αAlt, βIns, ɣH] is only specious.

From the above list it appears that the thematic vowel which usually is
taken as defining the different conjugation classes does not have a decisive
function. There is no natural classification of vowels in phonological
theory which would (nor should) permit the grouping of *a* and *i* as fundamentally different for palatalizing purposes from *e* such that the former
would block the rule whereas the mid vowel would induce it. The rule
applicability conditions are much more crucial for this purpose.

The thV acquires importance only for characterizing irregular verbs.
It is no accident that the reported irregularities only occur with verbs

exhibiting a front thV. Since all the variations can be arranged around palatalization and glide formation, it is to be expected that the crucial phonetic element supporting these alternations is inherently capable of undergoing or inducing the relevant processes. Therefore we cannot find such alternations with traditional class I verbs (thV a). But notice at the same time that beyond the specification of [-back] the exact phonetic content of the thV does not matter. Verbs or the traditional categories II and III ($\bar{e}$ vs. $\check{e}$) can be seen to be of no importance whatever either for regular or much less for irregular verbs; the opposition has to be neutralized under any analysis.

The presence vs. absence of the thV in irregular of alternating verbs does not make any difference for the fact that rule applicability conditions have to be stated for the various classes. Not even the presence of the thV in all forms of irregular verbs is sufficient, together with the knowledge that palatalization may apply, to predict the surface forms of the verbs. There are other rules which bring about additional variations. This all points strongly to the necessity for introducing another parameter than the ones at hand for controlling the derivation of paradigms. It has to allow for a principled treatment of the variations in rule applicability and the other observed phenomena.

III. IMPLICATIONS

The failure of conventional phonological theory[24] to give an adequate and interesting solution to the Italian problem is significant. There is no orderly way to predict the surface forms given knowledge of underlying representations and phonological processes in the language. Consider what may happen to the sequence $\bar{a} + \bar{\imath}$ # :

(42)　(a)　/ $\bar{a} + \bar{\imath}$ / : [e] ; e.g.　/ art + ist + $\bar{a} + \bar{\imath}$ / : noun, f. pl.
　　　　　 coalescence　　　　　　'artists'
　　　(b)　/ $\bar{a} + \bar{\imath}$ / : [i] ; e.g.　/ art + ist + $\bar{a} + \bar{\imath}$ / : noun, m. pl.
　　　　　 elision　　　　　　　　'artists'
　　　(c)　/ $\bar{a} + \bar{\imath}$ / : [ái]; e.g.　/ port + $\bar{a} + \bar{\imath}$ / : verb, 1 sg. passato
　　　　　 stress precedes　　　　'I carried'　　　　　　remoto
　　　　　 elision

It is crucial, not only for verbs, to have information about the specific morphological categories a given underlying representation belongs to. Only on this basis is it possible to choose the correct set of rules which will yield the surface forms.

For a conventional phonology this is a rather marked and unnatural state of affairs which will be penalized by the evaluation metric. Notice that in the case of Italian verbs most verb classes will have non-optimal derivations in that they have to be marked for undergoing a minor rule or for not undergoing a major rule.[25] The only group which would be entirely natural is the class of alternating verbs of the type of *vincere*. But this does not match at all with the fact that new verbs created in the language invariably belong to the class of regular, non-alternating verbs. The productive verb class then is not the one which is predicted by the theory as being natural, *vincere*, but a class whose derivations are marked for failing to undergo the general rule of palatalization. The prediction of unproductiveness for verbs which undergo minor rules on the other hand can be accepted as reasonable. These verbs are historical relics of earlier stages of the grammar. No wonder, therefore, that the rules needed for deriving the correct forms are ad hoc and highly limited.

Variable applicability of rules has been proposed in the past (and has to a wide degree also been used implicity) to account for relations between learned and native lexical items of a language. Saciuk (1969a and b) identifited the distinction [+native] vs. [-native] with a constant difference in the set of rules which may apply to a given underlying form. The difference between the native/non-native split of the vocabulary, and the several splits in the total number of verbs as I have proposed it is evident. The native/non-native distinction splits the whole lexicon in two parts based on factual observation without a clear functionality for the language such that it could be defined exclusively on these bases. On the other hand, here it is only a subpart of the lexicon (or two if we include consideration of the nominal paradigms) which is divided internally. All items belong to the same morpho-syntactic category. In addition this type of division has a clearly visible functionality. Whereas for the native/non-native split we are dealing with a synchronic reinterpretation of an essentially diachronic relation, here the function is to allow paradigmatically related surface forms to be generated in such a way that their transderivational proportions are maintained. In other words, the defining level for rule applicability is the resulting surface form in relation to cognate surface forms in the same paradigm. The rules applying to a particular form are not the real cause of its surface manifestation but only the means of producing it. The governing constraint is that a verb either has alternating forms of some type or that there is no alternation in the surface manifestations of the stem final consonant. Under this functionality interpretation it is much better imaginable that such utterly ad hoc rules like *Velarization* and *ThV shortening* are actually part of the grammar. They keep their place in the derivation exactly because of their function for a given class of derivation which is to maintain the set proportions in a particular paradigm. The fact that these rules do not and cannot find any outside motivation is just an artifact of the framework. It only provides for one or two types of expression of a regularity, processes and eventually also morpheme structure conditions, on the language particular level.

Some notion of *paradigm = related derivations* has to be introduced into the current theory to enable it to express the generalizations which can be observed in natural languages. The regularity of the overt form has to be a consequence of the overall regularity of a whole set of forms. It would be unsatisfactory to state the regularity just over the domain of one particular derivation. The two forms of a verb like *mancare:*

[máŋko] and [máŋki], are equally regular although the derivation of
[máŋki] is marked (cf. Miller (to appear)) with respect to palatalization
and the one of [máŋko] is not.

The precise applicability conditions of palatalization are not the
crucial point; they are rather accidental in the whole problem. However,
this does not mean that it is insignificant that exactly palatalization
behaves erratically with respect to verbal forms. Rather it is the case
that paradigmatic restrictions take into account the processes at disposi-
tion in the language in general, in non-paradigmatic forms. It is im-
material that palatalization is blocked for non-alternating verbs because
any process capable of altering the stem final consonant is blocked. But
then the rule of palatalization is at the base for establishing the paradigmatic proportion for alternating verbs. It is a basic alternation
between velar (or at least non-palatal) forms before back vowels (where
palatalization as a natural assimilatory process cannot apply) and palatal
(or at least non-velar) forms before front vowels (where palatalization
typically does apply). This condition has so much power as to induce the
language to create and later on keep alive a process which defines a velar
counterpart to palatal surface segments such as [ll] and [ññ]. The velarization process was even able to extend its domain to verbs which originally
did not show this alternation. This is an example of the content which
the evaluation metric has to be able to favor over straightforward unrelated simplicity of a single derivation.

The expression of paradigmatic binds between derivations in form of
functional rule applicability cannot be surprising. As in the examples
of functional cooperation of several processes ('conspiracies'; cf.
Kisseberth (1969) and (1970)) so far discussed in recent literature the
observational level of assuming such a convergence in function is the
surface level, the problem usually being connected with syllable structure.
Due to the particular form of phonological theory it is then necessary to
express the 'conspiracy' in terms of derivational processes and constraints
and underlying representations. As a consequence the formalism is no longer
able to capture the generalizations which go beyond its proper non-function-
al but formal domain. It is not clear to me how exactly the higher value
of functional relations is to be expressed, but this question might be
premature anyway.

The importance of the paradigmatic dimension is not new. It is usually
hidden behind a morphological statement. Given e.g. the morpheme /ya/ as
in our discussion, it would have been possible to state peculiarities of
its paradigm even in a conventional phonology by attaching to it some
feature X such that it will block glide-laxing.[26] But here it is the
case that /ya/ occurs in an open set of cases (i.e. it will occur with
any verb including the ones that will be introduced in the language only
later on); consequently this exceptionality cuts across-the-board (across
conjugation classes) in such a general way that its statement was provided
for in any phonological theory. On the other hand, the closed-set character
of genuine paradigms could be referred to only in case the paradigmatically

confined phenomenon correlated directly with the distribution of a morpheme; if this was not the case, the statement had to be ad hoc. Given that the present phonological theory is designed correctly for capturing the generalizations and for accounting for the open-set characteristics of language, it is not surprising that the assumption of the existence of important closed-set oriented phenomena which are not expressible on the lexical level will be made only when necessity imposes them on the linguist.

One other question could be asked finally: Why is the present theory of rule ordering, local or linear or any other proposed type, unable to handle the problem of paradigmatically related forms? Should it eventually be revised to include such phenomena?

Local ordering (Anderson 1969) as a three place function between two rules and a string to which the two rules are to be applied, although it is the most powerful ordering hypothesis available, has to fail here since it is defined over a single derivation whereas the problem of the paradigm is pluriderivational. But more importantly, the difference lies in the type of rules which have to be ordered. Local ordering may have its merits in ordering two rules with respect to one form where both possible orderings will yield derivations in which both rules have participated. But in our case the typical relation between rules and a given (set of) form(s) is that out of a number of rules only one can apply. The structural description of the competing rules cannot be met any longer. Only one of the competing rules is a general one, supported by independent motivation; the others have a highly limited domain. Consider the following rules:

(43) general   (a) elision   (b) palatalization
     special   thV shortening   velarization
     special   coalescence

Due to the bleeding character of the special rules and the restrictions of their applicability to defined verbal or nominal derivations, it does not make sense to talk about ordering and reordering of these rules in a synchronic grammar. Their ordering is given intrinsically as long as the rules exist as such, it has to be bleeding. What changes from one type of derivation to the other is the application or non-application of the rule. For these reasons, no specific proposal about rule ordering can possibly accomodate the true generalizations.

Ultimately, if it will prove advisable to include the paradigmatic dimension in the general theory, this revision will have to be designed in a way that it can take care of an old problem of historical linguistics: paradigm analogy. The attempts for explaining this phenomenon in the generative framework are futile as long as the paradigm as a surface configuation is only an accident of blindly applying rules and not a well defined network of transderivational statements limiting the power of the across-the-board phonological rules. Future research will asses the value of the present tentative introduction of the paradigm.

NOTES

*Research reported in this paper was supported in part by a Summer
Faculty Fellowship of the Graduate College of the University of Illinois
at Urbana-Champaign during Summer 1970.
        I would like to thank D. Gary Miller and Mario Saltarelli for their
valuable comments on an earlier version of this paper. Any errors are
my own.
   1.   The Italian data are taken from Battaglia-Pernicone (1963) for
nouns; for verbs especially Polcari (1909) proved very useful; lexical
data beyond the scope of these two publications were collected from
Zingarelli (1966); Rohlfs (1949) was also consulted.
        The Italian forms are often quoted in semi-phonetic representation
which indicates accent and palatalization as well as consonantal and
vocalic length.
   2.   Forms with overt rounded velars constitute an additional problem
for such an analysis: *akkwa* - *akkwe* 'water'; *seguire* 'to follow' etc.
   3.   It will be assumed that there are underlying palatal consonants
as in *gancio* and derived ones as in *amici*.
   4.   Certainly, it would be a monstrosity to claim that *amico* - *amici*
is non-native, *amica* - *amiche* on the other hand native. The remarks here
are only meant to be suggestive of possible directions to look for a
solution.
   5.   Historically there was a great amount of fluctuation in the palatalizing character of many nouns; unfortunately not even there is it possible
to detect major regularities nor do the old forms prove to be of any
relevance for the modern data.
   6.   Verbs with truly suppletive paradigms, e.g. *andare* - *vado* - *va*,
potere - *posso* - *puoi* etc., will not be considered here. Similarly, no
consideration will be given to the proper subcategorizing of strong verbs
with respect to the special stem in the *passato remoto*.
   7.   It has been argued in Wanner (forthcoming) that the *-o* in all 3 pl
forms is introduced epenthetically. The argument is based on accentual
properties of these forms.
   8.   Although the *passato remoto* has a great number of simple morphological exceptions, 2 sg, 1 and 2 pl forms are always predictable (weak forms).
   9.   In the same way the stem augmented forms of IIIb can be derived:
/ + isk + o /, / + isk + i / → [iŠŠi] by regular deaffrication, etc. For
the result [ŠŠ] cf. *koccio* 'pottery fragment' - *s + kocciare* 'to break';
čingere 'to gird' - *s + čingere* = [Šíngere] 'to loosen'.
   10. Notice that for this form it is necessary to claim that the coalescence rule operative for nouns is blocked, otherwise we would get the
wrong result **mánke*. For both forms it has to be assumed that elision
precedes stress assignment unless the results will be **mankáo, mankái*.
This last form is the correct result for pass. rem. 1 sg. where stress
has to precede elision.
   11. All the verbs mentioned here belong to IIIb and are derived from
adjectives. As Mario Saltarelli pointed out to me it could be imagined

that the internal syntactic structure has something to do with the failure
of palatalization to apply, i.e. that these verbs contain an internal word
boundary before the thV or the augment. The problem is that nouns derived
from adjectives do not behave in this way: *cieco - cecità*. Here (non-)
palatalization is a property of the suffix; by the same token it could be
a property of the suffix in the verbal derivation. In other words, the
suffix which forms class III does not induce palatalization, or palatalization is not applicable in III. The proposal has some intuitive appeal
to it, but it seems to fail as long as examples like *cecità* do not find
another explanation.

12. Not even the historical motivation for this morpheme is clear.
The original forms in *-ámo, -émo, -ímo* were perfectly adequate for the
indicative especially in the light of the 2nd person pl. which has a
parallel structure; at one point in the evolution (end XIII/beginning
XIV) the change took place rather abruptly at the same time that another
1 pl form, in the *passato remoto*, changed from the natural *-ámo, -émo,
-ímo* to *-ámmo, -émmo, -ímmo*. Cf. Castellani (1952), vol. I: Introduction.

13. The many changes in conjugation class in the historical evolution
of Italian and the other Romance languages also add plausibility to such
a proposal. Otherwise it would be hard to explain why usually all the
forms in a paradigm change in the same direction.

14. If the thV is inserted, then the syncopated infinitive forms such
as *pórre* (from *pon+re*), *condúrre* (from *conduc+re*) etc. exceptionally fail
to undergo insertion; in other words they are not unexpected and unexplainable irregularities. If on the other hand the thV were an integral part
of the underlying representation, a syncopation rule of completely unrelated nature to the thV question would be needed.

15. The distinction in the infinitive is purely accidental in terms of
present day Italian. Cf. also the Spanish situation where the two types
have merged: It. *temére*, Sp. *temér* 'to fear'; It. *préndere*, Sp. *prender*
'to take'; It. *cuócere*, Sp. *cocér* 'to cook'; It. *piacére*, Sp. *placér* 'to
like'.

16. It looks like an ad hoc statement is needed for adjusting the thV
as lax; otherwise the analysis whould have to become highly abstract by
claiming that the imperfect morpheme *v* followed by the imp. subj. morpheme
s causes the thV to lax; assimilation will then yield the surface form *ss*.

17. For reasons exposed in Saltarelli (1970a), Wanner (1970 and forthcoming) the particular syllable structure conditions of Italian have to be
stated in terms of the vowels rather than the more natural consonants.
The following conditions hold. In non-surface structure a *tense, long*
vowel may be followed by a short consonant or a weak cluster, but not by
a heavy cluseer or a long consonant. If the latter case holds, rule (24)
makes the vowel lax. Thus, a consonant has to have the opposite specification for tenseness and length than the immediately preceding vowel. On
the surface, length on vowels is eliminated except when the vowel is
stressed in an open syllable. -Graphically, a lower case vowel represents
a tense (long) one, a capital a lax vowel.

18. Even more facts point to the necessary degradation of this rule. The derived glides in the diphthongs *yǫ* and *wǫ* cannot act as environment and could not do so at any stage. There is a possibility that at one time the rule had an additional restriction so that it could apply only if the vowel to be laxed was also stressed. But this has disappeared completely: cf. dóppio 'double' - doppiétta 'double barreled gun' - raddoppiáre 'to double' etc. Finally, *r* had the detrimental characteristic of being elided exactly before a glide: *-ARIU > áyo, -ARI(I) > ári* Old Italian. In brief, there was a full 'conspiracy' to eliminate this rule. Cf. Rohlfs (1949), vol. I.

19. To regard this rule as a minor process has the advantage that it can be separated from the normal laxing rule (24). The two processes have completely different sets of exceptions (very many for (26), none for (24)). (24) can be ranged among the morpheme structure conditions of Italian.

20. Notice that even with this approach it is necessary to rely on lexical information for determining whether the glide-laxing rule can apply or not: cf. *cōpia* vs. *cóppia*.

21. The assumption of an underlying velar consonant is not crucial; the same arguments would hold for an underlying palatal.

22. All verbs in the traditional class II are classified as alternating regardless of the fact whether they alternate overtly or not; if they do not, it is not because they fail to undergo a rule which could make them alternating, but because there is no such rule in the language for their particular stem final consonant; cf. *redímere*. Even though they could be superficially non-alternating, no new verbs are created with thV *e* so that the proposed distinction has to be made in order to distinguish them from the truly non-alternating, productive class.

23. The nominal paradigms discussed to a certain extent in part I can be accounted for in a similar way. Since they do not lend themselves to clear generalizations due to the low number of forms in each paradigm we will not take them up again in the remainder of the paper.

24. For comprehensive expositions of a 'conventional' phonological theory, cf. Chomsky and Halle (1968), Postal (1968).

25. The notion of marked derivations is taken from Miller (to appear). A derivation is marked by (a) exceptionally not undergoing a categorial rule (e.g. *volere* and velarization); (b) undergoing a minor rule with cate-gorial information (e.g. probably the spread of /ya/); (c) by admitting more than one set of rules of competing optimality (no example here); (d) by undergoing a subcategorial rule. I.e. a marked derivation is different from what is expected on universal and language particular grounds.

26. This situation actually holds for /ya/: In 1 pl pres. ind. and 1, 2 pl pres. subj. the glide-laxing rule does not operate even in verbs which normally allow its application: [véŋgo - venyámo], not [*veŋgámo]. Only a few of these verbs allow sporadically the expected stem form: [pyáččo - pyáči - pyaččámo]. The paradigmatic constraint is broken by the exception-ality of the morpheme /ya/.

MARIO SALTARELLI
UNIVERSITY OF ILLINOIS

ITALIAN QUA NEO-LATIN

The purpose of this paper is twofold. I shall discuss (a) the phonology of modern standard Italian in a Neo-Latin perspective, and (b) some
theoretical considerations concerning the nature of phonological rules.
I shall be dealing fundamentally with a selected subset of phenomena
and the analytical problems which they raise. As these phenomena are to
a certain degree common to other Neo-Latin varieties I shall extend the
discussion to the larger Romance framework in as much as it may be relevant to the understanding of the particular phenomenon in question and in
the measure of my acquaintance with the subject matter.
It is my belief that a comprehensive view of Neo-Latin speech processes is not only an academically desirable endeavor but a crucial vantage point for a deeper understanding of any one present-day speech variety and a *sine qua non* for accuracy in inferred grammatical generalizations. In other words phenomena in the nature of Stress, Diphthongization, Palatalization, Tensing and Laxing, Vowel Shift and Reduction,
Assimilation, Apocope and Epenthesis, and the like are widespread and to
a certain degree similar in Romance. A widely different treatment and
characterization of the same phenomenon in so closely related languages
must be met with suspicion and can be accorded no more than provisional
grammatical status.
The search for settling differences may be a futile effort when rival
proposals adhere to diametrically opposed linguistic philosophies. I
shall therefore limit my discussion to recently proposed analyses which
assume approximately the same concept of language and phonological description.
In strict connection with the formulation of grammatical principles
for Italian phonology some theoretical and empirical questions will be
raised concerning the notion "phonological rule".
I shall discuss at some length and propose an informal evaluation
criterion for phonological rules. The present theory provides no explicit
(formal or informal) principle for ascertaining the import of alleged
grammatical rules (except for the vague terminological distinction between "major" and "minor" rule). As a consequence, argumentation on rival

hypotheses is often turned into fruitless quibbling since any formulation hatched by the linguist which seems to fit into or aid a proposal is accepted as a grammatical rule, without any principled way of assessing its viability as a bona fide grammatical statement.

In related languages like Romance, it is possible to find lexical regularities as evidence for most of the phonological phenomena which have differentiated Neo-Latin speech. One can find a body of data for formulating rules of Velar Softening, Diphthongization, Monophthongization, Vowel Shift, Syncope, Apocope, Metathesis, as well as Lenition, Spirantization, Assimilation, Vowel Reduction, Epenthesis, etc. Lexical regularities seem to constitute, at least from a methodological point of view, a motivation for the formulation of rules. It can be said then that a grammatical rule characterizes a lexical regularity. It is obvious, however, that the mere existence of a lexical regularity is not sufficient motivation for assigning its formulation a bona fide status as grammatical rule in any given language. No grammarian has suggested that all of the above lexical regularities should be characterized as rules in a grammar of present-day Italian.

At any one time the items in a lexicon constitute a closed domain. The characterization of a lexical regularity would therefore be restricted to a finite list irreconcilable with the commonly held concept of grammatical generalization. The formulation of a lexical regularity as a bona fide rule in a synchronic grammar must therefore be guided by some other criterion.

Grammatical rules have also been said to characterize the "productive" properties of language, in the structuralist's sense. As regards the definition of the speaker's linguistic capacity, they can be viewed as "predictive" generalizations in that they provide an explanation for rule government in novel expressive behavior. Such rules operate over a transfinite domain in which observed lexical regularities constitute only a finite subset.

Rules formulated on observed lexical regularities fall into two subsets. The subset of those formulations characterizing predictive generalizations and therefore defining an open (trans-finite) domain and those formulations defining a closed (finite) domain circumscribed to the existing lexicon.

Within a grammar concerned with the definition of a speaker's knowledge, the former type of rules are linguistically significant as they provide a principled explanation for the speaker's linguistic behavior. The latter have no obvious significance as they characterize a finite list, which is a definitely weaker, if not trivial, use of the notion of generalization.

Descriptively, predictive rules are more powerful than non-predictive ones by a clearly defined order of magnitude. The former describe a non-finite set, the latter a finite set. Note that this is an explicitly significant distinction that can be made with regards to the descriptive power of a rule. There is no similarly relevant differentiation that could be made within the subset of rules defining finite domains. No criterion is known (nor is forthcoming) for deciding how long a list of lexical items must be before it can be considered sufficient domain for grammatical rules. Consequently, all historical processes reflected in the established lexicon of a language at any one time would be equally motivated (or not motivated) for membership in a mentalistic phonology of that language. In particular, Diphthongization relating a rather long list of items like *cuore/coraggio/cuoricino* and *piede/pedone/piedino* is no more motivated, in an explicit sense, than, say, Syncope relating a much shorter list of items like *fredda/frigida* in a synchronic grammar of present-day standard Italian. As a matter of fact, I am inclined to believe that in accord with the present theory and knowledge, character- izations of finite lexical regularities are of no relevance to the mind works, and cannot be incorporated but provisionally in a synchronic grammar.

Finally, it will be argued that predictive formulations of a parti- cular phenomenon are higher-valued than non-predictive formulations. For the correct operation of the latter, a condition on rule application must be lexically defined in the form of a rule feature or another equivalent underlying distinction.

It seems to me that phonological treatises which have appeared in recent years, although adhering to a mentalistic philosophy of linguis- tics, have concentrated on lexical regularities but with less than overt mitigation in terms of a concern for the predictive value of phonological rules.

In the ensuing part of this paper we consider some empirical and ana- lytical problems arising in the formulation of rules for the characteriz- ation of lexical regularities in Italian, in the light of the above dimension of evaluation. It is surmised that such criterion will offer an explicit basis for ascertaining the relative value of grammatical formulations and an explicit scale in argumentation between rival propo- sals.

Owing to the nature of linguistic change, some historically general Romance phenomena reflected in present-day lexical regularities of Neo- Latin speech may be found to be fully or in part predictive in one lang- uage but not in another. This appears to be the case with respect to Velar Softening (Palatalization) in modern standard Italian and Spanish (Saltarelli forthcoming).

The phonological phenomenon which has received the most attention since the very beginning in generative analyses has been undoubtedly Stress. The claim that this feature need not be specified as an underlying dis- tinction, at least in Indo-European languages, has led to several propo- sals for Stress Assignment Rules, among them Foley (1965b), Harris (1969b), Cressey (1970a) and Saltarelli (1970b) for Spanish, Saltarelli (1966, 1970a), Wanner (forthcoming) for Italian, and of course Chomsky and Halle (1968) for English. The basic principle which underlies all of the above proposals are the conditions for stress assignment characterized in the Classical Latin Stress Rule: the length (or tenseness) of the vowel, and its position (in open or closed syllable). Aside from this fundamental similarity they differ widely.

The global generality which such rules contribute to the grammar of the language in question has been however often overstated. They do not "predict" stress, in the structualist's sense of the term. They "reduce" it to another classificatory feature, which hopefully allows the greater generalizations in the phonology as a whole: a much more modest achievement.

I shall first consider a new form of my original Primary Stress Rule (Saltarelli 1966, 1970a:81).

As a first approximation, the following subset of nouns and adjectives:

(1) Ia   IIa

     comodo   momento

     utile   foresta

     diacono   superbo

identify a proparoxyton stress type (Ia) and a paroxyton type (IIa). The stress alternation is predicted by the following principle:

(2) (i) if the penultimate vowel is in an open syllable,
           stress the antepenultimate

     (ii) otherwise stress the penultimate vowel

which can be abbreviated as follows:

(3) $V \rightarrow$ [+ stress] / ____ C_0 ($V C_0^1$) $V C_0 \#$

Rule (3) assigns stress to Ia items on its first pass (the longer environment), to IIa on its second pass (the shorter evironment). The governing generalization is the "weak cluster" condition.

As we consider additional data (4)

(4) IIb

     fucile

     amore

     remoto

we see that there are three-syllable items where the penult meets the weak cluster condition but receives primary stress in contrast to Ia in (1). Pursing the hunch that stress in Italian is normally attracted to the "strong" penultimate syllable, the phonetically supported hypothesis is proposed that the vowel in the penultimate syllable in IIb (4) is classificatorily [+length] as opposed to its counterpart in Ia (1) which is [-length]. The principle (2) must then be implemented as follows:

(5)　(i) if the penultimate vowel is in an open syllable and it is short, stress the antepenultimate

　　(ii) otherwise stress the penultimate vowel

whose corresponding formulation is

(6)　$V \rightarrow$ [+ stress]　/ ____ C_0 ($\breve{V} C_0^1$) $V C_0$ #

The governing generalization in (6) is still the weak syllable condition, as in (3), except that the properties of its condition involve the nature of the vowel as well as its position.

The principle of stress assignment defined by rules (6) for the Italian data presented so far is exactly the same as the stress assigning principle defined for Classical Latin. This is not surprising since items of the type Ia, IIa and IIb which largely characterized Latin:

(7)　Ia　　　　　IIa　　　　　IIb

　　inferum　　　honestum　　　Athēnīs

　　oppidum　　　ōrnāmentum　　mātūrē

　　fragilis　　　secundus　　　comētēs

have retained essentially the same syllable structure.

Before proceeding with the analysis of additional data relevant to stress assignment in Italian, I would like to direct your attention to a structural (surface) peculiarity of both Latin and Italian, which will lead us to a further refinement of (6) and to a sharper definition of the domain of stress.

It is a fact in both languages that the desinence or ending of words never receives stress. The independence of the desinence from its base needs not be motivated at length. In Latin it signals phonetically the partly structural and partly classificatory information of Gender, Number and Case, in Italian only the first two. There seems to be no reason for representing lexical items with their phonological desinence spelled out in the underlying representation. As a matter of fact, the information of case, gender and number is structurally determined for adjectives, and cannot be entered in the lexical representation of these items. The desinence can be introduced quite economically by a small, predictive set of spelling rules (Saltarelli 1970a:63,67), in the form of an Augment.

Thus for the purpose of stress assignment, the data given in (1), (4) and (7) is more properly represented without the final syllable (VC_0 #), which allows us to simplify the relative formulation (6) as

(8) $V \rightarrow [+ \text{stress}] \quad / \quad \underline{\hspace{1cm}} C_0 (\breve{V} C_0^1) \quad \#$

The implications of the above refinement of the stress principle lead us to a deeper understanding of this phenomenon in Latin and provide us with a more organized view of the apparently unwieldy Neo-Latin surface data.

The elimination of the desinence from the domain of the Stress Assigning Rule results in the reduction of practically all items by one syllable. Accordingly, the stress types considered so far, proparoxytons and paroxytons, become respectively paroxytons and oxytons. Furthermore, former two-syllable paroxytons as in

(9)   IIc   IId

       ponte   mano

       corto   casa

       pasta   pala

are reduced to monosyllables for stress assigning and lexical purposes and cease to be a proper subset of the alternating stress types. They are assigned stress by the second, unmarked environment of (8).

But what about the oxytonic type which distinguishes Italian from Latin on inspection of the following data?

(10)   IIIa   IIIb

       cittá   obló

       civiltá   bigné

       servitú   gigoló

as it is well known, IIIa are aboriginal items

(11)   IIIa

       cìvitātem

       cìvìlitātem

       servitūdo

which in the late middle ages underwent a truncation process. It is of
some significance that these forms are (or have been) produced by a
derivational process which is productive in present-day Italian by which
-*tá*, -*tú* affixal nouns are derived from nouns and adjectives. One might
be tempted then to restore the syllabic structure of these items to its
pre-truncation form and introduce the following rule into the grammar:

(12) delete that portion of the item which follows the
      stressed vowel in words which have the suffix
      -*tade*, -*tudo* (Saltarelli 1970a:86)

In support of (12) one can even find lexical regularities showing relics
of the pre-truncation situation like *città/cittadino*. The size of the
lexical subset which (12) would characterize is extremely limited, such
principle would therefore have no predictive value. Yet incorporating
such a rule in a synchronic grammar of Italian would generalize the stress
rule for all native items. Could then we claim that (12) is independently
motivated? I think not.

In the light of the just proposed no-desinence hypothesis of stress
assignment (8), items (11) are naturally accomodated without additional
machinery. In fact they fall into the domain of the rule which assigns
stress to types IIa and IIb (the second rule of the schema (8)). Naturally this set must be represented as it is in the lexicon, that is with its
final vowel. But this is not surprising since that vowel is not a desinence. They are in fact invariable as to gender and number. The invariable nature of a subset of the Italian lexicon is a fact which needs to be
accounted for somewhere in a grammar of Italian. Within the proposed
hypothesis it does not disturb in any way the Latin principle of stress
assignment, contrary to the commonly held view. It is incorporated in
the grammar as a lexical condition on desinence spelling, which seems
to me a more realistic account.

But since "there are exceptions to every rule" we must find some.
They are:

(13) Ic

      Lepanto

      Ofanto

      Otranto

place names of Greek origin with proparoxyton stress in spite of the fact
that its penultimate fails the weak cluster condition. Rules (8) would
in fact assign stress to the penultimate vowel. There is some informal
behavioral evidence to convince me that these are true exceptions to the
general stress principle which a speaker of Italian seems to internalize.
When items (13) are first learned through the print they are read with
penultimate stress.

Recently Dieter Wanner (forthcoming) has proposed a stress principle
for Italian which is quite different in nature from the one I have just
presented.

An earlier form of the no-desinence stress hypothesis has been presented informally for modern Spanish (Saltarelli 1970b, forthcoming), and
contested in Harris 1970a. The principle is stated on a condition of
"strong" syllable, rather than "weak" syllable as the above Italian Stress
Rule. The two forms, intuitively equivalent (as they retain the same
conditions as Latin), do not find an obvious equivalently-valued notational representation. Accordingly, the following underlying representation would be assigned to the three surface stress types.

(14)

I.		II.		III.	
marajá	/maraxā/	*árbol*	/ārbol/	*cómodo*	/kōmod/
pié	/ pe /	*útil*	/ūtil/	*antropólogo*	/antropōlog/
té	/ tē /	*caliente*	/kalent/	*aéreo*	/aēre/
papel	/papēl/	*momento*	/momēnt/	*atmósfera*	/atmōsfer/
		puente	/pont/		
		conde	/kōnd/		
		hacienda	/asend/		

The desinence spelling rules must incorporate, as in Italian, the "invariable" gender condition. Whereas in Italian this lexical condition characterizes the lexical traces of the historical process of truncation, in
Spanish it characterizes the similar process of apocope. To define non-
productive lexical regularities the proper mechanism appears to be that
of lexical conditions on predictive generalizations, rather than the
introduction of no longer operative historical processes among the set of
predictive rules.

The stress assigning principle could be stated simply as

(15)   stress the LONG vowel ([+length] or in closed syllable)

There is more than one type of infelicity in (15). First of all, why
not formulate it in the conventional Classical Latin form? Second, the
principle gives no indication as to which syllable stress is "naturally"
attracted in Spanish. Third, it does not appear very different from
marking stress directly. I shall attempt to present reasons which may
suggest that in Spanish the stress principle is plausibly stated in the

form (15), although I still hope that stronger evidence can be adduced in support of the weak syllable formulation.

A careful consideration of stress related phenomena supports the proposition that marking length is not equivalent to marking stress directly. Strong motivation in this connection is offered by the data of Diphthongization. That is if we choose to assign stress by the length principle, the lexical set of diphthongizing items is also perfectly defined. Short and stressed midvowels diphthongize. Thus /momēn-o, asend-a, kōnd-e, pont-e, kalent-e, papēl/ are correctly assigned primary stress either by the classificatory nature of the vowel or by its strong cluster position, and subsequently their short stressed midvowels are diphthongized. Evidence for the claim that the same classificatory feature is involved in stress assignment as well as in diphthongization is provided by proparaxytons. It seems to be a fact of Spanish that no diphthongs are ever found in items of the type III in (14), even though they may meet the condition for diphthongization (this observation is to be found also in Cressey 1970a). It must be assumed then that all of these midvowels are long. Such assumption would be independently motivated for stress assignment if the strong syllable condition characterized in (15) is assumed. Thus, such hypothesis provides an explanation for an otherwise curious fact.

Of course, the diphthongization could be defined as applying restrictedly to penultimate and ultimate syllables (ultimate in the no-desinence hypothesis), but this would be no explanation but a mere account of the facts which adds ad hoc complications to the Diphthongization rule. Besides it would be difficult to make an explanatory case for it, since one would have to justify the contradictory surface situation *puentecito* in Spanish and *uomini* in Italian.

It should be evident now that given the above hypothetical assumptions, marking length in the lexicon is not equivalent to marking stress. In fact, if stress were directly marked (or assigned in Spanish by Harris's 1969b principle) we would still need an additional lexical distinction for defining the set of diphthongizing midvowels in terms of length (or tenseness) or some other classificatory feature like [+Diphth] (cf. Harris 1969b:116).

The above seems then to offer provisional motivation for a strong syllable condition in the case of Spanish, as opposed to a weak syllable condition which I have proposed for Italian. If this turns out to be the case some explanation must be produced for the claim that the nature of the principle differs for the Italian and the Spanish speaker although an apparently similar domain is involved. What I have in mind at the moment is mere speculation.

If it is plausible to assume that the explanation for the weak syllable condition in Latin is that the marked stress type is the proparoxyton and the unmarked one is the paroxyton due to the preponderance of the latter set as opposed to the former, we can then follow this lead by considering the constitution of surface stress types in Italian and Spanish.

In Italian the situation is only slightly changed with respect to Latin. The preponderant stress type is the paroxyton. Next comes the proparoxyton. It is true that the language has acquired an oxyton type for its aboriginal vocabulary through an historical truncation process. However we have seen that truncation does not extend beyond the affixal formation in *-tá*, *-tú*. The domain of native oxytons is therefore extremely restricted. I am inclined to believe that the situation is unchanged in Italian.

In Spanish on the other hand the historical apocope process has brought about a massive shift from proparozytons to paroxytons on a smaller scale as in Sp. *árbol* It. *albero,* and from paroxytons to oxytons on a much larger scale as in Sp. *amor* It. *amore.* The effect of apocope, which concerned a large subset of the gender-unmarked class of nouns and adjectives, may have leveled any stress type preponderance: thus the absence of a characterization of markedness difference in the strong syllable formulation (15) in the case of Spanish.

If we accept the strong syllable principle for stress assignment in Spanish, the Diphthong lexical regularity is defined by the same classificatory feature, as we mentioned earlier. The diphthong rule could then be simply stated as follow:

(16) stressed, short midvowels are diphthongized

The operation of (16) is based on the classificatory feature length. The marking of each diphthongizing vowel coincides exactly in value with the strong syllable stress marking in proparoxytons like *cómodo* and in open syllable paroxytons like *barbero.* The marking of the vowel in blocked syllable paroxytons like *hacienda* (/asend-a/) as opposed to *momento* (/momēnt-o/), *puente* (/pont-e/) as opposed to *conde* (/kōnd-e/) and *pié* (/pe/) as opposed to *té* (/tē/) is of course methodologically impossible to ascertain since they are assigned stress by the strong cluster condition or by the convention which defines the unmarked set of monosyllables. In this relatively marginal sense, then, length marking is ad hoc as regards diphthongization in that it is a special specification, although not in the more arbitrary sense of diacritic features.

The characterization of the diphthong regularity observed in the established lexicon of Italian is markedly different. First of all the principle (16) must be restricted to open syllables:

(17) piede   festa

     buono   ponte

     maniera   recente

Furthermore, since Italian diphthongizes in open syllable paroxytons like *maniera, cavaliere, barriera* where Spanish does not and for stress assignment purposes that vowel must be long in accordance with the strong

as well as weak syllable hypothesis, this phenomenon cannot be characterized by the use of the classificatory feature length as in Spanish.
Even if Italian did not diphthongize in open syllable paroxytons (in
accord with Spanish), and we would switch to the strong syllable stress
principle our analysis would not be any better off. In fact, proparoxy-
tonic vowels would have to be marked long which, we have seen, is fine
for Spanish where they do not diphthongize, but not for Italian where
they do in some cases like *uomini*.

A characterization of the diphthong regularity observed in the established lexicon of modern standard Italian would be of a form equivalent
to the following:

(18) stressed, L_{Diphth} midvowels in open syllable are
      diphthongized

The lexical complications which Italian Diphthongization (18) requires
are entirely ad hoc (just for the purpose of the rule) and arbitrary
(no obvious phonetic/physiological criterion). This is not quite so in
the case of Spanish Diphthongization (16) where the lexical complication
is only in part ad hoc and not at all arbitrary. In view of the above
the lexical definition of Diphthongization is higher-valued for Spanish
than it is for Italian. The same can be said for the provisional characterization of the phenomenon. In both languages however the rules operate on a closed (finite) domain. Their predictive value is therefore
unassessed. Consequently their status and relevance as bona fide grammatical rules in a synchronic definition of the languages in question
remains undetermined.

The next phenomenon which I would like to discuss is length. We have
already seen its relation with respect to stress assignment and diphthongization. I shall now concentrate on the analysis of a particular phonetic
function obtaining between a stress vowel and the following consonant(s)
termed by Porena (1908) "metric syllable" and widely investigated since
the earliest studies of Italian pronunciation in the works of Bembo
(1549), Panconcelli-Calzia (1911), Josselyn (1901), Parmenter and Carman
(1932) among others (cf. Saltarelli 1970a:11).

The facts relevant to this discussion of length in Neo-Latin speech,
as far as known, can be summarized as follows:

(19)

```
early Latin
|                V̄ C̄          nūllus, vīlla
|  late Latin
|  |             V̆ C̆          fidem, gulam, focum
|  |  Italian
|  |  |          V̆ C̄          pullam, fissum, buccam
|  |  |  Spanish
|  |  |  |       V̄ C̆          mūrum, cārum, vīnum, vōcem
```

The above synopsis is restricted to geminate consonants. The type $\bar{V}\,\bar{C}$ in Latin included also non-geminate consonant clusters as in *frūctus*, which appears to have resisted longer than the geminate type. In Neo-Latin it coalesced with the $\bar{V}\,C$ type in Spanish and Italian. In the latter language there was consonantal assimilation of certain long cluster types like *ct* and *mn*. The only subtype of $V\,\bar{C}$ geminate clusters in Spanish is *rr*: Lat. *currĕre* Sp. *correr*. The following scheme traces informally the duration type reduction from Latin into Spanish and Italian:

(20)   Spanish

Latin $\bar{V}\,\bar{C}$, $\bar{V}\,C$, $\breve{V}\,\bar{C}$, $V\,C$

         Italian

It would appear possible that as a result of the particular type reduction in Italian (and to a minor extent in Spanish) to the complement relation between the vowel and the following consonant(s) VC/VC, the length of the vowel or of the consonant would need not be marked in the underlying representation. This entails substantial lexical simplification of the Italian lexicon with respect to Latin. The possible analytical solutions are two: either (a) the consonant is marked and the vowel is predicted by rule or, alternatively, (b) the vowel is marked and the consonant is predicted by rule. Although the choice of either (a) or (b) would appear equivalent on independent grounds, in fact the choice of one or the other solution has quite different consequences in the phonological analysis as a whole. Modern phonological tradition has assumed solution (a) without argument. The following are its implication. The Classical Latin stress principle is abandoned and the feature stress is introduced in the underlying representation for each item (cf. Saltarelli 1970a:26). In essence, the lexical specification required is as substantial as in Latin: the former marks stress, the latter length for each lexical item (in addition to specifying length for consonants). It is moreover less revealing from an explanatory point of view since the principled presentation of stress types is no longer characterized. Finally, the complement simplification of VC types is not taken into account.

In my doctoral dissertation (Saltarelli 1966, 1970a) the vowel length solution (b) has been proposed. An analysis of the same type but quite distinct in nature has been recently presented in Wanner (forthcoming).

In this paper, I discuss a more realistic appraisal of the vowel length solution in the light of the no-desinence weak syllable principle for stress assignment.

The vowel length hypothesis allows us to capture the $\bar{V}\breve{C}/\breve{C}\bar{V}$ types simplification which distinguishes modern Italian from Latin with massive

prediction of consonantal length, by relying on a consonant lengthening
principle which formalizes a predictive phonetic fact in the language:

(21) (a) the simple consonant which follows a short stressed
           vowel is long

      (b) the simple consonant which follows a long stressed vowel
           is short

Its inclusion in the grammar of Italian permits us to leave unmarked the
consonantal length in items of the type (22)

(22) (a) *villa*   /vil-a/   (b) *vile*   /vīl-e/

           fesso   /fes-o/   *riso*   /rīs-o/

           bocca   /bok-a/   *buca*   /būk-a/

           carro   /kar-o/   *caro*   /kār-o/

      (c) *frassino*   /frasin-o/ (d) *comodo*   /kōmod-o/

           pallido   /palid-o/   *ateo*   /āte-o/

           pettine   /petin-e/   *anatra*   /ānatr-a/

           Accamo   /akam-o/   *calice*   /kālič-e/

   Furthermore, all productive word formations with surface stress shifted
away from the base form vowel are explained by employing cyclically the
principle of Stress (8) and Length (21). For example *pallina,* the
diminutive of *palla,* and *bruttissimo*, the superlative of *brutto,* would
be derived as follows:

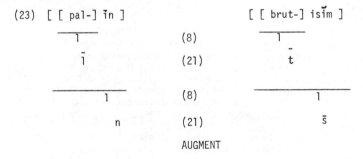

AUGMENT

Moreover, phrasal phenomena like *rafforzamento* (Saltarelli 1970a:86)
would be explained by marking the length of the governing vowel, significantly the surface monosyllables *a, da, e, la,* etc. as /a, dā, e, lā/
in my dialect. In fact the "metric syllable" which is constituted when
they are in a plurisyllabic phrasal formation reveals the nature of their
length composition. (In monosyllables length is phonetically leveled.)
Accordingly,

(24) *a casa* [ăkása]   *da casa* [dākása]

   e come [ĕkóme]   *la casa* [lākása]

   tra noi [trăñói]   *in alto* [ĭñálto]

   gassoso [gāsóso]   *per Ostia* [pĕróstya]

We have so far observed how (21) characterizes the Neo-Latin length
semplification in Italian VC̄/VC̆ in cases where C is either a single consonant or a geminate cluster. The vowel based consonant lengthening principle (21) allows us to leave the consonant unspecified as to the feature
length. The penultimate syllable would then have the following lexical
representation:

(25) [V, -length] [C, α length]

Accordingly, no consonant would be specified for the feature length (cf.
Saltarelli 1970a:29). In fact, this is true for the largest part of the
vocabulary, except for a well defined subset: that of plurisyllabic
paroxytons, like

(26) colonna

   madonna

   ombrello

If we represent (26) in accordance with (21) the penultimate syllable
would have the length composition (25). As it meets the weak syllable
condition, rule (8) assigns primary stress to the antepenultimate, which
is incorrect. Conversely, if we give the syllable the proper composition
[V, -length] [C, α length], it fails the weak syllable condition, stress
is correctly placed on the penultimate, but (21) incorrectly specifies the
consonant as [-length]. Thus the value of the feature length does not
coincide in this case in the assignment of stress and the determination of
the following consonant. This apparent failure of (21) is actually an
expected consequence of the stress assigning principle: in polysyllables
stress is placed on the penultimate vowel only if this is a "strong"
syllable by nature or by position. The lexical representation of subtype
(26) must therefore be

(27) [V, $a$length] [C, +length]

Such representation requires a consonant based vowel length principle

(28) (i)   a vowel which precedes a long consonant is short

(ii) a vowel which precedes a short consonant is long

which is the complement of (21). In this light, the difficulty presented by the type (26) evaporates. Since the lexical representations (25) and (27) are equivalently valued, no lexical complication is incurred. Rule-wise its cost is (28). But this rule is independently needed in order to specify vowel length in non-geminate clusters. Furthermore, and most significantly (21) and (28) together characterize the phonetic facts of Italian as to the distribution of duration in a speech sequence in terms of the so-called metric syllable where a complement ratio 1:2/2:1 obtains between the vowel and the following consonantal cluster.

The combined priciples (21) and (28) can also be viewed as a phonetic characterization on Italian speech output

(29) % ... [V,$a$length] [C, $\bar{a}$length] ...%

where % is pause boundary.

The volume of length specification can be gathered from the following sample list

(30) *Regular*

0 specification: conte, posta, momento, sergente, porta, colto, etc.

1 specification: *a*, gas, colo*nn*a, par*e*te, com*o*do, etc.

2 specifications: fra*ss*ino, pe*tt*ine, po*ll*ine, etc.

Irregular

1 specification: ca*rr*etto, ca*nn*one, To*mm*aso, ca*ff*é

2 specifications: ca*nn*e*ll*oni

The "regular" specifications are so defined because they are the basis for the regular processes of stress assignment and consonantal lengthening. Except for a small subset of the "regular" domain, items are either entirely unspecified or require one specification.

The "irregular" specification concern ad hoc consonant marking [+length].

They constitute a subset of the plurisyllabic set of the fixed lexicon in

the no-desinence hypothesis. Most of them are explained as irretrievable
word formations. That is, productively generated affixal formations which
have shifted from their derivational semantic form to new basic forms. For
example, *carretto* is a 'cart' in the present-day lexicon, although we may
infer that it is etymologically *carr-etto* 'small cart' in anology with
the derivational form *pal-etto* 'small post'. The same can be said about
cannellone which in the normal vocabulary is a type of food and not a
cann-ell-on-e 'large, little pipe'; the same is the case of *cannone* which
is not a *cann-one* 'large pipe'. It would certainly be questionable to represent such semantically shifted items in their affixal form just to
achieve maximun lexical regularity. This should lead us to the conclusion
that crucial support for predictive generalizations does not come necessarily from the fixed lexicon which includes all kinds of relics and unwieldy material which we learn as wholes, and which may be of undenyable
interest from the speaker's predictive principles of generalization. In
the latter respect we may find it useful to turn our attention from the
lexicon to the productive derivational processes of the language in the
search for grammatical generalizations.

A markedness characterization of length would include the following
conventions:

(31) I.   [mlength] $\rightarrow$ [αlength] / [αcons]

II. [ulength] $\rightarrow$ (a) [+length] (i) $\begin{bmatrix} V \\ -length \\ +stress \end{bmatrix}$ [————— $\begin{smallmatrix} C \\ \\ \end{smallmatrix}$]$_1^1$

(ii)[___V___]

(b) [-length] (i)[___V___] $\left\{ \begin{matrix} [\ C \ ]_2 \\ \# \end{matrix} \right\}$

(ii)[___C___]

In (31) I characterizes the claim that long consonants and short vowels
add to the complexity of the lexicon. The former account for "irregular"
specification, the latter for the less normal proparoxyton stress pattern.
In II (a-b), (i) defines the natural complement relation in "metric"
syllables, and (ii) states that vowels and consonants are otherwise normally long and short respectively.

In this light the stress rules (8) is quite consistently as converted:

(32) [V] $\rightarrow$ [+stress] / ___ C_0 ([mlength]^V C_0^1) #

One of the remarks that can be made at this point concerning length in Latin and in Romance is that the latter's lexicon is considerably lighter. This simplification is due to the historical type shift presented in (20) and characterized in a synchronic phonology of Italian in (34).

In Spanish the length type simplification is characterized by a phonetic principle similar to the one formulated for Italian:

(33)   (i)   the simple /r/ which follows a short stressed vowel is long

      (ii) the simple consonant which follows a short stressed vowel is short

    (iii) a vowel which precedes a LONG (a cluster of) consonant is short

      (i) a vowel which precedes a short consonant is long

The intuitively greater phonetic difference between Spanish and Italian is attributed to the fact that in the latter consonantal lengthening (33) (i) is substantially restricted as it applies only for /r/. Likewise the "irregular" consonantal specifications are limited to that segment: barril, ferrocarril, etc.

Another phenomenon closely connected with length and stress is the reduction of high vowels to glides (semivowels, semiconsonants) in unstressed position, with a concomitant shift of secondary stress:

(34) viola   [víola]   violenza   [vyolénza]

      miope   [míope]   miopia   [myopía]

      tuo   [túo]   tuoi   [twɔi]

      pio   [pío]   pio Nono [pyonóno]

      lui   [lúi]   lui stesso [lwistéso]

      paura   [paúra]   pauroso   [pàuróso]

      sua   [súa]   sua madre [swàmádre]

The principle that can be formulated is the following:

(35) (i) high vowels are reduced to glides when unstressed and adjacent to another vowel

$$
\begin{bmatrix}
-\text{ cons} \\
+\text{ voc} \\
+\text{ high} \\
-\text{ stress}
\end{bmatrix}
\rightarrow [\ -\text{voc}\ ]\ \ /\ \underline{\hspace{1.5cm}}\overline{V}
$$

(ii) "secondary" (reduced) stress is shifted to the adjacent vowel

Accordingly, we derive

(36)   [[sua] [madre]]

$$
\begin{array}{lll}
\overline{1} \quad \overline{\overline{1}} & & \text{STRESS} \\[6pt]
\overline{\hspace{3cm}1} & & \text{STRESS} \\[4pt]
\quad 2 & & \text{STRESS REDUCTION} \\[4pt]
\quad \text{w2} & & (35)
\end{array}
$$

[[paŭr] ōso]

$$
\begin{array}{lll}
\overline{1} & & \text{STRESS} \\[6pt]
\overline{\hspace{2cm}1} & & \text{STRESS} \\[4pt]
\quad 2 & & \text{STRESS REDUCTION} \\[4pt]
\quad 2\underset{\frown}{u} & & (35)
\end{array}
$$

The above glide reduction principle observed in word and phrase formations can be generalized to operated within a word.

(37)

   (a) *Mario*   / mari-o /   (b) *Maria*   / marī-a /

        piove   / piɔ̄v-e /   *pio*   / pi-o /

        Damiano   / damiān-o /   *bua*   / bu-a /

        fiume   / fiūm-e /   *mania*   / manī-a /

        uguale   / ugūāl-e /

   (c) *mai*   / mai /   (d) *paura*   / paūr-a /

        tiroide   / tirɔid-e /   *moina*   / moīn-a /

        baita   / bait-a /   *Balduina*   / balduīn-a /

        astronauta   / astronaut-a /

   (e) *tuoi*   / tuɔ̄-i /   (f) *aiuola*   / aiuɔ̄l-a /

        miei   / miɛ̄-i /

        buoi   / buɔ̄-i /

A phonetic distinction can also be made between on-glides [y, w] and off-glides [i̯, u̯]. In this connection there is a techincal problem concerning types (37) (f). It remains undetermined in accordance with the rule (35) whether in *aiuola* i is a a-offglide and u a o-onglide, or i is a u-onglide or u an i-offglide. It seems that a convention of non-high vowel "precedence" is a plausible way out, in accordance with which i is an a-offglide and u an o-onglide.

The above glide hypothesis presents another problem in connection with the stress principle (8). Items with offglides like *Claudio* / klaudi-o / would incorrectly receive primary stress on u. At least two solutions can be suggested. One is to specify such high vowels as short, and extend the weak syllable condition so that stress is thrown to the previous vowel (Saltarelli, 1970a). The second solution would be in terms of a V̄C/VC̄ constraint. Accordingly, short and high vowels adjacent to another vowel are reduced since -ūd- violates the length type constraint.

A final remark should be made about the phonetics of glide reduction in connection with boundaries. Consider the following data:

(38) *spianti*   / spi+ant-i /   "those who spy"

      spianti   / s+piant-i /   "you eradicate"

chi ama	/ ki#am-a /
chiama	/ kiam-a /
chi use	/ ki#us-a /
chiusa	/ kius-a /
da Irpino	/ da#irpino /
da Urbino	/ da#urbino /
dai tuoi	/ da#i#tuo-i / or / da≠i#tuo-i /
dai la chiave	/ da-i#la#kiav-e /

It seems that in accordance with the type of boundary (∅ segment, -desinence, +derivational, #word) a different degree of gliding occurs, ranging from highest at segment boundary to lowest at word boundary. In the speech output however such difference is obliterated as one accelerates from "largo" to "presto" style of prounciation, in the sense of Harris 1969b:7.

We have not memtioned in relation with glides the cases which are referred to as "dittonghi mobili" (Saltarelli 1970a:83). They have been considered briefly earlier in this paper as they concern stress assignment in Spanish and Italian.

In view of the length type reduction which occurred in Neo-Latin speech a principled explanation presents itself as regards the phenomenon of diphthongization.

We have seen that the type shift includes Lat. $\breve{V}\breve{C}$→It. $\bar{V}\breve{C}$: *gula*→*gōla*, a lengthening of the short vowel. In the case of short midvowels it can be speculated that such lengthening was achieved by the addition of another short vowel. Since this was done merely for the purpose of syllable length adjustment, the added vowel was the least distinct: an homorganic vowel. Thus Lat. *mel* ($\breve{V}\breve{C}$) became It. *miele* ($\breve{V}\breve{V}\breve{C}$).

Furthermore, if diphthongization is considered a length readjustment phenomenon, it seems to me to follow that it must have been a "once" process, limited to the established lexicon of the time, for reasons of lexical regularization. It is therefore clearer why Diphtongization is not a predictive generalization in present-day Neo-Latin speech, and why evidence is found only in the aboriginal vocabulary. If this is the nature of diphthongization, it would not be preposterous to claim that such a phenomenon is in principle not a predictive generalization.

As regard the general glide phenomenon (35), it might be useful to compare it with the situation in Latin. We find off-glides but no on-glides (except, if the interpretation is accepted, in word initial position). We can then set up the following glide reduction rule for Classical Latin:

(39) (short) high (and mid?) vowels are reduced to glides when
unstressed and preceded by another vowel or followed
by another vowel word initially

$$\begin{bmatrix} -\text{cons} \\ +\text{voc} \\ +\text{high} \\ -\text{stress} \end{bmatrix} \rightarrow [\ -\text{voc}\ ] \qquad /\#\ \underline{\quad} \ \overline{V}$$

which accounts for

(40) *Claudius*   / klaudi-us /   [kláu̯dius]

    laetitiae   / laititi-ai /   [laí̯titi̯ai]

    vetus   / uet-us /   [u̯étus]

    jussū̄   / iuss-ū /   [i̯ūsu]

Lexical evidence for the original off-glides seems to have been wiped
out entirely in Italian by an intervening vowel shift governed by the
glide and homorganic in nature: ai̯ → e, au̯ → o, (oe̯ ↛ e).

In comparison, the glide principle has thus been generalized to the
"hiatus" domain in modern Italian with resulting rule simplification.

Recapitulating, in this paper I have considered certain phenomena of
present-day standard Italian in a Neo-Latin perspective, in an attempt
to clarify a quite fundamental distinction between lexical regularities
and predictive generalizations.

I have focused on the intricate relation of length and stress, as it
affects also diphthongization and gliding in addition to other minor
phenomena in Italian, Spanish and Latin.

Concurrently, I have explored the nature of phonological rule in a
mentalistic grammar in view of an evaluation criterion distinguishing
between predictive and non-predictive generalizations, where the latter
concern only regularities in the established vocabulary of a language,
as opposed to the former which provide principled explanations about the
internalized grammar of a speaker.

It is concluded that a speaker's knowledge of his language is best
investigated in its productive derivational processes.

SANFORD A. SCHANE
UNIVERSITY OF CALIFORNIA, SAN DIEGO

HOW ABSTRACT IS FRENCH PHONOLOGY?

In what is perhaps the most celebrated recent unpublished paper, one that in the last couple years has certainly generated much phonological discussion, Paul Kiparsky (1968a) questioned the abstract nature of phonological representation.* In response to his query: How abstract is phonology?, there have been several interesting papers dealing with exotic languages, notably by Brame (1970) for Arabic, Hyman (1970) for Nupe, and Kisseberth (1970) for Yawelmani, all of which attempt to demonstrate the need for highly abstract phonological representations. In particular, these researchers show that their respective languages necessitate positing contrasting underlying segments which become totally neutralized at the surface level--that is, in all environments of occurrence, a situation of which Kiparsky was critical.

As for the Romance languages, if we are to obtain interesting insights about the morphology, then we too will need highly abstract phonological representations. In support of this view I shall present data exclusively from French, although one could reach the same conclusion from James Harris's work on Spanish. I shall not be overly concerned with total neutralization, for which I cannot find in French a great deal of evidence either for or against abstractness. Instead, I shall maintain that for Romance it is primarily the relationship between the nonlearned and the learned vocabulary which necessitates abstract representations. This peculiarity of Romance is of course due to the fact that much of both lexical strata historically have the same source--Latin.

In this presentation I shall try to accomplish two goals: (1) to give some idea of the abstractness of contemporary French, and (2) to suggest how such a system was able to evolve historically.

* * *

One of the central questions in a synchronic analysis is: Which forms are morphologically related? In general, forms which enter into the inflectional morphology--noun, verb, and adjective paradigms--pose little issue.

The thorny problems are found in the derivational morphology. As I pointed
out in my Introduction to *French Phonology and Morphology* (Schane 1968a:xix)
"In a language as morphologically complex as French, there are clear cases
of forms which should be related, and clear cases of forms which should not
be related, but there is also a significant number of forms where it is
difficult to reach a decision concerning relatedness, and accordingly we
can expect investigators to handle such cases differently." Consequently
there may be forms which I would relate but which you would not, but I do
not think it is worth arguing over them since for many cases we will be in
agreement and it is these cases on which the analysis must rest. As for
the marginal forms we can let them be decided by the overall complexity of
the description. "Can the forms in question be explained by existent rules?
If so, there is no reason to exclude them from the analysis. Will additional
rules explicate a large class of data which have not yet been accounted for,
or will they only explain some isolated forms? If rules will account for
a significant body of data, then forms which could be handled by such rules
are included as related forms. In general, we have not attempted to relate
forms which exhibit quite restricted phonological alternations. For example,
we do not give rules for the alternations: *mère, maternel* 'mother, maternal';
père, paternel 'father, paternal'; *frère, fraternel* 'brother, fraternal.'
Although within each pair the same alternation is exhibited, this alternation
is limited exclusively to these three pairs, so that any rule formulated cannot be extended beyond these three instances." (Schane 1968a:xix)

Although the underlying representations in *French Phonology and Morphology*
are highly abstract, they perhaps were not abstract enough, for according to
the criteria just mentioned, *mère, maternel; père; paternel;* and *frère,
fraternel* are to be related. Although it is true that the alternation /ɛr/:
/atɛrn/ is restricted to these three pairs, a deeper analysis than the one I
presented reveals that this alternation can be accounted for by an interaction
of rules, rules which are independently required to accommodate other forms
in the phonology. Assuming that the underlying representation for the stem
is equivalent to the learned alternant, an assumption to be subsequently
justified--that is, *matern, patern, fratern*--in order to derive the nonlearned
/mɛr/, /pɛr/, /frɛr/--four changes are required: the stem vowel *a* must be
fronted to ɛ, and the *t,e,* and *n* of the second syllable must all be deleted.
The vowels can be easily handled by two rules which were given in *French
Phonology and Morphology*.

(1)   Underlying *a* becomes ɛ in stressed position. This rule accounts
for alternations such as:

clarté	clair
maritime	mer
formalité	formel

américaniser	américaine
popularité	populaire

(2) Post-tonic nonlow vowels are deleted. For example:

populaire	peuple
mobilier	meuble
fabuleux	fable
sororité	soeur
circulaire	cercle

Since in *French Phonology and Morphology* I was not concerned too much with consonant alternation, I did not have rules for deleting the consonants. However, consideration of additional data shows the necessity for such rules.

(3) In nonlearned derivation certain noninitial dental and velar stops are deleted.

vital	vie
nudité	nu(e)
crudité	cru(e)
régal	roi
légal	loi
amical	ami(e)

It is this rule which will delete the *t* of *matern, patern,* and *fratern.*

(4) A nasal is deleted when preceded by a liquid and not followed by a vowel. This rule accounts for alternations such as:

corn-u	cor
journ-ée	jour
tourn-er	tour
hivern-al	hiver

infern-al	enfer
dorm-ons	dor-s

Although we are able to give rules which relate *mère, maternel; père, paternel;* and *frère, fraternel,* are we really justified in setting up such abstract representations? Semantically, there is no question that the members of each pair are related, but semantic considerations alone are not sufficient for deciding morphological relatedness. After all, English *mother, maternal; father, paternal;* and *brother, fraternal* have exactly the same semantic relationships as the corresponding French pairs, and would one want to derive these English pairs from unique underlying representations, a process which would necessitate a synchronic resurrection of Grimm and Verner. I do not believe that the two situations are parallel. We have shown that the four rules required to derive *mère, père,* and *frère* from underlying *matern, patern,* and *fratern* are all rules which can be justified independently of the forms in question, since the rules in any case are needed to accommodate other forms whose morphological relatedness is not in doubt. We then showed that it is precisely these *same* rules which handle the marginal forms. One would need to present equally strong evidence to support relating the English pairs and to show the necessity of the rules for clear cases of morphological relationship. Note, for example, that Chomsky and Halle(1968) do not consider such forms. In the absence of well-motivated rules, the members of each English pair would require separate listing, perhaps as native and learned suppletives.

For the remainder of the paper I want to concentrate on the abstractness of the underlying vowel system. In *French Phonology and Morphology* I derived the front rounded vowel *œ* from its back rounded partner ɔ. Actually, the rule which fronts *a* to ɛ also fronts ɔ to *œ*. It is this rule which accommodates alternations such as:

solitude	seul
mortel	meurt
floral	fleur
mobilier	meuble
sororité	soeur
professorat	professeur

Because / *œ* / was not needed as an underlying vowel but could be derived from ɔ, I then attempted to eliminate entirely front rounded vowels in underlying representations and in all cases to derive them from their back rounded

counterparts. This reasoning led me to derive all occurrences of the
high front rounded /y/ from underlying u, a procedure which was criticized
by N. V. Smith in his review in *Language* of *French Phonology and Morphology*.
"It is dubious, however, whether the arguments for deriving /y/ from |u|
enjoy the same cogency. It has been suggested by Kiparsky (1968) that
phonological theory should adopt what he calls an alternation condition...
to the effect that 'morphophonemic processes cannot apply to all occurrences
of a morpheme'. In other words, if there is no phonological alternation
among the different manifestations of a morpheme, this single form should
be entered in the lexicon.... In the case of /y/ above, as in *durons ~
dure*, every occurrence of this stem has /y/, and there is no alternation
with any other vowel. Accordingly, the underlying form should also be
/y/ rather than |u|. It should be noted that in Schane's treatment,
every underlying |u|, other than lexically marked exceptions, becomes /y/,
a process which Kiparsky's convention disallows." (Smith 1969:400)

Smith's critique is entirely justified. Because there are few good
alternations between u and y to parallel those between $\supset$ and *oe*, and
because the environmental conditions are not the same for both cases, my
argument for deriving all occurrences of /y/ from u was not a strong one.
Yet I still maintain that for modern French /y/ is to be derived from
underlying u, and I should now like to provide additional evidence to
support this claim, considerations not presented in *French Phonology and
Morphology*.

As everyone knows, the surface vowel system of French is very rich.
Depending on the particular style analyzed there are from eight to eleven
oral vowels plus a schwa, three or four nasalized vowels, and several
diphthongs. This rich vowel system is found primarily in the nonlearned
words. For a large majority of learned forms, however, we encounter a
different distribution of vowels. Consider the following sample of
learned words:

> maritime
>
> popularité
>
> américaniser
>
> circularité
>
> solitude
>
> sororité
>
> professorat
>
> musculature

There are five oral vowels--*i, e, a, o,* and *y* (the latter always represented by orthographic *u*) plus schwa which is nearly always restricted to the final syllable. Nasalized vowels may also occur in learned forms, but these need not concern us since they are always derived from sequences of oral vowel plus nasal consonant. Furthermore, the rules for deriving nasalized vowels apply to all aspects of the lexicon. What generally does not occur in learned stems are the dipthongs *wa* and *je.* the front rounded vowels *ø* and *œ* (although *ø* has a marginal occurrence in Greek stems such as *pseudo-*), nor the high back rounded vowel *u.* It should be noted that these restrictions on the distribution of vowels in learned forms apply primarily to stem vowels. (There are several productive "nonlearned" affixes which can be combined with "learned" stems: for example, nonlearned *meuble,* but learned *mobili-er,* where the stem is learned but the suffix is nonlearned, or *fable; fabul-eux.* Perhaps it would be more appropriate to refer to forms such as *mobilier* and *fabuleux* as "semilearned". Nonetheless I shall continue to call them "learned.")

The five basic vowels occurring in learned forms display an interesting asymmetry.

$$\begin{array}{ccc} i & & y \\ \\ e & & o \\ \\ & a & \end{array}$$

We are confronted with a five-vowel system where the rounded vowels do not conform to the expected pattern, what would be a more heavily marked five-vowel system within a theory of markedness. Furthermore if we consider *all* surface vowels, we find that for NONLEARNED forms, where *y* and *u* appear, that statistically *y* has a higher frequency of occurrence. If we add to these figures the LEARNED forms, where *u* as a surface vowel is virtually nonexistent, save for such non-Latin loans as *spoutnik,* then for the total vocabulary the statistical preponderance of *y* over *u* is overwhelming. It would appear, then, that in French *y* is FUNCTIONING as the high rounded vowel par excellence.

All of this indirect argumentation is necessary for lack of alternations between *y* and *u.* Interestingly enough, though, I have recently found a few such alternations--for example:

d*u*pliquer	d*ou*ble
dég*u*ster	go*û*ter
gén*u*flexion	gen*ou*

Although these *y-u* alternations are marginal, nonetheless, they exist.

As a consequence of these considerations--the statistical frequency of *y,* its occurrence as one of the basic five vowels in learned forms, the asymmetric system which one must recognize if *y* is an underlying vowel and the complexity of such a vowel system within a theory of markedness, the occurrence of a few alternations between this vowel and *u*, and finally, the relationship between this vowel and its cognate in the other Romance languages--I think we can conclude that within contemporary French, *y* is behaving as though it were *u*, that *u* in fact must be its abstract representation, and that any surface occurrence of *u* must have some other vowel as its source.

I present now what I believe to be the underlying vowel system of modern French, where there are five tense vowels and eight lax ones. This system is slightly different from that presented in *French Phonology and Morphology*.

	Underlying vowel	Principal surface manifestation	Example
TENSE			
	I	i	c*i*re
	E	e~ɛ	esp*é*rer, esp*è*re
	A	a	c*a*r
	O	ɔ~o	s*o*tte, s*o*t
	U	y	c*u*re
LAX			
	i	delete	mob*i*l*i* → meuble
	e	wa~ə	d*oi*vent, d*e*vons
	ɛ	jɛ~ə	v*i*ennent, v*e*nons
	ə	ə~ɛ	m*e*nons, m*è*ne
	a	ɛ	m*e*r
	ɔ	œ	fl*eu*r
	o	u	c*ou*r
	u	delete	fAb*u*l → fable

In learned derivation stem vowels become tense. As there are fewer tense vowels than lax ones, *e* and *ɛ* both become *E*, and *o* and *ɔ* both become *O*.

	Lax		Tense
i→I	mobili	(meuble)	mobIIIer
e↘			
E	leg	(loi)	lEgal
ɛ↗			
	pɛd	(pied)	pEdestre
a→A	mar	(mer)	mAritime
ɔ↘			
O	flɔr	(fleur)	flOral
o↗			
	tot	(tout)	tOtal
u→U	fAbul	(fable)	fabUleux

We see then that there are interesting morphological relations between corresponding pairs of tense and lax vowels.

How was it possible for this vowel system to have evolved, particularly since there are several strange things about it. First, whereas Latin had five tense (long) vowels and five lax (short) ones, the vowel system we posit for modern French has five tense vowels but eight lax ones. Where did the three extra lax vowels come from? Second, granted that there is the same number of tense and lax vowels, why are there more of the latter? If anything, one would expect the opposite situation--for there to be more tense vowels. Third, why do some of the lax vowels dipthongize--that is, *wa* and *jɛ* are derived from *e* and *ɛ* respectively? Is it not more natural for tense vowels to diphthongize?

It is well known that whereas Classical Latin had ten surface vowels, Vulgar Latin had seven: The Classical Latin lax vowels were lowered one step--*i* and *u* merged with *ē* and *ō* respectively, while *e* and *o* became *ɛ* and *ɔ*, and *a* merged with *ā*. The surface system of Vulgar Latin then was:

i		u
e		o
ɛ	a	ɔ

It is further maintained that with this new seven-vowel system there ceased to be *contrasts* between tense and lax vowels and that any differences in tenseness were now contextually determined: PHONETICALLY, vowels were tense when stressed and lax when unstressed.

Douglas Walker has shown that the seven-vowel surface system of Vulgar Latin could not also be the underlying vowel system. If, in Vulgar Latin, one is to predict stress placement and to account for vocalic alternation within the paradigm, then one must continue to posit a ten-vowel system-- five pairs of tense/lax vowels--with synchronic rules which lower the lax vowels and adjust teneness but only after stress has been assigned to the abstract vowels according to the well-known Latin stress rule. In fact, it is this underlying ten-vowel system of Vulgar Latin which has been inherited by present-day Spanish (cf. Foley 1965b, Harris 1969b).

The diphthongization of stressed *ɛ* and *ɔ* to *iɛ* and *uɔ* respectively began in Vulgar Latin. As already noted, as underlying vowels the sources of these diphthongs were PHONOLOGICALLY LAX. That underlying lax vowels should diphthongize in Romance is not paradoxical if it is understood that due to vowel lowering and stress the vowels had become PHONETICALLY tense, at which point, historically, they were ripe for diphthongization. Consequently, the diphthongization of phonologically lax vowels in the modern Romance languages is merely a continuation of what began in Vulgar Latin.

Modern French has a larger inventory of underlying vowels than Classical Latin or Vulgar Latin or even modern-day Spanish, and one can ask how such a vowel system came about. Walker has shown that at the earliest period of Old French there are five pairs of tense/lax vowels, exactly as in Vulgar

Latin. During this time there occurred extensive deletion of posttonic
vowels. In forms with original antepenultimate stress the penultimate
vowel underwent syncope, and for all forms a final unstressed vowel
(other than a), which did not support a consonant cluster, underwent
apocope, whereas a final a or a supporting vowel was reduced to schwa.

Latin	Modern French
perd*e*re	perdre
arb*o*re(m)	arbre
pop*u*lu(m)	peuple
mar*e*(m)	mer
dorm*i*t	dort
cant*a*t	chante

As a consequence of these deletions stress fell on the final syllable
unless its vowel was schwa, in which case the stress was on the penultimate. Because stress could now be assigned according to the surface vowels,
the tense/lax distinction was no longer necessary for stress placement.
The result was a restructuring in the direction of concreteness in the
underlying vowel system. The new vowel system which emerged was quite
similar to the surface vowel pattern of Vulgar Latin--seven vowels, but
in addition, a schwa.

In Old French the diphthongization of nonhigh vowels occurred in
stressed syllables where the vowel was followed by at most one consonant.
Therefore, nonhigh stressed vowels had two variants in complementary dis-
tribution--a diphthong or fronted vowel when in an open syllable or followed
by a single consonant, and a simple vowel when followed by two or more
consonants.

Underlying Stressed Vowel	Surface Manifestation	
	/___C_0^1	___C_2
i	i	i
e	ei	e
ɛ	iɛ	ɛ
a	**e**	a
ɔ	uɔ(uɛ)	ɔ
o	ou	o
u	y	u
(ə)	unstressed	y

This seven-vowel system plus schwa did not last very long. Two main
forces were responsible for the subsequent changes. First, many types of
consonant clusters were simplified: geminates were degeminated, and
clusters of nonhomorganic consonants were reduced through various processes to single consonants. Second, learned borrowings containing the

simple vowels of Latin were already entering the language. As a consequence of these effects nonhigh simple vowels and diphthongs were now
in contrast in open syllables or before single consonants. Hence it
became necessary to recognize two types of nonhigh vowels--those which
diphthongized and those which did not. For the moment I shall represent
the diphthongized vowels as underlying lax vowels and the simple vowels
as tense ones. I shall subsequently justify this distinction, which,
it should be noted no longer coincides exactly with the tense/lax distinction found in Latin.

	Underlying Vowel	Surface Manifestation
TENSE	i	i
	e	e
	ε	ε
	a	a
	ɔ	ɔ
	o	u
	u	y
LAX	e	(ei)→oi
	ε	iε
	a	(e)ε
	ɔ	(uɔ)→uε
	o	(ou)→eu
	ə	unstressed

   This underlying vowel system was to be reduced through two neutraliza-
tions. Whereas in early Old French, e and ε could contrast in a closed
syllable, by the end of the twelfth century this contrast was lost.
Hence it was no longer necessary to recognize both e and ε as underlying
tense vowels. Also by the end of the twelfth century the two diphthongs
uε and eu were both simplified to the front rounded vowel œ. Because
of this neutralization there was no longer any need for two different
underlying lax rounded vowels. The following underlying system emerged.

TENSE	i		u (y)
	e		o (u)
		a	ɔ
LAX	e (oi)→(we)		o (œ)
	ε (jε)	a (ε)	

   The underlying vowel system is now skewed--both the tense vowels and
the lax ones exhibit asymmetry. This asymmetry could be corrected in
either of two ways. One of the nonhigh rounded tense vowels could be
dropped from the tense vowel system and become integrated into the lax
vowel system. Conversely, one of the lax front vowels could become part

of the tense vowel system. In either case the resulting vowel patterns would be symmetrical. If we examine the distribution of surface vowels in lexical forms we note that the reflexes of all vowels occur in non-learned forms, whereas for the LEARNED vocabulary the reflexes of lax vowels are rarely found and among the tense vowels all of them except the reflex of underlying *o*--that is, surface /u/--can occur. Hence we see that LAX VOWELS become associated with the NONLEARNED vocabulary. But the underlying tense vowel *o* is also "functioning" as a lax vowel, i.e. in the sense that it occurs in nonlearned forms, and it is this vowel then which will drop out of the tense vowel pattern and integrate itself into the lax vowel system, thereby resolving the asymmetries previously noted.

TENSE   i   u (y)

              e   o (ɔ)

                      a

LAX   e (we)   o (u)

          ε (jε)   a (ε)   ɔ (œ)

Finally, at a later period underlying lax *i* and *u* enter the system. These vowels are always somewhat marginal but do account for alternations such as *meuble, mobilier; fable, fabuleux,* where they are deleted in the nonlearned forms. With the addition of these two vowels we arrive at the vowel system I advocated earlier for present-day French: five tense vowels and eight lax ones--that is, for the lax vowels the seven-vowel pattern plus schwa.

I have repeatedly alluded to the necessity for distinguishing two types of vowels--those which are diphthongized or deleted from those which are more stable; those which are part of nonlearned forms from those occur-ring throughout the vocabulary. To distinguish these two kinds of vowels I made use of the feature "tense"--underlying lax vowels are diphthongized or fronted or deleted whereas underlying tense vowels in general deviate less from their surface representations; underlying lax vowels, with the exception of final schwa, occur primarily in nonlearned forms, whereas underlying tense vowels are not so restricted. It remains to demonstrate that the feature "tense" is not being used arbitrarily as a diacritic for distinguishing these two classes, but rather that it has real phonological motivation.

Within the nonlearned morphology there are alternations between a stressed full vowel or diphthong and a pretonic schwa.

Underlying Lax	Stress	Pretonic
e	d*oi*vent	d*e*vons
ε	v*ie*nnent	v*e*nons
ə	m*ə*nent	m*e*nons
a	m*ai*n (cf. manuel)	m*e*notte

Schwa, a phonetically lax vowel, has only underlying lax vowels as its source. Hence, there is a correlation between phonetic laxness and phonological laxness. Underlying tense vowels, on the other hand, are never realized as schwa. They have only phonetic tense vowels as their surface manifestations.

We noted that due to the extensive syncope of posttonic vowels, for early Old French the Latin stress rule was no longer operative. Instead one stressed the penultimate vowel if the final vowel was schwa; otherwise the final vowel bore the stress. This stress rule could accommodate the incoming learned forms as well. However, with the introduction of large numbers of learned forms, new relationships were established between the nonlearned and the learned. Once there were these morphological relations the stress rule became inadequate for many of the nonlearned forms. For example, if *meuble* is to be derived from an underlying *mobili* (because of *mobilier*) or *père* from an underlying *patern* (because of *paternel*), the stress rule as given could not place stress on the first syllable for the nonlearned forms. However, the Latin stress rule could accommodate these forms providing that the noninitial vowels were lax. If they were tense they would of course attract the stress. Thus, stress shows that non-learned forms must contain lax vowels, which subsequent to stress placement, are either deleted or converted to schwa in posttonic position. Conversely, if learned forms, which are always stressed on one of the last two sylla-bles, are to be assigned stress by the same rule, then their underlying vowels must be tense so as to attract stress in those positions. The stress rule, then, for Modern French has once again become quite similar to the Latin stress rule, with one important difference. In polysyllables the Latin rule assigned stress to either the penultimate or the antepenult-imate vowel. In French, stress can also be assigned to the final syllable providing it contains a tense vowel.

* * *

It is my contention that the single most important factor in the evolu-tion of the present-day phonological system of French has been the massive introduction of learned Latin words. It is the learned vocabulary along-side of a cognate nonlearned one which is mainly responsible for the abstractness of the modern language. We saw that for a brief period in Old French, because of various historical processes, underlying represent-ations had become more concrete. With the introduction of the learned vocabulary there arose new sets of alternations between nonlearned and learned forms. As a consequence of these alternations those "concrete" nonlearned forms which were related to learned ones had to undergo a restructuring in their underlying representations. The underlying re-presentations became similar to the learned alternant--that is, the under-lying representations of these nonlearned forms became more abstract.

The French situation is quite different from English. Whereas the English learned vocabulary, like the Romance, is primarily Greco-Latin, or else borrowed from French, the indigenous vocabulary is Germanic. As Chomsky and Halle have shown, the interesting morphophonemic processes for English primarily· affect the Romance stratum. Forms such as *divine, divinity; serene, serenity;* etc. provide motivation for the stress rules, the rules of tensing and laxing, vowel shift, etc. Although occasionally there is alternation within the native lexicon, such as the vowel alternations for strong verbs, by and large, for English, the raison d'être for the majority of the morphophonemic processes resides in the Romance vocabulary--in general, WITHIN the learned part of the lexicon. In French, on the other hand, the interesting alternations are precisely BETWEEN the learned and the nonlearned, rather than entirely within the learned. It is the presence of cognate nonlearned and learned pairs which leads to a highly abstract phonology in French.

In conclusion, I should like to propose the following characteristics about phonological systems.

1. If a language acquires a substantial learned vocabulary whose direct source is the same as the indigenous vocabulary, and if as a consequence there are alternations between nonlearned and learned forms, then that language will have a highly abstract phonology.

2. Where there is alternation, the underlying representations can be deduced from the learned forms, or to put it differently, the underlying representations of nonlearned forms will be quite similar to the historically prior form in the source language.

3. The rules which convert the underlying nonlearned representations to their appropriate surface forms will be quite similar to the historically attested rules which led from the source language to the indigenous vocabulary.

NOTE

*This work was supported in part by the Délégation Générale à la Recherche Scientifique et Technique, contract number 69-01-591· Centre National de la Recherche Scientifique, Paris.

APPLICATION TO PEDAGOGY

JEAN CASAGRANDE
UNIVERSITY OF FLORIDA

THEORY, DESCRIPTION AND PEDAGOGY:
THE INTERRELATED PARTS OF A WHOLE

> *"Transformation grammar is nothing new*
> *to the language teacher; he has been*
> *using it for years."*

It is customary, in contemporary linguistic studies, to distinguish between description and pedagogical work. But this has not always been the case. In fact, this distinction has only been made of late--since the advent of the discipline of linguistics, a relatively recent development in a long tradition of thought about language.[1] This split is due to many factors most of which fall under the heading of awareness of language change and of linguistic relativity.

Like his contemporaries, Dionysius Thrax,[2] the great Alexandrian grammarian, was concerned about the changes--then incorrectly identified as "linguistic perversion"--that had taken place in Greek since Homeric time. Evidence of this concern is implicit in the opening remarks of Thrax's *Grammar*: "Grammar is the knowledge of the language employed by poets and writers" (Dinneen 1967:98). One of the purposes of Thrax's grammar was to show the Greeks the *correct* (Homer's) way to use the Greek language. Because the Alexandrians did not understand linguistic evolution they tried to reverse its trends and, to that end, they wrote normative grammars. Many grammars written since have the same goals: in some instances their models are closer in time--a prestigious social class, for instance-- and almost always they have been writers and poets. The contemporary equivalents of Thrax's *Grammar* are traditional grammars. Like Thrax's *Grammar*, they do not distinguish between the description of a language and the advice given to the reader to help him speak and write more like the writers and poets taken as models.

In many ways, Thrax's *Grammar* is the foundation of traditional grammar. In particular, he formalized the eight parts of speech which are still referred to in our classrooms. Thrax is not only responsible for establishing some basic principles of traditional grammar, but he also has given us a method in formal linguistics. The intellectual climate of the time, a controversy over the origin of language, led him to establish the identity of the parts of speech on the basis of their formal differences and only subsequently to give semantic corroboration to his findings. Identification of classes on purely formal terms has remained a basic tenet of descriptive linguistics.

With this glance over the earliest known grammar in Western civilization we can see that the distinction between the descriptive and didactic goals of linguistic studies was inexistent in Greek grammatical thought. Both the formal descriptive apparatus and advice about usage could be found in Greek grammars.[3] The distinction between description and pedagogical application is a very recent one. No clear-cut distinction to that effect is made in Roman, Medieval, Renaissance, or Philosophical grammars. Until the 1800's the two goals remained closely related. Even today, traditional grammars, the sole repositories of linguistic knowledge known to the layman, blend together the description of a language and the normative advice concerning the "proper" use of that language.

The normative tradition in linguistic studies was broken mid-way in the Nineteenth century when scholars, under the influence of the interest in the exotic generated by Romanticism, began to look for and discover the phenomenal diversity which exists in linguistic expression. The ancient Greek view that the rest of the world is made up of uninteresting barbarians, a view which for the most part has been prevalent for centuries, was set aside. Linguists studied languages previously ignored by or unknown to western linguistic tradition like Sanskrit, Persian, and Hittite, and began to understand the nature of linguistic change. The understanding that linguistic change is unavoidable, that change is an inherent part of the nature of language, gave rise, among the thinkers involved in these studies, to an element of tolerance toward linguistic diversity. This tolerance was also fostered by Romanticism, the prevalent thought of the time. Likewise today, we understand that the role of linguistic studies is not a prescriptive or normative one but rather one of description and explanation.[4] Some purists still do not tolerate linguistic change, particularly in their own language although they are, or should be, aware of the inescapable fact that language changes.[5]

The field of applied linguistics, and more specifically that branch of applied linguistics which is concerned with language pedagogy cannot simply be characterized by the term prescriptive. Those who work in linguistic pedagogy are not purists but linguists. In general they consider their roles to be to make available to the language teacher those insights which they or other linguists have gained in the study of language. In the next few pages I will point to some of the problems the applied linguist faces, and try to define his role. As in the rest of this volume, discussion is focused on the interaction of the Romance languages and generative transformational grammar.

As an illustration of how transformational descriptions can be utilized in pedagogy consider the following. The claim that non-restrictive relative clauses are derived from equivalent conjoined clauses provides a basis for a transformation drill like (1), where the student given a must provide b.

(1)   a. El hombre, y es racional, a veces comete graves errores.
       b. El hombre, que es racional, a veces comete graves errores.

       a. Los perezosos, y no tienen ningún escrúpulo, desean fracasar.
       b. Los perezosos, que no tienen ningún escrupúlo, desean fracasar.

The above would be an application for pedagogical purposes of a description
of Spanish syntax within transformational theory. As an example of the
application of phonological concepts to the teaching of pronunciation let
us suppose a drill based on a vocalic alternation in French.

(2)   meurt   mortel
            fleur   floraison
            moeurs   morale
            odeur   odorant
            seul   solitude

Table (2) gives phonological facts of French which lead the linguist to
pair the alternating sounds and to derive one from the other. Drills
based on alternations illustrated by (1) and (2) would have two purposes:
to point to kinship between words or between syntactic structures and to
underscore the obvious differences: a difference in sound -- which results
from the application of a rule of French phonology deriving the front
rounded vowels from the back rounded vowels--, and a difference in syntax--
which also results from a rule. Examples 1 and 2 sufficiently illustrate
the application of generative descriptions to pedagogical purposes to lead
us to conclude that drills, and particularly transformation drills, derived
from such descriptions will emphasize the related aspect of two sequences
rather than differences between sequences. This is an unavoidable result
of the theory itself; related sequences are formally related by rules
while unrelated sequences are so characterized by lack of formal relation.
Note therefore that a drill designed to differentiate between the pairs of
(3) would superficially be very similar to (2), while in its relationship
to generative theory it would be strikingly different.

(3)   meurt   mer
            fleur   flair
            soeur   serre
            seul   sel

In spite of its striking similarity to (2), (3) is theoretically different
in that the alternations exhibited in (3) are not such that a generative
phonology of French would relate the sounds in question by rule.[6] A
generative phonology of French cannot differentiate by means of a rule
between the vowels of the pairs in (3). The difference between the members
of pairs in (2) is not to be confused with the difference between the
members of the pairs in (3): in the former it is a result of derivational
morphology[7] while in the latter it is accidental. Generative grammar

attempts to characterize these differences by relating via rule the pairs
of (2) and not the pairs of (3). The meanings of the members of the pairs
of (3) are assigned independently, with no regard to the similarity in
sound between the numbers of these pairs, thus treating the accidents--
the minimal pairs[8] of (3)—precisely as accidents. A phonetic drill based
on (3), therefore, would not constitute a literal application of a phonology of French in the generative vein.

There are similar cases in syntax. Let us consider the one illustrated
by (4).

(4)   a. È la prima volta che viene a trovarLa?
        b. No, non è la prima volta.

        a. È lotano, il Palazzo Vecchio?
        b. No, non è lotano.

        a. È importante arrivare domenica prossima?
        b. No, non è importante.

This is a type of transformation drill with which teachers are all too
familiar. Among others, drill (4) illustrates two points: a part of a
question may be deleted when answering it; and, the negative particle
non precedes the verb. Because (b) is the answer to (a) it is often
assumed that the sentences (a) and (b) are related by rule. That's wrong.
Drill (4) is not *directly* derivable from a syntactic description of
Italian. There is no transformation which relates the declarative and
interrogative forms of (4). The theoretical model illustrated by Chomsky
(1957) could, and indeed was, so conceived as to transformationally relate
pairs of affirmative and negative sentences. Subsequent work has altered
the theory. The Katz-Postal principle (Cf. Katz and Postal 1964) that
transformations may not change meaning, makes the theory more consistent
with the treatment of meaning in the framework of generative transformational grammar, but, in a very indirect way it is also responsible for
the failure of descriptions applying that principle to be directly applicable to teaching. Because (a) and (b) are different in meaning they may
not be related by rule.

A relation established by a rule of grammar cannot be the sole criterion
for determining the appropriateness of a drill. In fact, it is not clear
whether it should be a criterion at all.[9] Pedagogically, items (3) and
(4) are, at least, equally as useful as (1) and (2). Drills like (4) are
used more commonly than drills based on the alternation shown in (1). It
is even possible that no drill based on (1) was ever used. The information
deduceable from a drill based on (1) is likely to be more general, likely
to apply to many languages--including the base and target languages--than
that of a drill like (4). Many rules of grammar reflect universal processes.
These processes are shared by many (hopefully all) language users. No
drills may be needed for those. On the other hand, language specific facts,
need to be drilled.[10] A drill similar to (4), but on negatives in French,

for example, would require the insertion in the proper place of the two commonly used negative particles *ne* and *pas*, while only one particle is needed in other Romance languages. Some useful drills may not even reflect any rule of language.

Another problem for the direct application of generative grammar must be raised with reference to examples (2) and (3). Descriptive phonological grammars within the theory of generative phonology do not distinguish between the first vowel sounds of *seul* and *solitude* in the same way as they distinguish between the vowel sounds of *seul* and *sel*. In so doing the theory aims at representing the competence of a native speaker of French. However, for an adult (or an adolescent) attempting to learn French as a second language, the distinction between these two sets of vowels seems to be of equal difficulty both from the auditory and the articulatory viewpoint. Hence, a device of a different nature than of classical generative phonology is needed to teach the distinction illustrated in (3).[11]

From all that precedes, it is clear that the area of applied linguistics concerned with foreign language pedagogy is not to be viewed as a set of mechanical procedures which apply the formal devices used in the description of a language L directly to the teaching of L.[12] To conceive of the role of the applied linguist in those terms is both an error and an injustice. All too often the latter has been self-inflicted. The work of the applied linguist can be viewed as either that part of linguistics which covers the research and writing of pedagogical grammars,[13] or simply as an extension of the descriptive work of linguists who make available to the teaching profession some insights gained through their work on language. These are, of course, not mutually exclusive definitions of the role of the applied linguist: often there is overlap. These definitions, however, involve some fundamental differences in viewpoint and need to be discussed here.

If the goal of applied linguists is to write pedagogical grammars, the purpose of which is to present descriptions which lend themselves to the teaching of particular languages, then the applied linguists are faced with a fundamental problem: eclecticism We have seen above that the direct application of descriptions based on one of the most promising theories known to linguists falls short of the goal. As a consequence of this shortcoming the applied linguist who wants to write a comprehensive pedagogical grammar will be forced into an eclectic mold. He will choose to apply to different aspects of a language L descriptions based on the theories which can best capture those different aspects of L.[14] If, on the other hand, the role of the applied linguist is to make available some insights gained while engaged in the study of the structure of a language, then he need not face the question of eclecticism in description. Eclecticism will, of course, still be with the teacher. It is not known whether an eclectic pedagogical method is or is not detrimental in foreign language pedagogy. Most of us, who have studied a foreign language in school, have learned by means of traditional grammar, the epitome of eclecticism, and no one has ever learned a language via the application of a description based on a single theory since no complete grammar of any language has ever been written. As it looks, pedagogical eclecticism will long be with us.

It should be clear, however, that pedagogical eclecticism does not
imply a total reliance on traditional grammar exclusive of other grammatical
points of view. What is needed is an improvement of the descriptive devices
on which we base our pedagogy. Transformational descriptions, among others,
afford us with improvements over the work of traditional grammarians. One
such improvement resides in the explicitness of the descriptive device of
transformational grammar. Like the linguist, the teacher can discover in
the explicit description of the language he teaches concepts which he sus-
pected to exist, which he misunderstood, or which only his subconscious
had grasp of.[15] After reading works on transformational grammar like the
ones in this volume, after giving thought to some aspects of the syntax
of, say, French and English, he may reach a new awareness. For instance, he
may come to realize that (5) cannot mean (6) but rather that the French
equivalent of (5) is (7) while the English equivalent of (6) is (8).

(5)   John was certain to win.
(6)   Jean était certain de gagner.
(7)   Il était certain que Jean gagnerait.
(8)   John was certain that he would win.

The realization on my part of the differences of meaning illustrated in
the preceding paragraph is a result of work in transformational grammar.
This realization on the part of anyone else need not have resulted from
work in transformational grammar. Clearly, transformational grammar is
not a necessary condition for understanding this meaning distinction, but
it helps to have as a tool an instrument not quite as blunt as traditional
grammar when attempting to dissect the highly complex and abstract system
we call language. Armed with a descriptive fact, with an insight which
he has gained in the study of the structure of language, the teacher can
then convey to his students information which they might not otherwise
acquire. In doing so, he is applying not the letter but the spirit of
transformational grammar.
We saw above that a literal (narrow, mechanical) application of a
linguistic description is of little use to language teaching. Instead
it appears that we should apply to language pedagogy the spirit of transformational descriptions. This application should take the form of the
literal application in those instances where it can be useful, as was the
case for (2), and also take the form of extrapolations resulting from a
host of possible facts, one of which was illustrated in (5)-(8). The
spirit of transformational grammar as it concerns language pedagogy would
then yield understanding of language that traditional grammars fail to
bring out and which can be of use to language teaching in that they provide
the language learner with insight possibly unavailable otherwise.
It is those additional benefits that Brown, Goldin and Valdman discuss
in this volume. Brown shows that classroom drilling needs to bring out
certain semantic and syntactic relationships. If this is done the student
will be able to understand subtle shades of meaning, puns, and the like.

Goldin distinguishes between ground rules which are langage specific and conceptual rules which "call for understanding and analysis of a philosophical nature: examining situations and determining the roles of participants." He proposes that the teacher distinguish between the two types of rules not only in the explanation of linguistic principles but in the types of exercises employed to teach them. Valdman points to the close relationship that exists between abstract phonological representation and French orthography. His paper deals not with the teaching of French to speakers of other languages but with the teaching of French orthography to French speakers. He underlines the eventual role of generative descriptions as a worthwhile set of guidelines for spelling reforms, should the proper climate arise.

In the late 1950's and early 1960's, when Chomsky's *Snytactic Structures* was first scrutinized by the linguistic world, reactions were generally negative, with criticism coming from various quarters. The epigraph of this paper represents the attitude of a number of linguists who had been involved in applied linguistics. Their criticism was more readily accepted by other linguists because transformational grammar was new, and still little understood. It is likely that the analogy noted between the new theory and the pedagogical practice was the notion of transformation, a rule in the former and a type of drill in the latter. In retrospect, such an analogy appears superficial, but an interesting conclusion can be drawn. Some of the critics of transformational grammar had attempted, with little success, to apply their conception of language to language pedagogy. Despite their influence in a number of "techniques" which often sidetracked the class, the basic tool remained the trusty traditional grammar. Little did they know that in their putative indictment of transformational grammar they were forecasting what would eventually be claimed by the transformationalists themselves: transformational grammar is but the continuation, the formalization, and hopefully the amelioration of traditional grammar.

NOTES

1.   No specific date can be given to identify the advent of the discipline in its modern form. What is referred to here is the period which marks the development of comparative historical linguistics. This is elaborated on briefly below.

2.   Dionysius Thrax (ca. 150BC) is considered to be the best grammarian of Ancient Greek. He codified aspects of Homeric Greek several centuries after the assumed period of composition of the Illiad and the Odyssey (Ca. 800 BC). Thrax lived in Alexandria, a Greek settlement in Egypt. He was thus separated both by time and by geographic distance from the models of usage that he chose to use.

3.   The concepts of applied work in modern linguistics and that of didactic advice about the "proper" forms to use are not to be confused. The distinction between those two concepts is made clear below.

4.   It is true that not all scholars working in the field of linguistics accept explanation as a goal of linguistics. This difference is a result of widely diverse philosophical viewpoints. Theoretical linguistic literature, particularly Noam Chomsky's writings, is pregnant with discussions on this topic. See Chomsky (1964 and 1965).
5.   Purists (see, for example, Etiemble 1964) often claim to be defending the purity of their language. There are, of course, in all of us certain tendencies toward purism--in our role as linguistic models for our children, as language teachers, in certain social situations which demand a more formal style or expression--but these are tendencies. They should not preclude us from using neologisms issued from foreign borrowing, or from including in our usage expressions which earlier generations just did not happen to sanction as appropriate.
6.   For discussion of rule related alternations in Romance see Harris 1969b, Saltarelli 1970a, Schane 1968a, and in this volume, Schane's article, a good part of which addresses itself to how alternations are determined to require a rule.
7.   Derivational morphology is a technical term covering relationship as illustrated in (2). The rules of derivational morphology change both the shape and the category of an item. Hence the rules relating *seul* and *solitude* change the shape (the morphology) of the words and their categories (parts of speech): adjective ↔ noun. Derivational morphology is often opposed to inflexional morphology whose rules change only the shape and not the categories of words: e.g. *cuento* ↔ *contamos*.
8.   A minimal pair in the phonological theory of American structuralism is a set of two similar sound sequences which differ in only one segment and which are different in meaning. Hence *seul, sel; habit, abbé; dix, six;* and *fleur, flore* are minimal pairs. Pairs *seul, solitude; fils, puce; fleur, frère* are not minimal: they differ in more than one phonological segment.
      Minimal pairs are accidents. They depend on the (accidental) existence of a word in the vocabulary of a language. There is, for example, a noun *miembro* in Spanish but no word *miembre,* although the word is possible. If *miembre* existed, there would be a minimal pair *miembro, miembre.*
9.   We can only speculate that a thorough understanding of the nature of language, on the one hand, and a thorough understanding of the nature of learning on the other, can be combined to mechanically provide a language teaching technology. For this marriage to be successful we need the added requirement that the two ideals be arrived at in complete harmony with each other. Chomsky (1966) says that it is too early for a teaching methodology to arise from the meager accomplishments of psychology and linguistics. It seems that a language teaching technology derived mechanically from psychology and linguistics is highly unlikely ever to come about. Newmark (1963) says that direct application of a theory of language to language teaching is neither necessary nor sufficient.
10.   There are universal facts that an explicit grammar must state, such as *penser* requiring a human subject, *effrayer* an animate object, etc...

These facts hardly need to be pointed out to students learning French as a second language. In fact, the students expect such facts to remain unchanged across languages. Nevertheless, to say that no drills are needed for universally distributed facts and processes may appear an exaggeration and requires an explanation. There are universal processes, relative embedding for example, which can be used successfully in drills. Embedding is a process of transformational grammar which allows the generation of complex sentences.

Recently, Grant Brown made a most enlightening demonstration of a relative embedding drill to a group of French teachers at the Annual Meeting of the Florida Chapter of the American Association of Teachers of French. Having elicited short descriptive sentences about a subject, he then asked the audience to integrate these sentences into a larger one. The sentences (a) were relativized, the proper deletion rules applied, and the adjectives were placed in either pre- or post-nominal position, yielding (b).

    a.   C'est une algérienne.
          Elle est jeune.
          Elle est bien habillée.
          Elle entre dans un magasin.
    b.   Une jeune algérienne bien habillée entre dans un magasin.

Because sentences are embedded in all languages, an exercise which would drill relative embedding exclusively (if such an exercise could be con- structed) would serve little purpose. What Brown was drilling was the language specific rules relating a and b.

11. For examples of works in classical generative phonology see Chomsky and Halle (1968), Schane (1968a), Harris (1969b). See also Valdman (1961 and 1964) where the notion of contrast is utiltized extensively for pedagogical purposes.

12. We should be careful not to assume that applied linguistics, as it concerns itself with language pedagogy, is an application of a theory. Instead, it is the application of a description which, in turn, is itself the application and the test of the theory within which it is written.

13. This is the role of the applied linguist as defined by Valdman (1967).

14. Cf. Valdman (1967:25): "A pedagogical grammar--an applied grammar-- attempts to describe individual areas or features of a language in as insightful a manner as possible, and to do so it will apply to the individ- ual problem those techniques of analysis that seem most appropriate."

15. Cf. Note 10.

T. GRANT BROWN
THE FLORIDA STATE UNIVERSITY

CASE GRAMMAR AND THE TEACHING OF FRENCH

Linguistic theory has been claimed to have a number of important implications for foreign language teaching. The strongest claim, proposed by structural linguists during the development of the audiolingual method, was that theories of language structure should prescribe the methods and techniques for language teaching. A second, much weaker claim is that more adequate theories of language structure, which are capable of capturing generalizations with greater accuracy than earlier theories, may be used to provide improved text materials to help the learner to internalize these generalizations. Since the possibility of basing a pedagogical theory directly on linguistic theory has been seriously questioned (Chomsky 1966), this paper will be limited to an investigation of the application of one theory of linguistic structure to French syntax and the use of the resulting generalizations in the classroom.

OUTLINE OF CASE THEORY

Until recently, it had been assumed that the notions of subject and object of a sentence were basic in the description of at least the Indo-European languages. This linguistic tradition was carried on in the earlier works in transformational grammar which defined, in effect, these functional notions by phrase structure rules (Chomsky 1965:68-74). However, there are many other syntactic relations in the sentences of natural languages which involve noun phrases, including indirect objects, prepositional phrases, and adverbial phrases containing nouns. Thus, it was necessary to include many additional rules in the phrase structure to generate these constructions.

Ultimately, research on the syntactic and semantic relations involved in constituents of this kind led many linguists to reject the notion of a deep structure generated by phrase structure rules and, consequently, the notion of deep subject and object (Fillmore 1968a). These linguists proposed versions of syntactic theory in which the deepest level of analysis consists of an abstractly described semantic representation

which resembles the predicate calculus in many important respects. That
is, verbs, adjectives, and predicate nominals are described as predicates
which may make an assertion about the arguments (noun phrases) associated
with them (Fillmore 1968b). The particular version developed by Fillmore
(1968a:24-5) differs in one important respect from the predicate calculus:
The noun phrases which represent the arguments bear case labels to account
for their semantic function in the sentence and the selectional requirements of the verb. Since these case labels are important in the discussion
of French grammar which follows, they are defined briefly and illustrated
below:

Agent (A), the animate cause of an action or state.

Instrument (I), the inanimate cause of an action or state.

Dative (D), animate being affected by an action or state.

Locative (L), location affected by or identified with an action or state.

Objective (O), inanimate noun affected by an action or state.

The semantic roles of these cases are illustrated in the following French
sentences:

       (A)   (O)   (I)
(1) Jean a coupé le pain avec un couteau.

       (O)   (A)
(2) Le pain a été coupe par Jean.

       (I)   (O)
(3) Le sel a abîmé la table.

       (A)   (D)
(4) Henri a tué Jean.

       (D)
(5) Jean est mort.

       (A)   (L)
(6) Jean a frappé à la porte.

       (D)   (O)
(7) J'ai peur de cela.

       (A)   (O)   (D)
(8) Marie a donné le livre à Jean.

Associated with each case in the deep structure is a case marker. In
French, as in English, each case marker is a preposition. In general,
these case marking prepositions are deleted when that case becomes the
surface subject or direct object. From the example sentences above, the
following paradigm of cases and their corresponding prepositions can be
given:

Agent . . . . par

Instrument . . . . avec

Dative . . . . à

Locative . . . . à

Objective . . . . de

Each verb and adjective requires a lexical entry which specifies the
cases which must be associated with it as well as those which may optionally occur with it. The verb *break* has a lexical entry of the form:

break, + [___ (A) (I) O]

since it occurs in sentences of the forms:

        (O)
(9)   The window broke.

      (A)   (O)   (I)
(10) John broke the window (with a hammer).

      (I)   (O)
(11) The wind broke the window.

Since this verb only requires one case, the objective, it is a one-place
predicate. The verb *hit*, however, is a two-place predicate, since at
least two cases must occur with it, e.g.:

(12) John hit the door (with the paper).

(13) The paper hit the door.

but not,

(14) *The door hit.

This verb has a lexical entry of the following form, where the linked
parentheses indicate that either the instrument or the agent may be missing,

but not both (Fillmore 1968a:28):

hit, +[___ (A)(I) 0]

Using sentence (3) as an example *(Le sel a abîmé la table)*, the process of sentence generation in a case grammar begins with the specification of an abstract semantic entity consisting of the predicate and its associated cases:*

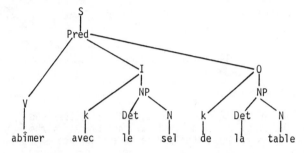

The surface structure subject and direct object are selected by the transformational component, giving:

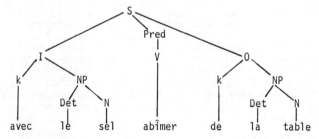

The case marking prepositions for the subject and object are then deleted, affix attachment rules are applied giving the surface structure of sentence (3).

THE REFLEXIVE CONSTRUCTIONS

Perhaps one of the most difficult syntactic problems which faces the beginning student of French is the use of the reflexive. This difficulty is due in large part to the numerous syntactic and semantic relationships which require the use of the reflexive. Most text materials treat thoroughly the use of the reflexive with the common verbs dealing with daily activities such as getting up in the morning and personal grooming, and other activities where the person performing the action is identical with the affected person.

Representative of these common verbs is *laver* which has syntactic properties that are similar to the other reflexive verbs generally taught in the first level. In addition to occurring in reflexive construction, these verbs also occur non-reflexively in sentences like:

(15) Jacques lave la voiture.

(16) La merè lave le bébé.

Instrumental adverbial phrases may also occur with verbs like *laver*, as in:

(17) Jacques lave la voiture au savon.

In case terminology, *Jacques* and *la mère* are agents, both *la voiture* and *le bébé* are in the objective case, and *le savon* is an instrument. Verbs like *laver* may also have an instrumental noun phrase as the surface structure subject, as in:

(18) Les grosses vagues de l'orage lavent la côte.

It should be noted, however, that nouns which denote tools and other objects that are typically understood as requiring human manipulation do not usually occur as the surface structure subject with verbs that accept the instrument case as subject. In general, the instrument case may occur as the subject only if its head noun is one which denotes a force of nature or some object which may produce effective action without human manipulation. However, this fact is related to presuppositions of the nature of forces of nature and of tools and not the syntactic properties of the verb. Notice that (19) is rejected by many native speakers due to the presupposition of required human manipulation of *le savon*, while these same native speakers readily accept (20):

(19) *Le savon a lavé la voiture.

(20) Une machine automatique a lavé la voiture.

In addition to noting those cases which may occur with verbs like *laver*, it is necessary to determine the minimum number of cases which must be associated with them. All of the examples above contain both a subject, which may be either an agent or instrument, and a direct object, which is a deep structure objective case. The following sentences are all rejected:

(21) *Henri lave.

(22) *Les grosses vagues lavent.

(23) *La voiture lave.

Therefore, verbs like *laver* are two-place predicated with a lexical entry of the following form:

laver, + [___ (A)(I) O]

The reflexive use of verbs like *laver*, as in:

(24) Jean s'est lavé.

is described in case grammar by the fact that the noun *Jean* occurs in objective case as well as in the agent case. The agent is raised as the subject; the objective, as direct object. Both case markers are deleted and pronominalization rules apply to the second occurrence of Jean to produce the reflexive structure. It is important to note that this generalization blocks the formation of ungrammatical sentences like:

(25) *La voiture s'est lavée.

since this structure would require two objective cases in the deep structure, which is a violation of the restriction that no case may occur twice with a predicate (Fillmore 1968a:22).

Although this analysis of verbs like *laver* offers little, if any, advantage to language teaching, the generalizations presented here are necessary for the description of other reflexive constructions and for the analysis of the uses of *de* and *par* in passive sentences. Thus, while (25) is not a grammatical sentence, there are fully grammatical sentences in French which have identical surface structures, e.g.:

(26) La fenêtre s'est brisée.

Since this type of reflexive construction is one which tends to be rather difficult for students, it is clearly worthy of analysis.

Verbs like *briser* (one sub-class of the change-of-state verbs) occur in sentences like (26) and the following:

(27) La fenêtre est brisée. (stative)

(28) Henri a brisé la fenêtre (avec une branche).

(29) Une branche a brisé la fenêtre.

From these examples, it is possible to characterize the information required in the lexical entries for verbs of this class. First of all, it is clear that verbs like *briser* may occur with an agent, an objective, and an instrument. Second, both the agent and instrument are optional as can be seen in (27); these verbs are, therefore, one-place predicates with the following lexical entry:

briser

casser
, + [___ (A) (I) 0]
fermer

etc.

This information, however, is not sufficient to account for either the description of (26) or for the difficulty that students have with similar sentences. Obviously, sentence (26) cannot be understood as parallel in meaning to (24), nor can it be understood as a substitute for the passive voice, as the following examples show:

(30) On a brisé la fenêtre.

(31) La fenêtre a été brisée.

but not,

(32) *La fenêtre s'est brisée, mais je ne sais pas qui était responsable.

Sentence (30) asserts that there was an agent who caused the action, although the agent is indefinite. Sentence (31) is a close paraphrase of (30); it, too, implies a cause. In short, there is an agent present in the deep structure of both these sentences. Notice, too, that the second clause of (32) may be added to both (30) and (31) with both resulting sentences being fully grammatical.

(33) On a brisé la fenêtre, mais je ne sais pas qui était responsable.

(34) La fenêtre a été brisée, mais je ne sais pas qui était responsable.

It can only be concluded, therefore, that (32) is rejected since the two-clauses are contradictory. The first clause asserts simply that a change of state affected a physical object without a cause, whereas the second clause implies that there was, indeed, a cause. In short, the reflexive use of verbs like *briser* is the translational equivalent of the intransitive use of English change-of-state-verbs. The reflexive pronoun serves as

a dummy direct object to fulfill the surface structure constraint that
change-of-state verbs in French must be transitive.

Perhaps the most obvious pedagogical implication in this generalization
lies in its ability to clarify the semantic interpretation of sentences
of this kind. A clear presentation of the meaning of such sentences (by
whatever method) can avoid having the student conclude that this use of
the reflexive is equivalent to the use of the reflexive with verbs like
laver as well as the more subtle, but incorrect, conclusion that the
reflexive is a substitute for the passive.

However, there is a second, more important facet to this generalization
which is equally significant for both the student and for an adequate
description of French. A grammar which generates deep structures by the
use of phrase structure, rejecting notions of case, must contain at least
two lexical entries for each change-of-state verb to satisfy strict-
subcategorizational requirements. That is, *briser*, etc., would require
an entry for *briser₁*, the transitive, and *briser₂*, the reflexive:

briser$_1$, + [NP ___ NP]

briser$_2$, + [NP se ___ 0]

It is interesting to note that the student of French who has been denied
the generalization given above for change-of-state verbs faces an identical
problem. He must memorize one by one each of the change-of-state verbs
in both its transitive and reflexive form. However, if he is permitted
this generalization, he need only learn one form of each verb and apply
one rule to derive the reflexive form of each verb in this group. Obviously, this results in a fifty per cent reduction of memory load for this
rather large group of verbs.

In addition to the change-of-state verbs, many other common verbs in
French occur in reflexive constructions. However, the use of the reflexive with many of these verbs differs somewhat from the change-of-state
verbs. Notice:

(35) Le théâtre se trouve en face de l'église.

(36) La Seine se jette dans la Manche.

Although I am unable to state a precise generalization for this type of
reflexive, it is clear that, as with the change-of-state verbs, that
these sentences are statements about nouns in the objective case with no
agent or instrument present in the deep structure. That is, they are not
substitutes for the passive, as is seen by:

(37) On a trouvé le théâtre en face de l'église.

(38) Le théâtre a été trouvé en face de l'église.

Clearly, sentence (35) is a statement about the permanent location of *le théâtre*. It does not imply, as do (37) and (38), that it was lost and has just been found. Similar attempts to paraphrase (36) with either (39) or (40) are equally anomalous.

(39) On jette la Seine dans la Manche.

(40) La Seine est jetée dans la Manche.

Reflexives also occur in sentences like:

(41) Ça ne se dit pas ici.

(42) Ça se voit partout au Canada.

(43) L'apéritif se boit debout dans les cafés.

Although these sentences may be paraphrased, at least to some extent, by either the use of *on* in active sentences, or by a passive sentence, they, too, are statements about nouns in the objective case with no agent implied. In addition, both this group (41-43) and the preceding group (35,36) imply action that is, in some sense, continuing or stative. While this kind of vague statement is of little help to the learner in deciding when to use such sentences, he should be aided somewhat in understanding such sentences provided that he already has firm command of the semantics of the change-of-state verbs.

PREPOSITIONS IN PASSIVE SENTENCES

Perhaps the most difficult problem with French passives which presents itself to the student is the choice of the prepositions *de* and *par*. As will be shown below, this choice is significant in that it depends on several factors: the lexical class of the verb, the presence or absence of an agent in the deep structure, and whether the participle is used to express an action or is used adjectivally to describe a state.

The most straight-forward uses of *de* and *par* are found in passive sentences with verbs like *briser*, e.g.:

(44) La fenêtre a été brisée par Henri.

(45) La fenêtre a été brisée par une branche.

(46) La fenêtre a été brisée avec une branche.

(47) La fenêtre a été brisée d'un coup de marteau.

The following sentences are rejected:

(48) *La fenêtre a été brisée d'Henri.

(49) *La fenêtre a été brisée avec Henri.

(50) *La fenêtre a été brisée d'une branche.

(51) *La fenêtre a été brisée par un coup de marteau.

(52) *la fenêtre a été brisée avec un coup de marteau.

From (44), (48), and (49), it is clear that the only possible preposition with the agent is *par*. The instrument, however, may select *de, par, avec*. The preposition *de*, however, may occur only with abstract nouns in the instrument case, as *un coup de quelque chose*. Concrete nouns offer a choice between *par* and *avec*, although with different underlying semantic interpretations. Notice that (46) is a paraphrase of (53) but not of (54):

(53) On a brisé la fenêtre avec une branche.

(54) Une branche a brisé la fenêtre.

whereas (45) is a paraphrase of (54) but not of (53). Thus, it can be concluded that the use of *avec* in (46) implies that there is an unspecified agent in the deep structure and, therefore, that the action was purposeful. On the other hand, sentence (45) implies that there was no agent in the deep structure and asserts only that one physical object caused a change in another physical object without animate manipulation.

Unfortunately, the choice of prepositions with verbs like *blesser* is not as clear cut, since both concrete and abstract instruments may occur with *de*,e.g.:

(55) Paul a blessé Jean avec une flèche.

(56) Paul a blessé Jean d'une flèche.

(57) Jean a été blessé avec une flèche.

(58) Jean a été blessé d'une flèche.

(59) Jean a été blessé par une flèche.

The consensus of my informants regarding these sentences is that *par* and *avec* in sentences (55), (57), and (59) function in the same manner as they do in passives with verbs like *briser*, and that *de*, while occurring in sentences whose deep structure contains an agent, does not carry as strong a notion of purposeful action as does *avec*. This is, however, insufficient evidence to warrant a conclusion, and the question must remain open.

Before continuing with the analysis of *de*, *par*, and *avec* in French passives, it is necessary to point out one additional property of French syntax. That is, there is a systematic ambiguity with the past participle in sentences like:

(60) la porte est fermée.

This sentence can be interpreted in two ways. The first interpretation is stative, with the form *fermée* given verbal force, as in:

(61) James Bond entre dans le salon et, tout à coup,
      la porte est fermée derrière lui.

Clearly, *est fermée* in this sentence is a present passive with full verbal force and not a stative adjective.

Given this fact, it is possible to continue the analysis of the passive voice with verbs like *aimer*, *respecter*, *estimer*, etc. These verbs are different from verbs like *briser*, *fermer*, etc. in several important ways. First, these verbs are two-place predicates and they do not accept the instrument case. Second, the stative interpretation of the past participle is possible in passive sentences with either one or two noun phrases present in the surface structure, whereas the past participle of verbs like *briser* cannot be understood statively with more than one noun present in the surface structure.

In contrast to verbs like *briser* and those like *blesser*, the agent case may take either *de* or *par* in passives with *estimer*, etc. However, there is a marked difference in semantic interpretation which depends on the preposition chosen, e.g.:

(62) Jean est estimé par tout le monde.

(63) Jean est estimé de tout le monde.

Notice the similarity of the above examples with *de* to the following adjectival predicates:

(64) Jean est rouge de colère.

(65) Le plancher est couvert de sable.

(66) Marie est habillée de soie.

Clearly, the use of *de* with the agent in (63) rules out the passive action sense. This sentence must be understood statively with the past participle having adjectival force. Sentence (62), however, is understood

statively with the past participles having adjectival force. Sentence
(62), however, is understood as a passive action and the participle has
verbal force.

The pedagogical implications of this analysis are obvious. If the
student is presented (by whatever method) these generalizations and
given sufficient practice to internalize them, then he will better be
able to understand subtle shades of meaning in both conversation and
reading. In addition, he will be able to produce in spoken or written
form utterances which are correct syntactically and appropriate in
meaning. In addition, it is interesting to note that, as was the case
with reflexives with verbs like *briser*, this analysis provides a simplification of the lexicon. That is, a grammar which relies on phrase structure to produce a level of deep structure where lexical insertion takes
place will require two lexical entries for each verb which can take *de*
or *par* with the agent in the passive voice. Furthermore, the generalization that most, if not all, two-place predicates behave in this fashion
is missed. The situation with the learner is essentially the same. He
must memorize each verb in the language which can take either *de* or *par*
with the agent in passive sentences, which doubles the load on his
memory.

CASE IN THE CLASSROOM

While the generalizations which were developed above have significant
theoretical implications for second language teaching, a practical treatment for use in the classroom must be shown if these implications are to
be taken seriously. Clearly, one of the obstacles which must be overcome
is that of terminology, which is of doubtful value in classrooms which
emphasize practice rather than involved analysis and discussion of grammar. This, however, is not a difficult task since the concepts involved
are so basic; it is easy to find synonyms in common usage with adolescents
for the necessary terms.

Another problem which must be solved if generalizations of this kind
are to be made suitable for the classroom is the manner of presentation.
Since it is not the purpose of this paper to suggest changes in methodology, the proposed manner of presentation which follows is one variation
on the audiolingual approach. Therefore, let us imagine the following
situation:

A small boy is playing *boules* in the living room. He makes a bad
toss and the mirror breaks with a loud crack. The boy's mother
rushes into the living room and inquires about the preceding events.

Note that the meaning of the French sentences can be cued by the use of
appropriate visuals or by the use of English paraphrase.

La mère: Jacques! Qu'est-ce que tu fais?

Jacques: Pas grand-chose, Maman.

La mère: Et regarde le miroir! Qu'est-ce qui se passe ici?

Jacques: Le miroir s'est cassé.

La mère: C'est évident! - et la boule?

Jacques: Oui, la boule a cassé le miroir, Maman.

La mère: Et toi, tu n'as rien fait?

Jacques: Si, j'ai cassé le miroir avec la boule.

La mère: Jacques, tu sais bien ce que je t'ai dit!
          Ne joue pas aux boules dans le salon.

After the dialogue has been practiced and the structures well drilled,
the students may be led to a statement of the generalization by a technique of leading questions. Such a generalization might take the following form:

Teacher: What did Jacques say to his mother when she pointed
          out the broken mirror?

Volunteer: Le miroir s'est cassé.

Teacher: Did he tell her how it happened?

Volunteer$_2$: No.

Teacher: O.K., he just told her what happened to the mirror.
          Well, what did he say when she pointed out *la boule?*

Volunteer$_3$: La boule a cassé le miroir.

Teacher: Did he tell her who threw it?

Volunteer$_4$: No, he just said: La boule a cassé le miroir.

Teacher: What did he say when she said: Et toi, tu n'as rien fait?

Volunteer$_5$: He finally admitted throwing it.

Teacher: When he said: Le miroir s'est cassé.
          What form of the verb did he use? [Note that students
          would already have seen reflexives with verbs like *laver*]

Volunteer$_6$: The reflexive.

Teacher: O.K., did he tell anything about who or what was responsible?

Volunteer: No.

Teacher: Either asks class to summarize the generalization, or states it himself.

Although the generalizations concerning the use of *de*, *par*, and *avec* in French passives are more involved than this one, the same techniques-- as well as a variety of other techniques--can be easily applied. With the passive, however, each of the subgeneralizations on various classes of verbs would need to be done separately to allow students time to practice and internalize each one. In short, complex grammatical theory does not have to be taught in the classroom, only the generalizations that the theory makes possible need to be taught.

NOTE

*Notice that the structural diagrams in this paper are somewhat oversimplified.

MARK G. GOLDIN
INDIANA UNIVERSITY

INDIRECT OBJECTS IN SPANISH AND ENGLISH

What has linguistics to do with teaching foreign languages? The answers which I would like to suggest come from the point of view of the teacher's preparation. It is common to talk about what a teacher does in terms of *subject matter* and *pedagogy*. Under subject matter are included such things are the teacher's own competence in the foreign language, his knowledge about the phenomenon of language, his knowledge of the foreign culture, and other things. Since someone who teaches foreign language as a skill never needs to teach linguistics, his knowledge of linguistics as subject matter is useful to him only in the way that calculus as subject matter is useful to a junior high school mathematics teacher. He studies it not because he will ever have to explain it to his students, but in order to gain a global idea of how the search for knowledge proceeds in his chosen field, and of the kind of questions with which the field deals. While there are no doubt many arguments in favor of the language teacher's learning linguistics for this reason, I am not going to advance any of them here.

The area of pedagogy I would divide into two parts, *planning* and *execution*. By execution I mean what the teacher actually does inside the classroom. I do not know of any important way in which generative grammar can help the teacher in this regard, unless one considers that the concept of "transformation" is used to construct drills changing one sentence into another. However, language teachers did not need to know linguistics to devise such drills, since they used transformations in that sense long before linguists did.

If there is to be any question of whether generative grammar is helpful to language teachers, it must be raised in the area of *planning*. By planning, I refer to the very general, wide-ranging questions a teacher asks himself about how he should deal with his subject matter. This is the area in which a teacher connects what he knows about his subject matter with what he does in the classroom. For example, a teacher has to decide whether to have his students learn language forms deductively, by first hearing an explanation and then solving problems; or inductively, by first observing samples of language and thereby discovering the principles that underlie the samples. Transformational grammar, with its emphasis on the

centrality of the notion of "rule", probably suggests the former course
(see Campbell 1970 for an elaboration).

The decisions that a teacher makes in the area of planning affect
mostly everything that he does. What I want to do here is to propose
a question that a teacher needs to ask in course planning; namely, *what
sorts of knowledge must be acquired by the students*. To show how generative grammar as a particular approach to language can help a teacher
answer this question, I will outline a problem in Spanish, and discuss
the implications of the information contained in the description.

Spanish indirect object constructions can be recognized by the presence
of one of the so-called indirect object pronouns, including *le* (sing.)
and *les* (pl.). Since the construction is in part a reflex of the Latin
dative, it has also been called the dative in Spanish. However, since
it is not quite like the Latin dative or the English indirect object,
American grammarians have used the additional names *adverb of interest*
(Stockwell, Bowen, and Martin 1965) and *involved entity* (Bull 1965). I
use the name *indirect object* because I want to contrast this construction
with the similarly-named one in English.

The English indirect object construction is characterized by two noun
phrases directly following the verb. Unlike the Spanish indirect object
construction, no pronoun is required, but the two postverbal nouns are
required.

Recognition of Spanish indirect object structures is sometimes confusing
because the first and second person forms *me, te, nos, os* are identical
to direct object pronouns whose syntactic behavior is somewhat different.
For this reason all of my examples are third person forms. Furthermore,
there is some important dialect variation in the use of the third person
forms *le* and *les*. All varieties of Spanish use *le* and *les* for indirect
objects regardless of grammatical gender. Many dialects, including the
most prestigious one in Spain, also use *le* and *les* for direct objects which
are semantically male. In order to avoid any confusion, and in order that
my examples may be uniquely applicable to indirect objects for all Spanish
speakers, I present them so that the referent of the indirect object pronoun is always both grammatically and semantically feminine; namely, a
woman.

The following Spanish sentences contain indirect objects:

(1)   Ricardo le hizo una cena a Juana
       'Dick made Jane a dinner'

(2)   Ricardo le dio un regalo a Juana
       'Dick gave Jane a gift'

(3)   Ricardo le robó un conejo a Juana
       'Dick stole a rabbit from Jane'

(4)   Ricardo le vio la braga a Juana
       'Dick saw Jane's underpants'

(5)   Ricardo le gusta a Juana
      'Dick appeals to Jane', or 'Jane likes Dick'

The situations that these sentences describe can be stated following
McCawley (1968, 1970), Fillmore (1968b,1970), and Langendoen (1970), as
logical propositions containing a predicate and various arguments.
Predicates are nouns, verbs, or adjectives; arguments may be either a
noun or another proposition.

Situation A (sentence 1)
made (dinner, Dick, Jane)

Situation B (sentence 2)
gave (gift, Dick, Jane)

Situation C (sentence 3)
stole (rabbit, Dick, Jane)

Situation D (sentence 4)
saw (underpants, Dick, [underpants (Jane)]])

Situation E (sentence 5)
appeal (Dick, Jane)

The English schematic representations are intended to correspond to both
the English and Spanish sentences. The order in which the arguments are
listed is entirely arbitrary.
    Some of the sentences (1)-(5) have paraphrases representing what I will
call the *prepositional phrase* pattern. Prepositional phrase sentences
contain no indirect object pronoun; the noun corresponding to the indirect
pronoun appears as the object of a preposition. This is also a common
pattern in English, as is seen from the translations of (3) and (5).
    Situation A produces a prepositional phrase sentence with the prep-
osition *para* 'for'.

(6)   Ricardo hizo una cena para Juana
      'Dick made a dinner for Jane'

Many dialects of Spanish allow prepositional phrase sentences, as well
as indirect object sentences, for situations B and C.[1] English allows
both patterns only for situation B, requiring a prepositional phrase for C.

(7)   Ricardo dio un regalo a Juana
      'Dick gave a gift to Jane' (compare (2))

(8)   Ricardo robó un conejo a Juana
      same translation as (3)

There is a prepositional phrase sentence which can correspond to situation D. However, it covers a wider range of semantic possibilities than does sentence (4).

(9)   Ricardo vio la braga de Juana
      same translation as (4)

Specifically, sentence (4) implies that the garment under consideration was on Jane when Dick saw it; (9) does not imply this.
There is no possible prepositional phrase sentence in Spanish for situation E.
Taking both Spanish and English into account, then, the five situations demonstrate five combinations of the two syntactic patterns. Situation A yields indirect object and prepositional phrase sentences in both languages. Situation B yields both patterns in English, the indirect object pattern in all Spanish dialects and the prepositional phrase pattern in some dialects. Situation C has the same realizations in Spanish as B, but produces only prepositional phrase sentences in English. Situation D corresponds to indirect object sentences, and in part to prepositional phrase sentences, in Spanish; and to possessive phrases in English. Situation E results in indirect object sentences in Spanish and a variety of constructions in English, often prepositional phrase sentences.
The possible sentence types corresponding to a given situation are determined by a combination of lexical and semantic factors. The semantic information necessary is most importantly the nature of the *role* played by the indirect object argument in the situation. Looking first at situation B, the indirect object argument is the physical *receiver* of one of the other arguments. Compare the following examples of situation B.

(10)   le mandó una carta   'he sent her a letter'

(11)   le trajo una copa   'he brought her a drink'

(12)   le pegó una paliza   'he dealt her a blow'

(13)   le ofreció un trabajo   'he offered her a job'

In situation C, the indirect object argument is the physical *loser* of one of the other arguments.

(14)   le quitó el empleo   'he deprived her of work'

(15)   le sacó una muela   'he pulled a tooth from her'

(16)   le pidió un dólar   'he asked her for a dollar'

(17)   le soltó su pájaro   'he let loose her bird on her'

Skipping to situation E, we see that the indirect object argument has a *psychological* relationship to another argument.

(18) le fue agradable el concierto 'the concert was pleasing to her'

(19) le entusiasmó la corrida 'she got enthused about the bullfight'

(20) le interesó mi opinión 'my opinion was of interest to her'

(21) le pareció bien la canción 'the song seemed good to her'

It will be noted that situations B and C are separated on the basis of their syntactic results in English. Both situations produce the same sentence patterns in Spanish. Furthermore, the situational role involved in E has been rather unclearly stated. Actually, the syntactic patterns corresponding to situations B, C, and E are apparently determined as much by lexical properties of the main predicate as by elements of situational role. The categories receiver, loser, and psychological role all make up what Fillmore (1970:116) has called *experiencer*, which he defines as "the entity which receives or accepts or experiences or undergoes the effect of an action". (States should be included as well as actions; cf. (18)-(21).) The names receiver, loser, and psychological role are language-particular categories corresponding to combinations of syntactic patterns determined by individual lexical items.

Situations A and D, on the other hand, do not involve lexical determination. The indirect object argument in situation A can be called *benefactor;* it represents the person for whose benefit, or at whose instigation, the action of the main predicate is performed by someone else. Benefactor indirect objects are limited to action predicates.

(22) le repararon el coche 'they fixed the car for her'

(23) le plantó unos pinos 'he planted some pine trees for her'

(24) le podaron el árbol 'they pruned the tree for her'

(25) le cerró la carta 'he sealed the letter for her'

Situation D involves possession. Due to the special interpretation of indirect object possession sentences, they are best described as involving *inalienable possession;* that is, cases in which the object possessed is uniquely indentified with its owner (compare sentences (4) and (9)). Davis (1969) points out that the vast majority of these possession situations involve clothing or body parts, although other forms of possession are found.

(26) un escalofrío le sacudió el cuerpo 'a chill shook her body'

(27) le secó las lágrimas 'he dried her tears'

(28) le cubrió la cabeza 'he covered her head'

(29) le apuntaron el número de Seguro Social
      'they took down her Social Security number'

Considering that the situational roles of experiencer, benefactor, and inalienable possessor can produce indirect objects in Spanish, it is interesting to observe what happens when more than one of these roles is present in a situation. There is evidently a hierarchical relationship between experiencer[2] and benefactor, since if both are present an indirect object can correspond only to the experiencer.

(30) Ricardo le compró flores a Juana

In this sentence, Jane can be interpreted either as experiencer-loser (Dick bought flowers from Jane), or as benefactor (Dick bought flowers for Jane). If Dick bought flowers from Jane for Alice, then the experiencer-loser, Jane, is the only argument that could correspond to an indirect object pronoun. The benefactor, Alice, can be realized only as a prepositional phrase.[3]

(31) Ricardo le compró flores a Juana para Alicia
      'Dick bought flowers from Jane for Alice'

If an inalienable possession is involved in the same situation as an experiencer or benefactor, there is a possibility for two indirect objects to occur in a single sentence.

(32) Me le robaron una muñeca a mi hija
      'They stole a doll from my daughter'

This corresponds to the following propositional structure:

stole (doll, they, daughter, [daughter (me)])

in which the argument *daughter* fills the experiencer role and the argument *me* is the inalienable possessor of the predicate *daughter*, and both correspond to indirect object pronouns. The fact that double indirect objects occur when possession is involved along with one or the other of the indirect object roles, but that double objects do not occur unless possession is involved, seems to be evidence for the analysis of possession as a separate proposition.

What has all this to say to the teacher of Spanish to English-speaking students? A contrastive analysis of the sort that language teachers have been doing since they began to ask what linguistics has to offer them would reveal essentially the distributional information summarized above. This is certainly important, and it may imply something about the relative difficulty for English speakers of the various Spanish indirect object patterns. Practical experience would confirm or deny this. But it seems to me that the contrastive data are not the most valuable contribution of generative grammar for the language teacher.

A rather large amount of conceptual information has been set forth regarding the structure of situations and the participants in them. To complete the inventory of what a speaker must learn in order to correctly produce Spanish indirect object sentences, there are two principles of a somewhat different sort. These require no semantic or situational information, and apply to all indirect object sentences.

(R1) An indirect object pronoun is obligatory in indirect object sentences, whether or not the referent noun is stated in the sentence.

(R2) If the indirect object noun is stated, it must be preceded by the preposition a.[4]

These two rules I call *ground rules*. They are arbitrary conventions regarding sentence formation in Spanish, and use of them requires no knowledge of how situations are structured into sentences in Spanish.

The most important contribution that generative grammar can make to teaching is that it separates the ground rules from the *conceptual rules*. A language student, in order to dominate Spanish indirect objects, needs to be able to manipulate both the conceptual and grammatical principles. However, the kind of understanding required of the student is quite different for the two kinds of principles. Conceptual rules call for understanding and analysis of a philosophical nature: examining situations and determining the roles of participants. Ground rules require only the ability to mechanically manipulate syntactic constituents. They call for no analysis of an intellectual variety.

If the teacher is able to separate the conceptual from the mechanical tasks, he can plan to use appropriate techniques for teaching both. The conceptual principles can be explained and practiced by intellectual exercises such as translation, partial translation, or even analysis of situations in English to determine which noun corresponds to a Spanish indirect object. All of these activities require the student to make the same kind of decision that a Spanish speaker intuitively makes when he selects the indirect object sentence pattern.

On the other hand, no amount of sophisticated explanation or analysis can help teach a student to manipulate the ground rules. These are probably the type of linguistic phenomena that can be mastered by systematic or unsystematic exposure to them, including mechanical or repetitive drills.

All of this is brought out to suggest an area of language pedagogy in which generative grammar can help the teacher answer important questions

of course planning. The recognition by the teacher of two types of knowledge involved in language use can help him determine the appropriate
approach to teaching each.

NOTES

1. I have no definite information on which dialects allow the
prepositional phrase sentences. Peninsular Spanish speakers tend
to use them, while Mexican and Caribbean speakers do not.

2. The fact that receiver, loser, and psychological roles never
cooccur in a single proposition is further evidence that they represent
a single underlying role category.

3. Some dialects may allow two indirect objects in certain cases
where the benefactor and experiencer roles are present. Some speakers
can be convinced to accept *¿Se le dices eso?* 'Will you tell him that
for her?', but I have not observed such a sentence spontaneously produced.

4. R2 is actually a special case of a more general rule concerning
direct and indirect objects.

ALBERT VALDMAN
INDIANA UNIVERSITY

ON THE APPLICABILITY OF GENERATIVE PHONOLOGY TO PROBLEMS OF FOREIGN LANGUAGE LEARNING

Applied linguistics is concerned primarily with the preparation of pedagogical grammars. These present facts and important generalizations about the structure of the target language in a form accessible to the foreign language material developers and teachers. Because linguistic theories are concerned with linguistic competence rather than performance, it would be a mistake to look to them for precise guidance in the elaboration of pedagogical strategies in the teaching of the language arts or of foreign languages (Lamendella 1969). As has been amply demonstrated, too literal an application of any linguistic theory can only interfere with learning (Newmark 1966). Though it does not bear directly on "how" a language should be taught (or learned), applied linguistics can contribute significantly in determining "what" is taught and is particularly relevant in the selection and the ordering of the subject matter.

The contribution of structural linguistics to the selection and ordering of phonological data--I use the term to include morphophonemics--has been considerable in the case of the teaching of a language such as French where erroneous attitudes toward language and its representation by the conventional orthography interfered with the description of the language as a set of verbal symbols and with the extraction of important generalizations. What can generative phonology do that has not already been done by structural phonetics, phonemics, and morphophonemics?

The generative view of phonological structure differs from the structural view in three principal respects. First, it claims that significant generalizations about phonological structure can only be made in terms of a set of universal distinctive features rather than phonemes. Second, every lexical item is given a single representation in terms of a sequence of distinctive feature matrices mapped onto phonetic realizations by a set of general rules whereas in a structural description lexical items with variable phonetic realization are represented by several phonemic strings or given a single representation by the use of ad hoc morpho phonemes. Third, a strong form of the generative

view claims that the abstract underlying forms and the distinctive
features of which it is constituted have a psychological reality and
correspond to cognitive structures. Pedagogically oriented structural
descriptions of spoken French have on the whole incorporated the deep-
seated generalizations highlighted in a generative phonology, and it is
doubtful that the latter could uncover much about the functioning of
the French phonological system that would be relevant to the teaching
of listening comprehension and speaking. But the primary objectives in
the teaching of a second language are seldom listening comprehension and speaking proficiency exclusively. Even programs that
emphasize these objectives do not deprive the learner of access to the
conventional orthography for any significant length of time, so that
materials developers and teachers are confronted at every step with the
task of relating the conventional orthography to speech sounds. The
conventional French orthography, like the abstract underlying representations of lexical items posited by generative phonologists, is only
indirectly related to speech sounds or an intermediate phonemic level,
and thus generative phonologists are eminently qualified to describe the
relationship between the conventional orthography and speech sounds on
the one hand, and between it and lexical items on the other. In this
paper I will attempt to show, first how a generative view of the conventional French orthography contributes to the teaching of the reading and
writing of French as a second language and, second, how that view needs
to be significantly qualified within the context of the teaching of
these skills to native speakers of the language.

THE CONVENTIONAL FRENCH ORTHOGRAPHY AS AN UNDERLYING REPRESENTATION

Structural linguists, by and large, continued in the footsteps of
late nineteenth century phoneticians who viewed writing as a representa-
tional system secondarily derived from speech and proposed as the ideal
writing system a type of biunique phonemic representation. From this
standpoint, the conventional orthographies of English and French could
only strike them as inconsistent, inefficient and replete with extraneous
graphic features, fossils from previous stages of the language, and it
was not surprising that these linguists joined the movement for total
spelling reform. Their treatment of spelling within the context of
audio-lingual-oriented foreign language instruction shed little light
on the linguistic problems involved and was of little utility to
foreign language material developers and teachers. Typically, discussions of spelling problems in structurally oriented applied linguistics
handbooks took the form of phoneme to grapheme correspondences of a very
primitive type. For instance, Politzer (1965:85-7) states that French
[f] is represented by *f* (*faim*), *ff* (*siffler*), and *ph* (*téléphone*) and
that [e] is represented by *ez* (*parlez*) and *er* (*parler*) as well as by
e (*essai*), *é* (*parlé*), *ai* (*parlai*) and *ei* (*neiger*). Such rules, on the
one hand, fail to indicate that there are autonomous principles that

underlie graphic structure; for instance, that *ff* does not occur word-initially or finally, that *ph* does not occur word-finally; on the other hand, since these rules are implicitly bidirectional, they fail to account for the fact that whereas a graph such as *é* corresponds uniquely (by and large) to /e/[1], *er* and *ez* correspond each to two phonemic representations:

(1)   Voulez-vous danser [dãse]?
but

(2)   Voulez-vous danser [dãse] ∿ [dãser] avec moi?
and

(3)   Vous voulez [vule] ce crayon?
but

(4)   Vous voulez [vule] ∿ [vulez] un crayon?

If the conventional French spelling is viewed as an abstract, underlying form mapped onto phonetic realizations by a set of general principles available to speakers of the language, the final consonant letter of *danser* and *voulez* or of *petit*, *grand*, and *gros* cannot be considered useless silent letters, for they stand for zero or some consonant realization depending on the phonological and syntactic environment. Similarly, the *e* of *petit* and *faible* is to be converted to zero or a vowel in the range [φ ↔ oe]. This interpretation of the final consonant letters and so-called mute e of the conventional French spelling as latent segments goes back several centuries, but it is the merit of the generative view to have underscored the abstractness of these graphic features. Not only do orthographic representations subsume the phonetic variants of individual morphemes but they note features which may not occur overtly in the base form of morphemes but which appear in inflectionally and derivationally related forms. For example, the final consonant of *froid* does not represent a latent consonant proper since in the isolated form it does not correspond to a consonant articulation, but it is realized as a [d] when it occurs in derivatives such as *froideur* and inflected forms such as *froide*. In this way the spelling *froid* differentiates that form from its homophones *foi* 'faith,' *fois* 'times,' and *foie* 'liver' whose phonetic reflexes do not share its total range of phonetic realizations.

The interpretation of latent consonants and mute e as abstract symbols that trigger the obligatory application of liaison and elision rules provides a lucid explanation for the pronunciation and distribution of adjective and verb forms (Valdman 1963, 1970a). Compare the spelling and underlying representations of the four distinct morphophonemic forms of the adjective *petit* given on the left of Table I to their pronunciation given on the right. The latent *t* of the base is

Table I

Distribution of Underlying Representation
and
Spoken Forms of the Adjective *petit*

Spelling			Pronunciation		
Sg	Pl		Sg		Pl
			V	C	V
petit	*petits*	Masc		[pti]	[ptiz]
petit	petit-z		[ptit]		
petite	*petites*	Fem			[ptitz]
petit-e	petit-e-z				

realized as [t] when it is "protected" by the mute *e* of the feminine inflection and when it occurs immediately preceding a vowel in the masculine singular as in *un petit oiseau*. It is not realized in the masculine plural since in all environments it is followed by latent *s* of the
plural inflection (*les petits oiseaux*, *les petits chats*) nor of course
in the singular when it occurs before a consonant (*un petit chat*). The
latent *s* of the plural inflection is only realized when it occurs before
a vowel in both the masculine and the feminine form: *les petites
hirondelles*, *les petits oiseaux*.

In addition to liaison rules which also account for the phonetic
realizations of underlying consonants in all paradigmatically related
forms, generative phonologists have posited for French a set of rules
of wide generality which change the features of vowels immediately
preceding so-called liaison consonants (*Mid Vowel Adjustment*, *Vowel
Nasalization*, etc. Schane, 1968a). The conventional spelling captures
these generalizations by providing a single representation for vowel
alternations to which these rules apply.

(5)   sain   [sɛ̃]   sain-e   [sɛn]
      bain   [bɛ̃]   baign-e   [bɛñ]

(6)   fin   [fɛ̃]   fin-e   [fin]
      vin   [vɛ̃]   vign-e   [viñ]

The alternations between nasal and oral vowels in (5) and (6) are predictable from the morphophonemic environment by *Vowel Nasalization* and
are subsumed by the use of a single graphic representation. Although
they contain the same overt vowel, the morphologically simple forms of
(6) differ from the corresponding forms of (5) in that in addition to
Vowel Nasalization some other general principle applies that relates
[ɛ̃] and [i], and consequently a different underlying vowel must be
postulated. On the other hand, the conventional spelling differentiates
homophones that show contrastive vocalism in derived or inflected forms
and for which different underlying vowels would need to be posited. For
instance, the graph *o* represents an underlying vowel with three phonetic
outputs [o ɔ ö][2] whereas the graph *au* represents an underlying vowel
with a single phonetic output:

(6') sot   [so]   saut   [so]
      sotte   [sɔt]   saute   [sot]
      sottise [sötiz]   sauter   [sote]

THE GENERATIVE VIEW OF THE CONVENTIONAL ORTHOGRAPHY AND THE TEACHING OF READING AND SPELLING

I will attempt to show below that, at least in regard to French,
claims that conventional orthographies "correspond fairly closely to a
linguistically significant level of representation" and that abstract
lexical representations such as those posited by generative phonologists provide "a natural orthography for a person who knows a language" (Chomsky 1970a:281-3) are somewhat overstated; nonetheless, since
persons engaged in various phases of language teaching have no choice
but to accept existing conventional orthographies, an interpretation of
French spelling as some sort of abstract morphophonemic representation
is more applicable to various aspects of teaching reading and spelling
than that adopted by most structural linguists.
Within the context of foreign language teaching, "reading" subsumes
two types of skills: the ability to assign the correct meaning to
written sentences and the ability to assign the correct phonological
interpretation to their constituent morphemes. Though it is seldom
stated explicitly, the primary objective of the teaching of French in an
academic setting in this country is the comprehension of written sentences. In what way would a correct view of French spelling contribute
to the teaching of reading comprehension? Graphic representations of
linguistic forms are more redundant than phonemic representations in
that they provide information not present in spoken utterances, such as
liaison consonants which enables the reader to relate individual
morphemes to other members of their paradigm and thus facilitates
identification. Consider the case of a reader who has only learned the
feminine form of the adjective *sot* (*sotte*[sɔt]) and who is presented with
the written sentence *Ce garçon est vraiment incroyable: quel sot!* Assume

further that he is unable to deduce the meaning from the syntactic structure and the context. On the basis of the phonemic representation /so/
he could not eliminate from consideration the homophones *seau* 'bucket'
and *saut* 'jump', but the representation of the liaison consonant "t" by
the graphic form would serve to disambiguate the sentence. It would
appear that some sort of training in relating forms consisting of the
simple form of a morpheme to paradigmatically related forms on the basis
of graphic information would facilitate the acquisition of the most
highly valued skill in language instruction.

"Reading aloud" is probably the most widely used form of pronunciation
practice. While it hardly will contribute to the acquisition of good
accent on the part of the learner, it will teach him the correct phonological representation of lexical items, a far more important aspect of
audio-lingual proficiency than the acquisition of near-native control of
sub-phonemic and suprasegmental features. Unless the learner is trained
to view certain graphic features as abstract representations which can be
mapped onto phonetic realizations only by the application of certain con-
version rules, he will need to memorize lists which match the graphic and
the phonological representations of whole morphemes, a strategy that
precludes the learner's assigning the correct phonological representation
to morphemes he has never seen before. A list of grapheme to phoneme
correspondences would be inadequate since the learner would be able to
provide only part of the phonological representation of words. For example,
in *un grand immeuble* only knowledge of the fact that *d* represents an underlying consonant realized as [t] in that phonological and syntactic environment would enable the reader to provide the correct representation [grãt]
rather than [grã] or [grãd] although the first three segments are adequately specified by grapheme to phoneme correspondences. This is not to
rule out completely the use of the latter type of rules in teaching students
to convert letters to sounds; indeed, an analysis of French spelling would
consist of the formulation of a small set of rules, analogous to the
liaison and elision rules of a generative phonology of French, operating
on graphic features viewed as abstract entities and a large set of grapheme
to phoneme correspondences.

In the teaching of spelling, pedagogical strategies whose input are
phoneme to grapheme correspondences are not likely to be particularly efficient. Consider the problem of spelling the sentence *Ils sont sots*,
pronounced normally: [isõso], and assume that the learner knows the
meaning of the constituent morphemes and can assign the correct deep-level
syntactic interpretation. Unless he can relate the phonetic realization
of the pronoun ([il]) to other realizations of the constituent morphemes: [il]
in *il a* and [iz] in *ils ont*, he cannot provide the *l* and *s* short of memorizing
the spelling of the individual morphemes. Similarly, providing the final *t*
of *sont* requires comparison of the form in question with that which occurs
optionally in *Ils sont en face,* for instance. The final *s* of the adjective
sots is most efficiently specified by considering it the representation
of the plural morpheme since it must be inferred from the syntactic structure and meaning rather than the auditory signals. Finally, the *t* and *o*

of *sot* are provided by relating that form to its derivatives of the
feminine form. To spell *saut* in the sentence *Quel saut!* correctly the
foreign learner needs to relate it to the derived verb *sauter* which
contains the overt [t] and the tense vowel [o] indicating that the vowel
graph must be either *au* or *ô* but not *o* or *eau* (compare *seau*).

THE CONVENTIONAL ORTHOGRAPHY AS THE MOST SUITABLE REPRESENTATION FOR FRENCH

The applied linguist who works exclusively within the context of the
teaching of French as a second language has no choice but to accept the
conventional spelling as a fairly coherent system. His task consists in
making accessible to material developers and teachers a correct characterization of it and to state its relationship to the various levels of
linguistic structure. But we are witnessing currently in France a
rapprochement between the teaching of French as a second language and the
teaching of and about that language to its speakers. Also problems in
the teaching of reading and spelling in the schools of France and other
francophone countries are the subject of lively controversy. Applied
French linguists concerned with problems of phonological representation
can hardly ignore the lively controversies in these areas, particularly
since the issues under debate turn on the proper characterization of the
conventional orthography and its suitability as an efficient means of
graphic representation for the majority of its speakers.
I now return to the consideration of two claims about the relationship
between lexical representation and conventional orthographies put forward
by generative phonologists. In his remarks in the meeting on Project
Literacy Chomsky (1970a) states:

1. "there is no reason to expect any significant set of phoneme-
    grapheme correspondences since it seems that phonemes are
    artificial units, having no linguistic status, whereas the
    'graphemes' of the conventional orthography do correspond
    fairly closely to a linguistically significant level of
    representation."

2. "... a lexical representation provides a natural orthography
    for a person who knows the language. It provides just the
    information about words that is not predictable by phonological
    rule or by syntactic rules that determine the phrasing of a
    sentence...conventional orthography, in English, as in every
    case of which I have knowledge, is remarkably close to optimal,
    in this sense."

Turning first to the second claim, it is easy to read into the characterization of a lexical representation, i.e. an abstract underlying form,
as the "natural orthography" for native speakers the additional claim
that systematic phonemes have a psychological reality and are directly

involved in the acquisition, storage, and use of language. The discussion
of such a claim is outside of the domain of applied linguistics, and I
will address myself to the statement that conventional orthographies are
optimal in the sense that they provide information about words that is
not predictable by phonological or syntactic rule.

My first counterexample to the claim that conventional orthographies
do not indicate phonetic distinctions predictable by phonological and
syntactic rule is from French. In that language the high back vowel [u]
and the corresponding glide [w] contrast only before [a]; elsewhere they
are either in free variation or predictable from the phonological context.

(7) loi   [lwa]   'law'   lou-a [lua] ∿ [lwa]
                                              '(he) rented'
     trois   [trwa]   'three'   trou-a [trua] ∿ [trwa
                                              '(he) punctured'

(8) louer   [lue] ∿ [lwe]   'to rent'
     fouet   [fuɛ] ∿ [fwɛ]   'whip'

(9) oui   [wi]   'yes'
     louis   [lwi]   'a type of coin'
     ouate   [wat]   'wadding'

In (7) the digraph *ou* corresponds to free variation between the vowel and
the glide whereas the digraph *oi* corresponds to the obligatory pronunciation of the glide. In (8), where *ou* occurs before graphs representing
vowels other than /a/ or /i/, it also corresponds to free variation between
the vowel and the glide but there is no possibility of contrast with a
form realized only with the glide   followed by a vowel other than /a/
or /i/. Finally in (9) *ou* occurring at the beginning of a word or before
the vowel /i/ corresponds to the obligatory pronunciation of the glide.
In its use of *ou* in (8) and (9) the conventional orthography provides an
optimal lexical representation, for the phonetic features it subsumes are
either predictable or in free variation. But in (7) the forms containing
the digraph *ou* differ from those containing the digraph *oi* by the presence
of a morphemic boundary. The forms containing the digraph *oi* could be
rewritten *oua* and the pronunciation predicted in terms of morphological
structure:

(10) loua [lwa] 'law'vs.lou-a [lua]   [lwa] '(he) rented'

Ou followed by *a* is pronounced [w] if no morphological boundary intervenes
but as either [u] or [w] if a morphological boundary intervenes.

By providing two contrastive graphs where phonetic output is predictable
from the morphplogicalcontext the conventional orthography fails to meet
the condition for optimality stated by Chomsky.

Chomsky admits that not all speakers might perceive speech exclusively
in terms of abstract underlying phonological units and provides an example

of the notation of a subphonemic distinction on the part of a child:
When she was five years old one of his daughters insisted that the
aspirated and unaspirated /k/'s of *cocoa* be written with different
symbols. I should like to offer evidence that even for linguistically
mature speakers an abstract underlying phonological representation might
not constitute the most natural or optimal spelling.

Haitian Creole, a language 90% of whose vocabulary is derived from
Northern French dialects closely related to Standard French, has only
recently been provided with a systematic orthography. Before, it had
been written down in a highly variable etymologizing notation based on
French since French, spoken by the bilingual elite, is the official
language of Haiti.

(11a) z'herbe sèche la [zɛbsɛšla] *cette herbe sèche*
'grass dry that'

(12a) pied cocoyé ha [pjekokojea] *ce cocotier*
'tree coconut tree that'

(13a) jodi ya [žodija] *aujourd'hui*
'today'

(14a) l'argent han [lažãã] *l'argent*
'money the'

(15a) morne nan [mɔnnã] *le morne*
'hill the'

The first systematic orthography for Haitian Creole, the McConnell-Laubach
system, was a phonemically based orthography that departed considerably
from French spelling conventions.

(11b) zèb sèch-la

(12b) pyé kokoyé-a

(13b) jodi-a

(14b) lajã̂-ã̂

(15b) mòn-nã̂

Needless to say, this orthography aroused the ire of the elite, literate
in French, and today a modified system adopting many of the phoneme-
grapheme correspondences of the French conventional orthography is used
by all groups that prepare Creole material; and that orthography, called
the ONAAC orthography, can today be considered the conventional orthography for Haitian Creole.[3]

(11c) zèb sèch la

(12c) pié kokoyé a

(13c) jodi a

(14c) lajan an

(15c) mòn nan

In Haitian Creole the definite determiner occurs postposed to the determined noun or NP and shows phonological variation determined by the last segment of the preceding morpheme and statable in terms of consonant deletion and nasalization rules of fairly extensive generality. It would be expected that native speakers of the language who devised the representations (a) and (c) above would not indicate the predictable nasalization of the vowel in (14) and (15) and that they might represent the determiner of (15) with l instead of n particularly since in that context there is wide variation between the realizations [lã] and [nã]. In a formal generative treatment one could justify an underlying representation of the definite determiner as la and account for all phonetic realizations by a set of general rules. One would expect that if native speakers tend to write down their language on the basis of their intuitive awareness of its general phonological principles, graphic distinction would be made by native scribes at most between post-vocalic and post-consonantal variants of the Haitian Creole determiner.

(11d) zèb sèch la

(12d) pié kokoyé a

(13d) jodi a

(14d) lajan a

(15d) mòn la

It is particularly noteworthy that the linguistically naive scribe who devised notation (a) noted the intervocalic glide [j] which occurs obligatorily in sequences involving any high front or mid vowel.

(16a) [krejɔl] 'Creole'   McConnell-Laubach Kréòl

(17a) [ajit'i] 'Haiti'   Aiti

(18a) [blije]   'to forget'   blié

In fact the representation of this predictable intervocalic glide is one
of the few moot points in the use of the ONAAC orthography. While the
phonemically based McConnell-Laubach orthography does not represent it
and assumes implicitly that native readers will insert it automatically,
current texts insist that it be noted explicity.

(16c) kréyòl

(17c) ayiti

(18c) bliyé

The glide [j] must be given phonemic status in Haitian Creole and postulated at the underlying level since there are contrasts involving its
presence or absence.

(19) [fɛ]   'to do'   [fɛj]   'leaf'
     [kaja] 'a type of vegetable' [kaa]   'that case'

In teaching monolingual speakers of Haitian Creole to spell it is necessary
to teach them to represent [j] in items where it could not be recovered
by phonological rules.

(20) [fɛj]   'leaf'   [fuje]   'to dig'

Once they are taught to note it in such words, it is pedagogically
uneconomical to teach them a rule stating that it is not represented
when it occurs between two vowels the first of which is [i] or [e] or
the second [i] as in (16)-(18). It has been reported to me that the
non-representation of the predictable intervocalic glide also presents
problems in the identification of written forms. When presented with
the graphic representations

(21) *mai*   [maji]   'corn' *péi* [peji] 'country'

monolingual speakers failed to identify the words unless their pronunciation was given.[4]

I now turn to the claim that the "'graphemes' of the conventional
orthography correspond fairly closely to a linguistically significant
level of representation." In numerous instances the conventional French
orthography provides an abstract representation of words which cannot be
mapped onto phonetic realizations by general rule and whose sole function
within the present-day graphic system is the differentiation of homophones
for the eye.

(22) doit   'he must'

(23) doigt   'finger'

The *g* in (23) does correspond to an actualized /ž/ occurring in *digital* 'digital', and in this way (23a) shows a pattern of alternation in the shape of the base form of a morpheme parallel to that of (24).

(23a) doigt [dwa]   digital [dižital]

(24) camp [kã] 'camp'   camper [kãpe] 'to camp'

But in addition to the alternation between zero and [ž], the forms in (23a) show an alternation in vocalism that cannot be accounted for in terms of a general phonological rule and which is not shared by all forms showing the sequence [wa] in their base form.

(23b) doigt [dwa] 'finger' dé [de] 'thimble'
      digital [dižital] 'digital'

(25) poids [pwa] 'weight' peser [pəze] 'to weigh'
      pondérer [põdere] 'to balance' pèse [pɛz] 'he weighs'

It is in the vowel alternations [wa] ∿ [e] or [wa] ∿ [ə] that the generative phonologist would look for a general phonological rule, and it is clear that the *g* and *d* of *doigt* and *poids* relate forms which in a generative phonology of French would need to be assigned to two different underlying forms.

One might be tempted to characterize such graphic superfluities as "flagrant archaisms" (Schane 1967b:8). Diachronic studies of the conventional French orthography show conclusively, however, that at the time that these letters were added to the graphic representation of the words by scribes they did not correspond to any phonetic or morphophonemic phenomena (Blanche-Benveniste and Chervel 1969:56-66).[5]

Whereas the examples given in the preceding discussion involve the linking of two levels of vocabulary--the learned *digital* and the 'popular' *doigt, doigté*, etc., for instance--by means of the spelling, there are cases of the reverse: the distinction effected by the orthography between popular and learned forms whose morphophonemic behavior is identical.

(26) sonn- [sõ∿sɔn∿sön]: sonner, sonneur, sonné, sonnette

(27) son- [sõ∿sɔn∿sön]: sonore, résonance, dissoner

From all forms of (26) and (27) can easily be extracted the common feature "sound", but the forms of (26) are secondary derivatives on the popular verb *sonner* 'to ring' whereas those of (27) are learned forms derived from the base form *son*.

Not only does the conventional French orthography note lexical relationships which are outside of the scope of a generative phonology, but it also fails to capture some of the important generalizations underscored by that type of phonological analysis.

(28) sel [sɛl] 'salt' saline [salin] 'salt marsh'

(29) meurt [moer] 'he dies' mourons [murɔ̃] 'we die'
          mort [mɔr] 'death'

(30) deux [dɸ] '2' douze [duz] '12'

In addition to morphophonemic alternations between words of the popular lexicon illustrated by (28)-(30), there are others which relate popular base forms and learned derivatives.

(31) ciel [sjɛl] 'sky' céleste [selɛst] 'celestial'

(32) loi [lwa] 'law' légal [legal] 'legal'

(33) fleur [floer] 'flower' floral [flöral] 'floral'

If the graphemes of the conventional orthography corresponded to systematic phonemes and if the orthography were primarily an abstract representation of the type posited by generative phonologists, we should expect that the vowel of the base form be spelled alike at least in the popular words of (28)-(30) since the differences in phonetic realization between related forms are predictable from the phonological environment and are statable in terms of a general rule: the vowel is fronted whenever it occurs in stressed, i.e. final position (Schane 1968a).

THE CONVENTIONAL ORTHOGRAPHY AND LEVELS OF LANGUAGE

The evidence I have presented suggests that, on the one hand, conventional alphabetic orthographies do not correspond to abstract underlying phonological representations, and that on the other, the fact that these orthographies do show a significant set of phoneme-grapheme correspondences indicates that it would be hazardous to look for direct correspondences between phonological units linguists posit and those which have psychological reality for speakers of a language. But there is another reason why applied linguists should not be cast as defenders of the conventional orthographies of such languages as English or French. Chomsky tempers his claims about the suitability of the conventional English orthography by the following qualification (1970a:283):

"The conventional orthography corresponds closely to a level of representation that seems to be optimal for the sound system of a fairly rich version of standard spoken English. Much of the evidence that determines, for the phonologist, the exact form of this underlying system is based on considerations of learned words and complex derivational patterns. It is by no means obvious that a child of six has mastered this phonological system in full--he may not have been presented with all the evidence that determines the general structure of the English sound pattern."

Might not it be the case that not only children but also the majority of mature speakers of English and many so-called languages of culture have not been presented with the evidence necessary to internalize a grammar of a rich version of the standard language?

There are many French linguists who maintain that, if all languages are mixed, French is more mixed than all others. Pierre Guiraud in particular (1965, 1969) sets up two levels of French available to varying degrees to French speakers and which differ in terms of structural, sociolinguistic, functional, and diachronic factors. These two levels of Standard French-"cultivated" and "popular French"-constitute according to Guiraud two separate systems from which speakers draw depending on a variety of factors,many obviously of a sociolinguistic nature. Cultivated French has a rich phonological structure characterized by the morphophonemic alternations (31)-(33) and perhaps also (28)-(30) which is not shared by popular French. If that is the case, learning to use the conventional orthography for the majority of the children of France and the francophone countries involves,in a sense, learning a new language. Consider the problems native speakers of popular French would have in spelling the first member of each of the following triads.

(34) sain [sɛ̃] saine [sɛn] sanitaire [sanitɛr]

(35) plein [plɛ̃] pleine [plɛn] plénitude [plenityd]

(36) faim [fɛ̃] famine [famin]

To correctly spell the vocalic portion of *sain, plein,* and *faim* they must relate them not only to their feminine counterparts in the case of (34) and (35), but also to their derivatives. This information being unavailable to them, they have no resort but to memorize the spelling of the individual items, a pedagogically costly alternative indeed.

Only two underlying vowels realized under certain conditions as [ɛ̃] need to be recognized for popular French, and *sain, plein,* and *faim* could be respelled

(6) fin [fɛ̃] fine [fin]

(34a) sein [sɛ̃] seine [sɛn]

(35a) plein [plɛ̃] pleine [plɛn]

(36a) fin   [fɛ̃]

If the phonological behavior of French speakers can only be accounted for in terms of two co-existent systems, and if one adopts the now prevalent view that early education must be imparted in the language or dialect the child uses at home, then exposing him immediately to an orthography that corresponds to a richer version of his language is indefensible on pedagogical grounds. The problems of teaching reading and writing are complex and beyond the scope of the applied linguist. As is the case for foreign language teaching, he can contribute by making available to specialists in these fields more accurate and insightful descriptions of the subject matter they have to impart--the conventional French orthography and its relations to the phonological system. Spelling reform is a socially and politically sensitive area in which applied linguists ought to tread warily. The advocacy of an abstract representation commits one to partial reform and to playing the apprentice sorcerer. Generative phonologists have helped to point out that the conventional French orthography is a very complex coherent system. As study of the latest timorous proposal for spelling reform in France shows (*Rapport* 1965), the elimination of an unmotivated feature often results in the adoption of some other arbitrary feature in another part of the system. It is the great merit of the generative view of the conventional French orthography to have brought to light its many morphophonemic features and the large number of rules that must be brought into play to decode it and to encode into it. Should the social and political climate in France ever be ripe for the total spelling reform that present pedagogical problems demand, we could look forward to more realistic proposals than those that issued from the ranks of nineteenth century phoneticians. In the meantime, more study is needed of the conventional orthography as a self-consistent system and its relations to the phonological system including its role in levelling variation from the orthoepic norm.

NOTES

    1. In such verbs as *répéter, préférer,* etc., *é* may correspond to [ɛ] for many speakers.
    2. The symbol [ö] stands for a centralized slightly rounded vowel often indistinguishable from [ə].
    3. ONAAC - Office National d'Alphabétisation et d'Action Communautaire.
    4. Oral communication from Father Yves Dejean to whom I am also indebted for several of the key Creole examples.
    5. Blanche-Benveniste and Chervel point out that many final consonant letters were introduced to differentiate ambiguous graphs. For example *pie* at one time represented both [pi] 'magpie' and [pje] 'foot'. The final *d* was added to the representation of the latter word to provide two distinct representations, and this resulted in linking the word to its derivatives *pedale, pédestre,* etc.

BIBLIOGRAPHY

Entered in this bibliography are only items which (1) treat Romance languages from a generative view point, (2) discuss theoretical problems with most illustrations drawn from the Romance languages, and (3) are referred to in any of the contributions herein. We are deeply indebted to R. Joe Campbell for making available to us many of the items below, as retrieved from his Computerized Bibliography of Spanish Linguistics, a comprehensive work which is to be published by the Research Center in Anthropology, Folklore and Linguistics, Bloomington, Indiana.

ADAMS, DOUGLAS, et al. (eds.). 1971. Papers from the Seventh Regional Meeting of the Chicago Linguistic Society. Chicago: Chicago Linguistic Society.

AGARD, FREDERICK B. 1967. Stress in four Romance languages. Glossa 1:150-200.

ALARCOS LLORACH, EMILIO. 1961. Fonología española. Madrid: Gredos.

ALBURY, DONALD H. In progress. Nominals as complements. Gainesville, Florida: University of Florida dissertation.

ALINEI, MARIO. 1971a. Primi appunti per una descrizione generativo-transformazionale del nesso temporale. Grammatica Transformazionale Italiana 13-22.

___. 1971b. Il tipo sintagmatico quel matto di Giorgio. Grammatica Transformazionale Italiana 1-12.

ALLEN, JOSEPH H. D., JR. 1964. Tense/Lax in Castillian Spanish. Word 20.295-321.

ANAIS DO I CONGRESSO DA LÍNGUA FALADA NO TEATRO. 1958. Rio de Janeiro: Ministério da Educacão.

ANDERSON, J. 1961. The morphophonemics of gender in Spanish nouns. Lingua 10.285-96.

ANDERSON, STEPHEN R. 1969. West Scandinavian vowel systems and the ordering of phonological rules. Cambridge, Massachusetts: MIT dissertation.

ANDERSON, STEPHEN R. 1970. On Grassmann's law in Sanskrit. Linguistic
Inquiry 1.387-96.

ANDREWS, AVERY D. 1971. Case agreement of predicate modifiers in
Ancient Greek. Linguistic Inquiry 2.127-52.

ANTINUCCI, FRANCESCO, MAURIZIO CRISARI and DOMENICO PARISI. 1971.
Analisi semantica di alcuni verbi italiani. Grammatica Transformazionale Italiana 23-46.

ANTINUCCI, FRANCESCO, and ANNARITA PUGLIELLI. 1971. Struttura della
quantificazione. Grammatica Transformazionale Italiana 47-62.

ASSELIN, CLAIRE. 1968. Negation in French. Chicago: University of
Chicago dissertation.

___. 1970. Review of Ruwet (1967). IJAL 36.52-5.

AUGEROT, JAMES E. 1968. A study of Romanian morphophonology. Seattle:
University of Washington dissertation.

___. 1971. Romanian phonology: a transformational view. Bucharest:
Romanian Academy of Sciences.

BABCOCK, SANDRA S. 1970a. Pattern-meaning in syntactic structures.
Language Sciences 10.13-7.

___. 1970b. The syntax of Spanish reflexive verbs: The parameters of
the middle verb. The Hague: Mouton.

BACH, EMMON and ROBERT T. HARMS (eds.). 1968. Universals in linguistic
theory. New York: Holt, Rinehart and Winston.

BAKER, CARL LEROY. 1968. Indirect questions in English. Urbana:
University of Illinois dissertation.

___. 1970. Notes on the description of English questions: the role
of an abstract question morpheme. Foundations of Language 6.197-
219.

BAKER, C. LEROY and MICHAEL K. BRAME. 1972. Global rules: a rejoin-
der. Language 48.52-75.

BARRUTIA, RICHARD, et al. 1970. Modern Portuguese. New York: Knopf.

BATTAGLIA, SALVATORE and VINCENZO PERNICONE. 1963. La grammatica
italiana. Torino: Loescher.

BELASCO, SIMON. 1961. The role of transformational grammar and tagmemics in the analysis of an old French text. Lingua 10.375-90.

BELCHIŢĂ, ANCA. 1967-1968. Morpheme structure rules in the generative grammar of the Romanian language. Revue Roumaine de Linguistique 12.507-22 and 13.29-47.

___. 1968. Les semi-voyelles dans la grammaire transformationnelle de la langue roumaine. Cahiers de Linguistique Théorique et Appliquée 5.7-21.

___. 1969. Flexiunea nominală în gramatica transformaţionala̋ a limbii române. Studii şi Cercetări Lingvistice 20.415-26 and 20.509-31.

___. 1970. Flexiunea verbala în gramatica transformaţionala̋ a limbii române. Studii şi Cercetări Lingvistice 21.171-203.

BEMBO, PIETRO. 1549. Prose della volgar lingua. Ed. by Mario Marti. Padova: Liviana editrice, 1955.

BERSCHIN, HELMUT. 1971. Sprachsystem und Sprachnorm bei spanischen lexikalischen Einheiten der Struktur KKVKV. Linguistische Berichte 12.39-46.

BIERWISCH, MANFRED and KARL E. HEIDOLPH (eds.). 1970. Progress in linguistics: a collection of papers. (Janua Linguarum, series maior 43) The Hague: Mouton.

BIERWISCH, MANFRED, F. KIEFER and N. RUWET (eds.). Forthcoming. Generative grammar in Europe. Dordrecht: Reidel.

BINKERT, PETER JOSEPH. 1970. Case and prepositional construction in a transformational grammar of Classical Latin. Ann Arbor: University of Michigan dissertation.

BINNICK, ROBERT I, et al. (eds.). 1969. Papers from the Fifth Regional Meeting of the Chicago Linguistic Society. Chicago: Department of Linguistics, University of Chicago.

BLANCHE-BENVENISTE, CLAIRE and ANDRÉ CHERVEL. 1969. L'orthographe. Paris: Maspéro.

BOLINGER, DWIGHT. 1967. A grammar for grammars: the contrastive

structures of English and Spanish. (Review of Stockwell et al.
1965) Romance Philology 31.206.

BOONS, JEAN-PAUL. 1971. Métaphore et baisse de la redondance.
Langue française 11.15-16.

BORILLO, ANDRÉE. 1971. Remarques sur les verbes symétriques français.
Langue Française 11.17-31.

BOURCIEZ, ÉDOUARD. 1956. Éléments de linguistique romane. 4th ed.
Paris: Klincksieck.

BOWEN, J. DONALD and TERENCE MOORE. 1968. The reflexive in English
and Spanish: a transformational approach. TESOL Quarterly 2.12-26.

BRAINERD, BARRON. 1967. A transformational-generative grammar for
Rumanian numerical expressions. Cahiers de Linguistique Théorique
et Appliquée 4.35-45.

BRAME, MICHAEL. 1970. Arabic phonology: implications for phonological
theory and historical Semitic. Cambridge, Massachusetts: MIT
dissertation.

BRASINGTON, R. W. P. 1971. Noun pluralization in Brazilian Portuguese.
Journal of Linguistics 7.151-77.

BRESNAN, JOAN W. 1970. On complementizers: towards a syntactic theory
of complement types. Foundations of Language 6.297-321.

BRIGGS, LUCY T. 1969. Poetry as transformation: a grammar of Arte
poética by Jorge Luis Borges. Washington: Georgetown University M.A.
thesis.

BROWN, T. GRANT. 1971. On emphasizing syntax. The Modern Language
Journal 60:271-6.

BULL, WILLIAM. 1965. Spanish for teachers: applied linguistics.
New York: Ronald Press.

BURSTYNSKY, EDWARD N. 1967. Distinctive feature analysis and diachronic
Spanish phonology. Toronto: University of Toronto dissertation.

___. 1968. Quelques observations de phonologie générative appliquées
au français canadien. In Léon, 9-17.

BUSCHERBRUCK, K. 1941. Zur Entwicklung der französischen Wortstellung. Germanisch-Romanische Monatschrift 29.139-45.

CALBOLI, GUALTIERO. 1971. Costrittori, nelle proposizioni a complemento: i modi del verbo e l'infinito. Grammatica Transformazionale Italiana 63-96.

CALVANO, WILLIAM J. 1966. A phonological study of four Ibero-Romance dialects. Ithaca, New York: Cornell University M.A. thesis.

___. 1969. Synchronic relationships: five Romance dialects. Ithaca, New York: Cornell University dissertation.

CAMPBELL, MARY ANN, et al. (eds.). 1970. Papers from the Sixth Regional Meeting of the Chicago Linguistic Society. Chicago: Chicago Linguistic Society.

CAMPBELL, RICHARD JOE. 1966. Phonological analyses of Spanish. Urbana: University of Illinois dissertation.

___. Forthcoming. Computerized bibliography of Spanish Linguistics. Bloomington, Indiana: Research Center in Anthropology, Folklore, and Linguistics.

CAMPBELL, RUSSELL. 1970. An evaluation and comparison of present methods of teaching English grammar to speakers of other languages. TESOL Quarterly 4.37-48.

CÁRDENAS, DANIEL. 1960. Introducción a una comparación fonológica del español y del inglés. Washington: Center for Applied Linguistics of the Modern Language Association of America.

CASAGRANDE, JEAN. 1968. On negation in French. Bloomington: Indiana University dissertation.

___. 1969. On the sources of some universals. Papers in Linguistics 1.76-90.

___. 1970. A case for global derivational constraints. Papers in Linguistics 2.449-59.

___. 1971. Review of Roulet (1969) and Lamérand (1970). The French Review 44.788-90.

___. Forthcoming a. Fossilization in French syntax. In Saltarelli and Wanner.

CASAGRANDE, JEAN. Forthcoming b. Review of Nivette (1970). To appear in Papers in Linguistics.

CHAFE, WALLACE. 1970a. A semantically based sketch of Onandaga. (Supplement to International Journal of American Linguistics 36. No. 2). Baltimore: The Waverly Press.

___. 1970b. New and old information. Papers from the Fourth Annual Kansas Linguistics Conference, 37-65, Lawrence, Kansas.

___. 1971. Meaning and the structure of language. Chicago: Chicago University Press.

CHOMSKY, NOAM. 1957. Syntactic structures. The Hague: Mouton.

___. 1964. Current issues in linguistic theory. In Fodor and Katz 1964.

___. 1965. Aspects of the theory of syntax. Cambridge, Massachusetts: MIT Press.

___. 1966. Linguistic theory. In Mead, 43-9 and in Lester, 51-60.

___. 1966'. Cartesian Linguistics. New York: Harper and Row.

___. 1970a. Comments for project literacy. In Lester, 277-83.

___. 1970b. Remarks on nominalization. In Jacobs and Rosenbaum, 181-221.

___. 1971. Conditions on Transformations. Mimeo paper.

CHOMSKY, NOAM and MORRIS HALLE. 1968. The sound pattern of English. New York: Harper and Row.

CÎRSTEA, MIHAELA. 1969. Les propositions à prédicats nominaux dans la langue italienne comtemporaine. Cahiers de Linguistique Théorique et Appliquée 8.137-57.

___. 1970. La generazione della forma atona ci nella lingua italiana comtemporanea. Revue des Langues Romanes (Montpellier) 15.345-67.

CLARIS, JEAN-MAX. 1971. Notes sur les formes en -rait. Langue Française 11.32-8.

CLÉDAT, L. 1928. L'inversion du sujet. Revue de Philologie Française 40:2.81-99.

CLIVIO, GIARENZO P. 1970. Possibilità di applicazione della grammatica transformazionale agli studi dialettologici. Atti del VII convegno del Centro per gli studi dialettali italiani, Torino, 58-62.

___. 1971. Vocalic prothesis, schwa-deletion, and morphophonemics in Piedmontese. Zeitschrift für Romanische Philologie 87.334-44.

CLOSS, ELIZABETH. 1965. Diachronic syntax and generative grammar. Language 41.402-15. Also in Reibel and Schane (1969), 395-405.

COHEN, VICTOR B. 1971. Foleyology. In Adams et al. 316-22.

COLOMBO, ADRIANO. 1971. Appunti per una grammatica delle proposizioni completive. Grammatica Transformazionale Italiana 135-61.

CONTRERAS, HELES. 1967a. La gramática transformacional y la lingüística aplicada. Estudos Lingüísticos 2:1/2.39-42.

___. 1967b. Sobre gramática transformacional. In Carrillo Herrera, Gastón (ed.) Lengua, literatura, folklore: estudios dedicados a Rodolfo Oroz. Santiago: Univ. de Chile, Facultad de Filosofía y Educación, 125-41.

___. 1968. The structure of the determiner in Spanish. Linguistics 44.22-8.

___. 1969a. Simplicity, descriptive adequacy and binary features. Language 45.1-8.

___. 1969b. Vowel fusion in Spanish. Hispania 52.60-2.

___. 1970. Review of Goldin 1968. Lingua 25.12-29.

___. (ed.) Forthcoming. Gramática transformacional: lecturas. México: Siglo XXI.

CONTRERAS, HELES and SOL SAPORTA. 1960. The validation of a phonological grammar. Lingua 9.1-15.

CONTRERAS, LIDIA. 1963. Las oraciones condicionales. Boletín del Instituto de Filología de la Universidad de Chile 15.33-109.

COSTABILE, N. 1967. Le strutture della lingua italiana: grammatica generativo-transformativa. Bologna.

COYAUD, M. 1965. Transformations linguistiques et classification lexicale. Cahiers de Lexicologie 6.25-34.

CRESSEY, WILLIAM W. 1966. A transformational analysis of the relative clause in urban Mexican Spanish. Urbana: University of Illinois dissertation.

___. 1968. Relative adverbs in Spanish: a transformational analysis. Language 44.487-500.

___. 1969. Teaching the position of Spanish adjectives: a transformational approach. Hispania 52.878-81.

___. 1970a. Is stress predictable in Spanish? Mimeo paper.

___. 1970b. A note on specious simplification and the theory of markedness. Papers in Linguistics 2.227-38.

___. 1970c. Relatives and interrogatives in Spanish: a transformational analysis. Linguistics 58.5-12.

___. 1971a. Review of Harris (1969b). General Linguistics 11.63-70.

___. 1971b. The subjunctive in Spanish: a transformational approach. Hispania 54.895-6.

___. Forthcoming. Teaching irregular verbs in Spanish: a transformational approach. Hispania.

CRISARI, MAURIZIO. Domenico Parisi e Annarita Puglielli. 1971. Le congiunzioni temporali spaziali e causali in italiano. Grammatica Transformazionale Italiana 117-34.

D'ADDIO, WANDA. 1971. Suffissi derivativi aggettivali dell'italiano: analisi semantica. Gramatica Transformazionale Italiana 163-75.

DAMOURETTE, J. and E. PICHON. 1934. Des mots à la pensée: essai de la langue française. Vol. 4. Paris: D'Artrey.

DARDEN,BILL J.et al. 1968. Papers from the Fourth Regional Meeting of the Chicago Linguistic Society. Chicago: Department of Linguistics, University of Chicago.

DAVIS, J. CAREY. 1969. The indirect object of possession in Spanish. University of South Florida Language Quarterly 7.2-6.

DE CORNULIER, BENOÎT. 1972. A peeking rule in French. Linguistic Inquiry 3.226-7.

DELISLE, GILLES L. 1968. First persons plural from Latin to French. Glossa 2.175-84.

DELL, FRANÇOIS. 1970. Les règles phonologiques tardives et la morphologie dérivationelle du français. Cambridge, Massachusetts: MIT dissertation.

DELL, FRANÇOIS. Forthcoming. Two cases of exceptional rule ordering.
In Bierwisch, et al. (forthcoming.).

DIACONESCU, PAULA. 1968. Morphologie et grammaires génératives.
Revue Roumaine de Linguistique 13.401-5.

DIEZ, FRIEDRICH. 1836-1843. Grammatik der romanischen Sprachen. Bonn:
A. Marcus.

DINGWALL, WILLIAM O. (ed.). 1971. A survey of linguistic science.
Baltimore: University of Maryland.

DINNEEN, FRANCIS P. (ed.). 1966. Report of the Seventeenth Annual
Round Table Meeting on Linguistics and Language Studies. Washington:
Georgetown University Monograph.

___. 1967. An introduction to general linguistics. New York: Holt.

DI PIETRO, ROBERT J. 1967. Phonemics, generative grammar and
the Italian sibilants. Studia Linguistica 21.96-106.

___. 1971a. Language structures in contrast. Rowley, Massachusetts:
Newbury House Publishers.

___. 1971b. Review of Saltarelli (1970a). Language 47.718-30.

DONALDSON, WEBER D., JR. 1970a. Code-cognition approaches to language
learning. In Newel 51-9.

___. 1970b. The syntax of French pronominal verbs: a case grammar
description. Bloomington: Indiana University dissertation.

___. 1971. Review of Lamérand (1970). Modern Language Journal 55.539.

DOUGHERTY, R. C. 1970. A grammar of coordinate conjoined structures:
I. Language 46.850-98.

___. 1971. A grammar of coordinate conjoined structures: II. Language
47.298-339.

DRESSLER, WOLFGANG. 1971. An alleged case of nonchronological rule
insertion: flōrālis. Linguistic Inquiry 2.597-9.

DUBOIS, JEAN. 1969a. Grammaire générative et transformationelle.
Langue française 1.49-57.

___. 1969b. Grammaire structurale du français. Vol. 3: La phrase
et les transformations. Paris: Larousse.

DUBOIS, JEAN and FRANÇOISE DUBOIS-CHARLIER. 1970. Eléments de linguistique française: syntaxe. Paris: Larousse.

DUCROT, O. 1968. Description sémantique des énoncés en français et la notion de présuposition. L'homme 37-53.

DUGAS, ANDRÉ, et al. 1969. Description syntaxique élémentaire du français inspirée des théories transformationnelles. Mimeographed manuscript: University of Quebec and University of Montreal.

DUGAS, DONALD GÉRARD. 1969. Some functions of de in French: a case analysis. Ann Arbor: University of Michigan dissertation.

ELCOCK, W. D. 1960. The Romance languages. London: Faber and Faber.

EMONDS, JOSEPH. 1969. Root and structure-preserving transformations. Cambridge, Massachusetts: MIT dissertation.

ENGWER, T. 1933. Umstellung und Endstellung des grammatischen Subjekts. Zeitschrift für Französische Sprache und Literatur 57.163-86.

___. 1935. Zur Deutung von Textstellen. Zeitschrift für Französische Sprache und Literatur 59.150-64.

ERNOUT, ALFRED and FRANÇOIS THOMAS. 1953. Syntaxe latine. 2nd rev. ed. Paris: Klincksieck.

ETIEMBLE, RENÉ. 1964. Parlez-vous franglais? Paris: Gallimard.

EWERT, ALFRED. 1943. The French language. 2nd ed. London: Faber and Faber.

FALK, JULIA S. 1968. Nominalizations in Spanish. (University of Washington Studies in Linguistics and Language Learning, 5.) Seattle: University of Washington.

FAUCONNIER, GILLES R. 1971a. Theoretical implications of some global phenomena in syntax. La Jolla: University of California San Diego dissertation.

___. 1971b. Unexpanded noun phrases and indexing transformations. Mimeo paper.

FILLMORE, CHARLES J. 1966a. A proposal concerning English prepositions. In Dinneen 19-33.

FILLMORE, CHARLES J. 1966b. Toward a modern theory of case. The
Ohio State University project on linguistic analysis, Report
13.1-24.

___. 1968a. The case for case. In Bach and Harms 1-88.

___. 1968b. Lexical entries for verbs. Foundations of Language
4.373-93.

___. 1970. Types of lexical information. In Kiefer, 109-37.

___. 1971a. Some problems for case grammar. In O'Brien, 35-56.

___. 1971b. Verbs of judging: an exercise in semantic description.
In Fillmore and Langendoen, 273-89.

___. 1971c. Les règles d'inférence dans une théorie sémantique.
Cahiers de Lexicologic 19.3-24.

FILLMORE, CHARLES J. and T. LANGENDOEN. 1971. Studies in linguistic
semantics. New York: Holt.

FLORA, RADU. 1962. Dijalektološki profil rumunskih banatskih govora
sa vršačkog produčja. Novi Sad.

FODOR, JERRY A. and JERROLD J. KATZ. 1964. The structure of language.
Englewood Cliffs, New Jersey: Prentice Hall.

FOLEY, JAMES A. 1965a. Prothesis in the Latin verb sum. Language
41.59-64.

___. 1965b. Spanish morphology. Cambridge, Massachusetts: MIT
dissertation.

___. 1966. Latin second singular imperative. Canadian Journal of
Linguistics 11.114-9.

___. 1967. Spanish plural formation. Language 43.486-93.

___. 1971. Phonological change by rule repetition. In Adams et
al. 376-84.

___. Undated. Spanish verb endings. Mimeo paper.

FONTANELLA, MARÍA BEATRIZ. 1967. La "s" postapical bonaerense.
Thesaurus: Boletín del Instituto Caro y Cuervo 22.394-400.

FORD, ALAN J. 1971. Aspects de la grammaire espagnole à la lumière
de la théorie chomskienne. Aix: thèse, Université d'Aix-Marseilles.

FOSTER, DAVID W. 1970. Spanish so-called impersonal sentences.
Anthropological Linguistics 12.1-9.

FOULET, LUCIEN. 1921. Comment ont évolué les formes de l'interrogation.
Romania 47.243-348.

___. 1930. Petite syntaxe de l'ancien Français. Paris: Champion.

FRANZÉN, T. 1939. Etude sur la syntaxe des pronoms personnels sujets
en ancien français. Uppsala: Almquist.

FRAZER, BRUCE. 1970. Some remarks on the action nominalization in
English. In Jacobs and Rosenbaum, 83-98.

GAATONE, D. 1970. La transformation impersonnelle en français.
Le Français Moderne. 389-411.

GARCIA, ERICA C. 1963. Review of a Phonological grammar of Spanish,
by Sol Saporta and Heles Contreras. Word 19.258-65.

GIRY, JACQUELINE. 1971. Remarques sur un emploi du verbe faire comme
opérateur. Langue Française 11.39-45.

GOLDIN, MARK. 1968. Spanish case and function. Washington: Georgetown University Press.

GOLOPENŢIA-ERETESCU, SANDA. 1967a. Alternanţe vocalice în gramatica
transformaţională. Studii şi Cercetări Lingvistice 18.407-12.

___. 1967b. Règles de structure de la phrase en roumain actuel.
Cahiers de Linguistique Théorique et Appliquée 4.65-71.

___. 1968. La génération des constructions modales en roumain.
Cahiers de Linguistique Théorique et Appliquée 5.67-81.

GORDON, DAVID and GEORGE LAKOFF. 1971. Conversational postulates. In
Adams et al., 63-84.

GRAMMATICA TRANSFORMAZIONALE ITALIANA. 1971. Roma: Bulzoni.
(Pubblicazioni della Società di Linguistica Italiana, No. 3).

GRANDGENT, CHARLES H. 1907. An introduction to Vulgar Latin. Boston:
Heath. Reprinted, New York: Hafner, 1962.

GREEN, GEORGIA M. 1970. Review of R. Lakoff (1968). Language 46.149-67.

___. 1971. A study in pre-lexical syntax: the interface of syntax and
semantics. Chicago, Illinois: University of Chicago Ph.D. dissertation.

GREENBERG, JOSEPH H. (ed.). 1963. Universals of language. Cambridge, Massachusetts: MIT Press.

GROSS, MAURICE. 1967. Sur une règle de cacophonie. Langages 7.105-18.

___. 1968. Grammaire transformationnelle du français: syntaxe du verbe. Paris: Larousse.

___. 1969. Remarques sur la notion d'objet direct en grammaire traditionnelle et transformationnelle. Langue Française 1.63-73.

___. 1971. Grammaire transformationnelle et enseignement du français. Langue Française 11.4-14.

___. 1972. Méthodes en syntaxe, 1. Grammaire des complétives du français. Paris: Herman.

___. Forthcoming. On grammatical reference. In Bierwisch, Kiefer, Ruwet.

GUILLET, ALAIN. 1971. Morphologie des dérivations. Langue Française 11.47-60.

GUIRAUD, PIERRE. 1965. Le français populaire. (Que sais-je, No. 1172). Paris: Presses Universitaires de France.

___. 1969. Français populaire ou français relâché. Le Français dans le Monde 69.23-7.

GULSTAD, DANIEL E. 1971. Verb classes, adverbs, and case. Some observations on explicitness and redundancy. Presented at the Mid-America Linguistics Conference, November 12-13, Lawrence.

HAASE, A. 1969. Syntaxe française du XVIIe siècle. Paris: Delagrave.

HADLICH, ROGER. 1971. A transformational grammar of Spanish. Englewood Cliffs, New Jersey: Prentice-Hall.

HALLE, MORRIS. 1962. Phonology in generative grammar. Word 18.54-72. Also in Fodor and Katz, 334-52.

HAMP, ERIC P. 1968. Unele concluzii de fonologie generativă în legătură cu palatalizarea consoanelor. Studii şi Cercetări Lingvistice 19.493-6.

HAMP, ERIC P., FRED W. HOUSEHOLDER, and ROBERT AUSTERLITZ. 1966. Readings in linguistics II. Chicago: University of Chicago Press.

HARRIS, JAMES W. 1969a. Sound change in Spanish and the theory of markedness. Language 45.538.52.

___. 1969b. Spanish phonology. Cambridge, Massachusetts: MIT Press.

___. 1970a. A note on Spanish plural formation. Language 46.928-30.

___. 1970b. Paradigmatic regularity and naturalness of grammars. Paper read at the Winter meeting of the Linguistic Society of America, Washington, D. C.

___. 1970c. Sequences of vowels in Spanish. Linguistic Inquiry 1.129-34.

___. 1970d. Distinctive feature theory and nasal assimilation in Spanish. Linguistics 58.30-7.

___. Forthcoming a. On the order of certain phonological rules in Spanish.

___. Forthcoming b. Two notes on Spanish verb forms.

___. Forthcoming c. Aspectos del consonantismo español. To appear in Contreras.

HARRIS, ZELLIG S. 1970. Papers in structural and transformational linguistics. New York: Humanities Press.

HENSEY, FRITZ. 1968. Questões de fonologia gerativa: as regras de pluralização. Estudos lingüísticos 3.1-10.

___. 1971. Portuguese inflectional morphology. To appear in the University of South Florida Language Quarterly.

___. Forthcoming. As regras da morfosintaxe verbal. To appear in the Proceedings of the Second Congress of the Latin American Association of Linguistics and Philology (ALFAL).

HIRSCHBÜHLER, PAUL. 1970. Traitement transformationnel de l'interrogation et de quelques problèmes connexes en français. Bruxelles: thèse, Université Libre de Bruxelles.

HOFFMAN, ROBERT J. 1969. The derivation of Spanish hypocoristics. In Binnick et al., 366-73.

HUDDLESTON, RODNEY and ORMOND UREN. 1969. Declarative, interrogative and imperative in French. Lingua 22.1-26.

HYMAN, LARRY M. 1970. How concrete is phonology? Language 46.58-76.

IONESCU, LILIANA. 1969. Unele probleme de fonologie în gramatica transformaţională a limbii române. Studii şi Cercetări Lingvistice 20.69-74.

___. 1971. Transformational grammar and dialect typology. Language Sciences 15.15-9.

IORDAN, IORGU and MARIA MANOLIU. 1965. Introducere în linguistica romanică. Bucureşti: Editura Didactică şi Pedagogică.

JACKENDOFF, RAY S. 1968. An interpretive theory of pronouns and reflexives. Unpublished paper reproduced by the Linguistics Club, Indiana University.

___. 1970. On some questionable arguments about negation and quantifiers. Unpublished paper reproduced by the Linguistics Club, Indiana University.

JACOBS, RODERICK A. and PETER S. ROSENBAUM (eds.). 1970. Readings in English transformational grammar. Waltham, Massachusetts: Ginn.

JORET, CHARLES. 1877. Un signe d'interrogation dans un patois français. Romania 6.133-4.

JOSSELYN, FREEMAN M. 1901. Études expérimentales de phonétique italienne. Paris: Publications de La Parole, Institut de Laryngologie et Orthophonie.

JUILLAND, ALPHONSE and MARILYN J. CONWELL. 1963. Louisiana French grammar. The Hague: Mouton.

KAHANE, HENRY R. and ANGELINA PIETRANGELI (eds.). 1959. Structural studies on Spanish themes. (Illinois Studies in Language and Literature, 38) Urbana: University of Illinois Press.

KATZ, JEROLD J. 1966. The philosophy of language. New York: Harper and Row.

KATZ, JEROLD J. 1967. Recent issues in semantic theory. Foundations of Language 3.124-94.

___. 1972. Semantic theory. Cambridge, Massachusetts: MIT Press.

KATZ, JERROLD J. and JERRY A FODOR. 1963. The structure of a semantic theory. Language 39.170-210.

KATZ, JERROLD J. and PAUL M. POSTAL. 1964. An integrated theory of linguistic descriptions. Cambridge, Massachusetts: MIT Press.

KAYNE, RICHARD S. 1969. On the inappropriateness of rule features. MITQPR 95. 85-93.

___. 1971. A pronominalization paradox in French. Linguistic Inquiry 2.237-41.

___. Forthcoming a. The evolution of subject-verb inversion in French.

___. Forthcoming b. French relative and interrogative 'que'.

___. Forthcoming c. The syntax of 'on'.

___. Forthcoming d. The transformational cycle in French syntax. Cambridge, Massachusetts: MIT Press.

KESSLER, ANN CAROLYN. 1969. Deep to surface contrasts in English and Italian imperatives. Language Learning 19.99-106.

KIEFER, F. (ed.). 1970. Studies in syntax and semantics. Dordrecht: D. Reidel.

KING, ROBERT D. 1969. Historical linguistics and generative grammar. Englewood Cliffs, New Jersey: Prentice Hall.

KIPARSKY, PAUL. 1965. Phonological change. Cambridge, Massachusetts: MIT dissertation.

___. 1967. A propos de l'histoire de l'accentuation grecque. Langages 8.73-93.

___. 1968a. How abstract is phonology? Mimeo paper. Duplicated by the Indiana University Linguistics Club.

___. 1968b. Linguistic universals and linguistic change. In Bach and Harms, 170-202.

KISSEBERTH, CHARLES W. 1969. Implications of Yawelmani phonology. Urbana: University of Illinois dissertation.

KISSEBERTH, CHARLES W. 1970. On the functional unity of phonological
rules. Linguistic Inquiry 1.291-306.

KLEIN, PHILIP W. 1968. Modal auxiliaries in Spanish. (University
of Washington Studies in Linguistics and Language Learning, 4)
Seattle: University of Washington.

KLIMA, EDWARD S. 1964. Relatedness between grammatical systems.
Language 40.1-20. Also in Reibel and Schane (1969), 227-46.

___. 1964'. Negation in English. In Fodor and Katz, 246-323.

___. 1965. Studies in diachronic transformational syntax. Cambridge,
Massachusetts: Harvard dissertation.

KOOPMAN, W. 1910. Die Inversion des Subjekts im Französischen.
Gottingen dissertation.

KOUTSOUDAS, ANDREAS. 1966. Writing transformational grammars. New York:
McGraw-Hill.

KOVACCI, OFELIA. 1968. Las proposiciones en español. Filología
(Univ. de Buenos Aires, Instituto de Filología) 11.23-39. [vol.
11 was published in 1968 with 1965 date].

KRENN, HERWIG. 1971. Per un'analisi generativa dell'enfasi in italiano.
Grammatica Transformazionale Italiana 177-90.

KURODA, SIGE-YUKI. 1969-1970. Remarks on the notion of subject with
reference to words like also, even or only. University of Tokyo,
Faculty of Medicine, Research Institute of Logopedics and Phoniatrics
Annual Bulletin 3.11-30 and 4.127-52.

___. 1971. Two remarks on pronominalization. Foundations of Language
7:2.183-98.

KURYŁOWICZ, JERZY. 1945-1949. La nature des procès dits 'analogiques'.
Acta Linguistica 5.121-38. Also in Hamp, et al (1966), 158-74.

___. 1968. The notion of morpho(pho)neme. In Lehmann and Malkiel
65-81.

LABOV, WILLIAM. 1963. The social motivation of a sound change.
Georgetown University Monograph Series on Languages and Linguistics
18.91-114. Also in O'Brien (1968), 259-82.

LACKSTROM, JOHN E. 1967. Pro-forms in the Spanish noun phrase. (University of Washington Studies in Linguistics and Language Learning, 3). Seattle: University of Washington.

LAKOFF, GEORGE. 1966. A note on negation. Mathematical Linguistics and Automatic Translation. NSF Report 17.I.1-9.

___. 1968. Counterparts, or the problem of reference in transformational grammar. Mimeo paper. Duplicated by the Indiana University Linguistics Club.

___. 1969. Generative Semantics. Unpublished.

___. 1970a. Global rules. Language 46.627-39.

___. 1970b. Irregularity in syntax. New York: Holt, Rinehart and Winston. (Originally titled 'On the nature of syntactic irregularity' this work was available as early as 1965 under the form of a Harvard Computation Laboratory Report).

___. 1972. The arbitrary basis of transformational grammar. Language 48.76-87.

LAKOFF, GEORGE and DAVID M. PERLMUTTER. MS. Gender agreement in French. Unpublished.

LAKOFF, GEORGE, and J. R. ROSS. 1966. Criterion for verb phrase constituency. The Computation Laboratory of Harvard University, Report No. NSF-17. Cambridge, Massachusetts.

LAKOFF, GEORGE and JOHN R. ROSS. 1968. Is deep structure necessary? Mimeo paper. Duplicated by the Indiana University Linguistics Club.

LAKOFF, ROBIN T. 1968. Abstract syntax and Latin complementation. Cambridge, Massachusetts: MIT Press.

___. 1969. Review of Arnauld and Lancelot, Grammaire Générale et Raisonnée. Language 45.343-64.

___. 1970. Tense and its relation to participants. Language 46.838-49.

LAMENDELLA, JOHN T. 1969. On the irrelevance of transformational grammar to second language pedagogy. Language Learning 19.255-70.

LAMÉRAND, RAYMOND. 1970. Syntaxe transformationnelle des propositions hypothétiques du français parlé. Bruxelles: AIMAV.

LANGACKER, RONALD W. 1965. French interrogatives: a tranformational description. Language 41.587-600.

___. 1966a. A transformational syntax of French. Urbana: University of Illinois dissertation.

___. 1966b. Les verbes faire, laisser, voir, et cetera. Langages 3.72-89.

___. 1968. Observations on French possessives. Language 44.51-75.

___. 1969a. An analysis of English questions. Unpublished paper.

___. 1969b. Mirror image rules I. Language 45.575-98.

___. 1969c. Mirror image rules II. Language 45.844-62.

___. 1969d. Review of Ruwet (1967). Language 45.97-104.

___. 1970. English question intonation. In Sadock and Vanek, 139-61.

___. 1970'. Review of Goldin (1968). Language 46.167-85.

___. 1971. Review of Roulet (1969). The Modern Language Journal. 55.37-40.

LANGENDOEN, D. TERENCE. 1970. Essentials of English grammar. New York: Holt, Rinehart and Winston.

LEÃO, ANGELA VAZ. 1961. O período hipotético iniciado por se. Belo Horizonte: Imprensa da Universidade de Minas Gerais.

LEBIDOIS, R. 1952. L'Inversion du sujet dans la prose contemporaine. Paris: D'Artrey.

LECLÈRE, CHRISTIAN. 1971. Remarques sur les substantifs opérateurs. Langue Française 11.61-76.

LEES, ROBERT B. 1960. The Grammar of English nominalizations. Bloomington, Indiana: Research Center in Anthropology, Folklore, and Linguistics.

LEHMANN, WINFRED P. 1962. Historical linguistics: an introduction. New York: Holt, Rinehart and Winston.

LEHMANN, WINFRED P. and YAKOV MALKIEL. 1968. Directions for historical linguistics. Austin: University of Texas Press.

LEON, PIERRE R. (ed.). 1968. Recherches sur la structure phonique du français canadien. Paris: Didier.

LERCH, E. 1934. Historische französische Syntax III. Leipzig: Reisland.

LESTER, MARK (ed.). 1970. Readings in applied transformational grammar. New York: Holt, Rinehart and Winston.

LEUSCHEL, DONALD A. 1960. Spanish verb morphology. Bloomington: Indiana University dissertation.

LLEÓ, CONCEPCIÓN. 1970. Problems of Catalan phonology. (University of Washington Studies in Linguistics and Language Learning, 8) Seattle: University of Washington.

LOY, ARTHA SUE. 1966. Historical rules in the development of modern French from Latin. Urbana: University of Illinois dissertation.

LOZANO, ANTHONY G. 1970. Non-reflexivity of the indefinite "se" in Spanish. Hispania 53.452-7.

MALKIEL, YAKOV. 1968. The inflectional paradigm as an occasional determinant of sound change. In Lehmann and Malkiel, 21-64.

MANCAŞ, MIHAELA. 1967. Aspects de la grammaire de coordination en Roumain. Cahiers de Linguistique Théorique et Appliquée 4.107-41.

MÁNCZAK, WITOLD. 1958. Tendances générales des changements analogiques. Lingua 7.298-325 and 7.387-420.

MARTINET, ANDRÉ. 1952. Function, structure, and sound change. Word 8.1-32.

___. 1955a. Economie des changements phonétiques. Berne: Francke.

___. 1955b. Review of Fonología española, by Emilio Alarcos Llorach. Word 11.112-7.

MATTOSO CÂMARA J., JR. 1970. Estrutura da língua portuguêsa. Petrópolis: Vozes.

MAYERTHALER, WILLI. 1971. Anmerkungen zur Pluralbildung im Spanischen. Linguistische Berichte 12.47-52.

MCCAWLEY, JAMES D. 1968a. Lexical insertion in a transformational grammar without deep structure. In Darden et al., 71-80.

___. 1968b. The role of semantics in a grammar. In Bach and Harms, 125-69.

MCCAWLEY, JAMES D. 1970. Where do noun phrases come from? In Jacobs and Rosenbaum, 166-83.

___. 1970'. English as a VSO language. Language 46.286-99.

___. 1971. Prelexical Syntax. In O'Brien, 19-34.

___. In Press. Syntactic and logical arguments for semantic structures. In the Proceedings of the Fifth International Seminar on Theoretical Linguistics. Tokyo: the TEC Corp.

MCCOY, ANA. 1970. A case grammar classification of Spanish verbs. Ann Arbor: University of Michigan dissertation.

MEAD, ROBERT C., JR. (ed.). 1966. Northeast Conference on the Teaching of Foreign Languages. Working Committee Reports.

MEILLET, ANTOINE and J. VENDRYES. 1948. Traité de grammaire comparée des langues classiques. 2nd ed. Paris: Champion.

MEL'CUK, IGOR A. 1965a. Fonología y morfología. Omagiu lui Alexandru Rosetti la 70 de ani, 551-3. Bucureşti: Editura Academiei Republicii Socialiste România.

___. 1965b. O fonologičeskoj traktovke 'poluglasnyx' v ispanskom jazyke [On the phonological treatment of 'semivowels' in Spanish]. Voprosy Jazykoznanija 14:4.92-109.

___. 1965c. Ob avtomatičeskom morfologičeskom sinteze (na materiale ispanskogo jazyka) [On automatic morphological synthesis (based on data from Spanish)]. Naučno-texničeskaja informacija 3:4.35-43.

___. 1967. Model' sprjaženija v ispanskom jazyke [A conjugation model in Spanish]. Mašinnyj perevod i prikladnaja lingvistika 10.21-52.

MENDELOFF, H. 1969. A manual of comparative Romance linguistics. Part I. Washington: Catholic University Press.

MENZEL, PETER. 1969. Propositions, events, and actions in the syntax of complementation. Los Angeles: UCLA dissertation.

MEYER-LÜBKE, W. 1893-1902. Grammatik der romanischen Sprachen. Leipzig.

___. 1901. Einführung in das Studium der romanischen Sprachwissenschaft. Heidelberg: Winter.

MICHELSON, D. 1969. An examination of Lakoff and Ross's criterion for verb phrase constituency. Glossa 3.146-64.

MIHĂESCU, H. 1960. Limba latină în provinciile dunărene ale imperiului roman. Bucureşti: Editura Academiei Republicii Populare Romîne.

MILLER, D. G. Forthcoming. On the motivation of linguistic change.

MILNER, J. C. G. 1967. French truncation rule. Quarterly Progress Report of the Research Laboratory of Electronics, Massachusetts Institute of Technology, 86.273-83.

MOELLERING, WILLIAM. 1971. On the indefinite "se". Hispania 54.300.

MOLINA, HUBERT. 1970. Scientific and pedagogical grammars. Hispania 53.75-80.

___. 1971. The learner, the teacher, the grammar and the method in designing an instructional program. Hispania 54.439-44.

MOORE, TERENCE H. 1967. The topic-comment function: a performance constraint on a competence model. Los Angeles: University of California Los Angeles dissertation.

MOREAU, M. L. 1970. Trois aspects de la syntaxe de C'EST. Thèse. Université de Liège.

___. 1971. L'homme que je crois qui est venu. Qui, que: relatifs ou conjonctions. Langue Française 11.77-90.

MORGAN, JERRY L. 1969. On the treatment of presupposition in transformational grammar. In Binnick et al., 167-77.

MORIN, YVES CH. 1972. The phonology of echo-words in French. Language 48.97-108.

NAJAM, EDWARD W. (ed.). 1966. Language learning: the individual and the process. The Hague: Mouton.

NARO, ANTHONY J. 1968a. History of Portuguese passives and impersonals. Cambridge, Massachusetts: MIT dissertation.

NARO, ANTHONY J. 1968b. Para o estudo da gramática transformacional. Estudos Lingüísticos 3.18-36.

___. 1970a. Binary or n-ary vowel height features?: historical evidence. In Campbell et al (eds.), 533-42.

___. 1970b. A note on elision of yod in Spanish. Linguistic Inquiry 1.543-5.

___. 1971a. Directionality and assimilation. Linguistic Inquiry 2.57-67.

___. 1971b. The history of e and o in Portuguese: a study in linguistic drift. Language 47.615-45.

___. 1971c. Resolution of vocalic hiatus in Portuguese: diachronic evidence for binary features. Language 47.381-93.

___. 1971d. Review of José G. Herculano de Carvalho, Estudos Lingüísticos. Vol. 1: Lisboa, Verba (Colecção Presenças 3), 1964. Vol. 2: Coimbra, Atlântida, 1969. Foundations of Language 7.148-55.

NEWELL, SANFORD (ed.). 1970. Dimension: 1970. Proceedings of the Sixth Annual Southern Conference on Language Teaching. Spartanburg: Converse College.

NEWMARK, LEONARD. 1963. Grammatical theory and teaching English as a foreign language. In Lester 1970.

___. 1966. How not to interfere with language learning. In Najam, 77-83.

NEWMEYER, FREDERICK. 1970. The derivation of the English action nominalization. In Campbell, et al., 408-15.

___. 1971. The source of derived nominals in English. Language 47.786-96.

NIVETTE, JOSEPH. 1970. Principes de grammaire générative. Paris: Fernand Nathan.

NØJGAARD, M. 1967. Le rôle de la négation dans les exclamations introduites. Actes du 4e Congrès des Romanistes Scandinaves (Revue Romane No. spécial 1). Copenhague: Akademisk Forlag, 94-112.

O'BRIEN, R. J. 1968. Georgetown round table selected papers in linguistics 1961-1965. Washington: Georgetown University Press.

___. 1971. Report of the twenty-second annual round table meeting on linguistics and language studies. Washington: Georgetown University Press.

ORLOPP, W. 1888. Ueber die Wortstellung bei Rabelais. Jena
    dissertation.
OTERO, CARLOS. 1970. The syntax of "mismo". Acte du deuxième
    congrès internationel des linguistes, Vol. 2.1145-51.
___. 1972. Acceptable ungrammatical sentences in Spanish. Linguistic
    Inquiry 3.233-42.
PAFF, TOBY. 1970. Restrictive and non-restrictive relative clauses.
    Unpublished paper.
PANCONCELLI-CALZIA, GINLIO. 1911. Italiano. Leipzig.
PAPIĆ, M. 1970. L'Expression et la place du sujet dans les essais de
    Montaigne. Paris: Presses Universitaires de France.
PARIS, GASTON. 1877. Ti, signe d'interrogation. Romania 6.438-42.
PARMENTER, C. E. and J. N. CARMAN. 1932. Some remarks on Italian
    quantity. Italica 9.103-8.
PATIÑO, CARLOS. 1965. The Development of Romance Syntactic Studies.
    Ann Arbor: University of Michigan dissertation.
PATTERSON, GEORGE W. 1969. A comparative study of the vocalic system
    of standard French and the dialect spoken at Falher. Edmonton:
    University of Alberta M.A. thesis.
___. 1971. (Dissertation in Progress) University of Alberta.
PERCIVAL, KEITH. 1968. The notion of usage in Vaugelas and in the
    Port Royal grammar. In Darden, et al., 165-76.
PERLMUTTER, DAVID. 1969. Les pronoms objets en espagnol. Langages
    14.81-133.
___. 1970. Surface structure constraints in syntax. Linguistic
    Inquiry 1.187-255.
___. 1971. Deep and surface structure constraints in syntax. New York:
    Holt, Rinehart and Winston.
PETERS, P. S. and R. W. RITCHIE. Forthcoming a. On the generative
    power of transformational grammars. To appear in Information Control.
___. Forthcoming b. On restricting the base component of a transforma-
    tional grammar. To appear in Information Control.

PHELPS, E. 1972. Catalan vowel reduction--alpha, braces, or angled brackets? Linguistic Inquiry 3.246-9.

PHILIPPSTHAL, R. 1886. Die Wortstellung in der französischen Prosa der 16 Jahrhunderts. Halle dissertation.

PICABIA, LÉLIA. 1971. Des adjectifs et de quelques problèmes de formalisation du lexique. Langue Française 11.91-101.

POLCARI, E. 1909. I verbi italiani. Milano: Hoepli.

POLITZER, ROBERT L. 1965. Teaching French: an introduction to applied linguistics. 2nd ed. Boston: Blaisdell.

POPE, MILDRED K. 1966. From Latin to modern French. Rev. ed. London: Butler and Tanner.

PORENA, MANFREDI. 1908. Sillabe brevi e sillabe lunghe nella poesia italiana. In Note di Lingua e Stile. Napoli.

POSNER, REBECCA. 1970. The generative generation and French phonology: Sanford Schane, French Phonology and Morphology. Romance Philology 14.625-33.

POSTAL, PAUL M. 1964. Constituent structure: a study of contemporary models of syntactic description. The Hague: Mouton.

___. 1966. The so-called 'pronouns' in English. In Dinneen 176-206.

___. 1968. Aspects of phonological theory. New York: Harper and Row.

___. 1971a. Cross-over phenomena. New York: Holt.

___. 1971b. On the surface verb "Remind". In Fillmore and Langendoen, 181-270.

___. 1972. A global constraint on pronominalization. Linguistic Inquiry 3.35-59.

POTTIER, BERNARD. 1970. Review of Stevens 1966, Lackstrom 1967, Klein 1968, and Falk 1968. Bulletin Hispanique 72.241-2.

PRICE, GLANVILLE. 1966. Contribtuion à l'étude de la syntaxe des pronoms personnels sujets en ancien français. Romania 87.476-504.

PUGLIELLI, ANNARITA. 1968. The predicate phrase in Italian: a transformational approach. Ithaca, New York: Cornell University dissertation.

PUGLIELLI, ANNARITA. 1970. Strutture sintattiche del predicato in italiano. Bari: Adriatica Editrice.

QUANG PHUC DONG. 1971. The applicability of transformations to idioms. In Adams, et al., 198-205.

QUERIDO, ANTONIO A. MARTINS. 1967. Introduction à une grammaire transformationelle du portugais. Paris: Ecole des Hautes Etudes.

___. 1969a. Anaphore et deixis. Revue Canadienne de Linguistique 14.91-107.

___. 1969b. Grammaire I: description transformationnelle d'un sous-ensemble du français. Proceedings of the International Conference on Computational Linguistics, Sanga-Saby, Sweden.

RAMEH, CLEA A. 1970. Toward a computerized syntactic analysis of Portuguese. Washington, D.C.: Georgetown University dissertation.

RAPPORT GÉNÉRAL SUR LES MODALITES D'UNE SIMPLIFICATION EVENTUELLE DE L'ORTHOGRAPHE FRANÇAISE. 1965. Paris: Didier.

REIBEL, DAVID and SANFORD A. SCHANE (eds.). 1969. Modern studies in English. Englewood Cliffs, New Jersey: Prentice-Hall.

RENCHON, H. 1967. Etudes de syntaxe descriptive II: la syntaxe de l'interrogation. Bruxelles: Palais des Académies.

RIVERO, MARÍA-LUISA. 1969. The Spanish quantifiers. Rochester: University of Rochester dissertation.

___. 1970a. La concepción de los modos en la gramática de Andrés Bello y los verbos abstractos en la gramática generativa. Mimeo.

___. 1970b. Estudio de una transformación en la gramática generativa del español. Español Actual 17.14-22.

___. 1970c. A surface structure constraint on negation in Spanish. Language 46.640-66.

___. 1971. Mood and presupposition in Spanish. Foundations of Language 7.305-36.

___. Forthcoming a. A note on "Postponed main phrases". To appear in the Canadian Journal of Linguistics.

RIVERO, MARIA-LUISA. Forthcoming b. Remarks on operators and modalities. To appear in Foundations of Language.

ROHLFS, GERHARD. 1949. Historische Grammatik der italienischen Sprache und ihrer Mundarten. Bern: Francke.

ROHRER, CHRISTIAN. 1967. Definition of locutions verbales. The French Review 41.357-67.

___. 1968a. L'analyse transformationelle des prepositions relatives du français. Mimeo paper. Read at the 12th International Congress of Romanists in Bucharest, Rumania.

___. 1968b. Das französische Vokalsystem. Festschrift for Hans Marchand. The Hague: Mouton.

ROLDÁN, MERCEDES. 1965. Ordered rules for Spanish. Bloomington: Indiana University dissertation.

___. 1970. Ser and estar in a new light. Language Sciences 12. 17-20.

___. 1971. The double object constructions of Spanish. Language Sciences 15.8-14.

ROLLAND, E. 1878. Ti, signe d'interrogation. Romania 7.599.

ROMEO, LUIGI. 1968. The economy of diphthongization in early Romance. The Hague: Mouton.

RONJAT, JULES. 1937. Grammaire historique des parlers provençaux modernes, III. Montpellier: Société des Parlers Romans.

ROSENBAUM, PETER S. 1967. The grammar of the English predicate complement construction. Cambridge, Massachusetts: MIT Press.

ROSS, JOHN R. 1967a. Auxiliaries as main Verbs. Dittographed manuscript. In print since 1969 in Todd.

___. 1967b. Constraints on variables in syntax. Cambridge: MIT dissertation. Reproduced by the Indiana University Linguistics Club.

___. 1970. On declarative sentences. In Jacobs and Rosenbaum, 222-72.

ROULET, EDDY. 1969. Syntaxe de la proposition nucléaire en français parlé: étude tagmémique et transformationnelle. Bruxelles: AIMAV.

RUWET, NICHOLAS. 1966. Le constituant 'auxiliaire' en français moderne. Langages 4.105-21.

___. 1967. Introduction à la grammaire générative. (Recherches en sciences humaines, 22) Paris: Plon.

___. 1970. "Note sur la syntaxe du pronom EN et d'autres sujets apparentés", in Langue Française, 6.

SABLESKI, JULIA A. 1965. A generative phonology of a Spanish dialect. Seattle: University of Washington M.A. thesis.

SACIUK, BOHDAN. 1969a. Lexical strata in generative phonology (with illustrations from Ibero-Romance). Urbana: University of Illinois dissertation.

___. 1969b. The stratal division of the lexicon. Papers in Linguistics 1.464-532.

___. 1970. Some basic rules of Portuguese phonology. In Sadock and Vanek, 197-222.

SADOCK, JERROLD M. and ANTHONY L. VANEK (eds.). 1970. Studies presented to Robert B. Lees by his students. (Papers in Linguistics Monograph Series, 1) Edmonton: Linguistic Research.

SAID ALI, M. 1964. Gramática histórica da língua portuguêsa. São Paulo: Edições Melhoramentos.

ST. CLAIR, ROBERT N. 1971. Dislocation in Rumanian. Language Sciences 16.32-4.

SAINTE-MARIE, MICHELINE. 1971. La grammaire structurale du français de Jean Dubois. La Linguistique 7:103-14.

SALTARELLI, MARIO. 1966. A phonology of Italian in a generative grammar. Urbana: University of Illinois dissertation.

___. 1966'. Romance dialectology and generative grammar. Orbis 15.51-9.

___. 1968. Marsian vocalism: intelligibility and rules of grammar. Orbis 17.88-96.

___. 1970a. A phonology of Italian in a generative grammar. The Hague: Mouton.

SALTARELLI, MARIO. 1970b. Spanish plural formation: apocope or epenthesis? Language 46.89-96.

___. 1970c. Fonologia generativa dell'algherese. Actele Celui de-al XII Congres Internaţional de Lingvistică şi Filologie Romanică 311-4.

___. 1971. Per una semantica generativa delle coordinate. Grammatica Transformazionale Italiana 203-7.

___. Forthcoming. On epenthesis, velar softening and stress.

SALUS, PETER H. 1969. Pre-Pre-Cartesian linguistics. In Binnick, 429-434.

___. 1971. The modistae as proto-generativists. In Adams, 530-4.

SANDFELD, K. 1965. Syntaxe du français contemporain I. Paris: Champion.

SAPORTA, SOL. 1959. Morpheme alternants in Spanish. In Kahane and Pietrangeli.

___. 1963. Phoneme distribtuion and language universals. In Greenberg 48-57.

___. 1965. Ordered rules, dialect differences, and historical processes. Language 41.218-24.

SAPORTA, SOL and HELES CONTRERAS. 1960. The validation of phonological grammar. Lingua 9.1-15.

___. 1962. A phonological grammar of Spanish. Seattle: University of Washington Press.

SCHANE, SANFORD A. 1964. The historical development of the French syntactic construction: ce + être + noun or pronoun. MIT Research Laboratory in Electronics Quarterly Progress Report, 75.

___. 1966. The morphophonemics of the French verb. Language 42.746-58.

___. 1967a. La phonologie du groupe verbal en français. Langages 7.120-8.

___. 1967b. L'élision et la liaison en français. Langages 8.37-59.

___. 1967c. Review of La linguistique synchronique: études et recherches, by André Martinet. International Journal of American Linguistics 33.178-83.

SCHANE, SANFORD A. 1968a. French phonology and morphology. Cambridge, Massachusetts: MIT Press.

___. 1968b. On the abstract character of the French e muet. Glossa 2.150-63.

___. 1968c. On the non-uniqueness of phonological representations. Language 44.709-16.

___. 1970. Phonological and morphological markedness. In Bierwisch and Heidolph (eds.), 286-94.

___. 1971a. Natural rules, strategies, and language change. In Tsiapera, 55-72.

___. 1971b. The phoneme revisited. Language 47.503-21.

SCHANE, SANFORD A. and DIETER WANNER. 1969. Why the i in Italian? Mimeo paper.

SHOLES, GEORGE NICKELL. 1958. Transformations in French grammar. Bloomington: Indiana University dissertation.

SMITH, CARLOTA S. 1971. Sentences in discourse: a stylistic analysis of an essay by Bertrand Russell. To appear in Journal of Linguistics.

SMITH, N.V. 1969. Review of Schane 1968a. Language 45.398-407.

SOEMARMO, MARMO. 1970. Subject-predicate, focus-presupposition, and topic-comment in Bahasa Indonesia and Javanese. Los Angeles: UCLA dissertation.

SOUBLIN, FRANÇOISE. 1971. Sur une règle rhétorique d'effacement. Langue Française 11.102-9.

SPITZER, L. 1941. De l'inversion absolue. PMLA 56.1150-62.

STEFANINI, JEAN. 1971. A propos des verbes pronominaux. Langue Française 11.110-25.

STEPHANY, URSULA. 1970. Adjektivische Attributkonstruktionen des Französichen. München: Fink.

STEVENS, CLAIRE. 1966. A characterization of Spanish nouns and adjectives. (University of Washington Studies in Linguistics and Language Learning, 2) Seattle: University of Washington.

STOCKWELL, ROBERT, J. DONALD BOWEN, and JOHN W. MARTIN. 1965. The
grammatical structures of English and Spanish. Chicago: University
of Chicago Press.

STROHMEYER, F. 1935. Endstellung und Umstellung des Subjekts. Zeitschrift
für französische Sprache und Literatur 59.129-49.

STURTEVANT, EDGAR H. 1947. An introduction to linguistic science.
New Haven, Connecticut: Yale University Press.

SWENSON, MARIA GIUSEPPINA SCAIOLA. 1969. The nominal phrase in Italian:
a transformational approach. Ithaca, New York: Cornell University
dissertation.

SZEMERÉNYI, OSWALD. 1960. Studies in the Indo-European system of numerals.
Heidelberg: Winter.

THOMAS, EARL. 1969. The syntax of spoken Brazilian Portuguese. Nashville:
Vanderbilt University Press.

THOMASON, SARAH G. 1969. On the nature of analogical change. New Haven,
Connecticut: Yale University Press.

TODD, WILLIAM (ed.). 1969. Studies in philosophical linguistics, series
one. Evanston, Illinois: Great Expectations.

TSIAPERA, MÁRIA (ed.). 1971. Generative studies in historical linguistics.
Edmonton: Linguistic Research Incorporated.

VALDMAN, ALBERT. 1961. Applied linguistics: French--A guide for
teachers. Boston: D. C. Heath.

___. 1963. Not all is wrong with French spelling. The French Review
37.213-23.

VALDMAN, ALBERT, et al.. 1964. A drillbook of French pronunciation.
New York: Harper and Row. (2nd revised edition in 1971).

VALDMAN, ALBERT. 1967. Introduction to the structure of French. (Unpublished manuscript).

___. 1968. Normes pédagogiques: les structures interrogatives du
Français. International Review of Applied Linguistics 5.3-10.

___. 1970a. Competing models of linguistic analysis: French adjective
inflection. The French Review 43.606-23.

VALDMAN, ALBERT. 1970b. Le E muet et la hierarchie structurale du
français. Actes du Xe Congrès international des linguistes.
Bucharest: Edition de l'Académie de la république socialiste de
Roumanie.

VALESIO, PAOLO. 1969. The synthetic future again: phonology and morpho-
syntax. Lingua 24.181-93.

___. 1971a. The distinction of active and passive. Linguistic Inquiry
2.407-14.

___. 1971b. Osservazioni sui verbi attivi e i verbi passivi. Grammatica
Transformazionale Italiana 225-45.

VASILIU, EMANUEL. 1966. Towards a generative phonology of Dacorumanian
dialects. Journal of Linguistics 2.79-98.

___. 1967. Considérations typologigues sur la phonologie transforma-
tionnelle des dialectes Daco-Roumains. Cahiers de Linguistique
Théorique et Appliquée 4.253-60.

VASILIU, EMANUEL and SANDA GOLOPENŢIA-ERETESCU. 1969. Sintaxa transformaţională a limbii române. Bucureşti: Editura Academiei
Republicii Socialiste România.

VOGT, ERIC E. 1970. Topics in Catalan phonology. Cambridge, Massachusetts:
Harvard University Bachelor's thesis.

___. 1971. Catalan vowel reduction and the angled bracket notation.
Linguistic Inquiry 2.233-6.

WALKER, DOUGLAS C. 1971. Old French phonology and morphology. La
Jolla: University of California San Diego M.A. dissertation.

WALL, ROBERT E. 1971. Mathematical linguistics. In Dingwall, 682-716.

WANNER, DIETER. 1970. Substratum as a special case of simplification.
Papers in Linguistics 2.415-48.

___. 1971. Review of Puglielli (1970). Papers in Linguistics 4:
395-404.

___. Forthcoming. Is stress predictable in Italian? To appear in
Papers in Linguistics in honor of Henry and Renée Kahane. Urbana:
University of Illinois Press.

WATKINS, CALVERT. 1970. A case on non-chronological rule insertion. Linguistic Inquiry 1.525-7.

WEINREICH, URIEL, WILLIAM LABOV, and MARVIN I. HERZOG. 1968. Empirical foundations for a theory of language change. In Lehmann and Malkiel, 97-188.

WILLIS, BRUCE E. 1967. The diachronic study of Spanish vowels. Urbana: University of Illinois M.A. thesis.

___. 1969. The alternation of so-called learned/popular vocabulary in a phonological description of Latin American Spanish. Urbana: University of Illinois dissertation.

___. 1970. Stress assignment in Spanish. In Sadock and Vanek (eds.), 303-12.

WILSON, JACK L. 1970. A generative phonological study of Costa Rican Spanish. Ann Arbor: University of Michigan dissertation.

WOLFE, DAVID L. 1966. A generative-transformational analysis of Spanish verb forms. Ann Arbor: University of Michigan dissertation.

WONDER, JOHN P. 1971. Complementos de adjetivo del genitivo. Hispania 54.114-20.

WYATT, JAMES LARKIN. 1965. An automated Portuguese-to-English transformational grammar. Austin: University of Texas dissertation.

ZINGARELLI, NICOLA. 1966. Vocabolario della lingua italiana. Novissima edizione minore, redatta e aggiornata da Giovanni Balducci. Bologna: Zanichelli.

ZULL, CAROLYN G. 1966. A formal system for generating French verb paradigms: a study in distinctive features. Madison: University of Wisconsin dissertation.